# LOST LANGUAGES

# LOST LANGUAGES / THE ENIGMA OF THE WORLD'S UNDECIPHERED SCRIPTS

## / ANDREW ROBINSON /

 Thames & Hudson

First published in the United Kingdom in 2009 by Thames & Hudson Ltd,
181A High Holborn, London WC1V 7QX

www.thamesandhudson.com

British Library Cataloguing-in-Publication Data
A catalogue record for this book is available from the British Library

ISBN 978-0-500-51453-5

Printed and bound in China by SNP Leefung Printers Ltd

# CONTENTS

# PREFACE

The first edition of *Lost Languages* went to press in late 2001. Since then, none of its undeciphered scripts has been deciphered, and so the book remains fundamentally up to date. However, there have been some new discoveries of inscriptions—the lifeblood of archaeological decipherment—of which three are particularly intriguing.

In India, a stone celt apparently bearing four signs in the undeciphered Indus script (see chapter X) was accidentally discovered in 2006 by a school teacher digging a pit in his backyard in southern Tamil Nadu, almost at the tip of the subcontinent. This location—far away from the Indus Valley—lends further support to the longstanding but unproven theory that the language of the Indus script is Dravidian.

The other two discoveries concern hitherto-unknown scripts. In Mexico, in the Olmec heartland, an inscription on a stone block was discovered and published in *Science* in 2006 by seven scholars after intensive study. The block had been spotted, along with Olmec pottery fragments and figurines, by road builders quarrying fill from an ancient mound at Cascajal in the Isthmus of Tehuantepec. If the inscription is of the same age as the accompanying artifacts, then it dates from 900 BC. This would make it the oldest example of writing in the New World, predating the Zapotec and Isthmian scripts (see chapter IX)—which it does not resemble—by several centuries. Since the Cascajal inscription comprises a mere 62 characters consisting of 28 signs, there is no hope of deciphering it at present, as with the solitary Phaistos disc from Crete (see chapter XI). But it is generally agreed to be the first definitive example of writing from the highly influential Olmec civilization.

In Turkmenistan, a single seal was found by an archaeologist at Anau, on the northern borders of Iran and Afghanistan, and published in 2002. It belongs to the Bronze Age "Oxus civilization". Radiocarbon dating puts its date in the middle of the third millennium BC, comparable in age to the Indus seals. Its signs look sophisticated and a bit Chinese, but since no other sample has been found, it is far too soon to declare that the Anau seal is definitely writing. Yet it suggests that there may have been communication between Asian cultures even at this very early period, as with the much later Silk Road. To be highly speculative, could the seal be a link in a chain that propagated the idea of writing from Mesopotamia to China?

The enigma of the world's undeciphered scripts continues to tantalize us.

————

I dedicate this book jointly to the late John Chadwick, author of *The Decipherment of Linear B*, and to Michael Coe, author of *Breaking the Maya Code*. In my view these are the two best books on archaeological decipherment: the first for its intellectual clarity, the second for its lively humanity. Both John and Mike offered generous encouragement to me, especially in connection with my earlier book, *The Story of Writing* (1995), which appeared in a new edition in 2007.

Many scholars gave invaluable help with my research and writing. I owe a special debt to those who commented on individual chapters in draft: John Baines of Oxford University (Egyptian hieroglyphs); Tom Palaima of the University of Texas at Austin (Linear B); Michael Coe of Yale University (Mayan glyphs); Peter Shinnie of the University of Calgary and Robin Thelwall (the Meroitic script); Larissa Bonfante of New York University (the Etruscan alphabet); Yves Duhoux of the Catholic University of Louvain and Maurice Pope (Linear A); Robert Englund of the University of California at Los Angeles (the proto-Elamite script); Jacques Guy (Rongorongo); Michael Coe, Stephen Houston of Brigham Young University and now Brown University, Martha Macri of the University of California at Davis and Javier Urcid of Brandeis University (the Zapotec and Isthmian scripts); Asko Parpola of the University of Helsinki (the Indus script); and Maurice Pope (the Phaistos disc).

In addition, a number of other scholars helped me to obtain published and unpublished work by themselves and others, in particular: John Bennet, Emmett Bennett Jr., Margalit Finkelberg, Steven Roger Fischer, Nikolai Grube, Fred Hiebert, John Justeson, Mark Kenoyer, John Killen, James Lamb, Jean Leclant, Iravatham Mahadevan, Nicholas Millet, Jean-Pierre Olivier, John Ray, George Stuart, Bryan Wells and Derek Welsby. Michael Zach of the University of Vienna offered selfless assistance with the Meroitic script.

London, March 2008

# Writing Systems, Coded Civilizations and Undeciphered Scripts

# INTRODUCTION

*"[Michael] Ventris was able to discover among the bewildering variety of the mysterious signs, patterns and regularities which betrayed the underlying structure. It is this quality, the power of seeing order in apparent confusion, that has marked the work of all great men."*

JOHN CHADWICK
*The Decipherment of Linear B*

May 1953 was an extraordinary month for human endeavor. Two scientists, Francis Crick and James Watson, announced in *Nature*, the world's leading scientific journal, their discovery of the 'double helix' structure of DNA, the basic molecule of life, and outlined its genetic implications. Two climbers, Edmund Hillary and Tenzing Norgay, finally made it to the top of Mount Everest, the world's highest mountain. At the same time, the architect Michael Ventris's tentative decipherment of 'Minoan Linear Script B'—writing first discovered in 1900 on clay tablets in the 'Palace of Minos' at Knossos in Crete—was triumphantly proved right when it produced incontrovertible readings of new tablets just excavated from a site in mainland Greece. At long last, the tantalizing signs in the clay yielded up their meaning: Linear B, perhaps Europe's first fully functional writing system, dating from the middle of the 2nd millennium BC, was shown to write an archaic dialect of ancient Greek.

The London *Times* soon ran a leader entitled "Men and mountains", which hailed "a story that will live as long as courage and comradeship are honoured...". Immediately below it was a second leader, "On the threshold?", that spoke of the potentially imminent revelation of an ancestral language and culture pre-dating the Trojan war, "as distant from the Greek of Homer as is the English of Chaucer from that which we speak today." The decipherment of Linear B was quickly dubbed, "the Everest of Greek archaeology."

Whichever of these three achievements you regard as the most challenging or significant, "there can be no question which of them belongs to the rarest category of achievement," writes Maurice Pope in *The Story of Decipherment*, his respected account of the successful decipherments of ancient scripts. The prize in this category must go to the decipherment of Linear B. For there have been dozens of earth-shaking scientific discoveries over the past two millennia, hundreds of courageous 'firsts' in the even longer history of exploration, but only a handful of classic archaeological decipherments, all of which date from the past two centuries.

The earliest, of course, was the decipherment of the Egyptian hieroglyphs—made possible by what is probably the world's most famous inscription, the Rosetta stone. Discovered by French soldiers of Napoleon in Egypt in 1799, and subsequently taken as a trophy of war to the British Museum in London, the Rosetta stone provided a decipherment key, because it was a bilingual inscription. The part of it written in the Greek alphabet in the language of ancient Greece (which could easily be understood), was a translation of the other parts written in the unknown ancient Egyptian language in two clearly different unknown scripts, hieroglyphic and demotic. This alone was not enough to decipher the individual signs of the scripts, but now a brilliant French Orientalist, Jean-François Champollion, guessed that the language of the pharaohs was not totally unknown, because it might be related to the Coptic language used in post-pharaonic Egypt and even today in the Coptic church. Through clever analysis of proper names identifiable in the unknown scripts of the Rosetta stone and other Egyptian inscriptions, such as Alexander, Ptolemy, Caesar, Cleopatra and Ramesses, combined with the evidence of the ancient Greek and Roman historians and his knowledge of Coptic, Champollion could work out the sounds and meanings of the hieroglyphic and demotic words. Suddenly, in 1823, the span of recorded history expanded by some two millennia; the pharaohs began to speak to us directly through their stone monuments, wall paintings and papyrus manuscripts; and scholars could begin to reconstruct a whole new mental universe. "Such study is the closest one can come to speaking with the dead," writes a current British Museum curator of the Rosetta stone.

This breakthrough was followed by the 'cracking' of the Babylonian and other cuneiform writings of Mesopotamia, the 'cradle of civilization', in the mid-19th century; the decipherment of various Near Eastern and European scripts, such as Hittite, Ugaritic and Linear B, in the early to mid-20th century; and, in our own time, the breakneck decipherment of the Mayan glyphs of Central America. Since the 1970s, scholars, working chiefly in the United States, have revealed an astonishing truth: the New World, too, had a great, sophisticated, literate civilization at the time of the Roman empire: that of the Maya—a millennium and a half before Columbus reached America.

*The major ancient scripts, with their approximate earliest dates of use. Deciphered scripts are designated in black, undeciphered or partially deciphered scripts in blue. Today most of the world except China and Japan writes in an alphabet.*

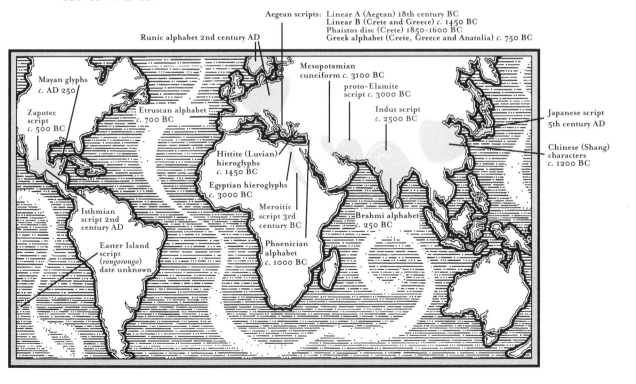

Aegean scripts:  Linear A (Aegean) 18th century BC
Linear B (Crete and Greece) *c.* 1450 BC
Phaistos disc (Crete) 1850-1600 BC
Greek alphabet (Crete, Greece and Anatolia) *c.* 750 BC

Runic alphabet 2nd century AD

Mayan glyphs *c.* AD 250

Zapotec script *c.* 500 BC

Etruscan alphabet *c.* 700 BC

Mesopotamian cuneiform *c.* 3100 BC

proto-Elamite script *c.* 3000 BC

Indus script *c.* 2500 BC

Japanese script 5th century AD

Chinese (Shang) characters *c.* 1200 BC

Hittite (Luvian) hieroglyphs *c.* 1450 BC

Egyptian hieroglyphs *c.* 3000 BC

Isthmian script 2nd century AD

Meroitic script 3rd century BC

Brahmi alphabet *c.* 250 BC

Easter Island script (*rongorongo*) date unknown

Phoenician alphabet *c.* 1000 BC

With its hint of genius, the successful decipherment of a major script carries a whiff of glamour and immortality about it, seldom found in the world of academic scholarship. The Nobel prize-winning physicist Richard Feynman tried his hand at deciphering the Mayan numerals and calendar just for the fun of it (he knew he was not the first) and said: "You get one hell of an excitement, just like a physics discovery or something." For the decipherer who succeeds, it is like winning a Nobel prize in literature or a solo Nobel in science—indeed perhaps of wider prestige when one thinks of the public fascination with ancient Egypt.

Ventris, the decipherer of Linear B, was only 34 when he died in a car crash in 1956, but he left behind him an inimitable reputation that is still growing half a century later. Among my prized papers is an offprint of Ventris's 1954 article, "King Nestor's four-handled cups", signed by Ventris and illustrated by him with Linear B characters in a hand so neat and appealing that, as a fellow scholar quipped, "Mr. Ventris would have had no trouble getting a job as scribe for King Minos". In this paper, Ventris published his full translation of the Linear B tablet from Greece first deciphered in May 1953 that refers beyond any doubt to a four-handled drinking cup—just as Homer does in *The Iliad*, before the old warrior Nestor sets off for the Trojan war: "a magnificent beaker adorned with golden studs... It had four handles... Anyone else would have found it difficult to shift the beaker from the table when full, but Nestor, old as he was, could lift it without trouble."

The paper reminds me of two anecdotal footnotes to the decipherment not to be found in today's copious academic studies of Linear B. It was gifted to me by an old man, Ventris's former classics master, Patrick Hunter, now no more. In his precise, understated way, Hunter told me a story about Ventris: of how in 1936 he had taken a party of schoolboys including the fourteen-year old Michael to a London exhibition on the Minoan world where they had the luck to be guided around by the 85-year-old Sir Arthur Evans, discoverer of Knossos; and of how, when they reached the Linear B tablets, Michael "piped up" and very politely questioned the grand old archaeologist, "Did you say they haven't been deciphered, Sir?" This was the moment, said Hunter, when Ventris became hooked on the problem that would obsess him, until one day in June 1952, when the fog lifted and he finally perceived that Linear B was written in Greek. That evening—this is the second footnote—Ventris and his wife Lois were due to give dinner at their ultra-modern flat to an architect friend and his wife, Prudence. She told me of how she and her husband arrived on time and started chatting to Lois Ventris, but there was absolutely no sign of Michael; only after a long time, when dinner was ruined, did he appear from a nearby room, his hair uncharacteristically ruffled, and excitedly inform them that he had just, that very day, worked out the language of Linear B. Being a BBC radio producer, Prudence Smith promptly persuaded Ventris to make a broadcast. Thus it was, that on 1 July 1952, the world—including the world of classical scholarship which would normally expect such a discovery to be announced at a conference or in a journal—first came to hear from 'the schoolboy who beat the experts' of the probable decipherment of Linear B. (One of those listening was John Chadwick, a classicist, who soon contacted Ventris, collaborated with him intensively for three years, and after his death wrote the well-known book, *The Decipherment of Linear B*, as a tribute to Ventris's rare mind.)

In addition to fanatical perseverance and devotion to detail and wide linguistic and cultural knowledge, the successful archaeological decipherer has required a high order of intellectual power of analysis, the courage to follow his or her intuition rather than the conventional wisdom, and the luck to come along at the right moment: which generally was when sufficient examples of the script to be deciphered had become accessible. Champollion and Ventris had these advantages in abundance, and so, to a lesser degree perhaps, did Sir Henry Creswicke Rawlinson, chief decipherer of Babylonian cuneiform, and Yuri Knorozov, Russian pioneer of the Maya decipherment in the 1950s. None of them, however, could have achieved success without the prior labor of many others, such as the celebrated physicist Thomas Young (Egyptian hieroglyphs), the great archaeologist Evans (Linear B) and the Mayanist Sir Eric Thompson—scholars as remarkable as those who eventually took the prize.

Human nature being what it is, decipherers and would-be decipherers did not always admit their debts. Rivalry, sometimes with a touch of skullduggery, is endemic in archaeological decipherment. Champollion was certainly influenced by Young's pioneering work—but never gave it due acknowledgement, and took pains to diminish it in his chief book. Rawlinson never explained his decipherment properly—and it is now plain from study of his notebooks that he borrowed without attribution from the work of a humbler scholar, Irish clergyman Edward Hincks. Both Evans and Thompson, for different reasons, did their best to discourage, and even ridicule, most of the aspirant decipherers; Evans by denying them access to the tablets he had discovered, Thompson by branding Knorozov a 'cold warrior', which was a serious slur in the United States of the 1950s and 60s. Even Ventris, an amateur of exceptional modesty who originally saw himself as an enabler of the decipherment by professional classicists, failed to mention in his BBC broadcast the seminal contribution of the American scholar Alice Kober, who had died prematurely just two years earlier (raising the possibility, somewhat like Rosalind Franklin in the DNA story, that Kober might have beaten Ventris to it, had she lived).

These 'rival' scholars all made vital contributions to the eventual decipherment. What, therefore, is it that disqualifies them—and those who periodically claim to have deciphered the world's remaining undeciphered scripts—from being admitted to the small pantheon of successful decipherers? What, in fact, do scholars have in mind exactly, when they say that an ancient script has been 'deciphered'?

In normal conversation, to decipher someone's 'indecipherable' handwriting means to make sense of the meaning; it does not imply that one can read every last word. In its more technical sense, as applied to ancient scripts, 'deciphered' means different things to different scholars. At one extreme, everyone agrees that the Egyptian hieroglyphs have been deciphered—because every trained Egyptologist would make the same sense of virtually every word of a given hieroglyphic inscription (though their individual translations would still differ, as do all independent translations of the same work from one language into another). At the other extreme, (almost) every scholar agrees that the script of the Indus Valley civilization is undeciphered—because no one can make sense of its seals and other inscriptions to the satisfaction of anyone else. Between these extremes lies a vast spectrum of opinion. In the case of Mayan writing, for example, most scholars agree that a high proportion, as much as 85 per cent, of the inscriptions can be meaningfully read, and yet there remain large numbers of individual glyphs that are contentious or obscure.

Scholars can, for instance, often decipher the numerical system and arithmetical and calendrical systems of an ancient script without knowing its underlying language. Even a layperson can sometimes obtain accurate sense merely from the pictographic/iconic quality of certain signs, such as the recognizable humans, creatures, objects and actions in some Egyptian hieroglyphs:

'old man'      'birds, fowl'      'to be stood      'to plough'      'cut open'
                                  on one's head'

And the vast majority of readers of this book would be quite confident in interpreting the following 'icons', no matter which country or language they appeared in:

When the late Linda Schele, a key figure in the Maya decipherment, was asked how much of the script had been deciphered, she would always answer that it depended what you meant by 'deciphered'. Writing in the 1993 notebook for the XVIIth Maya Hieroglyphic Workshop, a vibrant meeting of professionals and amateurs she led annually at the University of Texas at Austin, Schele remarked:

" Some glyphs can be translated exactly; we know the original word or its syllabic value. For other glyphs, we have the meaning (for example, we have evidence that a glyph means 'to hold or grasp'), but we do not yet know the Mayan words. There are other glyphs for which we know the general meaning, but we haven't found the original word; for example, we may know it involves war, marriage, or perhaps that the event always occurs before age 13, but we cannot associate the glyph with a precise action. For others, we can only recover their syntactical function; for example, we may know a glyph occurs in the position of a verb, but we have no other information. To me the most frustrating state is to have a glyph with known phonetic signs, so that we can pronounce the glyph, but we cannot find the word in any of the Mayan languages. If a glyph is unique or occurs in only a few texts, we have little chance of translating it. "

In other words, there can no shibboleth by which we judge a script to be undeciphered or deciphered; we must instead talk about *degrees* of decipherment. The most useful criterion is the degree to which the proposed decipherment can generate consistent readings from new samples of the script, preferably produced by persons other than the original decipherer. Here is a specific example from the early days of the Maya decipherment:

The pair of signs were read as the glyph for 'dog' by both Thompson and Knorozov, but they gave wholly different reasons for thinking so. According to Thompson, the sign on the left was an *iconographic* depiction of the ribs of a dog, as known from other Maya imagery, for example:

—while the sign on the right could be shown from its other contexts to be the glyph for death. The combined meaning of 'dog' was implied by the fact that the dog was known in Maya belief to be closely associated with the underworld. ('Iconographic', not 'iconic', because the ribs are so artistically stylized that only a reader trained in the aesthetics of Maya symbolism will recognize them; 'iconic' symbols are more universal, like those on page 17.)

Knorozov, by contrast, taking help from a Spanish account of Mayan writing, simply read these two signs *phonetically* as the syllables *tzu* and *lu,* which together spelt 'tzul', meaning 'dog' according to the modern Mayan language dictionaries. Knorozov commented on Thompson's particular 'decipherment': "It...cannot help us make sense out of any other hieroglyph." Whereas his own syllabic reading should work equally well when the two signs were used independently in other glyphs, like our letters of the alphabet which freely substitute in different words. In due course, other scholars proved that Knorozov was right, and the degree of decipherment of the Mayan script increased dramatically.

The degree would be 100 per cent if all the signs of a historically used script were to match the sounds and meanings of a historically known or at least linguistically plausible underlying language: this is the holy grail for the archaeological decipherer. It distinguishes the *epigrapher* (as such students of ancient scripts are known) from the cryptanalyst, who breaks the secret codes and ciphers used by the armed forces in wartime, and governments and commercial organizations in peacetime. The epigrapher and the cryptanalyst are certainly both decipherers, but the epigrapher works with a script not originally designed to baffle the reader and an underlying language which the reader may or may not know, whereas the cryptanalyst tackles a code or cipher designed from the outset to baffle him but an underlying language (such as German, ciphered by the famous Enigma machines in the second world war) which is generally obvious. To paraphrase Einstein's famous comment about God, "Ancient languages [written and spoken]...may be subtle, but they are not malicious"—writes the American computer scientist Whitfield Diffie, one of the inventors of public-key cryptography in a joint contribution with his Egyptologist wife to *Cracking Codes*, the catalogue of a British Museum exhibition celebrating the bicentenary of the discovery of the Rosetta stone. Diffie adds: "What cryptographic systems lack in subtlety, they make up for in malice." According to him, cryptanalysis is fundamentally easier than archaeological decipherment. Perhaps that is why cryptanalysts-turned-scholars, such as John Chadwick (though not his collaborator Ventris, who also served in the second world war but *not* as a cryptanalyst), for all their important contributions to archaeological decipherment, seldom become the ones who finally 'crack' an ancient script.

But we are getting ahead of ourselves. Ancient scripts are indeed complex and subtle, much more so than our modern alphabets—at least they seem that way because very few of us know how to read them! Nor do we understand the cultures they encoded, an almost equally important part of being able to read ancient languages. Decipherment certainly involves the chief attributes that made Sherlock Holmes such a formidable detective: persistence, powers of logical deduction and more than an occasional flash of intuition—but it also demands a wide and varied knowledge of linguistics, literacy and ancient civilizations. It was Champollion's deep knowledge of Coptic and his passion for all things Egyptian that gave him his crucial edge over the scientifically minded Thomas Young. So, before going further into the methods and challenges of decipherment, we shall take a broad look at writing systems, ancient and modern. We need to know what writing has been used for in different societies over five millennia, as well as something of the evolution of early written communication and the principles of 'visible speech' more generally: in other words, how various writing systems work graphically and linguistically, and the relationship between historical scripts and the languages they write. You may be surprised to discover that Egyptian hieroglyphs and our modern alphabets are fundamentally similar.

———

Writing is among the greatest inventions in human history, perhaps *the* greatest invention, since it made history possible. Yet it is a skill most writers take for granted. We learn it at school, building on the alphabet, or (if we live in most of the Far East) the Chinese characters. As adults we seldom stop to think about the mental-cum-physical process that turns our thoughts into symbols on a piece of paper or on a video screen, or bytes of information in a computer's memory. Few of us have any clear recollection of how we learnt to write.

A page of text in a foreign script such as Arabic or Japanese, totally incomprehensible to us, reminds us forcibly of the nature of our achievement. An extinct script, such as Egyptian hieroglyphs or one of the undeciphered scripts in this book, may strike us as little short of miraculous. By what means did those pioneering writers of several millennia ago learn to write? How did their symbols encode their thought and speech? Do today's writing systems work in a completely different way from the ancient scripts? What about the Chinese and Japanese scripts—are they like ancient hieroglyphs? Do hieroglyphs have any advantages over alphabets? Finally, what kind of people were the early writers, and what kind of information, ideas and feelings did they make permanent?

Writing and literacy are generally seen as forces for good. It hardly needs saying that a person who can read and write has greater opportunities for fulfillment than one who is illiterate. But there is also a dark side to the spread of writing that is present throughout its history, if somewhat less obvious. Writing has been used to tell lies as well as truth, to bamboozle and exploit as well as to educate, to make minds lazy as well as to stretch them.

Socrates pinpointed our ambivalence towards writing in his story of the Egyptian god Thoth, the mythical inventor of writing, who came to see the king seeking royal blessing on his enlightening invention. The king told Thoth:

> **"** You, who are the father of letters, have been led by your affection to ascribe to them a power the opposite of that which they really possess... You have invented an elixir not of memory, but of reminding; and you offer your pupils the appearance of wisdom, for they will read many things without instruction and will therefore seem to know many things, when they are for the most part ignorant. **"**

In a 21st-century world drenched with written information and surrounded by information technologies of astonishing speed, convenience and power, these words spoken in antiquity have a distinctly contemporary ring.

Political leaders, especially autocrats and dictators, have always used writing for propaganda purposes. Nearly 4000 years and a totally different script separate the famous black basalt law code of Hammurabi of Babylon (1792-1750 BC) from the slogans and billboards of its modern equivalent in Iraq at the beginning of the third millennium AD—but the message is (regrettably) similar. Hammurabi called himself, in purest Babylonian cuneiform, "King, King of Babylon, King of the whole country of Amurru, King of Sumer and Akkad, King of the Four Quarters of the World"; and he promised that if his laws were obeyed, then all his people would benefit. "Writing", wrote H. G. Wells in his *Short History of the World*, "put agreements, laws, commandments on record. It made the growth of states larger than the old city states possible. It made a continuous historical consciousness possible. The command of the priest or king and his seal could go far beyond his sight and voice and could survive his death."

The urge for immortality has always been of the first importance to writers. Most of the thousands of known fragments written by the Etruscans, for instance, are funerary inscriptions. We can read the names of the deceased and of his or her relations, and often the age of death, because the signs are a simple adaptation of the Greek alphabet; but that is almost all we know of the enigmatic language of this important people, who borrowed the alphabet from Greece and handed it on to the Romans, who in turn gave it to the rest of Europe. The Etruscan *script* is therefore deciphered—we can pronounce Etruscan words—but the decipherment of the Etruscan *language*—i.e. the establishing of what the words actually mean—is like trying to learn English by reading nothing but gravestones.

Another purpose for writing was to predict the future. All ancient societies were obsessed with what was to come. Writing allowed them to codify their worries. Among the Maya it took the form of bark-paper books elaborately painted in color and bound in jaguar skin (which in the 20th century would prove vital to the decipherment of Mayan glyphs); the prognostications were based on a written calendrical system so sophisticated it extended as far back as five billion years ago, more than our present scientifically estimated age for the earth. In China, on the other hand, during the Bronze Age Shang dynasty, questions about the future were written on turtle shells and ox bones, so-called 'oracle bones'. The bone was heated with a brand until it cracked, the meaning of the shape of the crack was divined, and the answer to the question was inscribed. Later, what actually transpired might be added to the shell or bone.

But most ancient writing was probably comparatively mundane, destroyed, like last year's newspapers, by the ravages of time. It provided, for instance, the equivalent of an identity card or a property marker. The cartouche enclosing the name of Tutankhamun was found on objects throughout his tomb, from the grandest of thrones to the smallest of boxes. Anyone who was anyone among ancient rulers required a personal seal for signing clay tablets and other inscriptions. So did any merchant or other person of substance. (Today, in Japan and China, a seal, rather than a western-style signature, is standard practice for signing business and legal documents.) Such ancient name-tagging has been found as far apart as Mesopotamia, China, Central America and the Indus Valley, although in the latter case we cannot be sure of the purpose, as the exquisite symbols engraved on the Indus seal stones remain stubbornly undeciphered.

Much more common than name-tagging was writing used for accountancy. The earliest writing of all, on clay tablets from ancient

Sumer in Mesopotamia, and the slightly later tablets from neighboring Iran (ancient Elam)—a partially deciphered script known as proto-Elamite—concerns lists of raw materials and products, such as barley and beer, lists of laborers and their tasks, lists of field areas and their owners, the income and outgoing of temples, and so forth: all with calculations concerning production levels, delivery dates, locations, payments and debts. And the same is true, generally speaking, of Linear B—and probably, too, of its companion script Linear A ('probably', because we cannot yet decipher much of it). Ventris's famous Linear B tablet deciphered in May 1953 was simply an inventory of tripod cauldrons—one of them with its legs burnt off—and of goblets of varying sizes and numbers of handles.

How did writing begin? The favored explanation, until the Enlightenment in the 18th century, was divine origin. Today many, probably most, scholars accept that the earliest writing evolved from accountancy, though it is puzzling that accountancy is little in evidence in the surviving writing of ancient Egypt, China and Central America (which is no guarantee that once upon a time there was not a great deal of bureaucratic record keeping on perishable materials in these civilizations). In other words, some time in the late 4th millennium BC, the complexity of trade and administration in the early cities of Mesopotamia reached a point where it outstripped the power of memory of the governing elite. To record transactions in an indisputable, permanent form became essential. Administrators and merchants could then say the Sumerian equivalent of "I shall put it in writing" and "May I have this in writing?"

Some scholars believe that a conscious search for a solution to this problem by an unknown Sumerian individual in the city of Uruk (biblical Erech) in about 3300 BC, produced writing. Others believe writing was the work of a group, presumably of clever administrators and merchants. Still others think it was not an invention at all, but an accidental discovery. Many regard it as the result of evolution over a long period, rather than a flash of inspiration. One particularly well-aired theory holds that writing grew out of a long-standing counting system of clay 'tokens' (such 'tokens'— varying from simple, plain discs to more complex, incised shapes whose exact purpose is unknown—have been found in many Middle Eastern archaeological sites): the substitution of two-dimensional symbols for these tokens, with the symbols resembling the appearance of the token, was a first step towards writing, according to this theory.

The first written symbols are generally thought to have been *pictograms*: iconic drawings of, say, a pot, or a fish, or a head with a bowl (representing the concept of eating):

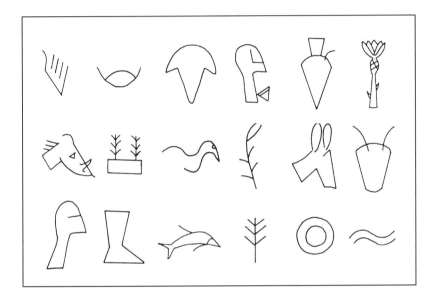

*Sumerian pictograms, c. 3000 BC. Try to guess their meanings before reading the answers printed below.*

| 'hand'  | 'day'         | 'cow'  | 'eat'    | 'pot'    | 'date-palm' |
|---------|---------------|--------|----------|----------|-------------|
| 'pig'   | 'orchard'     | 'bird' | 'reed'   | 'donkey' | 'ox'        |
| 'head'  | 'walk, stand' | 'fish' | 'barley' | 'well'   | 'water'     |

These have been found in Mesopotamia and Egypt dating to the mid-4th millennium BC and even earlier in China, according to the (doubtful) claims of some Chinese archaeologists. In many cases, their iconicity soon became so abstract that it is barely perceptible to us. But these signs were insufficient to express the kinds of words, and their constituent parts, that

*The symbol in the top left-hand corner of this Sumerian tablet is a pictogram representing the Sumerian word for 'reed', pronounced* gi; *it thus stands here for the concept 'reimburse', which is also pronounced* gi. *In Sumerian, 'reed' and 'reimburse' are homophonous, like 'son' and 'sun' in English.*

cannot be pictured. Essential to the development of full writing, as opposed to limited, purely pictographic 'proto-writing', was the discovery of the *rebus* principle. This radical idea, from the Latin meaning 'by things', enables phonetic values to be represented by pictographic symbols. Thus in English, a picture of a bee with a picture of a tray might stand for 'betray', a bee with a figure 4 might (if one were so minded) represent 'before', while a picture of an ant next to a buzzing bee hive, might (less obviously) represent 'Anthony'. Egyptian hieroglyphs are full of rebuses, for instance the 'sun' sign, $\odot$, pronounced *R(a)* or *R(e)*, is the first symbol in the hieroglyphic spelling of the pharaoh Ramesses. In an early Sumerian accounting tablet we find the abstract word reimburse represented by a picture of a reed, because 'reimburse' and 'reed' shared the same phonetic value *gi* in the Sumerian language.

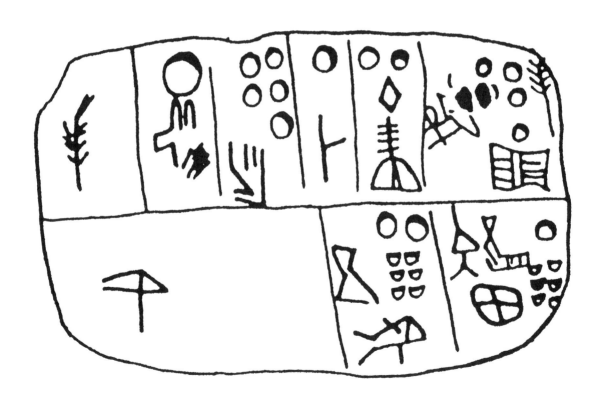

Once writing of this 'full' kind, capable of expressing the full range of speech and thought, was invented, accidentally discovered or evolved—take your pick—did it then diffuse throughout the globe from Mesopotamia? The earliest Egyptian writing dates from 3100 BC, that of the Indus Valley from 2500 BC, that of Crete from 1750 BC, that of China from 1200 BC, that of Central America—the undeciphered Zapotec script—from perhaps 500 BC (all dates are approximate). On this basis, it seems reasonable that the *idea* of writing, but not the symbols of a particular script, could have diffused gradually from culture to distant culture. It took 600 or 700 years for the idea of printing to reach Europe from China (if we discount the unique and enigmatic Phaistos disc of *c.* 1700 BC, found in Crete, which appears to be 'printed'), and even longer for the idea of paper to spread to Europe: why should writing not have reached China from Mesopotamia over an even longer period, or the Mesoamerican scripts not have been inspired by Old World writing diffusing across the oceans, as a few 'arch-diffusionist' scholars think possible?

Nevertheless, in the absence of any real evidence for transmission of the idea of writing, even in the case of the physically much nearer civilizations of Mesopotamia and Egypt, a majority of scholars chooses to think that writing developed independently in the major civilizations of the ancient world. The optimist, or at any rate the anti-imperialist, will prefer to emphasize the intelligence and inventiveness of human societies; the pessimist, who takes a more conservative view of history, will tend to assume that humans prefer to copy what already exists, as faithfully as they can, restricting their innovations to cases of absolute necessity. (Those geneticists and linguists who favor a single 'mother' language for all our modern languages take a comparable line about the origin of spoken languages, in which natural selection is hypothesized to work for languages as well as for genes.) Borrowing, rather than invention, is the preferred explanation for how the Greeks, near the beginning of the 1st millennium BC, acquired their alphabet; they took the idea of consonantal letters from the Phoenicians, and added in the process signs for the vowels not written in the Phoenician script. If ever the *rongorongo* script of Easter Island—the most isolated inhabited spot on earth—is deciphered, it may shed light on the fascinating question of whether the Easter Islanders invented *rongorongo* entirely unaided, brought the idea of their writing from Polynesia in their canoes during the mid-1st millennium AD, or borrowed it from Europeans who first visited Easter Island in the 18th century.

There can be no doubt about certain script borrowings, such as the Meroitic civilization of Sudan employing chiefly Egyptian hieroglyphs to represent the sounds of its unknown language, the Romans taking the Etruscan alphabet, the Japanese taking the Chinese characters during the 1st millennium AD, the Slavs taking the Greek alphabet and creating the Cyrillic script in the 9th century, and in the 20th century the Turks (under Kemal Atatürk) borrowing the Latin script and abandoning their Arabic script. Changes were made to a borrowed script because the new language had sounds in it that were not found in the language for which the script was being used originally (hence the umlaut on the 'u' of Atatürk). This idea is easy enough to grasp when the two languages are similar, like English and Latin, but it can be extremely awkward to follow when the two languages differ vastly, as Japanese does from Chinese. In order to cope with the different sounds of Japanese, the Japanese script has *two* entirely distinct sets of symbols: Chinese characters known as *kanji* (thousands), and 50 or so Japanese syllabic signs known as *kana*, forming what is generally regarded as the most complicated contemporary system of writing.

Europeans and Americans of ordinary literacy must recognize and write around 52 alphabetic signs (lower and upper case), and sundry other symbols, such as numerals, punctuation marks (:, ?, !, etc.) and 'whole-word' semantic symbols, for example +, &, $, £, %, @, which are often called *logograms* (from Greek 'logos' meaning 'word') and sometimes ideograms (a term we shall avoid because it is generally more ambiguous than logogram). Japanese people, by contrast, are supposed to know and be able to write some 2000 symbols, and, if they are highly educated, must recognize 5000 symbols or more. The two situations, in Europe/America and in Japan, appear to be poles apart. But in fact, the European and Japanese writing systems resemble each other more than appears.

*All* scripts that are full writing—that is, a "system of graphic symbols that can be used to convey any and all thought" (to quote John DeFrancis, a distinguished American student of Chinese in his book *Visible Speech*)—operate on one basic principle, contrary to what most people think, some scholars included. Both alphabets and the Chinese and Japanese scripts—and indeed the Egyptian hieroglyphs and Babylonian cuneiform—use symbols to represent sounds (i.e. signs with phonetic values); and similarly all writing systems use a mixture of phonetic signs and semantic signs standing for words and concepts (i.e. logograms). The higher the proportion of phonetic symbols in a script, the easier it is to guess the pronunciation of written words. In English the proportion is high, in Chinese it is low. Thus English spelling represents English speech sound by sound more accurately than Chinese characters represent Mandarin speech (Putonghua); but Finnish spelling represents the Finnish language even better. The Finnish alphabetic script is phonetically highly efficient, while the Chinese (and Japanese) *logosyllabic* script is phonetically seriously deficient; and cryptographic codes, which frequently use numbers to represent words in the underlying language, have a phonetic efficiency of almost zero: an undecoded number reveals nothing about the pronunciation of the word it encrypts.

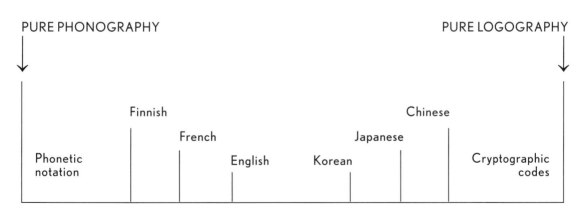

*All writing systems are a mixture of phonetic and logographic elements. In Finnish, phoneticism predominates, while the Chinese script is chiefly logographic, though it contains more phoneticism than many people think.*

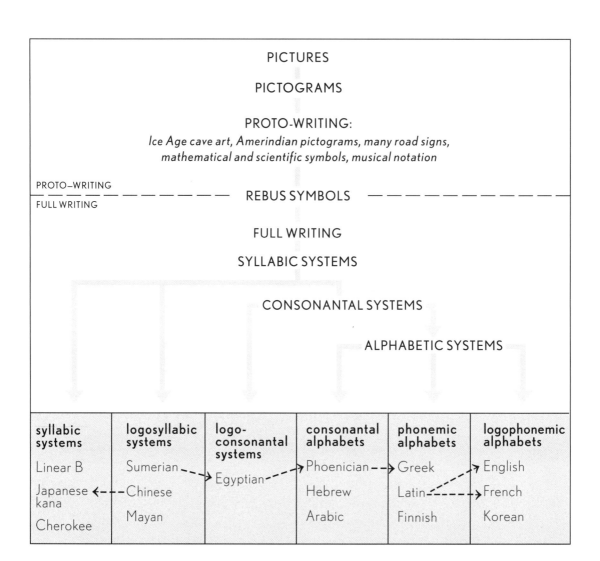

The classification of writing systems. This tree divides writing systems according to their nature, not according to their age; it does not show how one writing system may have given rise to another historically. (The dashed lines indicate possible influences of one system upon another.) How best to classify writing systems is a controversial matter. The root of the problem is that there is no such thing as a 'pure' writing system—i.e. a system that expresses meaning entirely through syllabic signs or alphabetic letters or logograms. Nevertheless, labels such as 'logosyllabic' involving these three concepts are useful to remind us of the predominant nature of different systems, along with one further concept, the phoneme, defined in linguistics as "the smallest contrastive unit in the sound system of a language". (Examples of vowel phonemes in English are /e/ and /a/ in the words set and sat, while English consonantal phonemes include /b/ and /p/ in the words bat and pat.) However, it is not necessary to understand the details of these labeled classifications in order to understand decipherment.

The difficulty of learning the Chinese and Japanese scripts cannot be denied. It takes a Chinese or Japanese person several years longer than a western counterpart to achieve fluency in reading and writing. That said, there are many millions of westerners who have failed to learn to read and write. Japanese literacy levels are higher than in the West (though probably not as high as is said). The logosyllabic intricacy of the Japanese script has not stopped the Japanese from becoming a great economic power and winning Nobel prizes in science; nor has it caused them to abandon their use of Chinese *kanji* in favor of a much smaller set of signs based on their syllabic *kana*—a theoretically feasible move. (In China, it is true, the government has introduced *pinyin*, meaning 'spell-sound', a romanised script based on the sounds of Chinese—but *pinyin* is yet to come anywhere near replacing the character-based script.)

Are the huge claims ritually made for the efficiency of the alphabet then perhaps misguided? Maybe writing and reading would work best if alphabetic scripts contained more logograms—some of them pictographic—representing whole words and concepts, as in Chinese and Japanese writing and (less so) in Egyptian hieroglyphs? Why is it necessarily desirable to have a *sound*-based, phonetic script? What, after all, has sound to do with the actual process of writing and reading?

We have only to look around us to see that 'hieroglyphs' are striking back—beside highways, at airports, on maps, in weather forecasts, on clothes labels, in machine operating handbooks, and, most visibly, on computer screens and keyboards. Instead of 'move cursor to right', there is a simple logogram ⇨; instead of chunks of text with alphabetic instructions to press a certain set of keys, there are computer 'icons' at which we point and click a mouse, and carry out complex operations as if by magic.

Some people, beginning with the philosopher and mathematician Gottfried Leibniz and the fellows of the Royal Society in the 17th century, even like to imagine that we can invent an entire written language for international communication based on 'universal' signs that all of us will intuitively recognize. (The influential, if controversial linguist Noam

Chomsky believes in a similar idea about speech: that all natural languages share a set of innate universal principles, which are hard-wired into our brains at birth.) The new 'universal' written language would aim to be independent of any of the spoken languages of the world, dependent only upon the concepts essential for high-level philosophical, political and scientific communication. If music and mathematics can achieve it, so the thought goes—why not more generally?

But music, and its various notation systems, is not in fact a language that can "express any and all thought"; ditto mathematics, which requires linking sentences to explain its flow of argument (look at any high-level mathematics text, listen to a mathematician lecturing). Leibniz's dream, appealing as it is—and that of some software and graphic designers—can never become a reality. Writing and reading are intimately and inextricably bound to speech, whether or not we move our lips. Chinese characters do *not* speak directly to the mind without the intervention of sound, despite centuries of assertion to the contrary by the Chinese and some western scholars. Nor do Egyptian hieroglyphs or Mayan glyphs, notwithstanding the beauty of their symbols and the fact that we can recognize people, animals, objects and the natural world depicted in them both iconically and iconographically. One needs to know the Chinese, Egyptian or Mayan languages.

Aristotle called the basic unit of language—by which he meant both spoken *and* written language—*gramma*. Ferdinand de Saussure, the founder of modern linguistics, said of language that it might be compared to a sheet of paper. "Thought is one side of the sheet and sound the reverse side. Just as it is impossible to take a pair of scissors and cut one side of the paper without at the same time cutting the other, so it is impossible in a language to isolate sound from thought, or thought from sound." We have just begun, in the last few decades, to understand the neurological processes occurring when we speak, we understand still less about those involved in reading and writing, but we may be sure of this: 'full' writing cannot be divorced from speech; words, and the scripts that employ words, involve both sounds *and* signs.

And that is what makes archaeological decipherment so complex and fascinating. To decipher an ancient written language means to be able both to pronounce the sounds and words represented by the signs, *and* to understand the original meaning of those words in an ancient, and possibly long-extinct tongue. Decipherment means both *transliteration* of signs into sounds, and translation of sounds into meaning. Let us now have a tour, an overview, of the main avenues open to the decipherer that are currently being explored in the attack on undeciphered scripts, before we take a look at some successful decipherments in detail in part one.

————

The first-ever reference to 'deciphering'—written by an Englishman, Thomas Herbert, in 1677—referred to the cuneiform inscriptions of the Persian king Darius at Persepolis, a wonder of the world which was then almost entirely mysterious. Herbert called them "well worthy the scrutiny of those ingenious persons that delight themselves in the dark and difficult Art or Exercise of deciphering".

Nearly three centuries later, Michael Ventris summarized the process so masterfully that I cannot resist quoting him in full:

❝ Each operation needs to be planned in three phases: an exhaustive *analysis* of the signs, words and contexts in all the available inscriptions, designed to extract every possible clue as to the spelling system, meaning and language structure; an experimental *substitution* of phonetic values to give possible words and inflections in a known or postulated language; and a decisive *check*, preferably with the aid of virgin material, to ensure that the apparent results are not due to fantasy, coincidence or circular reasoning. ❞

Remember these wise words of Ventris: "fantasy, coincidence or circular reasoning". In the second part of this book you will come across examples of all three situations masquerading as true decipherments.

'Pseudo-hieroglyphic' script (as yet
undeciphered) from Byblos on the
Phoenician coast of modern Lebanon,
2nd millennium BC.

One of the truths of archaeological decipherment is that it attracts both geniuses and cranks; and it is not always easy to tell the two apart. Sometimes, a successful decipherer of one script gets it into his head that he can decipher other scripts and becomes a crank–a fear that seems to have haunted Ventris and kept him from tackling Linear A after his triumph with Linear B. Undeciphered scripts, the Easter Island *rongorongo* scholar Jacques Guy unceremoniously declares, are "powerful kook attractors".

What are the minimum conditions for any degree of decipherment to be feasible? According to Ventris again, "Prerequisites are that the material should be large enough for the analysis to yield usable results, and (in the case of an unreadable script without bilinguals or identifiable proper names) that the concealed language should be related to one which we already know."

Perhaps the most significant fact about all the successful decipherments has been this: the would-be decipherers had masses of text to work with–eventually, even if not initially. Alas, there is not a big mass of text available for any of the undeciphered scripts; and some of what is available is repetitious. The largest corpus belongs to Etruscan, with some 13,000 inscriptions (many of them fragmentary or graffiti) mainly of a funerary nature, scattered over central Italy; the smallest is that of the Phaistos disc, with a mere 242 characters of text consisting of 45 different signs. (Note here the crucial distinction between *characters* and *signs*; the two words are often used interchangeably in writing about writing, which can sometimes be confusing.) Since the Phaistos disc signs write a language of which we know nothing, there is absolutely no hope of deciphering the disc unless and until more of the script turns up in excavations–though this has not stopped dozens of people, including a few classical scholars, from claiming to have deciphered the disc since its discovery in Crete in 1908. By the same token,

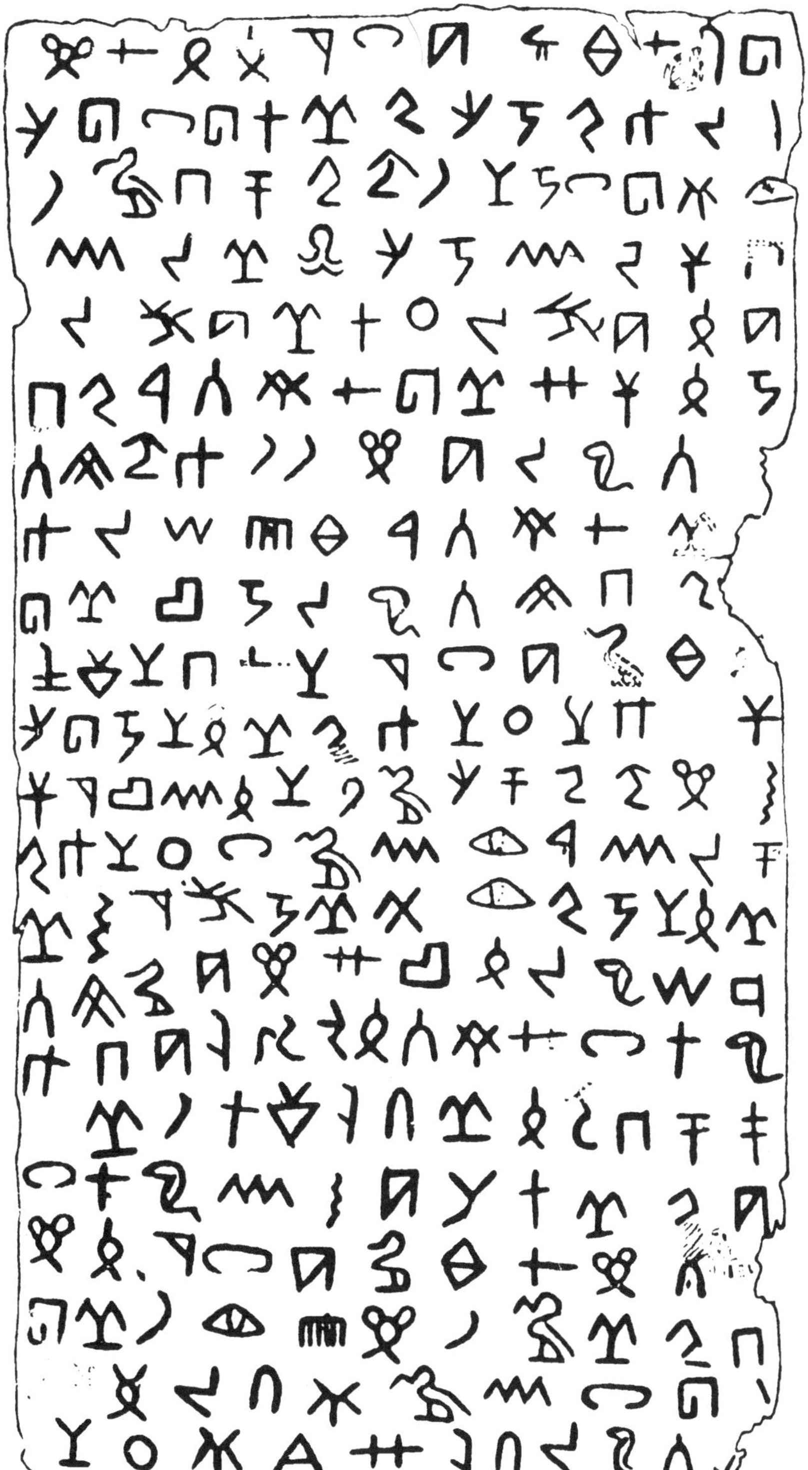

it is also impossible to decipher the tantalizing 'pseudo-hieroglyphs' found at Byblos (the ancient center of papyrus production that gave the Greeks their word for 'book' and hence the West its 'Bible') on the coast of modern Lebanon, which date from the 2nd millennium BC and consist of 1038 characters classifiable into 114 signs.

Linear B was in fact only decipherable by Ventris when, following Arthur Evans's death, the Linear B inscriptions of Knossos were finally published in 1952, half a century after Evans dug the tablets out of the ground, and were supplemented by a second major 'injection' of tablets from mainland Greece (including the tablet with the four-handled cups). Ventris's collaborator Chadwick explained to me in a letter in 1989, distilling a lifetime's thought on the subject, his view that there is a 'critical mass' in decipherment:

> " Since the invention of the atomic bomb, the concept of critical mass has become familiar; but it is not realized that this applies to decipherments too. By this I mean the quantity of text which will ensure that a few correct guesses will produce a chain reaction leading to more solutions. There is no formula known to me for determining the critical mass; it depends of course on the complexity of the script, and I should guess that it contains n squared where n is the number of different signs in the script. But this means that the Phaistos disc, with about 250 characters of text and 45 different signs, is undecipherable. Linear B was deciphered in 1952 precisely because a sufficient corpus of material had just been made available. "

Chadwick was not saying that if you had n-squared text characters, a script would definitely be decipherable. But he was suggesting that since 45 squared equals 2025, and this number is nearly ten times 250, a Phaistos disc decipherment is almost certainly impossible. With Linear B, by contrast, there were several tens of thousands of text characters of Linear B available to Ventris by mid-1952—which was several times bigger than 7569, the square of 87, the number of basic Linear B signs.

Other decipherment experts are highly skeptical of Chadwick's 'n-squared' formula, and think it extremely unlikely there is a single decipherment formula applicable to all scripts, because there are too many variables in decipherment. They stress that what works for a syllabic script like Linear B is unlikely to apply directly to an alphabetic script and, even less likely to apply to a more complex logosyllabic script like Egyptian hieroglyphic. Each sign in an alphabet, for instance, stands (ideally if not in practice) for only one sound–vowel or consonant–whereas each sign in a syllabic script represents an inherent vowel *and* consonant: that is twice as much phonetic information per sign and a correspondingly higher chance of setting off a chain reaction when a few syllabic signs have been correctly identified. Then there is the question of the underlying language of the script, also mentioned by Ventris as a "prerequisite", in the absence of bilinguals or identifiable proper names. "One must remember that the moment at which Ventris 'deciphered' Linear B was the moment at which he recognized that it was Greek–a language he knew to some extent," comments Elizabeth Barber, the author of *Archaeological Decipherment: A Handbook*. "If it had been some lost language that we do not know from any other sources, it would have required far more text even to get a toe-hold (as with Etruscan). So 'n squared' does not help us there."

It is a fact that in each successful decipherment, the language was assumed to be related to a known language: for example, Coptic (Egyptian hieroglyphs), Semitic languages (Mesopotamian and Ugaritic cuneiform) and Avestan/Sanskrit (Persian cuneiform), Greek (Linear B), and various Mayan languages of Central America (Mayan glyphs). With the ancient scripts that are still to be deciphered, the best hope lies in identifying a modern language that is likely, on firm historical and cultural grounds, to be related to the script's concealed language: a licence for scholars to attempt to reconstruct the ancestor of the modern language.

There is much uncertainty in such reconstructions, given the magnitude of change in languages over the centuries and millennia; and scholars have to be careful not to rely too much on apparent similarities between words of similar meaning in different languages—the so-called 'method of resemblances' or 'etymological method'—when in fact the resemblance is only accidental. (There are bound to be occasional such deceptive coincidences between unrelated languages, as a result of the limited set of sounds that the human vocal apparatus can produce.) Better, because more rigorous, is the 'comparative method', which looks for regular *patterns* of sound correspondence between languages that may be projected back into their earlier forms; patterns are not so subject to coincidence as individual words, and they change more slowly over time. But the comparative method requires more data, and hence more time and effort in collection and analysis, than the etymological method.

A whole sub-discipline, historical linguistics, is devoted to reconstructions. Its best-known product is a proto-Indo-European language, spoken perhaps 8000-6000 years ago, reconstructed from structural similarities between words in Sanskrit, Greek, Latin and other European languages. (For example, the correspondence between English *t* and German *z*: *ten/zehn*, *tooth/Zahn*, *timber/Zimmer*, *tell/zahlen*.) Reconstruction of the language of Easter Island's *rongorongo* inscriptions is theoretically possible given the strong likelihood that it is closely related to well-known Polynesian languages. But efforts to reconstruct the Etruscan language from Indo-European languages, especially Latin and Greek, have proved fruitless. Etruscan seems to be an 'isolate', unrelated to any Indo-European language. (So too is Sumerian, but it has proved to be reconstructable through the extensive bilingual inscriptions written in both Sumerian and Akkadian cuneiform, the second of which can be read because Akkadian is a Semitic language, closely related to Babylonian. Unfortunately, we lack extensive bilinguals for Etruscan.)

To return to the signs themselves, independent of considerations of the language, there are numerous possibilities for analysis of the kind mentioned above by Ventris. But before the epigraphers can get properly started, they need high-quality photographs and, as important, scrupulous drawings of the inscriptions. This may seem obvious, yet it is surprising how much labor has been expended on attempting to decipher unclear texts. The careful photographing and drawing of inscriptions is unglamorous work, involving painstaking fieldwork and collaboration between scholarly editors and the (often-scattered) institutions that contain the inscriptions—but without all this hard work, analysis is seriously handicapped. Only in the last decade or so have Linear A and Indus script decipherers had available to them a reliable corpus of images, and the latter is not yet complete. *Rongorongo* decipherers do not yet have reliable photographs at their disposal; they are still, so to speak, looking through the dusty glass of museum cases, regrets Jacques Guy.

There are two elements of an unknown script that usually yield up their secrets without too much effort. The first is the direction of writing: from left to right or from right to left, from top to bottom or from bottom to top. Clues to the direction include the position of unfilled space in the text, the way in which characters sometimes crowd (on the left or on the right), and the direction in which pictographic signs face. However, there are certain scripts that are written *boustrophedon* (from the Greek for 'as the ox turns', when ploughing), in other words first from left to right (say), then from right to left, then again from left to right, and so on. There are even reverse-boustrophedon scripts, in which the writer turned the original document through 180 degrees come the end of each line; *rongorongo* is an example of this.

The second element is the system of counting. Numerals frequently stand out graphically from the rest of the text, especially if they are used for calculations (which helpfully suggests that the non-numerical signs next to the numerals are likely to stand for counted objects or people). Easily visible numerals are a particular feature of the Linear B and Mayan scripts and, among the undeciphered scripts, of the proto-Elamite script; and the numerical system is obvious in the Etruscan script, Linear A and the Zapotec and Isthmian scripts, fairly clear in the Indus script, but seems to be largely absent from the Meroitic script and *rongorongo*, and not at all evident in the Phaistos disc. Of course, in working out a system of ancient numerals, one has to be aware that it may differ radically from our decimal, 'place-value' system; the Babylonians, for instance, used a sexagesimal system (from which we inherit 60 seconds in a minute and 360 degrees in a circle), and no zero.

More challenging than direction of writing or numerals is the analysis of the sign system as a whole. Suppose you were unfamiliar with the roman alphabet. If you were to take a typical chapter of an ordinary novel printed in English, it would be a fairly straightforward matter, by careful study and comparison of the thousands of characters in the text, to work out that they could be classified into a set of signs: 26 lower-case ones and a similar number of upper-case signs (though you might wonder whether letters with ascenders like b, d, f, h, k should be classified with the lower-case or the upper-case letters)–plus sundry other signs, mainly punctuation marks and numerals. Now imagine that the same text is handwritten. Immediately, the task of isolating the signs is far harder, because the letters are joined up and different writers write the same letter in different ways, also differently from its printed equivalent, and not always distinctly.

The same sign written in a variant form is known in epigraphy as an *allograph*. A key challenge for the epigrapher/decipherer–who naturally cannot be sure in advance that different-looking signs are in fact allographs of only one sign–is how to distinguish signs which are genuinely different, such as 'l' and '1', from signs which are probably allographs, such as 'a' and α (not to mention A). Judging by deciphered scripts, an undeciphered script may easily contain three or four allographs of the same basic sign. The would-be decipherer needs to be able to work out, say, which of the stick figures in this cipher-text from the Sherlock Holmes story "The Adventure of the Dancing Men", are allographs:

Ditto for these undeciphered Easter Island *rongorongo* signs:

Unless epigraphers can distinguish the allographs with a fair degree of confidence, generally by comparing their contexts in many very similar inscriptions, they cannot classify the signs in a script correctly, neither can they establish the total number of signs. Classification is self-evidently crucial to decipherment, but the number of signs is almost as important. Alphabets and consonantal scripts (like Hebrew and Arabic) number between 20 and nearly 40 signs (Russian has 36, Hebrew 22 signs). Essentially syllabic scripts, in which the signs stand for syllables not vowels or consonants, number between 40 and about 85-90 basic signs (Persian has 40 signs, Linear B 87 signs, and Japanese around 50 *kana*). More complex scripts, which mix relatively small numbers of phonetic signs with large numbers of logograms, such as Mayan and Egyptian hieroglyphs, and Babylonian cuneiform, number hundreds of signs, or even (as in Chinese characters and Japanese *kanji*) thousands of signs.

Once we know the number of signs in an undeciphered script, we can therefore get a fair idea of whether it is an alphabetic/consonantal script, a syllabary, or a mixture of syllables and logograms, i.e. a logosyllabic script—without having any idea of the phonetic values of the signs. This broad system of classifying scripts was first recognized in the 1870s and was taken up by 20th-century decipherers. The decipherers of Ugaritic, a cuneiform script from Syria (ancient Ugarit), quickly realized that it had only 30 signs and therefore could not be a logosyllabic script like Babylonian cuneiform. Ventris, on the basis of the number of Linear B signs, convinced himself that Linear B was a syllabic script, not an alphabet or a logosyllabic script, which was an important step in the direction of decipherment. A similar line of argument has been useful, since Ventris's time, in narrowing the range of possibilities for the still-undeciphered scripts: the script of the Phaistos disc, for instance, with a minimum of 45 signs (there may be a few more signs not shown in such a small sample as the disc), is likely to be a syllabary. The following table gives the numbers of signs in different (ancient and modern) scripts:

| Logosyllabic script | Number of signs |
| --- | --- |
| Chinese | 5000 + |
| Egyptian hieroglyphs | 2500 + |
| Mayan glyphs | 800 + |
| Sumerian cuneiform | 600 + |
| Hittite hieroglyphs | 497 |

| Syllabic script | |
| --- | --- |
| Linear B | 87 |
| Cherokee | 85 |
| Cypriot | 56 |
| Persian | 40 |

| Alphabetic and Consonantal scripts | |
| --- | --- |
| Russian | 36 |
| Sanskrit | 35 |
| Anglo-Saxon | 31 |
| Arabic | 28 |
| English | 26 |
| Hebrew | 22 |
| Etruscan | 20 |

If the signs of an undeciphered script can be correctly classified, with the allographs accurately identified—a big 'if', it has to be said—a numbered sign list can be made and each inscription can be written in terms of a sequence of numbers instead of the usual graphic symbols; the inscription can also be classified by computer in a *concordance*, i.e. a catalogue organized by sign (not by inscription) that under each sign lists every inscription containing the particular sign. (Literary concordances are used by scholars to research every instance of a particular word in, say, the entire works of Shakespeare.) Concordances offer important possibilities for analyzing the distribution of signs. Once all the text data has been computerized in a concordance, one can ask the computer to calculate the relative sign frequencies (e.g. which is the commonest sign, and which sign is the least common), or to list all the inscriptions in which a particular sign occurs; and, further, all the inscriptions in which a particular combination of signs occurs. If one suspects this combination of representing, say, a certain word or proper name, one can then analyze in exactly which contexts (e.g. at the beginning of inscriptions, in the middle of words, next to which other signs?) the combination occurs—within every inscription in a corpus.

Although such frequency analysis has been done by computer in the case of the Linear A, Meroitic and Indus script corpuses, the truth is that computers have made little impact on archaeological decipherment. They came along more or less too late for Ventris (who anyway does not appear to have been interested in computing), but none of the decipherers of the 1980s and 90s has found computers as useful as they hoped. One reason is the difficulty of discriminating between signs and their allographs, which is still a matter of human judgement; another is the great graphical complexity of, say, the Mayan script, which does not lend itself to the black-and-white, discrete nature of numerical classification; and yet another reason, more general, is that there is not really enough text available in the undeciphered scripts for computerized statistical techniques to prove decisive. On the whole, successful archaeological decipherment has turned out to require a synthesis of logic and intuition based, as already remarked, on wide linguistic, archaeological, historical and cultural knowledge that computers do not (and presumably cannot) possess.

This is especially relevant to the question of what constitutes 'sense' in the results of a decipherment. How do you judge whether the meaning is right—at the pivotal moment when, as Ventris earlier remarked, you conduct "an experimental substitution of phonetic values to give possible words and inflections in a known or postulated language"? For example: Knorozov's 'tzul', which meant 'dog' in Yucatec Mayan; Ventris's 'iereu', which clearly meant 'priest' (as in Greek 'hiereus', the root word in 'hiero-glyph', meaning 'sacred carvings'); not to mention the many names, such as Ptolemy, Cleopatra, Alexander, produced by substituting hypothesized phonetic values into Egyptian hieroglyphic words.

Those who approach decipherment expecting sensational revelations—of great battles and the fall of civilizations or grand philosophical discussions and astrological prognostications, leave aside visitations from E.T.'s as one *rongorongo* 'decipherer' has claimed—are likely to find their expectations confirmed in the mysterious signs of an undeciphered script, even if they have to invent an underlying language with no plausible relationship to any known language (the correctness of which can naturally never be proved or disproved). But as Chadwick, echoing Ventris, saw decipherment, "The simplest, most mundane and least surprising explanation of any inscription, is likely to be the correct one". That is, the most probable solution should be as economical with new assumptions about content and language as possible, and should fit, not contradict, the existing body of archaeological knowledge about ancient civilizations in general and the civilization under study in particular.

Thus it was reasonable to suppose that the undeciphered Linear B tablets would contain abbreviated bureaucratic accounts, not paeans to the gods or epic poetry like Homer's, for at least three simple reasons. First, the tablets plainly contained many numerals and pictograms of mundane objects (vessels, animals, chariots and so on); second, they were scratched on a cheap and relatively impermanent medium, clay, without much care for aesthetics, unlike the beautiful contemporary Minoan seals carved on gemstones; and lastly, they were discovered in what was obviously a palace archive, like the much larger palace archives of clay tablets found in Mesopotamia containing thousands of bureaucratic records in cuneiform. Here Chadwick liked to recall an incident from the early days of his joint work with Ventris on the decipherment. He had pointed out to Ventris that they had found the names of four classical Greek gods on a single tablet (such as 'poseda[o]', apparently an early form of Poseidon)—and Ventris had been horrified, because this was exactly the sort of too-good-to-be-true result that previous, eccentric attempts at decipherment had been offering as 'proof'. "He was quite right to be very skeptical, although I was later proved to be right", Chadwick observed. The numeral 1 also appeared on the tablet, so it was probably a record of something unknown, such as an animal for sacrifice, dedicated one apiece to the four gods: a fairly mundane explanation, consistent with ritual inscriptions in many early cultures.

Given the extraordinary interest of the texts revealed by the Egyptian hieroglyphic decipherment and the surprising and fascinating epigraphic revelations of life among the ancient Maya of the past two decades, I think Chadwick was being typically over-cautious about what we may find in the undeciphered scripts. (Linear B was perhaps the least exciting decipherment in terms of content, if the most intellectually demanding script to decipher.) But one must remember that Chadwick was a scholar who had been exposed, whether he liked it or not, to more examples of highly imaginative decipherment of the alluringly mysterious Phaistos disc probably than any man alive (as we shall see when we dip into his 'Disc' files in the final chapter of part two). Like Chadwick, readers of this book will have to examine the evidence for themselves and, in the final analysis, make up their own minds about what secrets—mundane, sensational, or otherwise—may be lurking in the undeciphered signs.

———

The most vivid way into the challenges posed by the undeciphered scripts is to see how some of the deciphered scripts were 'cracked'. Part one tells the stories, in three consecutive chapters, of three great decipherments: Champollion and the Egyptian hieroglyphs; Ventris and Linear B; and Knorozov and the Maya decipherment. These accounts of the elements essential to success demonstrate the main approaches used by decipherers, and show the often-surprising ways in which phonetic signs (syllabic and alphabetic) and logograms (pictographic and non-pictographic) make up functional writing systems. They also reveal the obstacles to decipherment—intellectual and emotional—and the somewhat disconcerting truth that decipherers occasionally make the right moves for the wrong reasons.

Many successful decipherments have been left out, such as those of the cuneiform scripts, the Hittite (Luvian) hieroglyphs of Anatolia and the most recent example of all, Carian, another Anatolian language written in a script that borrowed some of its letters from the Greek alphabet. Interesting though these are, the techniques involved were not unique, and this is not a book chiefly about deciphered scripts; every significant deciphered script is covered in the second (1999) edition of Maurice Pope's *The Story of Decipherment.*

The undeciphered scripts in part two have been organized according to the following basic principles, depending on the state of expert knowledge of the *script* relative to that of its underlying *language*. We shall begin with scripts that are comparatively well understood but which write unknown languages (i.e. languages that are apparently unrelated to any known language): the Meroitic, Etruscan, Linear A and proto-Elamite scripts. Then we shall move on to scripts that are not well understood but which are believed to write partially known languages: *rongorongo*, and the Zapotec and Isthmian scripts. Finally, we shall deal with unknown scripts which write essentially unknown languages (the toughest challenge of all): the Indus script, and the symbols on the Phaistos disc.

The minimal amount of text on this unique object, and the seemingly endless attempts to decipher it, suggest the title of the book's Conclusion, "The urge to decipher". Major newspapers and magazines, and international journals such as *Nature, Science, Scientific American, Antiquity, New Scientist* and *National Geographic*, regularly report claims of decipherment, sometimes in detail. There are also several high-quality websites devoted to undeciphered scripts (as well as a number of distinctly unreliable ones!). Why are so many people worldwide fascinated by the subject? In this last chapter, we shall see what we can learn, in the widest sense, from the decipherment challenge and from ancient writing systems as a whole.

Again, in part two some undeciphered scripts have been omitted, as also the special problems of reading the runic alphabet of northern Europe and ancient Chinese inscriptions ('oracle bones' and even older pottery marks), since most of the runic and all of the Chinese inscriptions are written in essentially familiar scripts and languages even if the meanings of some inscriptions are contentious. Among the omitted undeciphered scripts is the intriguing but scanty proto-Sinaitic script (c. 1500 BC) found by Sir Flinders Petrie in 1905 in the middle of the Sinai Peninsula, scratched on one or two small sphinxes and some rocks. Tentatively deciphered in 1916 by the Egyptologist Sir Alan Gardiner as signs resembling Egyptian hieroglyphs but written in a Semitic language, the proto-Sinaitic script is thought by some scholars to be a sort of 'missing link' between Egyptian hieroglyphs and the enigmatic origins of the alphabet in Palestine. (In 1993/94, two still earlier fragments of what may or may not be the very first alphabet, were discovered, this time in ancient Egypt proper, which reinforces Gardiner's suggestion that the alphabet may have been inspired by Egyptian hieroglyphs, and not invented in Palestine—though the debate is far from settled.) Omitted too is the Tangut script of north-western China, based on Chinese characters and introduced in 1036 AD to write the now-extinct Tibeto-Burman language. A final omission is that of the much-debated Voynich manuscript, 235 mysterious pages probably originating in medieval Europe which were donated to Yale University in 1969 by the book collector Wilfrid Voynich (some slight evidence suggests the author may have been Roger Bacon, which, if correct, would place the manuscript in the 13th century).

In the proto-Sinaitic case, there is simply not enough material to confirm, deny, or even seriously discuss a decipherment, while the Tangut culture is too insignificant for a non-specialist book, and the Voynich manuscript is really a challenge for cryptanalysts rather than archaeological decipherers and therefore outside the province of this book. Although all noteworthy undeciphered scripts (but not codes and ciphers) will get a mention somewhere in this book in the appropriate place, we shall concentrate on those that belong to significant cultures (such as the Etruscan alphabet), or that are undeniably fascinating (like *rongorongo*), or that offer some long-term prospect of decipherment (like the proto-Elamite script)—or that fulfil all three criteria (like the Indus script).

Finally, I ought perhaps to say, openly, that I do not believe any of the scripts in part two can be fully deciphered as of now. But I think that various degrees of progress are achievable, and if new material were to be discovered—as happened in recent decades with every script in this book except the *rongorongo* script and the Phaistos disc—especially if such material were to be substantial, then the prospects for a new decipherment could brighten. Then, readers with ambitions to follow in the footsteps of Michael Ventris could be in a position, with the help of the references to the scholarly literature at the end of this book and the resources of the world-wide web, to make their own advances.

# PART ONE
*Three Great Decipherments*

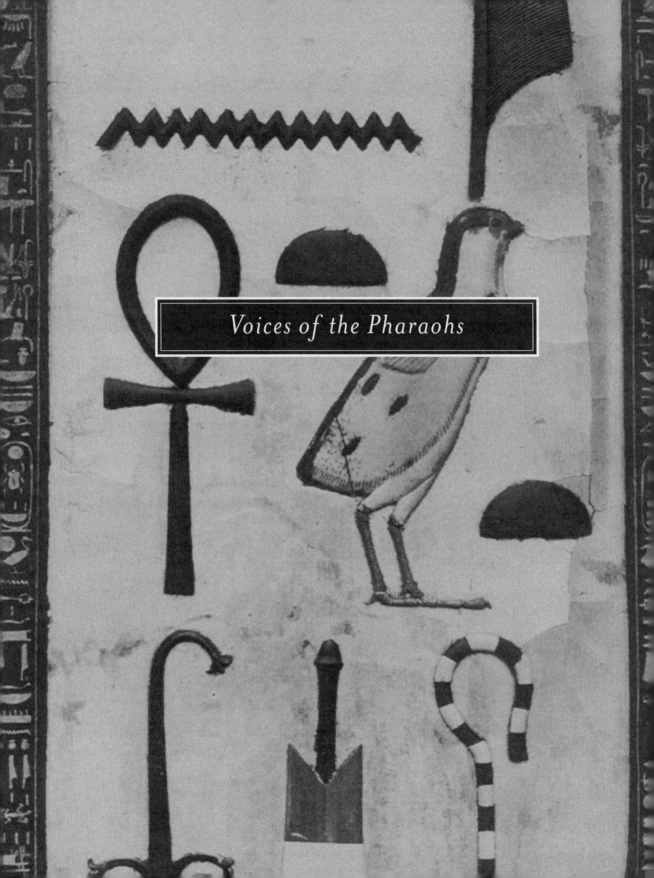

Voices of the Pharaohs

# I

## EGYPTIAN HIEROGLYPHS

Successful decipherments of ancient scripts have never sprung fully formed from the mind of one decipherer. They have arisen from an accumulation of insights achieved by many scholars working over many decades or even longer, often against the received wisdom of their time. The first great decipherment of all, that of the Egyptian hieroglyphs in 1823, had to sweep away centuries of erroneous thinking. To understand how the hieroglyphic code was 'cracked', we therefore have to go back into history as far

as classical antiquity, and follow each major step and obstacle (with one or two minor entertaining digressions) in order to reach the breakthrough in understanding of Jean-François Champollion.

The civilization of the pharaohs went into eclipse more than 2000 years ago when it was conquered by Alexander the Great and came under the Hellenistic rule of the Ptolemy dynasty. Such was its legendary magnificence, however, that the Greeks and Romans, especially the Greeks, regarded ancient Egypt with a

*Cynocephalus, a fabled dog-headed man, inspired by Horapollo, the chief classical writer on the Egyptian hieroglyphs. Many Renaissance artists drew hieroglyphs based on the descriptions of Horapollo. Left by Albrecht Dürer from a German edition, above from a French edition.*

paradoxical mixture of reverence for its wisdom and antiquity and contempt for its 'barbarism'. The very word hieroglyph derives, as we know, from the Greek for 'sacred carving'. Egyptian obelisks were taken to ancient Rome and became symbols of prestige; today, thirteen large obelisks stand in Rome, while only four remain in Egypt.

The classical authors generally credited Egypt with the invention of writing (though Pliny the Elder attributed it to the inventors of cuneiform). But none of them learnt how to read the hieroglyphs as they could read their Greek and Latin alphabet, despite the fact that hieroglyphic inscriptions continued to be written in Egypt as late as AD 394. They preferred to believe, as Diodorus Siculus wrote in the 1st century BC, that the Egyptian writing was "not built up from syllables to express the underlying meaning, but from the appearance of the things drawn and by their metaphorical meaning, learned by heart." Thus,

a picture of a hawk signified anything that happened swiftly, a crocodile signified all that was evil.

By far the most important authority was an Egyptian magus named Horapollo (Horus Apollo) supposedly from Nilopolis in Upper Egypt. His treatise, *Hieroglyphica*, was probably composed in Greek, during the 4th century AD or later, and then sank from view until a manuscript was discovered on a Greek island in about 1419 and became known in Renaissance Italy. Published in 1505, the book was hugely influential: it went through 30 editions, one of them illustrated by Dürer, and even remains in print.

Horapollo's readings of the hieroglyphs were a combination of the (mainly) fictitious and the genuine. For instance, "when they wish to indicate a sacred scribe, or a prophet, or an embalmer, or the spleen, or odor, or laughter, or sneezing, or rule, or judge, they draw a dog." Or consider his "What they mean by a vulture":

> " When they mean a mother, or boundaries, or foreknowledge...they draw a vulture. A mother, since there is no male in this species of animal... the vulture stands for sight since of all other animals the vulture has the keenest vision... It means boundaries, because when a war is about to break out, it limits the place in which the battle will occur, hovering over it for seven days. Foreknowledge, because of what has been said above and because it looks forward to the amount of corpses which the slaughter will provide it for food... "

This was largely fantasy—except for "mother": the hieroglyph for mother is indeed a vulture.

Fuelled by Horapollo, the Renaissance revival of classical learning brought a revival of the Greek and Roman belief in hieroglyphic wisdom. The first of many scholars in the modern world to write a whole book on the hieroglyphs was a Venetian, Pierius Valerianus. He published it in 1556, and illustrated his readings with delightfully fantastic 'Renaissance' hieroglyphs. The most famous of the early interpreters was the Jesuit priest Athanasius Kircher. In the mid-17th century, Kircher was Rome's widely accepted pundit on ancient Egypt. But his voluminous writings took him far beyond 'Egyptology'; "sometimes called the last Renaissance man" (*Encyclopædia Britannica*), Kircher attempted to encompass the totality of human knowledge. The result was a mixture of folly and brilliance—with the former easily predominant—from which his reputation never recovered.

In 1666 he was entrusted with the publication of a hieroglyphic inscription on an Egyptian obelisk in Rome's Piazza della Minerva. This had been erected on the orders of Pope Alexander VII to a design by Bernini (it stands to this day, mounted

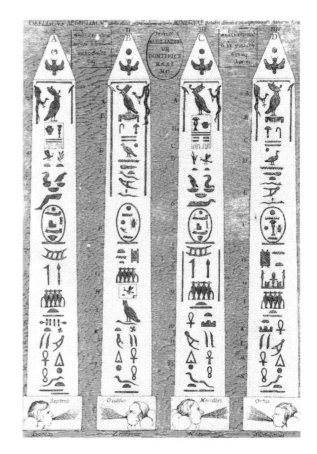

*Four faces of an obelisk brought from Egypt to Rome and erected in the Piazza della Minerva in 1667—as drawn by Athanasius Kircher. The oval rings are cartouches.*

on a stone elephant, encapsulating the concept 'wisdom supported by strength'). Kircher gave his reading of a cartouche, i.e. a small group of hieroglyphs in the inscription enclosed in an oval ring, as follows:

> " The protection of Osiris against the violence of Typho must be elicited according to the proper rites and ceremonies by sacrifices and by appeal to the tutelary Genii of the triple world in order to ensure the enjoyment of the prosperity customarily given by the Nile against the violence of the enemy Typho. "

*Coptic ostracon, 6th century AD: a pastoral letter
from a bishop. Coptic died out as a spoken language
around 1000 AD but is still the liturgical language
of the Coptic church.*

| | | |
|---|---|---|
| Ⲁ | alpha | a |
| Ⲃ | vita | v (b) |
| Ⲅ | gamma | g |
| Ⲇ | delta | d |
| Ⲉ | epsilon | e |
| Ⲍ | zita | z |
| Ⲏ | ita | i, e |
| Ⲑ | tita | th |
| Ⲓ | iota | i |
| Ⲕ | kappa | k |
| Ⲗ | laula | l |
| Ⲙ | mi | m |
| Ⲛ | ni | n |
| Ⲝ | xi | x |
| Ⲟ | omicron | o |
| Ⲡ | pi | p |
| Ⲣ | ro | r |
| Ⲥ | sima | s |
| Ⲧ | tau | t |
| Ⲩ | ypsilon | y, u |
| Ⲫ | phi | ph |
| Ⲭ | khi | ch, kh |
| Ⲯ | psi | ps |
| Ⲱ | omega | o |
| Ϣ | shei | s |
| Ϥ | fai | f |
| Ϩ | hori | h |
| Ϫ | djandja | g |
| Ϭ | chima | c |
| Ϯ | ti | ti |

*The Coptic alphabet, and its phonetic values.*

Today's accepted reading is simply the name of a pharaoh, Wahibre (Apries), of the 26th dynasty!

By contrast, Kircher genuinely assisted in the rescue of Coptic, the language of the last phase of ancient Egypt, by publishing the first Coptic grammar and vocabulary. The word Copt is derived from the Arabic 'qubti', which itself derives from Greek 'Aiguptos' (Egypt). The Coptic script was invented around the end of the 1st century AD, and from the 4th to the 10th centuries Coptic flourished as a spoken language and as the official language of the Egyptian church; after that it was replaced by Arabic, except in the church, and by the time of Kircher, the mid-17th century, the language was headed for extinction (though it is still used in the liturgy). During the 18th century, however, several scholars acquired a knowledge of Coptic and its alphabet, which consists in its standard form of the 24 Greek letters plus six signs borrowed from the (demotic) script of ancient Egypt. This knowledge would prove essential in the decipherment of the hieroglyphs in the 19th century.

Wrong-headed theories about ancient Egypt— even, were the Chinese Egyptian colonists?—still held sway, but during the Enlightenment some scholars began to question the classical/Renaissance view of the hieroglyphs, and make tentative, rational moves towards analyzing them. In Britain, William Warburton, the future bishop of Gloucester, was the first to suggest, in 1740, that all writing, hieroglyphs included, might have evolved from pictures, rather than by divine origin. The Abbé Barthélemy, an admirer of Warburton, then made a sensible guess that obelisk cartouches might contain the names of kings or gods—ironically, on the basis of two false observations (one being that the hieroglyphs in obelisk cartouches differed from all other hieroglyphs): a phenomenon we shall encounter more than once in considering successful decipherments.

Finally, near the end of the century, a Danish scholar, Georg Zoëga, hazarded that some hieroglyphs might be, in some measure at least, what he called "notae phoneticae", Latin for "phonetic signs", representing sounds rather than concepts in the Egyptian language. The path towards decipherment of the hieroglyphs was being cleared.

And now we have reached a turning point: the arrival of Napoleon's invasion force in Egypt in 1798 and the discovery of the Rosetta stone. The word cartouche, as applied to Egyptian hieroglyphs, dates from this fateful expedition. The oval rings enclosing groups of hieroglyphs visible within inscriptions on temple walls and elsewhere to any casual observer reminded the French soldiers of the cartridges ('cartouches') in their guns.

Fortunately, the military force was almost as interested in culture as in conquest. A party of French savants, including the celebrated mathematician Jean Baptiste Joseph Fourier, accompanied the army and remained in Egypt for some three years. There were also many artists, chief of whom was Domenique Vivant Denon. Between 1809 and 1828, he and others illustrated the *Description de l'Egypte*, and the whole of Europe was astonished by the marvels of the pharaohs. One of the French drawings shows the city of Thebes, with the columns of the temple of Luxor behind and highly inscribed obelisks in the foreground. The carved scenes depict the charge of chariot-borne archers under the command of Ramesses II against the Hittites in the battle of Kadesh (*c.* 1275 BC). Napoleon's army was so awestruck by this spectacle that, according to a witness, "it halted of itself and, by one spontaneous impulse, grounded its arms."

It was a demolition squad of French soldiers which stumbled across the Rosetta stone in mid-July 1799, probably built into a very old wall in the village of Rashid (Rosetta), on a branch of the Nile just a few miles from the sea. Recognizing its importance, the officer in charge had the stone moved immediately to Cairo. Copies were made and distributed to the scholars of Europe during 1800—a remarkably open-minded gesture considering the politics of the period. In 1801, the stone was shifted to Alexandria in an attempt to avoid its capture by British forces. But after a somewhat unseemly wrangle, it was eventually handed over, shipped to Britain, and displayed in the British Museum, where it has remained ever since (apart from an excursion to Paris in the 1970s on the 150th anniversary of Champollion's decipherment).

According to one of the museum's curators of Egyptian antiquities, Richard Parkinson (already quoted in the Introduction), the Rosetta stone is probably "the most popular single object in the British Museum". In his catalogue of the exhibition "Cracking Codes", celebrating the bicentenary of the stone's discovery, he writes: "Unfortunately, the Stone's iconic status seems to encourage visitors to reach out and touch the almost miraculous object." The familiar white characters on the black surface, polished by generations of visitors' hands until the stone looked more like a printer's lithographic stone (which it was actually used as, in the early 19th century) than a 2000 year-old monument, were mainly the result of chalk and carnauba wax rubbed into the surface by museum curators to increase visibility and aid preservation. In the 1990s, in time for the bicentenary, this policy was changed and the stone cleaned to reveal its natural color. It is now seen to be a dark gray slab of igneous rock (not basalt, as formerly believed), which sparkles with feldspar and mica and has a pink vein through its top left-hand corner; it weighs some three quarters of a ton.

The Rosetta stone, as it would originally have looked, before it was broken.

Cartouche ————————————————

*Drawing and photograph of the Rosetta stone, key to the decipherment of the Egyptian hieroglyphs. The stone was recently cleaned in time for the bicentenary of its discovery in 1799, and the familiar black-and-white surface restored to its true appearance (shown here). The hieroglyphic section is at the top, the demotic section in the middle, and the Greek section at the bottom. One cartouche is highlighted (above).*

Even a quick glance reveals that the stone is broken (this probably occurred before it came to Rosetta), both in the right-hand corner and, most obviously, at the top. So the inscription is incomplete. Fortunately, though, there exist other similar complete inscriptions (found after the decipherment), including a near-copy inscribed fourteen years later and now in the Cairo Museum, so we can visualize the Rosetta stone as it would originally have looked (see page 57).

From the moment of discovery, it was clear that the inscription on the stone was written in three different scripts, the bottom one being the Greek alphabet and the top one—the most badly damaged—Egyptian hieroglyphs with visible cartouches. Sandwiched between them was a script about which little was known. It plainly did not resemble the Greek script, but it seemed to bear at least a slight resemblance to the hieroglyphic script above it, without having cartouches. Today we know this script as demotic, a development (c. 650 BC) from a cursive form of writing known as hieratic used in parallel with the hieroglyphic script (hieratic itself does not appear on the Rosetta stone). The name demotic derives from Greek 'demotikos', meaning 'in common use'—in contrast to sacred hieroglyphic, which was essentially a monumental script.

The first step towards decipherment was obviously to translate the Greek inscription. It turned out to be a decree issued at Memphis, the principal city of ancient Egypt, by a general council of priests from every part of the kingdom assembled on the first anniversary of the coronation of the young Ptolemy V Epiphanes, king of all Egypt, on 27 March 196 BC. Greek was used because it was the language of court and government of the descendants of Ptolemy, Alexander's general. The names Ptolemy, Alexander, Alexandria, among others, occurred in the Greek inscription.

Much of the decree is taken up, to put it bluntly, with the terms of a deal by which the priests agreed to give their support to the new king (who was only thirteen) in exchange for certain privileges. While this was of some interest to historians of ancient Egypt and its religion, the eye of would-be decipherers was caught by the last sentence. It read: "This decree shall be inscribed on a stela of hard stone in sacred [i.e. hieroglyphic] and native [i.e. demotic] and Greek characters and set up in each of the first, second and third [-rank] temples beside the image of the ever-living king." In other words, the three inscriptions—hieroglyphic, demotic and Greek—were equivalent in meaning, though not necessarily 'word for word' translations of each other. This was how scholars first knew that the stone was a bilingual inscription: the kind most sought after by decipherers. The two languages were clearly Greek and (presumably) ancient Egyptian, the language of the priests, the latter being written in two different scripts—unless the "sacred" and the "native" characters concealed *two* different languages, which seemed unlikely from the context. (In fact, as we now know, the Egyptian languages written in hieroglyphic and demotic are not identical, but they are closely related, like Latin and Renaissance Italian.)

Since the hieroglyphic section was so damaged, attention focused on the demotic. Two scholars, a distinguished French Orientalist Sylvestre de Sacy (future teacher of Champollion) and a Swedish diplomat Johan Åkerblad, adopted similar techniques. They searched for a name such as Ptolemy, by isolating repeated groups of demotic symbols located in roughly the same position as the known occurrence of Ptolemy in the Greek inscription. Having found these groups, they noticed that the names in demotic seemed to be written alphabetically, as in the Greek inscription, i.e. the demotic names contained similar numbers of characters to the letters of their assumed Greek equivalents. By matching demotic sign with Greek letter, they were able to draw up a tentative alphabet of demotic signs. Certain other words, such as 'Greek', 'Egypt', 'temple', could now be identified using this demotic alphabet. It looked as though the entire demotic script might be alphabetic like the Greek inscription.

But in fact it was not, unluckily for de Sacy and Åkerblad. They could proceed no further, because they could not get rid of their idea that the demotic inscription was in an alphabetic script–as against the hieroglyphic inscription, which they took to be wholly *non*-phonetic, its symbols expressing ideas, not sounds, along the lines of Horapollo. The apparent difference in appearance between the hieroglyphic and demotic signs, and the suffocating weight of western tradition that Egyptian hieroglyphs were a 'conceptual' script, convinced them that the invisible principles of the two scripts, hieroglyphic and demotic, were wholly different: one conceptual, the other phonetic.

Except in one element. De Sacy deserves credit as the first to make an important suggestion: that the names inside the hieroglyphic cartouches, which he naturally assumed were Ptolemy, Alexander and so on, were also spelt *alphabetically*, as in demotic. He was led to this by some information given him by one of his pupils, a student of Chinese, in 1811. The Chinese script was generally thought in Europe to be a conceptual script like the hieroglyphs. Yet, as this student pointed out, foreign (i.e. non-Chinese) names had to be written *phonetically* in Chinese with a special sign to indicate that the Chinese characters were being reduced to their phonetic value without any logographic value. (Remember the name written as a rebus on page 26, in which the two pictographic symbols are used purely phonetically to spell the name Ant-hony.) Were not Ptolemy, Alexander and so on Greek names foreign to the Egyptian language, and might not the cartouche be the ancient Egyptian hieroglyphic equivalent of the special sign in Chinese? But as for the rest of the hieroglyphs not in cartouches, including any native Egyptian names, de Sacy was convinced they must surely be non-phonetic.

————

The person who broke this impasse–and really launched the decipherment–was the Englishman Thomas Young: 'Phaenomenon' Young, to his impressed, if amused contemporaries at Cambridge University where Young was a late-arriving student in the 1790s.

*Thomas Young (1773–1829), fellow of the Royal Society, physicist, physician, linguist and major contributor to the decipherment of Egyptian hieroglyphs.*

Although he was a formidable linguist (and inventor of the term Indo-European), who also contributed significantly to the problem of longitude at sea and the principles of life insurance, Young's primary fame rests on his scientific achievements, mainly in physics. He discovered the principle of interference of light, which put the wave theory of light on a firm experimental footing; his three-color theory explained how the structure of the eye's retina senses color; in mechanics, the ratio of stress to strain in the stretching of materials is known as Young's modulus—and this is not to mention his explanation of astigmatism and a mass of less enduring work. A current dictionary of scientific biography concludes a lengthy entry on Young with some words that are also relevant to his work on the hieroglyphs: "Thomas Young was a scientist who possessed an extraordinary range of talents and a rare degree of insight, and he was able to initiate important paths of investigation that others were to take up and complete."

He started work on the Rosetta stone inscription in 1814. Like de Sacy, with whom he was corresponding in his capacity as foreign secretary of the Royal Society, Young at first concentrated on the demotic script—partly because it was more complete but also perhaps because he felt, as a rational scientist (and Quaker), some aversion for the priestly mumbo-jumbo expected in Egyptian hieroglyphs. He compared the demotic with the Greek and drew up a substantial list of equivalent words and a demotic alphabet, following the lead of de Sacy and Åkerblad; but then he went on to make a crucial fresh observation by comparing the demotic characters with the hieroglyphs.

By dint of careful examination and analysis, Young noted a "striking resemblance", hitherto neglected, between some of the cursive demotic symbols and what he called "the corresponding hieroglyphs"—the first intimation that demotic might relate directly to hieroglyphic, somewhat as modern cursive alphabetic letters partly resemble their printed equivalents. Comparing the three Rosetta stone inscriptions systematically, Young correlated words in each, such as 'king' and 'Egypt', and correctly guessed the meanings of a surprising number of hieroglyphic word groups. But "none of these characters [i.e. the hieroglyphs] could be reconciled without inconceivable violence, to the forms of any imaginable alphabet", he further remarked. No surprise there, since no one (least of all the mystical Athanasius Kircher) had ever dreamt that hieroglyphs were alphabetic. Now for the punchline: Young concluded that the demotic script was therefore *not* an alphabet but must consist rather of "imitations of the hieroglyphics... mixed with letters of the alphabet." In other words, demotic was in some way derived from hieroglyphic and had to be, in modern terminology, a mixture of logograms and phonetic signs.

The Greek/demotic/hieroglyphic comparisons by Young and earlier workers had also established the direction of Egyptian writing on the Rosetta stone: right to left in demotic and hieroglyphic, as opposed to left to right in Greek. The direction in demotic was obvious from demotic papyri in which lines started at the right and there was blank space on the left; the hieroglyphic direction could be deduced from the order of signs in the cartouches compared with the sign orders of the equivalent words in demotic and Greek. (The vertical 'base' line drawn at one end of the cartouche was seen to mark the end, not the beginning, of a word.) A right to left direction turns out to be generally true for

Egyptian inscriptions, though with many exceptions; and the individual hieroglyphs, e.g. ![glyph], ![glyph], ![glyph], face in the *opposite* direction to the direction of reading, i.e. they generally face to the right. However, for ease of reading, Egyptologists always 'normalize' hieroglyphic inscriptions so that they are readable like our familiar alphabet, from left to right. This means that while the cartouches on the Rosetta stone itself should be read from right to left, with the 'base' line on the left, the drawings of the cartouches shown below should be read in the normalized reverse direction, with the 'base' line on the right and the signs facing leftwards. (Try comparing the actual cartouches with the drawings.)

Young went further in identifying words. He acted on Barthélemy's idea that the cartouches expressed royal or religious names and the suggestion made by de Sacy that some of the cartouches might be spelt phonetically where they represented foreign names. There were six cartouches in the Rosetta stone's hieroglyphic inscription which clearly had to contain the name Ptolemy (Ptolemaios, in Greek), three of them like this:

and three of them like this:

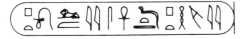

Young postulated that the longer cartouche wrote the name of Ptolemy with a title, as suggested by equivalents in the Greek inscription which read "Ptolemy, living for ever, beloved of Ptah".

This enabled him to match the hieroglyphs with English letters and phonetic values. Here is what Young himself recorded:

| Hieroglyph | Young value | Today's value |
|---|---|---|
| □ | p | p |
| ⌓ | t | t |
| ![glyph] | "not essentially necessary" | o |
| ![glyph] | lo or ole | l |
| ![glyph] | ma or simply m | m |
| ![glyph] | i | i or y |
| ![glyph] | osh or os | s |

By performing a similar analysis with the cartouche of a Ptolemaic queen, Berenike, he assigned phonetic values to four more hieroglyphs. (Her cartouche came not from the Rosetta stone but from an inscription in the temple complex of Karnak at Thebes.) Taken together, six of the values were correct, and three partly so: the beginnings of a hieroglyphic 'alphabet'. He also identified a classificatory logogram (soon to be named by Champollion a 'determinative') used to mark feminine names, and established various hieroglyphic numerical notations.

In 1819, Young published a magnificent article, "Egypt", in the supplement to the 4th edition of the *Encyclopædia Britannica*, summarizing his labors and offering English equivalents for 218 demotic and 200 hieroglyphic words, based on his equations with Greek. About 80 of these demotic-hieroglyphic equivalents have stood the test of time—an impressive record.

But now he came unstuck. The spell of Horapollo was a strong one. While Young could accept that the hieroglyphic script used an alphabet to represent non-Egyptian names—and indeed could apply this idea brilliantly—he was convinced that the remaining hieroglyphs, the part used to write the Egyptian names and the Egyptian language in general (rather than words borrowed into Egyptian from Greek), were *non*-phonetic. His fledgling hieroglyphic 'alphabet' would therefore not apply to the bulk of the hieroglyphic inscriptions, which remained mysterious. Young had made a vital move towards decipherment—and "surely deserves to be known as the decipherer of demotic" for this and later work, says the Egyptologist John Ray—but he would not be the person to break the hieroglyphic code.

Jean-François Champollion, the one who ultimately succeeded, was 17 years junior to Young, and differed greatly from him in both background and temperament. To oversimplify a complex matter: Young's primary fascination was with science, not the humanities, and he restlessly explored as wide a variety of scientific problems as possible; Champollion was passionate about human languages and societies, and became increasingly focused on, indeed obsessed with, only one goal: the unlocking of the world of ancient Egypt.

Born in 1790 during the French revolution, Champollion was initially unable to attend school. Instead, he received private tuition in Greek and Latin, and by the age of nine, it is said, he could read Homer and Virgil. Moving to Grenoble to attend the Lycée, he came into contact with Fourier, who had been the secretary of Napoleon's Egyptian mission. It was Fourier who launched the teenager into

*Jean-François Champollion (1790–1832), decipherer of Egyptian hieroglyphs. The portrait shows him holding his "Tableau des Signes Phonétiques" (see page 67) in 1823, the year of his breakthrough.*

Egyptology by showing him his collection of antiquities; according to the adult Champollion, they kindled in him the desire to read the hieroglyphs. In 1807, aged not yet 17, Champollion presented a paper on the Coptic etymology of Egyptian place names preserved in the works of Greek and Latin authors. He moved to Paris, where he saw a copy of the Rosetta stone in 1808, and spent three years studying Oriental languages and Coptic under de Sacy and others, displaying a rare linguistic gift. Then he returned to Grenoble to teach history at the Lycée, and began serious study of pharaonic Egypt. (Following the decipherment, he moved back to Paris as the first curator of the Egyptian collection at the Louvre and occupied the chair of Egyptian antiquities at the Collège de France.)

In 1814, the year in which Young became interested in hieroglyphs, Champollion wrote to the Royal Society requesting a cast of the Rosetta stone because his French copy differed from the one made by the Royal Society. Young, the foreign secretary, replied, and a correspondence began which lasted until Young's death in 1829. He duly checked some passages in the inscription for Champollion, but does not appear to have greeted the younger man's letter with enthusiasm. No doubt he became cooler still after receiving in 1815 from de Sacy, who had become disillusioned with his brilliant pupil, a letter which frankly advised him "to not communicate your discoveries too much to M. Champollion. It could happen that he might then claim to have been first." Nevertheless, Young did inform Champollion of the work which he later published in the *Encyclopædia Britannica* supplement—an influence that Champollion would be reluctant to admit at the time of his decipherment. Without doubt, the two scholars quickly came to regard each other as rivals, and an angry public controversy about Champollion's true debt to Young began in early 1823 when Young published *An Account of Some Recent Discoveries in Hieroglyphical Literature, and Egyptian Antiquities: Including the Author's Original Alphabet, as Extended by Mr. Champollion*. The argument has refused altogether to die down, nearly two centuries later. (Even Maurice Pope, in *The Story of Decipherment*, undervalues Young's contribution, as pointed out by John Ray in a recent balanced account.)

For a long while, though, Champollion ignored Young's proposals. He continued to believe that the hieroglyphs, including the foreign names in the cartouches, were *entirely* non-phonetic; as late as 1821 he published an article to this effect, "De l'écriture hiératique des anciens Egyptiens". What changed his mind—and became the key to further progress—was a copy of a bilingual obelisk inscription belonging to the English collector William Bankes, seen by Champollion around January 1822. It came from

Britain, where the obelisk had been dispatched after its removal from Philae in 1815.

The base-block inscription was in Greek, while the column inscription was in hieroglyphic script. This, however, did not make it a true bilingual, a second Rosetta stone, because the two inscriptions did not match. Notwithstanding, Bankes realized that in the Greek letters the names of Ptolemy and Cleopatra, Ptolemaic queen, were mentioned, while in the hieroglyphs two (and only two) cartouches occurred—presumably representing the same two names as written on the base.

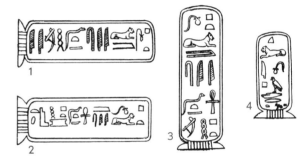

*Four cartouches drawn by Champollion: 1. Ptolemy (Rosetta stone); 2. Ptolemy with royal title (Rosetta stone); 3. Ptolemy (Philae obelisk); 4. Cleopatra (Philae obelisk).*

Champollion took the clue and ran with it. He saw that one of the Philae obelisk cartouches was almost identical to one form of the cartouche of Ptolemy on the Rosetta stone:

*Philae obelisk*

*Rosetta stone*

There was also the shorter version of the Ptolemy cartouche on the Rosetta stone:

Just as Young had done, Champollion decided that the shorter version spelt Ptolemy, while the longer Rosetta stone cartouche must involve some royal title, tacked on to Ptolemy's name. Again following Young, he now assumed that Ptolemy was spelt alphabetically, and so was Cleopatra on the Philae obelisk. He proceeded to guess the phonetic values of the hieroglyphs in both cartouches:

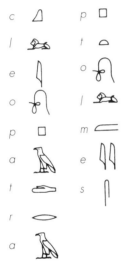

There were four signs in common, those with the values *l*, *e*, *o*, *p*, but the phonetic value *t* was represented differently. Champollion deduced correctly that the two signs for *t* were homophones, i.e. different signs with the same sound (compare in English **J**ill and **G**ill, **C**atherine and **K**atherine).

The real test, however, was whether the new phonetic values when applied to the cartouches in other inscriptions would produce sensible names.

Champollon tried them in the following one:

Substituting his phonetic values produced *Al?se?tr?*. Champollion now guessed Alksentrs = (Greek) Alexandros [Alexander]–again the two signs for *k*/*c* ( ⌒ and △ ) are homophonous, as are the two signs for *s* ( ⚊ and | ).

He went on to identify the cartouches of other rulers of non-Egyptian origin, such as Berenike (already tackled by Young) and Caesar, and a title of the Roman emperor, Autocrator:

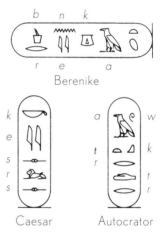

*(Opposite) Champollion's first decipherment. This table of demotic and hieroglyphic signs with their Greek equivalents was drawn up in October 1822 to accompany the printed version of Champollion's famous* Lettre à M. Dacier. *Note the extensive homophony, e.g. three different hieroglyphs corresponding to the Greek letter T (t). His own name appears in demotic script right at the bottom (highlighted), enclosed in a cartouche, though the cartouche is not easy to read using the demotic signs in the table.*

## Tableau des Signes Phonétiques
### des Écritures hiéroglyphique et Démotique des anciens Égyptiens

| Lettres Grecques | Signes Démotiques | Signes Hiéroglyphiques |
|---|---|---|
| A | | |
| B | | |
| Γ | | |
| Δ | | |
| E | | |
| Z | | |
| H | | |
| Θ | | |
| I | | |
| K | | |
| Λ | | |
| M | | |
| N | | |
| Ξ | | |
| O | | |
| Π | | |
| P | | |
| Σ | | |
| T | | |
| Υ | | |
| Φ | | |
| Ψ | | |
| X | | |
| Ω | | |
| ΤΟ. ΤΛ. | | |

On 27 September 1822, Champollion felt ready to announce these results at a meeting in Paris of the French Academy of Inscriptions, and to follow this with the publication in October of his celebrated *Lettre à M. Dacier*—Dacier was the secretary of the Academy—in which he unveiled his first shot at a complete hieroglyphic/demotic list of signs with their Greek equivalents, accompanied by a cartouche of his own name written in demotic script. (This understandable flourish, which he omitted from his later, more dignified publications, is something not easy to imagine from the pen of his more soberly scientific rival Thomas Young.)

But even his second announcement cannot be described as Champollion's great moment of breakthrough, because the vast majority of his readings, apart from a few prescient ones near the end of the *Lettre*, were still based on the premise that only *foreign* (i.e. non-Egyptian) names and words were spelt alphabetically in hieroglyphic and in demotic. The hoary idea, dating from classical times, that the hieroglyphs almost exclusively expressed only ideas, rather than ideas *and* sounds, still possessed Champollion's mind, as it did Young's. ("Ingrained preconceptions can be as ferociously guarded by scholars and scientists as a very old bone by a dog", the Mayanist Michael Coe reminds us in his story of a great 20th-century decipherment, *Breaking the Maya Code*.) Not until April 1823 did Champollion announce that he understood the principles of the hieroglyphs as a whole.

What had happened, then, in those crucial six months? The shift in Champollion's thinking is hinted at near the end of the *Lettre*, when he mentions, without giving any details, that he has recently succeeded in reading the names of some *Egyptian* names in the cartouches. These arose from copies of various reliefs and inscriptions in temples that he received only in mid-September. One of them, from the temple of Abu Simbel in Nubia, contained intriguing cartouches. They appeared to write the same name in a variety of ways, the simplest being as follows:

Champollion wondered if his new alphabet, derived from Graeco-Roman inscriptions, might apply to this set of purely Egyptian inscriptions. The last two signs were familiar to him, having the phonetic value *s*. Using his knowledge of Coptic, he guessed that the first sign had the value *re*, which was the Coptic word for 'sun'—the object apparently symbolized by the sign. Did an ancient Egyptian ruler with a name that resembled *R(e)?ss* exist? Champollion immediately thought of Ramesses, a king of the 19th dynasty mentioned in a well-known Greek history of Egypt written by a 3rd-century-BC Ptolemaic historian, Manetho. (The difference in the vowel was relatively minor.) If this guess was correct, then the sign **ⵏ** must have the phonetic value *m*.

Encouragement came from a second inscription:

Two of these signs were 'known' from the alphabet, while the first sign, an ibis, was a symbol of the god Thoth. Then the name had to be Thothmes, a king of the 18th dynasty also mentioned by Manetho (as Tuthmosis). The Rosetta stone appeared to confirm the value of 𝕸. The sign occurred there, again with ⎮, as an element with the Greek translation 'genethlia', 'birth day'. Champollion was at once reminded of the Coptic for 'give birth', 'mise'.

We now know that he was only half right about the spelling of Ramesses: 𝕸 does not have the value m, but the *bi*consonantal value ms (the Egyptian script records vowels consistently only in the spelling of foreign names), as implied by the Coptic 'mise'. Champollion was still unaware of this complexity. For despite his success with Egyptian names, he was yet to take the plunge and accept that *all* hieroglyphic words, not just proper names, might have phonetic elements. He never said what finally pushed him to change his mind about this crucial matter; after the decipherment, "He was naturally more concerned to give a rational and convincing account... than to trace the full sequence of ideas that had led him to it", writes Maurice Pope.

Having studied Champollion's writings, Pope suggests that a combination of factors was at work. For one thing, Champollion was clearly frustrated by the apparent disorder of the hieroglyphs, the way that pictographic symbols were combined with no discernible regard for their apparent meanings: "The most contradictory objects are put right next to each other, producing monstrous alliances." If the pictograms really represented the objects they depicted, the objects should surely relate to each other in a plausible way (like Thompson's 'decipherment' of the 'dog' glyph on pages 18-19). For another, Champollion was taken by the same Chinese clue that had impressed de Sacy: the fact that the Chinese script, with thousands of signs, nevertheless contains phonetic elements. Furthermore, it struck him that there were only 66 different signs among the 1419 hieroglyphic characters on the Rosetta stone; if the hieroglyphs were exclusively semantic (logographic) symbols, then, even allowing for repetition of words, many more than 66 different signs would have been expected, each one a logogram representing a different word.

Once the moment of illumination occurred, and he had accepted that the hieroglyphs were in their very nature a mixture of phonetic signs and logograms, Champollion could decipher the second half of the long cartouche of Ptolemy on the Philae obelisk. That is:

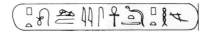

According to the Greek inscription on the Rosetta stone, as already said, the entire cartouche meant 'Ptolemy living for ever, beloved of Ptah' (Ptah was the creator god of Memphis). In Coptic, the word for 'life' or 'living' was 'onkh'; this was thought to be derived from an ancient Egyptian word 'ankh' represented by the sign ☥ (i.e. a logogram). Presumably the next signs ⌇ meant 'ever' and contained a t sound, given that the sign ⌒ was now known to have the phonetic value t. With help from Greek and Coptic, the ⌐ could be assigned the value dj, giving a rough ancient Egyptian pronunciation *djet*, meaning 'for ever'. The other sign ⚊ was silent, a determinative; it symbolized 'flat land'. (Even today, scholars do not understand its function here properly.)

| Sign | Transliteration | Sound value | Sign | Transliteration | Sound value |
|------|-----------------|-------------|------|-----------------|-------------|
|  | 3 | glottal stop |  | ḥ | emphatic *h* |
|  | ỉ | *i* |  | ḫ | *ch* as in Scottish loch |
|  | y | *y* |  | ẖ | slightly softer than last |
|  | ꜥ | gutteral, the ayin of the Semitic languages |  | s | *s* |
|  | w | *w* |  | š | *sh* |
|  | b | *b* |  | ḳ | *q* |
|  | p | *p* |  | k | *k* |
|  | f | *f* |  | g | hard *g* |
|  | m | *m* |  | t | *t* |
|  | n | *n* |  | ṯ | *tj* |
|  | r | *r* |  | d | *d* |
|  | h | *h* |  | ḏ | *dj* |

*Egyptian hieroglyphic 'alphabet' (above) and the cartouche of Tutankhamun (opposite), which appears on the upper part of an inlaid box found in his tomb. With the help of the 'alphabet' we can read Tutankhamun's name, working from the top down-wards, and also the name of Ramesses in the six cartouches on this page. (See also pages 68–69.) These cartouches were drawn by Champollion.*

The single reed is an alphabetic phonogram with the approximate value *i*.

The game board with playing pieces is a phonogram with the biconsonantal value *mn*.

Water is an alphabetic phonogram with the value *n*. Functioning (as here) as a 'phonetic complement', it reinforces the sound of the *n* in *mn*.

These three signs are therefore read *imn*, which is normally pronounced *imen* or, more commonly, *amon* or *amun*. (Vowels are mostly absent in hieroglyphic spelling.) Amun was the god of Luxor, regarded as the king of the gods during the New Kingdom. Out of respect, his name is placed first.

The half circle (familiar from the cartouche for Ptolemy) is an alphabetic phonogram with the value *t*. It appears twice in the cartouche.

The chick is a phonogram with the value *w*, a weak consonant similar to the vowel *u*.

This is the triconsonantal 'ankh' sign already seen in the cartouche of Ptolemy, meaning 'life' or 'living' (which later became the 'handled or eyed' cross, 'crux ansata', of the Coptic church).

These four signs are therefore read 'tutankh'.

The shepherd's crook is a logogram meaning 'ruler'.

The column is a logogram for Heliopolis, a city near Cairo.

This is the heraldic plant of Upper Egypt. It is a logogram for Upper Egypt.

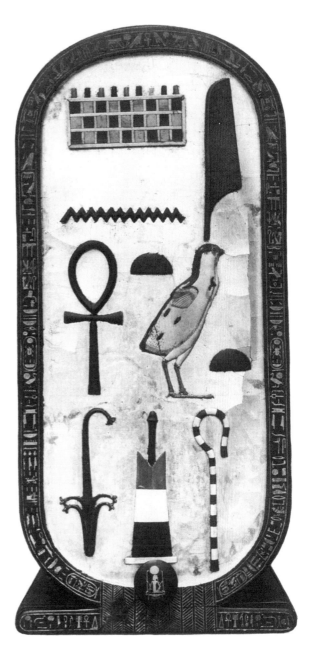

"Heliopolis of Upper Egypt" is another name for the city of Thebes. So the complete cartouche reads: 'Tutankhamun, Ruler of Thebes'.

Of the remaining signs ⬚𓀁𓏏 the first sign was now known to stand for *p* and the second for *t*– the initial two sounds of Ptah; and so the third sign could be given the approximate phonetic value *h*. The fourth sign–another logogram–was therefore assumed to mean 'beloved'. Coptic once more came in useful to assign a pronunciation: the Coptic word for love was known to be 'mere', and so the pronunciation of the fourth sign was thought to be *mer*. So, in sum, Champollion arrived at a rough pronunciation of the famous Philae/Rosetta stone cartouche: *Ptolmes ankh djet Ptah mer* (Ptolemy living for ever, beloved of Ptah).

————

In 1824, after many more months of intensive study of hieroglyphs in various Egyptian inscriptions including papyri, Champollion published his definitive statement of his decipherment, *Precis du Système Hiéroglyphique des Anciens Egyptiens*. In his introduction he made a point of stating what he saw as Young's contribution:

> ❝ I recognize that [he] was the first to publish some correct ideas about the ancient writings of Egypt; that he also was the first to establish some correct distinctions concerning the general nature of these writings, by determining, through a substantial comparison of texts, the value of several groups of characters. I even recognize that he published before me his ideas on the possibility of the existence of several sound-signs, which would have been used to write foreign proper names in Egypt in hieroglyphs; finally that M. Young was also the first to try, but without complete success, to give a phonetic value to the hieroglyphs making up the two names Ptolemy and Berenice [Berenike]. ❞

Though not inaccurate, this is damning with faint praise in its vague references to "correct ideas" and "correct distinctions". It fails to articulate Young's two key perceptions of general principles, published in 1819: first, that the demotic script to some extent resembled the hieroglyphic script visually and hence that one script was derived from the other; second, that the demotic script was therefore not an alphabet but a mixture of phonetic signs and hieroglyphic signs. This line of argument was what had led Young to suggest that the hieroglyphic script too might contain some phonetic elements (for spelling non-Egyptian names), more than two years before his rival. Champollion "knew that Young had reached this conclusion before him but he never admitted it in print", observes Carol Andrews, the British Museum curator regarded as the 'doyenne of the Rosetta stone'.

But of course it was Champollion, and Champollion alone, who took the next logical step and boldly cast aside his own earlier views to assume–courage of this kind is common to all successful decipherers–that the hieroglyphic script was fundamentally, not merely superficially, a mixture of phoneticism and logography. And Champollion who then, by brilliant application of his knowledge of Coptic and of ancient Egypt– both far superior to Young's–revealed a convincing *system*, in fine detail, behind the seeming hieroglyphic chaos. In this respect, says Richard Parkinson, "Young discovered parts of an alphabet–a key–but Champollion unlocked an entire language."

It must also not be forgotten that Champollion's decipherment was by no means complete on his death in 1832. Other scholars, notably Karl Richard Lepsius, now used Champollion's system to decipher new inscriptions successfully; but its basic validity was irrefutably confirmed only in 1866, when another bilingual text, containing the so-called Canopus decree, was discovered. When its hieroglyphic section was translated *à la* Champollion, it could be checked against its Greek equivalent with satisfactory results. Even then, there remained much in the hieroglyphs that was obscure to scholars. The language may have become readable, but what about the ancient Egyptian culture? Studying the hieroglyphs, *Cracking Codes* reminds us in its conclusion, "like any act of reading,...is a process of dialogue. The decipherment of the Rosetta stone and of ancient Egypt is a dialogue that has scarcely begun." The challenge for Egyptologists today is to interpret the full cultural meaning contained in the hieroglyphic inscriptions. But that is a task that takes them beyond the usual meaning of decipherment into literary criticism, theology, anthropology and several other disciplines. Nowadays, rather than 'cracking' codes like the pioneer Champollion and his immediate successors, scholars are immersed in decoding the nuances of an ancient, alien civilization.

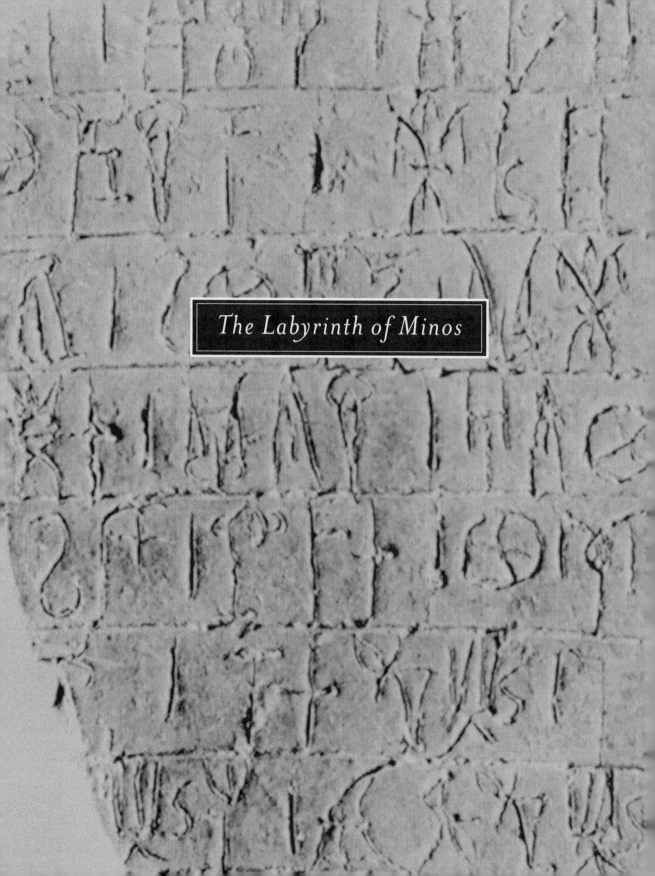

The Labyrinth of Minos

# II

# LINEAR B

In *The Odyssey* (Book 19), Homer sings:

" There is a land called Crete, set in the wine-dark sea, lovely and fertile and ocean-rounded. Those who live in this land are many, indeed past counting, and there are ninety cities there. The population speaks many tongues... Among the cities is mighty Knossos; its king was once Minos, who every ninth year took counsel with Zeus himself. "

Some two and half millennia after Homer, in 1900, the archaeologist Arthur Evans began to dig up and reconstruct the "great city" of Knossos in the northern part of central Crete. He discovered what he believed was the palace of King Minos, with its notorious labyrinth, home of the Minotaur. Over the next three decades, Evans spent his family fortune on reconstructing the palace including its brilliantly painted frescoes, and fell in love with 'his' Minoans. Just as they had enthralled Homer and the ancient Greeks, the Minoans dazzled Evans, too, and convinced him that Greece was "a Mainland branch of the Minoan culture", a mere "Minoan plantation". So much for the glories of classical Greece and the grandeur and treasures of Mycenae and Troy, excavated by Schliemann and others in the previous century, said

Evans, in effect: it was the Minoans, and not the Greeks, who had created the first great European civilization; and it was he who had revealed it to a wondering world.

If any classical specialist—such as the archaeologists digging in mainland Greece—disagreed with Evans, they seldom voiced their opinion, such was Sir Arthur's prestige and influence as one of the two or three best-known archaeologists of his time. When the director of the British School at Athens ventured to differ in 1923, he had to retire from his position and was excluded from digging in Greece for a considerable period. Minoan hegemony over Greece (and Evans's hegemony over practically every scholar in the field) became the orthodoxy. It would hinder the decipherment of Linear B for half a century—somewhat as the idea that Egyptian hieroglyphs were entirely conceptual hindered their decipherment for even longer. Both the idea of Greek ascendancy over the Minoans and the idea of hieroglyphic phoneticism were considered to be beyond the pale of intellectual respectability.

"Linear Script of Class B", which is nowadays dated to c. 1450 BC, two or three centuries before the Trojan war, was the name given by Evans to the fairly primitive characters scratched on clay tablets that he had discovered soon after he began digging; writing that was unknown in Crete (and of course in Bronze Age Greece, which was believed to have been illiterate). The label Class B was to distinguish the characters from similar-looking but nevertheless distinct characters on archaeologically older tablets Evans had labeled "Linear Script of Class A", which had been found at Knossos but chiefly at another Minoan palace excavation in southern Crete. "Linear" was attached not because the signs were written in sequence but because they consisted of lines inscribed on a surface, as opposed to the three-dimensional, engraved

images of a third, pictographic script, found chiefly on seal stones and only in the eastern part of Crete, which Evans dubbed "Hieroglyphic" but which actually did not much resemble Egyptian writing. (See chapter VI for both Linear A and Hieroglyphic.)

To be honest, Linear B tablets are uninspiring objects to the eye of the uninitiated, unlike Egyptian hieroglyphic inscriptions and many of the cuneiform tablets. They are flat, smooth pieces of clay, their color generally dull gray but sometimes like red brick (the result of greater oxidation when the tablet was burnt). Their sizes vary from small sealings and labels little more than an inch across to heavy, page-shaped tablets designed to be held in a single hand, the largest being as big as a fair-sized paperback. Evans found many of them in a fragile, even friable condition and once accidentally reduced a batch to an indecipherable muddy mess by leaving them overnight in a storeroom with a leaky roof.

Indeed, the first traces of Linear B he unearthed were so unimpressive that he copied them and filed them away in what he termed "a suspense account". Yet Evans, whose background was in epigraphy not archaeology until he started at Knossos, quickly became hooked on the problem of what the characters meant. They bore little resemblance to Egyptian hieroglyphs (though Evans detected some), and no resemblance to cuneiform or the later Greek alphabet. As for their underlying language, Evans was quite convinced, for reasons already given, that it could not be Greek: he therefore coined the term Minoan for it. He then spent the last 40 years of his long life hoping to decipher it—while keeping the large majority of the tablets away from other scholars, lest (as one is almost compelled to assume) they got to the answer before him.

*The first Linear B tablet published by Arthur Evans, in 1900. It was found in the palace of Minos.*

*'Hieroglyphs' from Crete. Most of this undeci-*
*phered Hieroglyphic script appears on seal stones.*
*It predates Linear A and B.*

But although Evans failed to decipher Linear B, he did take some comparatively straightforward yet significant steps in the right direction, which he published during his lifetime. For a start, as mentioned, he recognized the existence of at least three distinct scripts in Crete in the 2nd millennium BC: Linear A, Linear B and Hieroglyphic. Concentrating on Linear B, of which by far the most was available, he identified the short upright lines that frequently recurred near the horizontal lines that divide most tablets, as word dividers (highlighted):

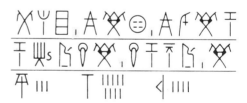

He also worked out the system of counting as follows:

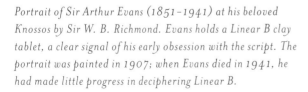

*Portrait of Sir Arthur Evans (1851–1941) at his beloved*
*Knossos by Sir W. B. Richmond. Evans holds a Linear B clay*
*tablet, a clear signal of his early obsession with the script. The*
*portrait was painted in 1907; when Evans died in 1941, he*
*had made little progress in deciphering Linear B.*

Here are two examples of numbers in Linear B tablets, 362 and 1350:

362

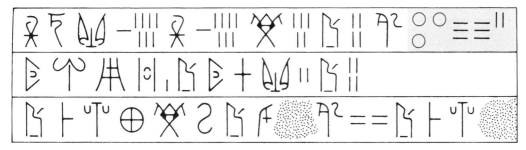

1350

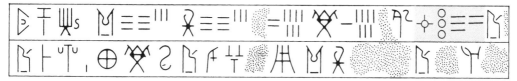

Evans also understood that the tablets were inventories, sometimes with a total at the bottom, often involving a pictogram. The fact that the number was a total could be established in the better-preserved tablets by adding up the separate entries above it. On the right is an example with the numerals highlighted (ignore the symbols in the top line that appear to be numerals; they are in fact word dividers). And Evans deduced that the two highlighted signs ₸ �**, sometimes ₸ ꓶ, common in the Linear B tablets, probably meant 'total'.

Many other pictograms had to be logographic, representing words; this was clear from their iconic qualities and the fact that they stood out by virtue

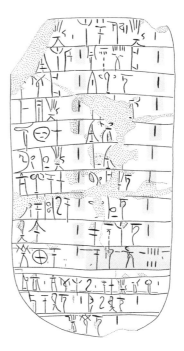

*Numerals and the 'total' signs on a Linear B tablet.*

'total'   man 17

of being accompanied by numerals and by being isolated from the majority of characters on the tablets:

| | Man | | Woman |
| | Horse | | Pig |
| | Tripod | | Cup |
| | Amphora | | Sword |
| | Spear | | Arrow |
| | Chariot | | Wheel |

The tablet (previous page), for instance, counts men.

And there were a number of pictograms that came in two forms:

Evans recognized that these stood for male and female animals, presumably counted for the palace of Minos. But he could not determine which pictogram was male and which female.

Such pictograms led Evans astray in respect of the Linear B signary. He succumbed, at least partially, to one of the commonest errors in decipherment: what might be called 'the pictographic fallacy'. Having gone looking for pictographic elements in the signs, he naturally found them, and then—under the influence of the determinatives found in Egyptian hieroglyphs (such as the shepherd's crook meaning 'ruler' in the cartouche of Tutankhamun on page 71)—he proceeded to treat his supposed Linear B pictograms as logograms referring only to the objects they depicted. Thus ⊤, a frequent sign at the beginning of a word, Evans decided stood for 'double-axe', a common Minoan object, and ⮕, which appears five times in the tablet below, stood for 'throne-and-sceptre'.

Given the shape and apparent significance of the double axes and the real throne (of Minos?) that Evans had found at Knossos, both these analogies were not unreasonable, yet his conclusion turned out to be fallacious: the linguistic function of the two signs was actually *phonetic*, not pictographic/logographic/determinative as he had postulated (though this fact was not established until well after Evans's death).

In search of further clues to the decipherment of Linear B, Evans turned east, to Cyprus. Here was another island on which an ancient script had been found, dating to about 800-200 BC. But unlike Linear B, the classical Cypriot script had been deciphered (in 1871), because it appeared alongside the classical Greek alphabet in a number of 'bilingual' inscriptions.

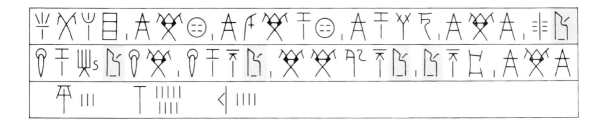

*Greek/Cypriot 'bilingual' stone inscription from Cyprus, with the Cypriot script drawn underneath. It is a dedication by Ellowoikos to Demeter and Kore. Some of the Cypriot signs resemble those of Linear B.*

To digress for a moment, the *language* represented in these 'bilinguals' is the same in the case of both scripts: Greek—a dialect of Greek in the Cypriot case. (Compare the hieroglyphic and demotic inscriptions on the Rosetta stone, which write basically the same Egyptian language.) The historical reason for this, according to classicists of Evans's day, was that Greek speakers fleeing the Trojan war had brought Greek to Cyprus. Since the sounds of the Greek alphabetic signs were known, the sounds of the Cypriot script could be deciphered and matched with their corresponding signs. But the Cypriot script turned out to be, not alphabetic, but *syllabic*, with 56 signs; an inconvenient way to represent Greek sounds, if manageable. The Cypriot syllabary is a so-called 'open' syllabary, in which a sign stands not for a consonant C but for a consonant with an inherent vowel, CV. (In 'closed' syllabaries, a sign stands for CVC.) This means that when an 'open' syllabic sign is used to represent a final consonant in a word, the sign's inherent vowel must be assumed to be silent, i.e. C(V). In classical Cypriot, therefore, the many words that finish with the syllabic sign ⊢ , *se*, have a silent *e* , and actually end in *s*; which agrees with a very common ending for words in classical

Greek, '-s' (e.g. logo**s**, Dionyso**s**). This was as expected in a dialect of Greek.

Evans, however, was not looking to the Cypriot script for its Greek connections—rather the opposite, given his Minoan predilections. His hope was that the *known* sounds of the Cypriot script could help him to decipher the *unknown* sounds of the Linear B script, but without assuming that the language of Linear B was Greek (or a dialect of Greek). His idea may seem somewhat perverse, but it was based on his theory that the Cypriot script was somehow derived from the 'Minoan' Linear B script, while the Cypriot language was *not* derived from the 'Minoan' language. (One might recall the modern Turkish script, which Atatürk derived from the roman script, even though the Turkish language is not derived from any European language written in the roman script.) According to Evans, 'Minoan'-speaking people, possibly traders to begin with, must have settled in Cyprus, bringing their script with them from Crete. That was why, he said, some of the Cypriot signs looked so similar to the Linear B signs, despite being up to a thousand or so years younger than Linear B.

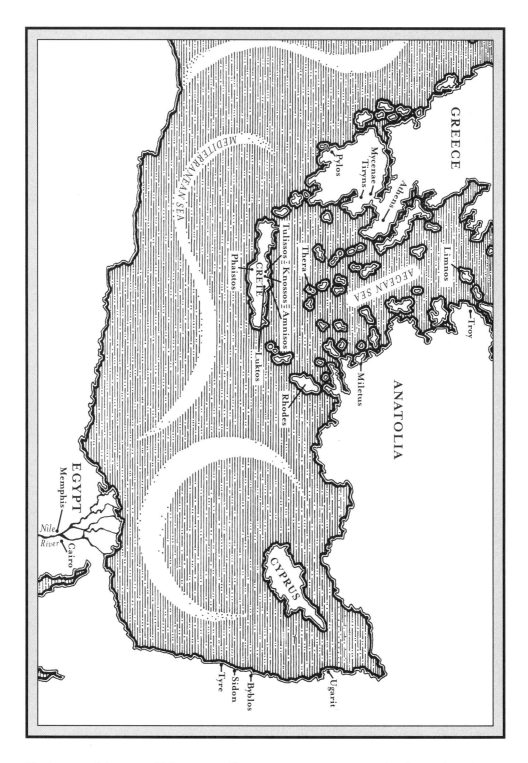

The Aegean and the eastern Mediterranean. There was constant movement and settlement throughout this area during the 2nd millennium BC and after, including between Crete and Cyprus.

Horse tablet from Knossos with partial drawing by Arthur Evans. It nearly convinced him that Linear B wrote Greek.

Here are the eight most similar signs and their syllabic phonetic values in Cypriot:

| Linear B | Cypriot | Cypriot sound values |
|---|---|---|
| ⫐ | ⫶ | *po* |
| ⊦ | ⊢ | *ta* |
| + | + | *lo* |
| ⊤ | ⊤ | *to* |
| ⊔ | ⊔ | *se* |
| ‡ | ‡ | *pa* |
| ⟨ | ⟨ | *na* |
| ⋀ | ⋀ | *ti* |

Evans decided to test these values on a promising-looking tablet from Knossos (above). He noticed on the tablet six horse heads, two of which were incomplete. (The join in the tablet was made years after Evans's death by John Chadwick, so Evans's drawing does not include the left-hand portion.) Of the four horse heads in the middle and on the right of the tablet, two had manes and two did not. The ones without manes, foals presumably, were preceded by the same pair of Linear B signs ⫐ +.

According to the Cypriot phonetic values, the two signs should read *polo*. What might 'polo' mean in the 'Minoan' language? Evans duly noted that it resembled the classical Greek word 'pōlos', young horse or foal, (and its dual form 'pōlo', two foals); in fact the English word foal comes from the same source as Greek 'pōlos'. If the 'Minoan' language and the Greek language were related after all, 'Minoan' 'polo' could easily be the equivalent of classical Greek 'pōlos'. The tablet would then mean:

horses 2       *polo* foals
*polo* foals 2      horses 4

Presumably, the word ⫐ + ('polo') had been added by the Minoan scribe to make it absolutely clear that the maneless pictogram was a foal and not an adult animal.

But Evans rejected this plausible beginning, almost out of hand. For one thing, he noted that, unlike Cypriot words, very *few* Linear B sign groups ended in the sign ⨳ (*se*), '-s', which suggested that 'Minoan' and Greek were not related. A logical enough deduction, and one that would trouble all subsequent decipherers including Michael Ventris. Less logical was that Evans simply could not accept that the Minoans spoke and wrote an archaic form of Greek, which they took with them to Cyprus. In Evans's view, it was Minos and the Minoans, *not* the mainland Greeks, who ruled the roost: the 'Minoan' language could not possibly be Greek. He dismissed the similarity of the Linear B and Cypriot signs in the case of 'polo' as a mere coincidence of the kind that, in fairness to Evans, must be admitted to be only too misleadingly common in historical linguistics and decipherment.

————

Evans died at the age of 90 in mid-1941, near Oxford, spared from the knowledge that the house he had built for himself at Knossos, the Villa Ariadne, had become the headquarters of the German occupation forces on Crete. With regard to Linear B, he left a disorganized legacy, which hampered attempts at decipherment as the man himself had hampered them while he lived. Of the more than 3000 tablets and fragments excavated by him and others at Knossos, some 200-300 had been published, most of them only in the 1930s, along with a sign list seriously flawed by Evans's falling for the pictographic fallacy (many of the signs he had read as pictograms/logograms were really phonetic signs). The arduous task of completing their publication from his drawings and photographs fell to Evans's colleague and friend, the emeritus professor of ancient history at Oxford, Sir John Myres, who was already well into his seventies. Myres labored at it for ten years with fading eyesight and help from a few others, chiefly the American classicists Alice Kober and Emmett Bennett Jr., but he was in an impossible position: trapped between a loyal desire to keep faith with the faulty sign list prepared by Evans and the clear perception of Kober, Bennett and others that a more logical, scientific approach to classifying the signs was required. (Ventris, too, was invited by Myres to help, in 1948, but declined.)

There was also the startling fact that more Linear B tablets had recently been discovered, and this time not in Crete but in mainland Greece, in the western Peloponnese. In 1939, the American archaeologist Carl Blegen, having completed a dig at Troy, had struck lucky with his first trial trench at a place he believed to be the site of ancient Pylos, the city made famous in Homer's *Iliad* as the seat of King Nestor. The result was almost 600 new pieces of Linear B– and a serious embarrassment to the Evans theory that Linear B was exclusively the writing of the Minoans. For if this were so, what were Linear B tablets doing in large quantity in mainland Greece? The 88-year-old Evans did not respond to the find, but his followers rapidly came up with explanations, such as that the tablets at Pylos were "loot from Crete" or that a Greek ruler had raided Minoan Crete and carried off its scribes to work in his own palace at Pylos. Whatever proved to be the truth, Blegen's discovery was bound to have a profound effect on all scholars working on the decipherment of Linear B.

*Where Linear B tablets were discovered, and when. According to Arthur Evans, Linear B should have been found only on Crete.*

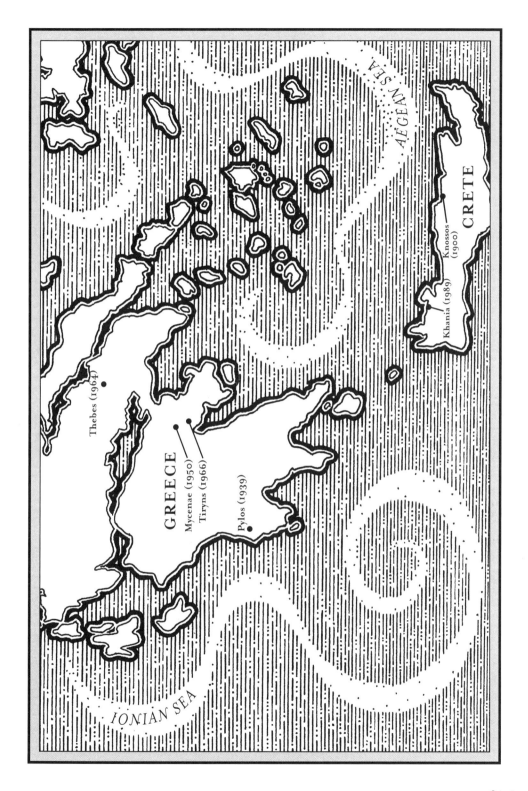

AEGEAN SEA

CRETE

Knossos
(1900)

Khania (1989)

Thebes (1964)

GREECE

Mycenae (1950)
Tiryns (1966)

Pylos (1939)

IONIAN SEA

There was just time before the second world war intervened for the new pieces to be cleaned, mended and photographed, and then deposited in the Bank of Athens, where they remained intact during the next few turbulent years. The photographs were taken to the United States on the last American ship to leave the Mediterranean in 1940, after Italy declared war. Blegen, who had found the tablets, entrusted their analysis to his student at the University of Cincinnati, Emmett Bennett, but Bennett could get down to the task only after doing his war service as a cryptanalyst.

Throughout the 1940s, the situation for active research on Linear B—as opposed to scholarly speculation—was therefore complicated and unsatisfactory. The tablets themselves were mostly inaccessible, in storage in Athens

*Key contributors to the decipherment of Linear B: Michael Ventris (1922-56), John Chadwick (1920-98), Emmett Bennett Jr. (1918- ) and Alice Kober (1906-50). Ventris and Kober were to some extent rivals, until Kober's premature death.*

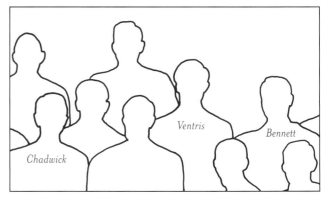

and Crete. Not very clear photographs and probably somewhat inaccurate drawings were under scrutiny in Britain and America by Myres, Ventris, Kober and Bennett, at first independently of each other (though keeping in touch by correspondence). Myres in Oxford was examining the entire Knossos tablets, but not those from Pylos, and would not publish them until 1952; Ventris in London could work only with the tablets published by Evans; ditto Kober in New York, until she began to help Myres in 1947; Bennett at Cincinnati and then Yale University had the Pylos archive, but comparatively little access to the Knossos tablets, which were obviously essential for comparison in compiling a definitive Linear B sign list. Overall, the situation was a mess, though not a hopeless one.

Nevertheless, during this time, both Bennett and Kober were able to carry out analyses that would be as vital to Ventris as Thomas Young's work was to Champollion. But the analyses were different in kind. Bennett's work may be likened to clearing the terrain of jungle and straightening the path; Kober's was more in the nature of proposing a methodology that would enable the decipherment to move forwards along the path of progress.

First, Bennett proved that while the numerical systems of Linear A and Linear B were very similar, the systems of measurement were not. Linear A has a system of fractional signs, e.g. $1/2$, $2/3$, $4/5$, while Linear B records fractional quantities in terms of smaller units, like dollars and cents or feet and inches. Besides being useful information, this added further weight to the suspicion that Linear B represented a language different from that of Linear A—probably from outside Crete since Linear B had been found in mainland Greece, unlike Linear A. (Evans had of course believed that both scripts wrote 'Minoan'.)

More important, though, was Bennett's wrestling with the thousands of text characters in the Pylos tablets, written by many different scribal hands, to produce a sign list in which some 89 signs—presumably (but not yet provably) phonetic in function—with their several allographs, were logically distinguished from each other and from a second class of signs, pictographic/iconic, which were apparently used as logograms (for instance, signs such as ⊢ and ⨝ on page 80). Without of course knowing what any of the 89 signs stood for, Bennett managed to classify correctly signs such as Evans's 'double-axe' and 'throne-and-sceptre'—which might have been thought to be logograms—among the 89 ?phonetic signs, *not* among the logograms. Besides painstaking visual comparisons of sign forms, Bennett achieved this sorting largely by using two techniques. One was a laborious comparison of the contexts of all the characters on the tablets; for example a lone sign which occurred only with numerals and was clearly iconic was almost certainly a logogram. The other involved frequency analysis of signs and sign combinations, which we shall discuss later in connection with Ventris's use of the same technique. "How difficult the task is only those who have tried can tell", wrote John Chadwick of Bennett's sign list compilation in *The Decipherment of Linear B*. The conclusion that there were 89 signs in the list, rather than a much smaller number such as 30-40, meant that the Linear B script probably was basically a syllabary, and definitely not an alphabet.

When *The Pylos Tablets, A Preliminary Transcription* was finally ready in 1951, Bennett packed up a copy and posted it from the USA to Ventris in London. At this time, six years after the end of the war, Britain still had rationing and a relatively austere regime; gifts from the United States were especially welcome, though carefully vetted by customs. As Bennett, now in his mid-eighties, recalls with a smile, he received a letter from Ventris explaining that when he went to pick up the packet,

| | | | | | | | | |
|---|---|---|---|---|---|---|---|---|
| 01 | da | | 30 | ni | | 59 | ta | |
| 02 | ro | | 31 | sa | | 60 | ra | |
| 03 | pa | | 32 | qo | | 61 | o | |
| 04 | te | | 33 | ra₃ | | 62 | pte | |
| 05 | to | | 34 | | | 63 | | |
| 06 | na | | 35 | | | 64 | | |
| 07 | di | | 36 | jo | | 65 | ju | |
| 08 | a | | 37 | ti | | 66 | ta₂ | |
| 09 | se | | 38 | e | | 67 | ki | |
| 10 | u | | 39 | pi | | 68 | ro₂ | |
| 11 | po | | 40 | wi | | 69 | tu | |
| 12 | so | | 41 | si | | 70 | ko | |
| 13 | me | | 42 | wo | | 71 | dwe | |
| 14 | do | | 43 | ai | | 72 | pe | |
| 15 | mo | | 44 | ke | | 73 | mi | |
| 16 | pa₂ | | 45 | de | | 74 | ze | |
| 17 | za | | 46 | je | | 75 | we | |
| 18 | | | 47 | | | 76 | ra₂ | |
| 19 | | | 48 | nwa | | 77 | ka | |
| 20 | zo | | 49 | | | 78 | qe | |
| 21 | qi | | 50 | pu | | 79 | zu | |
| 22 | | | 51 | du | | 80 | ma | |
| 23 | mu | | 52 | no | | 81 | ku | |
| 24 | ne | | 53 | ri | | 82 | | |
| 25 | a₂ | | 54 | wa | | 83 | | |
| 26 | ru | | 55 | nu | | 84 | | |
| 27 | re | | 56 | pa₃ | | 85 | | |
| 28 | i | | 57 | ja | | 86 | | |
| 29 | pu₂ | | 58 | su | | 87 | | |

*The sign list of Linear B, as agreed today. It is almost identical with Emmett Bennett's sign list of 1951. The order of the signs is based on their shapes and has nothing to do with their phonetic values, which were of course totally unknown to Bennett. Some values are represented by more than one sign.*

a suspicious postal official asked him: "I see the contents are listed as PYLOS TABLETS. Now, just what ailments are pylos tablets supposed to alleviate?" In practice, Bennett's sign list soon proved to be something of a Linear B cure-all: quickly adopted by Ventris, it remains the standard for Linear B research, with remarkably few modifications. Today's accepted figure for the signary is, as already remarked in the Introduction, 87 syllabic signs.

If Bennett was dedicated, Alice Kober, one senses, was driven; and it is hard to write about her without a certain pathos, for she died in 1950 of cancer at the age of only 43, just two years before Ventris announced his decipherment. It seems reasonable to compare her with Rosalind Franklin, the competitor of Crick and Watson in the DNA story, for Kober was theoretically well placed to have 'cracked' Linear B, besides sharing Franklin's caution and determination (even obstinacy). However, on the evidence of her published work, it seems doubtful she would have succeeded, as we shall now see.

Superficially, Kober's career was that of a typical classicist of her time. She studied Latin and Greek and took a PhD from Columbia University with a dissertation on "Color terms in the Greek poets", then she began teaching at a college. But as Bennett wrote after her death, in her mid-twenties Kober had developed a "consuming interest" in the undeciphered scripts of Crete. It would do her academic status no good (ditto for Bennett), yet as soon as she could, she set about learning as many ancient languages as possible, chiefly in order to be able to eliminate them as candidates for the languages of Linear A and B, while also studying archaeology in the field and, even more determinedly, mathematics (for its use in statistics) and physics and chemistry (for their methodology).

The result was a series of important, ruthlessly logical papers on the Cretan undeciphered scripts published between 1943 and her early death,

notably in the *American Journal of Archaeology*. Their distinctive feature was Kober's conviction that with enough material available, there was no absolute need for a bilingual: it should be possible, simply by an intelligent search for patterns in the unknown Linear B characters, to determine the nature of the 'Minoan' script and its language, and hence, if the language was in fact related to a known language, to decipher Linear B.

Her most important practical contribution to the decipherment came from a suggestion originally made by Evans: that there was evidence of declension in Linear B. Kober was of course familiar with declension in Latin and Greek, where nouns are inflected according to their case, nominative/accusative/genitive/dative (e.g. domin**us**/domin**um**/domin**i**/domin**o**), and verbs are inflected as they conjugate (e.g.am**o**/am**as**/am**at**/am**amus**/am**atis**/am**ant**). There is relatively little declension/conjugation in English (e.g. potato/potato**es**, love/love**s**), more in French (e.g. j'aim**e**/tu aim**es**/il aim**e**/nous aim**ons**/vous aim**ez**/ils aim**ent**). In Linear B, Kober identified five groups of words taken from various published Knossos tablets, with three words in each group—dubbed "Kober's triplets" by a slightly mischievous Ventris—which suggested to her the presence of declension. She could not know what the words meant, but their contexts in the tablets seemed to be the same, making them likely to be nouns, maybe personal names or place names. That they shared the same context was of course essential, otherwise she might have been comparing groups of three words that were visually similar but, unknown to her, were grammatically *dis*similar, which would have rendered a comparison invalid and potentially misleading. (A very rough equivalent might be a comparison between street names in three bus timetables for the same route, one for daytime, the second for nighttime and the third for

Sundays. This would be valid, whereas a comparison of daytime timetables for three somewhat different routes would be misleading, even though they might easily share some street names in common.)

Here are two of Kober's 'triplets':

We can see the inflection more clearly if we highlight the word endings:

An English parallel might be:

Ca-na-da                  Ar-ge(n)-ti-na
Ca-na-di-a(n)          Ar-ge(n)-ti-ni-a(n)
Ca-na-di-a(ns)         Ar-ge(n)-ti-ni-a(ns)

If such parallels were right (assuming that Linear B was syllabic, like the Cypriot script), $\top$ and $\lrcorner$ would have different consonants (C) but share the same vowel (V), like *da* and *na* in

Cana-**da** /Argenti-**na**, i.e.:

So would ⋀ and ⋕ like *di* and *ni* in Cana-**di**-a(n) /Argenti-**ni**-a(n):

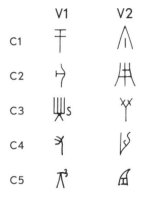

By the same token, using the other three 'triplets', Kober arrived at what she called "the beginning of a tentative phonetic pattern":

|  | V1 | V2 |
|---|---|---|
| C1 | 𐘇 | ⋀ |
| C2 | 𐙣 | ⋕ |
| C3 | 𐘂s | 𐘱 |
| C4 | 𐘂 | 𐙈 |
| C5 | 𐘃³ | 𐘌 |

The phonetic values of these syllabic signs were as yet undetermined, but their interrelationships, on the model of the blank square in a crossword where two words meet in which the shared letter is unknown yet must fit the two words—were (tentatively) established. This analytical principle, called a "grid" by Ventris and others, was seminal in organizing the bewildering mass of Linear B inscriptions for decipherment. The concept of a grid was not new—it had been used in the 19th century in the cuneiform and other decipherments—but it came into its own as a tool (and as a new coinage in decipherment) with Linear B.

Original as the above insight was, Kober somewhat spoilt it by giving a strong hint in one of her papers that she thought the 'triplets' were cases of a noun on the Latin model (e.g. domin**us**/domin**i**/domin**o**). She was wrong about this, as we shall see. On the other hand, careful scholar that she was, in a later paper she did not repeat the Latin parallel but instead contented herself with the observation that, "There is enough evidence to make it necessary to investigate the inflection theory thoroughly, and without prejudice. If it is right, more evidence will appear; if more evidence is not found, it is wrong."

One other result by Kober must be mentioned, without going into her detailed reasons. She demonstrated that the two Linear B words for 'total' (page 79), 𐀴 𐀸 and 𐀴 𐀥, are masculine and feminine variants of the same root word: the first appears with the 'man' logogram and male animals, the second with the 'woman' logogram and female animals. Since both words contain two signs, of which the first is the same, the variant was clearly formed by a change of vowel (or conceivably consonant) rather than by the addition of an extra syllable. The importance of this deduction lies in the fact that Indo-European languages are almost alone in this formation. Hence the language of Linear B was very likely to be Indo-European (which included Greek), and not Semitic or similar to Etruscan, a candidate favored by many scholars, including Ventris, because of an ancient tradition that the Etruscans came from the Aegean area to Italy.

During 1948, an already-ailing Kober virtually bowed out of the Linear B battle with these words, in her article "The Minoan scripts: fact and theory": "When we have the facts, certain conclusions will

be almost inevitable. Until we have them, no conclusions are possible." Ventris read the piece and criticized it to Myres for ending on "a rather pessimistic note".

Surely, Kober went too far here. No science, and certainly no archaeological decipherment, proceeds on such an arid, all-or-nothing basis. The scientist and the decipherer never have all the facts they need, but when they have sufficient to form sensible hypotheses, they can hope to test these hypotheses against existing knowledge and against new facts as these become available. This is where the element of creativity and courage comes in. Alice Kober was probably too restrained a scholar to have 'cracked' Linear B. In the words of Ventris written after the decipherment, her approach was "prim but necessary". To go further would require a mind like his that combined her perseverance, logic and method, with a willingness to take intellectual risks.

————

Michael Ventris's background was cosmopolitan and somewhat unorthodox, which were both factors in his success in tackling Linear B. And although he was not wealthy in the style of Arthur Evans, he had enough private means to concentrate exclusively on Linear B for substantial periods when he chose to. Ventris has often been described as an amateur in decipherment—unlike, say, Champollion or Knorozov—since his professional career was as an architect not a linguist and he never took any kind of academic post (nor attended university). While 'amateur' is a fair description, his was amateurism of a very special kind, more dedicated to the task than the professionals, and certainly in no way similar to that of a dilettante decoder.

He was the only child of an English army officer and a mother who was half-English; her father was a wealthy Pole named Janasz. Michael's extraordinary flair for learning languages began at the age of six when he taught himself Polish. Soon he picked up French, German and the Swiss-German dialect while at school in Switzerland; later he added Russian, Swedish, Italian and other European languages, in addition to a good grasp of classical Greek and Latin. It became a matter of pride to him to pick up languages within a matter of weeks. An English architect friend, Oliver Cox, while on holiday in Rome with Ventris in the late 1940s, remembers that he was able to get them into a part of the Vatican closed to the public by chatting to the Swiss Guards, in what they mistook to be the Swiss-German dialect of a native speaker.

When Michael was thirteen, his parents, who were by now divorced (his father died not long after from tuberculosis), sent him to Stowe, an English public school in Buckinghamshire. It was newly founded and not as conventional as many established public schools, which was fortunate for Ventris, who had no interest in team sports and 'hearty' socializing. His studies, involving little science and mathematics as was typical of the time, went well but not brilliantly; he was remembered by most of his contemporaries as always pleasant, sometimes amusing, but detached and somewhat withdrawn, with no obvious signs of 'genius'.

From childhood he had been attracted to ancient scripts. The interest in Linear B crystallized when he was fourteen and went on a school trip to the "Minoan World" exhibition, met Evans in person and saw undeciphered tablets, as described in the Introduction. Soon it became an obsession. But under the influence of his mother Dorothea and her artistic friends he was also attracted to architecture. Mother and son had moved into one of the most expensive flats in London at the top of Highpoint, a block of just-completed apartments inspired by Le Corbusier. The Ventris interior was the work of Marcel Breuer (of the Bauhaus), and there were Picassos on the walls; the whole flat was designed as the epitome of modernity. And so, in 1940, aged 17, Ventris became a student at the Architectural Association School, while continuing to study Linear B in his spare time.

How much did Ventris's training as an architect contribute to his work as a decipherer? There are some fairly obvious connections, such as his superb drafting skills with a pen and his ability to absorb, mentally compare and manipulate large quantities of written and visual information; but there are more subtle links too, which were almost entirely overlooked by John Chadwick in *The Decipherment of Linear B*. The American classicist Thomas Palaima, who is studying the links along with the architect Oliver Cox, emphasizes that Ventris combined crystal-clear analysis with "group working, hypothesizing and brainstorming." In other words, he did *not* believe in the idea of the genius who works solo and finally solves a problem by his own sheer, unaided brainpower.

What is certainly utterly exceptional—and absolutely contrary to the solo working methods of Champollion, and indeed most scholars of Linear B—is the way that Ventris explained in writing and in tremendous detail each stage of his attack on Linear B, and then circulated these neatly typed "Work Notes" (Ventris's name for them) to other scholars for comments and contradictions. Much of what he hypothesized turned out to be irrelevant or wrong, but this did not stop him from showing it to the professionals. And it appears that he did take this whole approach from his work as an architect. In 1948, he edited and published a conversation between five architects (including Cox) entitled "Group working", and himself joined in with the comment:

" There are three golden rules:–

1. Put down conceitedly every requirement, argument, inspiration and mind's eye picture that occurs during the design process, and put it down as concisely, enthusiastically and *pictorially* as possible.

2. Phrase your conclusions, set out and color your pictures, in such a way that they will mean the most to you (or to a colleague), at a second reading.

3. File everything where you will still find it fresh and clean tomorrow or in a year's time. Architecture needs paper in order to take form: enjoy and respect your material. "

Ventris's first published contribution to the debate on Linear B was a somewhat immature article, "Introducing the Minoan language", published by the *American Journal of Archaeology* as early as 1940, which he wrote while he was beginning to train as an architect. Its author was barely 18 (which he did not confess to the journal), and he may have rushed into print partly to escape his worrying personal uncertainties: his mother had committed suicide in June 1940 after the Nazi destruction of Poland, the London Blitz had begun, and he was sure to be drafted to fight.

His argument frankly took the Evans line: "The theory that Minoan could be Greek is based of course on a deliberate disregard for historical plausibility". And he speculated that 'Minoan' would eventually be found "to correspond...closely to Etruscan". Two years later, now a serviceman in the Royal Air Force, he maintained the same Etruscan hypothesis in letters to Myres (and remarked, quite presciently, "one can remain sure that no Champollion is working quietly in a corner and preparing a full and startling revelation, as no one has access to sufficient reproductions").

From 1951-52, his "Work Notes" are littered with Etruscan analogies. The truth is, that Ventris did not abandon the Etruscan hypothesis until the very last moment, in June 1952.

After the end of the war, he continued to study Linear B while finishing his training and beginning work as an architect, but his next real step as a decipherer came only in late 1949, when he felt that the publication of the Pylos and Knossos tablets was coming close. In an unusual move typical of the ethos of 'group working', Ventris sent a questionnaire to a dozen scholars known to be interested in the problem, such as Myres, Bennett, Kober and some continental Europeans, collated their answers and provided his own detailed commentary, and then sent everything back to them (and others) in mimeographed form. This became known as the *Mid-Century Report*, which Ventris concluded with the following words: "I have good hopes that a sufficient number of people working on these lines will before long enable a satisfactory solution to be found. To them I offer my best wishes, being forced by pressure of other work to make this my last small contribution to the problem."

But the problem gave him no rest. Another year, 1950, passed before Ventris decided to give up paid work for a while and apply his mind full-time to Linear B (and to the new house he and his wife had been designing on the edge of Hampstead Heath). The first of his 20 "Work Notes" is therefore dated 28 January 1951, not long before Bennett's publication of the Pylos tablets. It incorporated the first of Ventris's 'grids'. As the notes progressed, the grids steadily filled up with Linear B signs like words in a crossword–to which Ventris added guesses at the phonetic values of the vowels and consonants. Frequently, the position of the signs and the nature of the guesses had to be revised, but the grid endured.

# 'B' SYLLABARY PHONETIC 'GRID'

Fig. 1
MGFV

**1: State as at 28 Jan 51: before publication of Pylos inscriptions.**

| CONSONANTS | Vowel 1 — NIL? (-o ?) = typical 'nominative' of nouns which change their last theme syllable in oblique cases | Vowel 2 — -i ? = typical changed last syllable before -ẓ and -ᴴ. | Other vowels? — -a, -e, -u ? = changes in last syllable caused by other endings. (5 vowels in all, rather than 4 ?) | Doubtful |
|---|---|---|---|---|
| 1  t- ? | ag | aj | | ax (Sundwall) |
| 2  r- ?? | az | iw | ah / ol | |
| 3  ś- ?? | eg | aw | oc / oj | |
| 4  n- ?? / s- ?? | od | ok | ɩb· ez | is / oh |
| 5 | | ak | ef | |
| 6  l- ? | ac | ij | | |
| 7  h- ?? | ix | | if | |
| 8  θ- ?? | en | | id | ex |
| 9  m- ? / k- ? | ay | — if an enclitic "and". | | al |
| 10 | | | | om / av |
| 11 | | | | |
| 12 | | | | |
| 13 | | | | |
| 14 | | | | |
| 15 | | | | |

aj  ij
ak  il
aw  og
ej  oh
er  oj
ex  ok
ib  iw

group of syllables, including those occurring before -ᴴ on 'woman' tablet (Hr 44, PM fig 689), and those characteristic of alternating endings -ẓ & -ᴴ. About ¾ of these 14 signs very likely include vowel 2.

'Grid' from "Work Note" 1 by Michael Ventris, 28 January 1951. Vowels are plotted across the page, consonants down the page. Most of the sign positions proved to be wrong but the principle of using a 'grid' for decipherment was sound. (Ignore the labels such as 'ag', 'oc', 'en': they are nothing to do with the syllabic values of the signs.)

As Ventris and Chadwick commented much later:

**❝** The problem of decipherment is in this way reduced to the correct distribution of five vowels and twelve consonants to the columns of the grid; and since a proposed reading of only two or three words may, by a 'chain reaction', predetermine rigid values for almost the entire syllabary, a very severe discipline is imposed on the earliest stages of a decipherment. If the initial moves are wrong, it should be quite impossible to force any part of the texts into showing the slightest conformity with the vocabulary or grammar of a known language; even though that might be quite easy if one were free to juggle with the values of 88 mutually unconnected signs. **❞**

The "Work Notes" run to almost 200 pages of densely typed, often-technical analysis, hypothesis and experiment, which jump back and forth. There is no thread like Ariadne's running through the Linear B decipherment labyrinth. Even Ventris himself was unable to produce a coherent narrative of his method. So we must, I fear, be content with a summary of the basic techniques based on his own account, followed by a fuller explanation of what was unquestionably the moment of revelation.

His first technique was statistical. Using Bennett's transcription of the Pylos tablets, Ventris counted each sign group (word) with a distinct spelling, and discarded all repeated sign groups. (This was necessary to avoid distortion of the statistics by multiple occurrences of common words, including names.) It left him with 5410 total occurrences of signs. He then counted the number of occurrences of each of 79 signs, taken from Bennett's 89-sign list (the remaining 10 signs occurred too rarely for statistical analysis), and calculated their frequencies out of 1000. This enabled him to classify the 79 signs into three categories: Frequent (15 signs), Average (26 signs) and Infrequent (38 signs). In addition, he classified each sign according to its *position* in sign groups, such as initial, final, second or all positions. Here is the portion of Ventris's table dealing with the Frequent signs:

FIGURE 7 : Minoan B syllabary.

Ventris
WORK NOTE
1 May 51

## PYLOS SIGNS IN ORDER OF FREQUENCY

FREQUENT SIGNS

| | | | | | | | |
|---|---|---|---|---|---|---|---|
| 1 : om 44.0 | | FINAL, rare initial & second | 6 : an 34.0 | | final and penultimate | 11 : ij 31.2 | SECOND |
| 2 : af 38.2 | | penultimate | 7 : ac 33.8 | | final & second, rare initial | 12 : ik 30.3 | INITIAL & final, rare second |
| 3 : ak 37.7 | | INITIAL | 8 : ix 33.1 | | all positions | 13 : av 29.4 | FINAL rare initial |
| 4 : ig 37.2 | | INITIAL rare elsewhere | 9 : iw 32.5 | | final | 14 : ag 28.6 | final & second |
| 5 : eg 34.4 | | second and penultimate | 10 : if 32 3 | | second and initial | 15 : oj 28 1 | final and penultimate |

Note that the three signs ⚹, ⊤, and ℔, have high frequencies in the initial position. This suggested to Ventris that they were probably pure *vowels*. The reason is that in a syllabary of the CV ('open') type, the sign for a pure vowel will occur mainly at the beginning of word, because in every other position the vowel will normally be subsumed into the syllabic sign. Thus, in English, 'anagram' would be spelt syllabically **a**-na-g(a)-ra-m(a). A pure vowel would appear *within* a word only in examples such as 'initial', *i-ni-ti-**a**-l(a)*. Such words turn out to be comparatively infrequent, whatever the language under consideration.

Another sign ☺ ('currant bun') was found to occur with 'average' frequency but exclusively in the final position of sign groups. That the sign was a suffix and not part of the root was clear from the fact that there occurred pairs of sign groups of the following kind:

W-X-Y-Z
W-X-Y-Z-☺

This suggested to Ventris that the 'currant bun' might be a conjunction such as 'and', formed not in the English way as a separate word but as a syllable tacked onto the preceding word, like '-que' in the Latin phrase "Senatus Populusque Romanus" (SPQR), meaning "The Senate *and* People of Rome". In English, '-ly' is tacked on to adjectives to form adverbs in the same way.

Then there was the technique of scribal variation, in other words a search for variant spellings of the same word, such as 'infle**ct**ion/infle**x**ion' in English. One looked for pairs of sign groups which appeared in two slightly different spellings, for example:

and deduced that there was a close relationship between a sign in one group and the sign that had replaced it in the second group (perhaps a shared vowel but different consonant). For this technique to work, the two words had to be basically the same (bar one sign, or perhaps two signs), e.g. recogni**s**e/recogni**z**e, **sc**eptical/s**k**eptical, and not two words of completely different meaning, e.g. but**t**er/but**l**er, **y**ellow/**b**ellow, which happen to have one sign different. The problem, of course, was how to tell this when one could not read the language. The most promising examples came from pairs of long words, or from scribal erasures of spelling mistakes, in which it sometimes proved possible to read both the intended sign and the old, erased sign beneath it.

Plural forms too were useful. Where there were numerals on the tablets, singular and plural forms could be distinguished. Many, but not all, showed the addition of an extra syllable (highlighted):

An inflection of this kind resembled the formation of plurals in Greek.

But the most powerful technique was the search for patterns of inflection in what appeared to be nouns, as practiced on the tablets from Knossos by Kober in the 1940s. With the entire corpus of Pylos tablets now available, from 1951, the opportunities were much increased. For example, an exhaustive search of the Pylos sign groups yielded the fact that men's names appeared to inflect in at least six different 'declensions', each with three 'cases':

In late February 1952, having finished reviewing the Pylos tablets but before receiving Myres's long-awaited published edition of Evans's Knossos tablets, Ventris produced "Work Note" 17 complete with another grid:

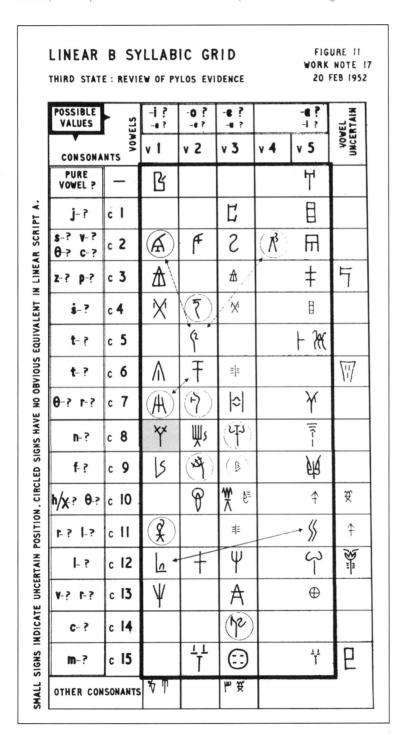

*'Grid' from "Work Note" 17 by Michael Ventris, 20 February 1952. Although the phonetic values were still very uncertain, some of Ventris's guesses proved right: for example, vowel 1 turned out to have the value i, consonant 8 the value n and the sign V1C8,*  Y *, had the syllabic value ni.*

A week later, he wrote to Myres about a fascinating experiment that he had tried over the weekend. For some time he had suspected that the Knossos tablets studied by Kober contained place names, and he knew that Myres agreed with him. In addition, he had noticed that Kober's 'triplets' occurred only in the tablets from Knossos, never in the tablets from Pylos. Could each 'triplet' refer to a different town in Crete? Now he noticed that if he made "only a little adjustment" to the phonetic values that he had guessed in the grid, and then substituted them for the corresponding signs in Kober's 'triplets', a very interesting result emerged: what appeared to be 'archaic Greek' names of three well-known Cretan cities, including Knossos! "This is one of those guesses it's best to keep up one's sleeve, because there's an extremely good chance of its being completely *wrong*", he told Myres cautiously. If correct, it meant, very probably, that the language of Linear B was basically Greek. Ventris must have felt like Evans with the foal tablet (page 83): each man looked the 'Greek solution' in the face for a moment but pulled back on the brink of accepting it because he preferred another solution—'Minoan' or Etruscan.

Three months later, after receiving Myres's massive edition, Ventris was forced to accept the truth. Here is how it happened.

By early 1952 Ventris knew that he had reached the point beyond which further sign analysis would be unproductive. There was no Linear B equivalent of the Rosetta stone, and no realistic prospect of finding one. "To wait for a *bilingual* to help us solve our problem is to cry for the moon", he had noted. If he was to establish the language behind the signs, he must now make a definite, educated guess at phonetic values for two or three signs and then see what phonetic values the 'grid' generated for many other signs.

He began by allotting *a* to the 'double-axe' ⑂, pure vowel 5 on the grid. Its high initial frequency in Linear B and similar behavior in other languages suggested this identification. For his second guess he turned to the Cypriot clue once tried by Evans: comparison of the shapes of Linear B signs with those of the Cypriot script (see chart on page 83). Ventris had studiously avoided using this comparison until now because (like Evans) he distrusted it; but he had continued to believe in some kind of historic link between the languages of Crete, Cyprus and the Aegean area. He now hazarded that Linear B ⍦ was equivalent to ⍑ –*na* in Cypriot, and that Linear B ∧ was equivalent to ↑ –*ti* in Cypriot. (He also adduced evidence from Etruscan, just to confuse right with wrong reasoning!) If these guesses were right, then consonant 8 on the grid must be *n* and vowel 1 must be *i*, which automatically meant that ⍭ was *ni*, according to the grid. (See previous page.)

Ventris's next step was inspired: a "leap in the dark," in the words of Chadwick. He decided to follow up his February hunch about the names of Cretan towns, and see where the hypothesis would lead him.

Amnisos he knew was the classical Greek name for the ancient port of Knossos. Amnisos spelt syllabically in Linear B would, he proposed, be *A-mi-ni-so*, with no final *s*—the 's' being a classical Greek inflection also found, as we saw earlier, in the Cypriot script. (Evans had had the same idea about Linear B spelling when he speculatively equated Linear B 'polo' with classical Greek 'pōlos'.) In introducing this assumption, that Linear B spelling might have omitted final *s* in nouns, Ventris was undoubtedly sticking out his neck, since he had no supporting linguistic evidence at all for such a difference between archaic Greek and classical Greek.

Written in Linear B, A-mi-ni-so would be:

⊤ – ? – ⋎ – ?

The first word in one 'triplet' was ⊤ ⩗ ⋎ ⫏. If it meant Amnisos, then ⩗ = *mi*  ⫏ = *so*.

Then, according to the grid, consonant 9 must be *m*, and vowel 2 must be *o*. This would mean, in turn (the so-called 'chain reaction') that ⫲s =*no*.

The first word in another 'triplet' was ⫐ ⫲s ⫏. Using the grid, this translated as ?-*no-so*. If ⫐ = *ko*, the name could be Knossos itself. Soon Ventris extracted from the five 'triplets' the names of three further known Cretan towns:

⫤ ⋇ ⫏     *Tu-li-so* (Tulissos)

⧾ ⫲ ⊤     *Pa-i-to* (Phaistos)

⫥ ⋎ ⊤     *Lu-ki-to* (Luktos)

An entire 'triplet' could now be transliterated as:

⊤ ⩗ ⋎ ⫏        *A-mi-ni-so* (Amnisos)

⊤ ⩗ ⋎ ⧆ ⫐      *A-mi-ni-si-jo* (Amnisian men)

⊤ ⩗ ⋎ ⧆ ⊟      *A-mi-ni-si-ja* (Amnisian women)

Ventris's proposed meanings of the second and third words, though as yet unproven by him, recalled words with similar inflections in Homeric Greek, and were therefore promising. It looked as if Kober's 'triplets' were *not*, after all, noun declensions but proper names and their ethnica (e.g. New York/New Yorkers, London/Londoners).

Thus proper names, vital in the Egyptian hieroglyphic decipherment, had proved vital in deciphering Linear B too. Instead of Ptolemy and Cleopatra, there was Amnisos and Knossos. But everything was still speculative, dependent on the initial assumptions. It was only when a still-cautious Ventris began to apply his new phonetic values for the signs to dozens of fresh words in the tablets, and obtained recognizable archaic Greek words, that the breakthrough began to seem real. He quickly identified, for instance, *po-me* (shepherd), *ka-ke-u* (smith), *ke-ra-me-u* (potter), *ka-na-pe-u* (fuller), *i-e-re-u* (priest) and *i-je-re-ja* (priestess); furthermore, the inflections of these words he had codified as unknown sign groups (like the 'triplets') since the beginning of 1951 were immediately explicable in terms of accepted archaic Greek declension.

On 1 June 1952, he typed his final "Work Note", number 20, titling it "Are the Knossos and Pylos tablets written in Greek?" Soon after, he wrote to Myres: "though it runs completely counter to everything I've said in the past, I'm now almost completely convinced that the ... tablets are in GREEK." On 1 July, in a measured and slightly diffident voice he announced his discovery on BBC radio, publicly renouncing his long-cherished Etruscan hypothesis and remarking that the language of Linear B was

| | | | | |
|---|---|---|---|---|
| a | e | i | o | u |
| da | de | di | do | du |
| ja | je | | jo | ju |
| ka | ke | ki | ko | ku |
| ma | me | mi | mo | mu |
| na | ne | ni | no | nu |
| pa | pe | pi | po | pu |
| qa | qe | qi | qo | |
| ra | re | ri | ro | ru |
| sa | se | si | so | su |
| ta | te | ti | to | tu |
| wa | we | wi | wo | |
| za | ze | | zo | |

*(Opposite) The fundamental Linear B syllabary, established by Ventris and Chadwick, with 60 signs. The order is based on phonetic values (shared vowel or consonant), not on sign shapes. Compare the sign list on page 88. (Right) Pylos tablet deciphered in May 1953, drawn by Ventris (see photograph on page 14).*

"a difficult and archaic Greek, seeing that it is 500 years older than Homer and written in a rather abbreviated form, but Greek nevertheless." As John Chadwick much later said of Ventris: "The most interesting fact about his work is that it forced him to propose a solution contrary to his own preconceptions."

Chadwick was about to become a junior lecturer in classics at Cambridge when he heard the BBC broadcast and promptly obtained Ventris's "Work Notes" from Myres. After a few days of skepticism, he contacted Ventris and they immediately began a collaboration, in which Chadwick's specialist knowledge of early Greek was important in translating more and more of the tablets. The editor of the most prestigious British journal of Hellenic studies, excited by the new, though unproven discovery, immediately accepted a Ventris/Chadwick article on the decipherment.

A few months later, in May 1953, came the bombshell tablet with the four-handled cups mentioned in the Introduction (see page 14). Ventris phoned Chadwick in Cambridge in a great state of excitement—"he rarely showed signs of emotion, but for him this was a dramatic moment", Chadwick recalled. Blegen, the excavator of Pylos, had used the Ventris syllabary to read a new Linear B tablet (see right), never seen by Ventris and Chadwick. Suddenly, the mute signs—writing that predated the Trojan war—were being compelled to speak after more than three millennia of silence.

*tiripode aikeu keresijo weke* 2
(tripod cauldrons of Cretan workmanship of the aikeu type 2)

*tiripo eme pode owowe* 1
(tripod cauldron with a single handle on one foot 1)

*tiripo keresijo weke*
(tripod cauldron of Cretan workmanship)

*apu kekaumeno kerea*
(burnt at the legs)

*qeto* 3
(wine jars 3)

*dipa mezoe qetorowe* 1
(larger-sized goblet with four handles 1)

*dipae mezoe tiriowee* 2
(larger-sized goblet with three handles 2)

*dipa mewijo qetorowe* 1
(smaller-sized goblet with four handles 1)

*dipa mewijo tirijowe* 1
(smaller-sized goblet with three handles 1)

*dipa mewijo anowe* 1
(smaller-sized goblet without a handle)

*Michael Ventris at work on Linear B, following his decipherment of the script in 1952.*

This was not the Greek of Homer, still less the classical Greek of Euripides or Plato—as modern English is not the English of Chaucer or Shakespeare. But it made good linguistic, archaeological and historical sense, once scholars overrode Evans's Minoan imperialism and accepted that Crete had been invaded by Greeks who invented Linear B. Many scholars immediately put the sign list and phonetic values to use and found that they worked; and although there were a few severe critics (including a former teacher of Chadwick), one of whom claimed that Ventris had 'fixed' the famous tablet with the four-handled cups, the fundamental decipherment was widely regarded as a *fait accompli* by 1953. As the details of the tablets were worked out over the next decades, they proved, alas, to contain nothing of literary value: they merely recorded prosaic details of palace administration, such as lists of names and their trades and lists of goods. Unlike Egyptian hieroglyphs and Mesopotamian cuneiform, Linear B tells us not one word about the names of kings and the deeds of heroes. But Greek the language certainly was, not Evans's 'Minoan'; and it predated the earliest-known (classical) Greek inscription by some 600 or 700 years. With characteristic modesty and pleasant irony, Ventris announced the fact to his old classics master at Stowe school, Patrick Hunter, who had introduced him to Linear B as a precocious teenager:

Not quite the Greek you taught me, I'm afraid!
Best wishes —— Michael

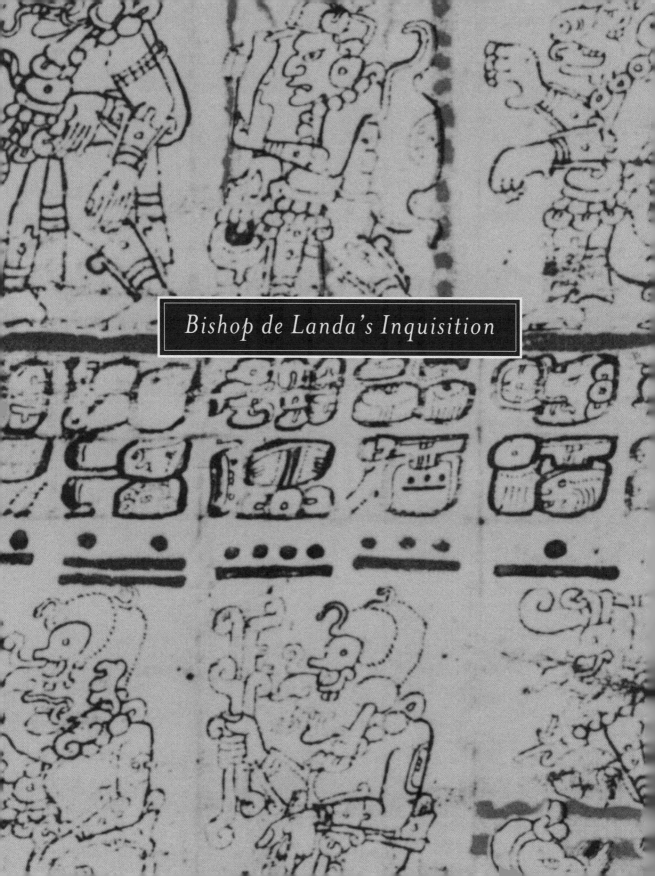

Bishop de Landa's Inquisition

# III

# MAYAN GLYPHS

The Dresden Codex (opposite) is one of only four surviving 'books' of the ancient Maya of Central America. It is also the best preserved. Probably created just before the Spanish conquest of Mexico in the 16th century, it consists of 39 leaves, making up a folding screen the size of a Michelin travel guide which opens out to a length of nearly twelve feet. On each leaf, which has been sized with a fine coat of lime, the artist has painted with extreme care a series of gods and animals, often in many colors, accompanied by 'hieroglyphic' symbols.

It is difficult to believe that these glyphs—as they are generally called—are part of a full writing system. They bear no resemblance to cuneiform, Linear B or even Egyptian hieroglyphs; they seem, rather, like cabalistic symbols, designed for the rituals of some esoteric cult. And that is exactly how Mayan glyphs were regarded until as recently as the 1970s. The three chief books on decipherment published for the general reader in the 1960s and 70s kept total silence about the Mayan glyphs—as if they were not writing to be deciphered.

J. E. S. (Sir Eric) Thompson, the leading Mayanist of the time, asserted in 1972: "Maya writing is not syllabic or alphabetic in part or in whole." Its intricacies had been created, according to Thompson's decades of immensely detailed research, for the purposes of a Maya theocracy of star-gazing astronomer-priests, who were time worshippers with a highly sophisticated calendar and a deeply spiritual outlook. Their ideal was "moderation in all things", their motto "live and let live", and their character had "an emphasis on discipline, cooperation, patience, and consideration for others." Maya civilization was unlike any other, said Thompson, who looked to it as a source of spiritual values in a modern world that placed far more importance on material prosperity.

As Sir Arthur Evans worshipped the noble, cultured Minoans, and sought to distance them from the comparatively vulgar Greeks, so Sir Eric Thompson revered the peace-loving ancient Maya and abstracted them from the brutal, human-sacrificing Aztecs who followed them. Only after Evans's death in 1941 was the myth fully exposed, and the mundane subject matter of the Linear B tablets revealed. Something similar happened in the years following Thompson's death in 1975. But the content of the glyphs turned out to be very much more intriguing and unexpected than the accounting tablets from the Old World.

Today we know, thanks to the recent decipherment of the glyphs, that the Maya, or at any rate their rulers, were obsessed with blood and war, and that both the rulers and the gods liked to take hallucinogenic or inebriating enemas using special syringes. "The highest goal of these lineage-proud dynasts was to capture the ruler of a rival city-state in battle, to torture and humiliate him (sometimes for years), and then subject him to decapitation following a ball game which the prisoner was always destined to lose," writes Michael Coe of Yale University, a long-time participant in the Maya decipherment, who chronicled it compellingly in *Breaking the Maya Code*. Time and religion and the movements of the heavenly bodies certainly did fascinate the Maya—Thompson was not wrong about that—but not at all to the exclusion of politics and material matters of earthly existence.

*J. E. S. (Sir Eric) Thompson (1898–1975), with the edition of the Dresden Codex he published in 1972.*

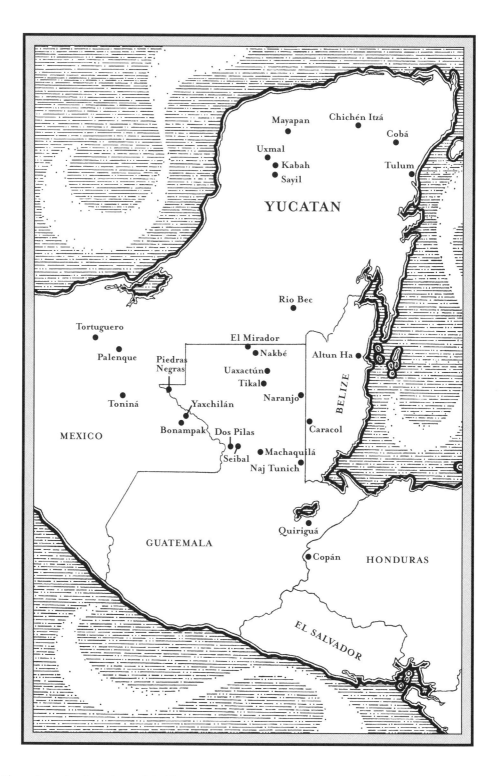

The major archaeological sites of the Maya area.

The story begins with the Spanish, who were the first Europeans to encounter the Maya, after their leader Cortés had subdued the Aztecs. Maya civilization had by then long since passed its glory (the so-called Classic period, 250-900 AD, as we now know). The conquistadors and missionaries left accounts of astonishing monuments buried in the jungles of the Central America, and they recorded invaluable clues as to the meaning of the glyphs. Subsequent travelers and visitors could not believe that the impoverished Indians they saw laboring like slaves for the Spanish could have any connection with these monuments, and so they proposed that Old World peoples, even the Lost Tribes of Israel, were the builders.

Not until the 1840s did the Maya enter modern consciousness: an intrepid American traveler (the first American to reach the 'lost city' of Petra in Jordan), John Lloyd Stephens, and his companion, the Englishman Frederick Catherwood, a brilliant illustrator, published what became one of the best-sellers of the 19th century, *Incidents of Travel in Central America, Chiapas, and Yucatan*. The authors felt that they had stumbled upon wonders comparable with that of ancient Egypt, a land where each had recently traveled and which Napoleon's scholars had explored 40 years before. Speaking of the ruined buildings of Palenque (in Chiapas state in southern Mexico), Stephens wrote that, "If a like discovery had been made in Italy, Greece, Egypt, or Asia, within reach of European travel, it would have created an interest not inferior to the discovery of Herculaneum, or Pompeii." Among the wonders were many stone inscriptions on buildings and stelae. Stephens was firmly (and presciently) convinced that the elaborate glyphs on these monuments, drawn by Catherwood, were writing: "No Champollion has yet brought to them the energies of his inquiring mind. Who shall read them?"

*Mayan glyphs, at Copán in Honduras, as drawn by Frederick Catherwood in* Incidents of Travel in Central America, Chiapas, and Yucatan *(1841). His co-author, John Lloyd Stephens, guessed that the glyphs formed a writing system like the Egyptian hieroglyphs deciphered in the 1820s, but his insight was effectively ignored until the 1950s.*

As Champollion had been aided by Coptic, the descendant of the language of the ancient Egyptians, so the decipherers of Mayan writing have been helped by the languages of the living Maya, and by their living traditions and cultures (none of which has survived in the ancient Egyptian

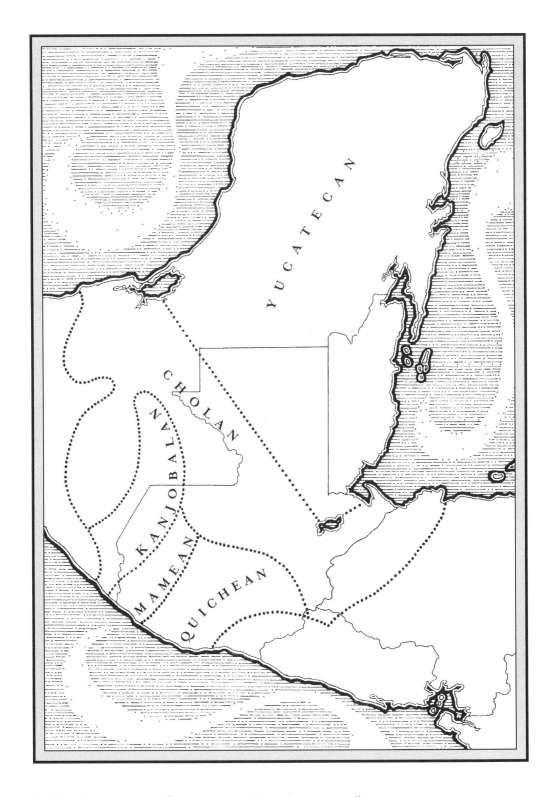

*The Mayan language groups. There are some 30 Mayan languages in all.*

case). Some six million Mayan-speakers dwell today in the same area as their ancestors. Although they are mostly Catholics, in consequence of the Spanish conquest, they speak various languages and preserve a distinctive culture; their relationships with the governments of the countries in which they live have been fraught with oppression and bloodshed. (Rigoberta Menchú, a Maya woman, received a Nobel peace prize in 1992 for her resistance work in Guatemala; in the 1994 Zapatista rebellion in Chiapas, the Maya predominated.) While they cannot read the glyphs of their ancestors, the modern Maya use vocabulary and syntax directly related to the words behind the glyphs in many cases.

The linguistic situation is very complex, however. Besides being difficult to learn (for speakers of modern European languages), modern Mayan languages number as many as thirty-one. Some of these are as close as, say, Dutch is to English, others differ as much as English does from French. The division between Cholan and Yucatec Mayan, the Mayan language of most of the Yucatan peninsula which has the greatest number of speakers, is a major one; Tzeltal and Tzotzil are spoken in Chiapas; Quiché and Cakchiquel in the highlands of Guatemala. The precise nature of the earlier Mayan language written in the ancient glyphs is controversial. Is it related to one modern language, to multiple modern languages or even, as many now think, to one now-extinct 'prestige' literary language, Cholti? (Compare Latin in Europe.) Whatever the real situation, dictionaries of the modern languages compiled in recent centuries have yielded words that fit the ancient inscriptions; and contemporary native speakers, with the help of North American and European epigraphers,

have been able to suggest insights into the glyphs based on their unique knowledge.

The first part of the Mayan writing system to be deciphered concerned numbers and counting; this was the work of scholars in the 19th century, notably Constantine Samuel Rafinesque and Ernst Förstemann, royal librarian of the electorate of Saxony, who had charge of the Dresden Codex. (The numbers were also the part that first attracted the attention of Feynman, the physicist, about a century later.) Rafinesque noted a system of dots and bars, as evident in the page of the Dresden Codex on page 106, that was patently numerical. Since there were never more than four dots together with a bar, he deduced that a dot stood for one and a bar for five. The mathematically minded Förstemann scrutinized the entire codex and demonstrated that the bars and dots could be used for calculations, as we shall show later, and that some of the calculations were based on the 584-day cycle of Venus as seen from Earth.

The numerical system in its entirety turned out to be remarkably sophisticated. The Maya (like the Hindus) were ahead of the Babylonians and the Romans in inventing a symbol for zero: a shell. Here are some examples of simple numbers, 0, 1, 4, 6 and 19:

Like us (and the Babylonians), the Maya used the idea of place value. But where we have a place value that increases from right to left in multiples of ten (i.e. 1, 10, 100, 1000, etc.), in the Maya system the place value increases in multiples of 20 (i.e. 1, 20, 400, 8000, etc.). And instead of it increasing horizontally from right to left, among the Maya the place value increased vertically from the bottom upwards. Here are five more examples, the numbers 20, 55, 249, 819 and 72,063:

| | | |
|---|---|---|
| • | = 1 (x 20) = | 20 |
| ⊂▥⊃ | = 0 (x 1) = | 0 |
| | Total: | **20** |
| • • | = 2 (x 20) = | 40 |
| ▬▬▬ | = 15 (x 1) = | 15 |
| | Total: | **55** |
| •• • | = 12 (x 20) = | 240 |
| • • • • | = 9 (x 1) = | 9 |
| | Total: | **249** |
| • • | = 2 (x 400) = | 800 |
| ⊂▥⊃ | = 0 (x 20) = | 0 |
| • • • •<br>▬▬▬▬ | = 19 (x 1) = | 19 |
| | Total: | **819** |
| • • • • | 9 (x 8000) = | 72,000 |
| ⊂▥⊃ | 0 (x 400) = | 0 |
| • • • | 3 (x 20) = | 60 |
| • • • | 3 (x 1) = | 3 |
| | Total: | **72,063** |

But this is not the end of the numerical system. Maya scribes loved decoration and complexity for its own sake, even more than the ancient Egyptian scribes. By comparing dates in Mayan inscriptions written entirely in bar-and-dot numerals with similar dates written in a mixture of such numerals and other glyphs, early 20th-century scholars worked

out a parallel system of Mayan numerals, 1-19, that employ pictures, so-called 'head variants'. Here are four examples:

—a hint of the daunting diversity of the non-numerical part of the writing system.

The Mayan inscriptions are full of numerals and dates, for the measurement of time was a Maya obsession, as already mentioned. Though it is not necessary to understand in detail the complicated Maya calendar and how it related to their astronomical observations in order to grasp the decipherment of the non-numerical glyphs, we do need to be acquainted with its broad principles.

The simplest part of the calendar combines the numerals 1-13 with 20 named days, producing a 260-day count. We can visualize this with two interlocking wheels; the days are on the upper wheel, with their glyphs and names given in Yucatec Mayan. (The wheels are simply a visual aid, and were not used by the ancient Maya; we do not know whether they had calculating 'machines'.) The date shown opposite is 1 Imix:

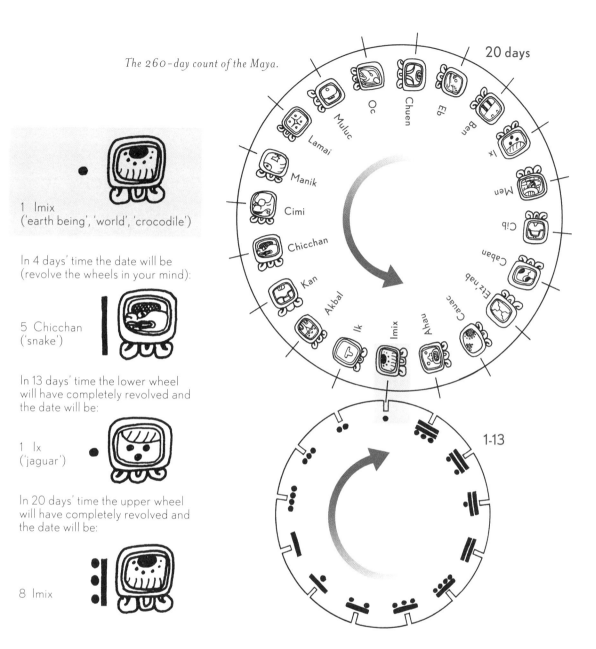

*The 260-day count of the Maya.*

**20 days**

Muluc · Oc · Chuen · Eb · Ben · Ix · Men · Cib · Caban · Etz'nab · Cauac · Ahau · Imix · Ik · Akbal · Kan · Chicchan · Cimi · Manik · Lamat

1 Imix
('earth being', 'world', 'crocodile')

In 4 days' time the date will be (revolve the wheels in your mind):

5 Chicchan
('snake')

In 13 days' time the lower wheel will have completely revolved and the date will be:

1 Ix
('jaguar')

In 20 days' time the upper wheel will have completely revolved and the date will be:

8 Imix

1-13

The Dresden Codex is full of time calculations like this, as we shall shortly see.

The Maya expanded the 260-day count by meshing the named days with a third wheel representing the approximate solar year of 365 days. It consisted of 18 named months (compare our 12 months, January, February, March,

and so on), each of 20 days' duration, and one month of 5 days called Uayeb, making altogether a 'vague year' of (18 × 20) + (1 × 5) = 365 days: 'vague' because the extra one quarter of a day in a solar year, which we solve by adding a leap year every four years, the Maya deliberately chose to ignore.

Pop    Uo    Zip    Zotz    Tzec

Xul    Yaxkin    Mol    Chen    Yax

Zac    Ceh    Mac    Kankin    Muan

Pax    Kayab    Cumku    Uayeb

*The 19 month glyphs with their names in Yucatec Mayan. Each month lasts 20 days, except for Uayeb which lasts only 5 days.*

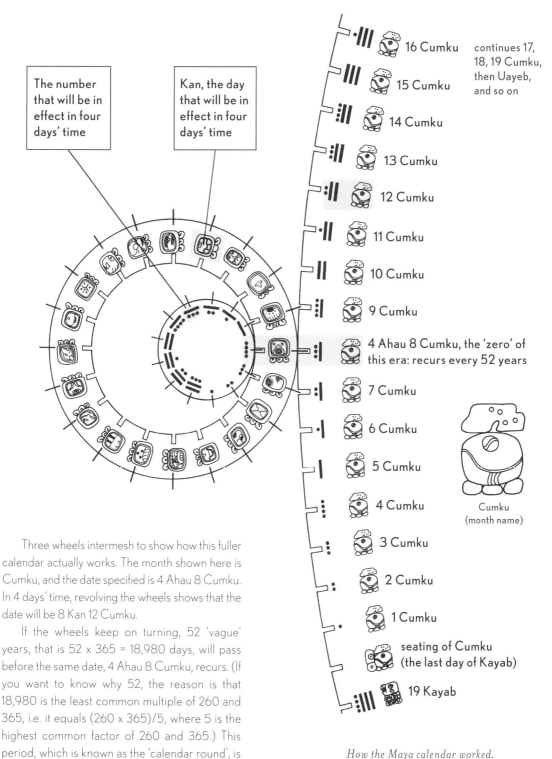

The number that will be in effect in four days' time

Kan, the day that will be in effect in four days' time

16 Cumku
15 Cumku
14 Cumku
13 Cumku
12 Cumku
11 Cumku
10 Cumku
9 Cumku

continues 17, 18, 19 Cumku, then Uayeb, and so on

4 Ahau 8 Cumku, the 'zero' of this era: recurs every 52 years

7 Cumku
6 Cumku
5 Cumku
4 Cumku
3 Cumku
2 Cumku
1 Cumku

seating of Cumku (the last day of Kayab)

19 Kayab

Cumku (month name)

Three wheels intermesh to show how this fuller calendar actually works. The month shown here is Cumku, and the date specified is 4 Ahau 8 Cumku. In 4 days' time, revolving the wheels shows that the date will be 8 Kan 12 Cumku.

If the wheels keep on turning, 52 'vague' years, that is 52 x 365 = 18,980 days, will pass before the same date, 4 Ahau 8 Cumku, recurs. (If you want to know why 52, the reason is that 18,980 is the least common multiple of 260 and 365, i.e. it equals (260 x 365)/5, where 5 is the highest common factor of 260 and 365.) This period, which is known as the 'calendar round', is

*How the Maya calendar worked.*

long enough to be sufficient for an average human life span, but not long enough for historical purposes. Imagine if our longest defined time period was 100 years: we would then date the beginning of the French revolution, the building of the Eiffel Tower and the fall of the Berlin Wall each as '89—clearly an unsatisfactory ambiguity.

So the Maya, like us, needed to invent an equivalent of our 'long count' of years, an endless march of time from the past into the future, which we anchor with BC and AD. Such a 'long count' will be independent of the 'calendar round' until the two counts are correlated at a particular day. The Maya chose to correlate their zero on the 'long count' with the date 4 Ahau 8 Cumku in the 'calendar round'. Why they selected this particular date for the beginning of the present creation is obscure. At any rate, it correlates with 13 August 3114 BC in our Gregorian calendar. (The figuring out of the correlation was done through some astute detective work in 1905 on the Maya codices and Spanish colonial records by Joseph Goodman, a Californian newspaper editor turned amateur Mayanist, perhaps the first of many such in the 20th century. It was then refined by Thompson and others.)

Mayanists give this zero date as 0.0.0.0.0.—which is the beginning of the current 'great cycle' of time, due to end on 23 December AD 2012. (The current 'great cycle' is of course part of an endless series of cycles in the past and to come, which the Maya marked, when required, by adding more digits to the left of the date.) The five positions in the date refer to numbers of five smaller cycles within the 'great cycle', as we have days, months, years, decades and centuries within our millennia. A Maya date therefore consists of a series of numerals, beginning on the left with the count of the largest cycles of time elapsed since the 'zero' point, working through the count of successively shorter cycles, and finally correlating with the 'calendar round'.

Take, for example, the date 9.15.4.6.4. 8 Kan 17 Muan. The first five numerals correspond to:

9 cycles of 144,000 days = 1,296,000 days
15 cycles of 7,200 days =108,000 days
4 cycles of 360 days =1440 days
6 cycles of 20 days =120 days
4 cycles of 1 day = 4 days
**Total: 1,405,564 days**

That is 1,405,564 days from the beginning of the current 'great cycle' (13 August 3114 BC): 3 December AD 735—a date in an inscription, correlating with 8 Kan 17 Muan in the 'calendar round'.

If the heavens were cyclical, for the Maya it followed that human affairs must be cyclical too. Much more than ancient societies in general, the Maya made no fundamental distinction between the natural and the supernatural, astronomy and astrology (this is part of the fascination of their mental universe for us moderns). Thus the Dresden Codex is an almanac full of 260-day counts, in which each day is linked to other days by calculations based on astronomical observations, using eclipses and the 584-day Venus cycle, and is thereby given an astrological significance—auspicious or otherwise—expressed in the deeds and moods of a bewildering variety of gods, goddesses and half-recognizable deified animals.

In the following typical page from the codex, each god and goddess is named with a glyph written above his or her portrait. We can think of the whole codex as being a bit like a strip cartoon about Maya gods and goddesses. Rather than the captions being written close to the human figures in a bubble, in the codex they are generally written above the figure. There are also not many dividing lines to tell readers of the codex that they have moved from one picture to the next (dotted lines have been added here, as a guide). Five dates have been extracted on the left of the codex to show how it was used to calculate; the month glyphs (Ik, Ix, Cimi, Etz'nab, Oc) have been drawn to show them more clearly. Above the codex are the numerals (20, 9, 13, 20, 3, 10) that the Maya diviners used for calculation with these dates.

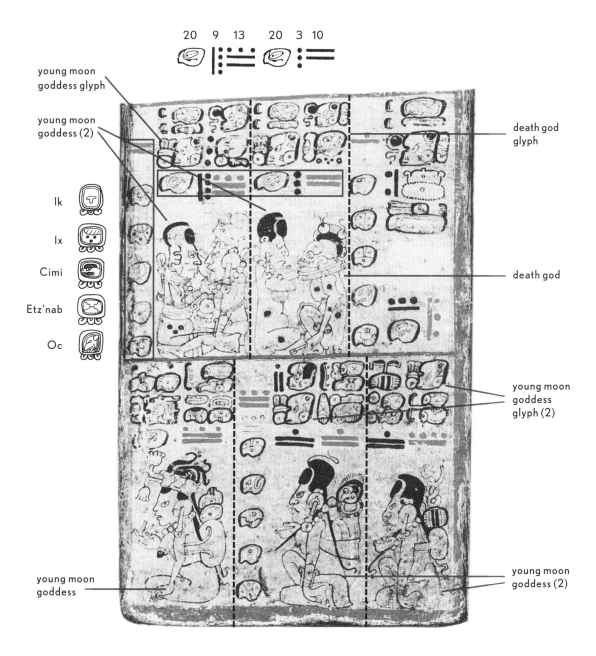

The Dresden Codex as a calculating machine.

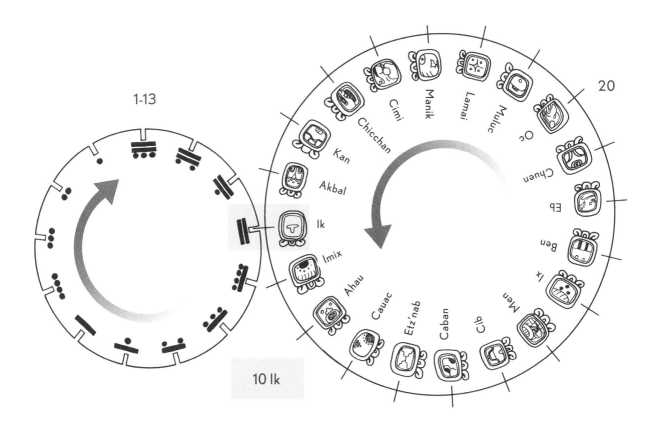

1-13

20

Cimi
Manik
Lamai
Muluc
Oc
Chuen
Eb
Ben
Ix
Men
Cib
Caban
Etz'nab
Cauac
Ahau
Imix
Ik
Akbal
Kan
Chicchan

10 Ik

These particular numerals connect the dates 10 Ik, 10 Ix, 10 Cimi, 10 Etz'nab and 10 Oc by means of the 260-day count. We start at 10 Ik. Revolving the wheels in our mind through 20 + 9 = 29 positions (day names), we reach 13 Chuen. Now revolve the wheels again through 20 + 3 = 23 (day names). You should find that the new date is 10 Ix. 10 Ix is 29 + 23 = 52 days after 10 Ik. If we repeat this calculation four more times, we move from 10 Ix to 10 Cimi to 10 Etz'nab to 10 Oc and back to 10 Ik. This part of the almanac therefore covers 5 x 52 = 260 days, a number vital to the Maya, as already explained.

Having acquired a good idea of the numerical system and the calendar, scholars of a century ago turned to the rest of the script. They had realized that the same basic numerical/calendrical system was used throughout the scripts of Mesoamerica (for example, by the Aztecs), which suggested that it was probably independent of the rest of the Mayan script and would not be of much help in deciphering the glyphs as a whole. So where were they to turn?

The techniques that had helped to decipher other ancient scripts (Egyptian hieroglyphs, Mesopotamian cuneiform and so on) were not easily available in the Maya case. To analyze the codices and stone inscriptions so as to produce a sign list was one possibility, eventually pursued by Thompson (it is used even today with modifications); but there seemed to be an endless galli-maufry of signs, with no obvious core group. To compare inscriptions and look for patterns, i.e. similar glyphs in a similar position, which might betray the structure of the script, was another possibility, if daunting; and it did eventually produce some results, as we shall see. A search for glyphs representing proper names, so fruitful with Egyptian hieroglyphs and cuneiform (and later with Linear B) seemed to be a non-starter, because no one knew the names of any ancient Maya rulers or places. The living Maya were completely clueless about the meaning of the glyphs; their knowledge had been wiped out in the years following the Spanish conquest and they now wrote their languages, if they wrote at all, in roman script. Finally, there was no bilingual: a Mayan inscription with a parallel text in a known language.

Or perhaps there was? A French priest who had served in Guatemala and become interested in the Maya, the Abbé Brasseur de Bourbourg, came upon a copy of a forgotten Spanish manuscript in a library in Madrid and published it in 1864. Entitled *Relación de las Cosas de Yucatán* (An Account of the Things of Yucatan), it was a detailed description of Maya society intended as an exculpation of charges of excessive zeal in converting the Maya brought by the Spanish authorities against a minor member of the Inquisition. The author, Fray Diego de Landa, was a Franciscan friar who served in Yucatan from 1547 and eventually, after being acquitted in Spain, became bishop of Yucatan until his death in 1579. One of the ironies of history is that this cleric, who tortured many Maya and did so much to destroy almost all their hieroglyphic writing by burning their codices as works of the devil, was also the man who noted down the essential clue to the decipherment of the glyphs four centuries later. In Yucatan today, there is a rather grim-faced statue of Landa outside the massive church that he founded at Izamal, the Spanish inscription of which both celebrates and excoriates him for his works.

*Fray Diego de Landa (1524-79), bishop of Yucatan from 1572 until his death. A fascinating, contradictory figure, Landa burnt most of the Mayan codices as being works of the devil, yet he gave posterity the key to understanding those few that survived. This portrait of Landa hangs in the cathedral of Izamal in northern Yucatan which was founded by him and where today crowds of Maya, descendants of those tortured by Landa, come to take Holy Communion.*

The most important thing in the *Relación* is the drawing Landa made in the section on native writing of what he called an "alphabet". Plainly it is no straightforward alphabet since it contains more than one sign for some letters as well as syllabic signs:

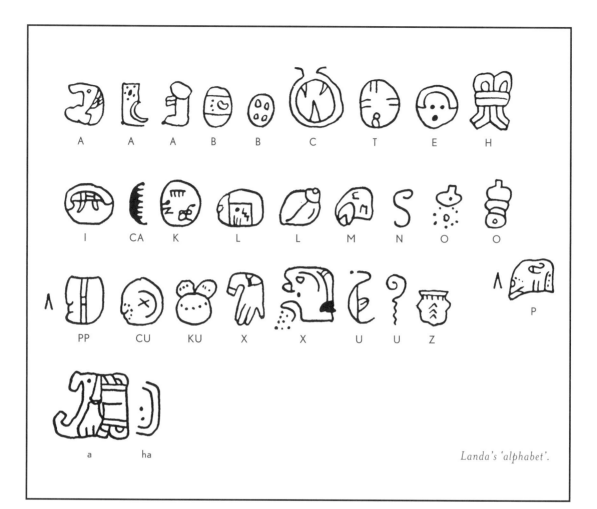

| A | A | A | B | B | C | T | E | H |

| I | CA | K | L | L | M | N | O | O |

| PP | CU | KU | X | X | U | U | Z | P |

| a | ha |

*Landa's 'alphabet'.*

We now know that Landa's 'alphabet' was a mixture of right and wrong interpretations, based on a fundamental misunderstanding. Landa, speaking in Spanish, had questioned a Maya noble named Juan Nachi Cocom with whom he was friendly, and neither man had properly understood the other. (The very name Yucatan is derived from 'uic athan'–the phrase spoken to the Spanish conquistadors by the Maya when asked what their land was called: it means 'what do you say, we do not understand you'.) Landa tended to assume that the Maya wrote like 16th-century Spaniards, using an alphabet. For instance, seeing a picture in a codex of a noose around the leg of a deer, and knowing from his understanding of Yucatec Mayan that 'noose' is pronounced *le* in that language, Landa must have pointed to the drawing and said: "Kindly show me how you write *le*. It has two letters." He must then have given the two letters their Spanish names (the first being *ele*, English *el*) and pronounced the complete word again: "*ele, e: le.*" This must have puzzled his Maya informant, who nevertheless obligingly transcribed exactly what Landa had said and therefore wrote:

 *le*

This in turn must have surprised Landa. How could *four* glyphs be required to spell *two* letters? And why was it necessary to repeat each glyph? The truth was that the writing was basically *syllabic* with an admixture of pure vowels:  had the value *e*, had the value *le*. Landa, never having encountered a syllabic writing system, was confused by his evidence, though one can see from his 'alphabet' that he obviously understood some of the glyphs to be syllables. He also knew that Mayan consonants could change their meaning depending on whether they were unglottalized or glottalized, that is, whether the throat was unconstricted or not. (Ordinary English uses the glottal stop at the beginning of 'apple' and in the middle of 'uh-oh!'; and the well-known Cockney English spoken in parts of London is full of glottal-ization.) The following examples are from Yucatec Mayan:

| Unglottalized | Glottalized |
|---|---|
| 'pop' (mat) | 'p'op' (to shell squash seeds) |
| 'cutz' (turkey) | 'kutz' (tobacco) |
| 'muc' (to bury) | 'muk' (to permit) |

Landa expressed the contrast by writing *cu* for , and *ku* for . However, his communication with his informant clearly broke down, as we can see from the following noted phrase:

| ma | i | n | ka | ti |
|---|---|---|---|---|

which means 'I don't want to'—presumably the informant's response to Landa on being request-ed to write further phonetic values of the mysteri-ous glyphs.

The moment that Landa's 'alphabet' was dis-covered, it was obvious that it had the potential to be a 'Rosetta stone' of the Mayan glyphs. But exactly how was it to be applied? Brasseur de Bourbourg, its discoverer, applied it as an alpha-bet to the glyphs of a new codex also discovered by him in Madrid, but the results were patently nonsense. A French Orientalist, Léon de Rosny, had slightly more success in 1876. He realized that the glyphs for certain animals, such as dog, turkey, parrot and jaguar, could be identified by examin-ing the glyphs above the pictures of these crea-tures (the same method used to identify the glyphs for gods and goddesses in the Dresden Codex). He now applied the Landa 'alphabet' to what seemed to be the first sign in the glyph for 'turkey' in the Madrid Codex:

*turkey glyph*       *turkey (Madrid Codex)*

Rosny read the first sign in the glyph as *cu*, by comparing it with Landa's:

 *cu*

He then hazarded a guess that the entire glyph might be read *cutz(u)*, since the Yucatec Mayan word for turkey is 'cutz'. (Recall the silent vowel in final consonants in classical Cypriot on page 81.) Rosny went on to propose that Mayan writing con-tained a phonetic system, based on syllables, but he suggested just this one reading, *cutz(u)*, no 'cross-readings' in which the same signs substituted in other glyphs succeeded in producing a consistent reading, in the manner of Ventris's 'grid'. Thus,

*Yuri Knorozov (1922-99), the Russian linguist who is chiefly responsible for the decipherment of the Mayan script. In the early 1950s, he demonstrated the existence of a phonetic system in the glyphs.*

although Rosny was right about 'cutz', he did not suggest any *system*.

There were a few other lucky shots in subsequent decades, but the majority of suggested readings based on Landa's 'alphabet' were gibberish. After about 1905, the phonetic approach became discredited for half a century (curiously like Alfred Wegener's contemporaneous theory of continental drift). In 1950, when he published his most important book, *Maya Hieroglyphic Writing*, Thompson had rejected Landa's 'alphabet' and phoneticism in the glyphs almost entirely. As we saw in the Introduction, Thompson favored a logographic (and slightly mystical) explanation of the glyph for 'dog', in which one sign represented 'ribs' and the other represented 'death'; and he came to regard the whole system of glyphs as essentially non-phonetic, perhaps not a full writing system at all. "It [was] as though the Rosetta stone had been known for a century before anyone got around to using it to decipher the Egyptian script"–remarks Michael Coe.

———

Then, in 1952, a new Champollion appeared– from an unexpected quarter, the Soviet Union in the final years of Stalin. Yuri Valentinovich Knorozov was the same age as Ventris, and his career too had been interrupted by war; he served in the Red Army and was present at the fall of Berlin in 1945. Curiously, it was a book about the Maya from Berlin's National Library taken to Moscow, and a pessimistic article on the chances of a decipherment by an old German scholar published in 1945, that triggered Knorozov's curiosity about the glyphs. The book was an edition of the Mayan codices published in Guatemala in the 1930s. Seeing Knorozov's interest, a professor at Leningrad's Institute of Ethnology encouraged him to write a dissertation on Landa's *Relación*, and see if he could put his belief that any writing system "made by a man can be cracked by a man", into effect.

Despite the war, Stalin's regime and his isolation from western scholars and from the Maya themselves—Knorozov did not actually visit Central America until after the fall of the Soviet Union—he was well up in the literature of the decipherment. But, like Ventris, he was an independent thinker, in a position, off-center, to look at the glyphs with a fresh eye. He noticed that the first sign in the dog glyph was the same as the second sign in the turkey glyph:

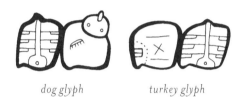

*dog glyph*          *turkey glyph*

If the first sign in the dog glyph had the phonetic value *tzu* (as proposed by Rosny), the second sign could be assigned the value *l(u)*, on the basis of its resemblance to Landa's symbol:

*l*

Hence the dog glyph might stand for *tzul*:

*tzu*                          *l(u)*

Was there a Yucatec word 'tzul' in the dictionary? There was. It meant 'dog'. (The principle that the vowel inherent in a final consonant should match the vowel in the previous syllable was termed *synharmony* by Knorozov; synharmony turned out to be generally but not universally obeyed.)

Knorozov was able to take his line of reasoning further. On a certain page of the Dresden Codex, instead of the expected bar and dot numeral for 11, or its equivalent god-face, there appears a glyph consisting of three signs:

(1 is damaged in the codex)

'Eleven' in Yucatec Mayan is 'buluc'. Could the glyph be made up of *bu*, *lu* and *c(u)*, as follows? (*bu* is damaged):

*cu*

A damaged glyph on another page of the Dresden Codex consisted of two signs that appeared, from Knorozov's line of argument, to mean *lub(u)*.

The word 'lub' in Yucatec Mayan means 'to fall' or 'to rain'. The drawing in the codex suggested that the idea might be correct: rain is shown falling on the central figure (see next page).

Knorozov produced a series of such phonetic decipherments, not all of which were to prove

*The 'rain' glyph in the Dresden Codex (highlighted).*

correct. (Today's accepted reading of  is *b(a)*, for example, not *b(u)*, which means that synharmony is not obeyed in the above spelling of 'lub'.)

He also criticized western scholarship on the Maya, including Thompson's, and couched some of this criticism in the phraseology obligatory for a Soviet scholar of the time: "bourgeois idealism", "class dominance", "super-reactionary", and so on. This, combined with Knorozov's heretical phonetic thesis, was bound to provoke, and the decipherments were bitterly ridiculed by Thompson, who began a kind of personal war, taking his tone from the cold war of the 1950s. One comment referred acerbically to "the

| | | | | | |
|---|---|---|---|---|---|
| 1 | | c(u) | 11 | | cutz |
| 2 | | tz(u) | 12 | | tzul |
| 3 | | l(u) | 13 | | buluc |
| 4 | | b(u) | 14 | | can tzuc |
| 5 | | k(a) | 15 | | lub |
| 6 | | m(a) | 16 | | kati |
| 7 | | t(i) | 17 | | kam |
| 8 | | u | 18 | | ukah |
| 9 | | h(a) | 19 | | pax |
| 10 | | p(a) | 20 | | Mam |

*Some Mayan glyphs as deciphered by Yuri Knorozov.*

Russian Knorozov, who, treading in the footsteps of so many discredited enthusiasts, claims to have discovered (nestling in the bosom of Marxist philosophy) the key to the decipherment of the Maya glyphs." But some of the younger Mayanists in North America, especially Coe (who had married the daughter of a Russian émigré), David Kelley and Floyd Lounsbury, decided that the Leningrad scholar was on to something important.

While it would be true to say that Knorozov's initial readings of the Mayan glyphs were as pivotal as Champollion's readings of the cartouches of Egyptian rulers or Ventris's decipherments of

Cretan towns in the Knossos tablets, subsequent progress proved to be very much slower in the Maya case. There was no immediate 'chain reaction' to Knorozov's nuggets—partly because of Thompson's hostility, but mainly because of the following combination of factors: the under-analysis (and paucity of reproductions) of the corpus of Mayan inscriptions; the mind-boggling graphic complexity of the system; its subtle combinations of logograms and phonetic symbols; and the general ignorance of the modern Mayan languages among epigraphers, which left them entirely dependent on dictionaries. Phoneticism in Mayan writing would remain a fringe theory until the late 1960s. In fact, the next steps forward had nothing to do with language; they came from analyzing patterns in the inscriptions.

To recap for a moment, recall that in the middle of the 20th century the Mayan inscriptions, both codices and stone monuments, were known to be full of dates, which could be fairly easily read. No one, however, had much idea of the significance of these dates to the Maya, apart from those which were used for astrological divination, as in the Dresden Codex. Then, in the late 1950s, a Harvard University researcher Tatiana Proskouriakoff (Russian, but settled in the United States), noticed a significant pattern in a set of sculpted inscriptions originally from Piedras Negras, a Maya site in Guatemala she had helped to dig in the 1930s. To simplify her evidence, we can say she found that with each depicted Maya human (or divine?) figure, among its many accompanying glyphs there were always two:

These two glyphs were adjacent to dates, and the date with the first glyph preceded that with the second glyph by a period of between 12 and 31 years. Proskouriakoff suggested that the figures depicted were rulers of Piedras Negras and that the first glyph referred to the birth date of a ruler while the second glyph referred to the ruler's date of accession.

All of a sudden, by this simple and credible hypothesis, it became clear that the Maya had recorded history on their monuments. The Piedras Negras dates were the dates of rulers and dynasties, nothing to do with the dedication of temples (as Thompson had suggested). "In retrospect, the idea that Maya texts record history, naming the rulers or lords of the towns, seems so natural that it is strange it has not been thoroughly explored before," wrote Proskouriakoff in 1961, no doubt thinking of Thompson, who had written in *Maya Hieroglyphic Writing* that such an idea was "well nigh inconceivable". But she was careful to add: "It is not at all certain that a completely linguistic rendering of hieroglyphic passages is possible." For she did not wish to side openly with Knorozov and cause an irreparable breach with her long-time colleague Thompson.

A second important non-linguistic insight based on structural analysis of patterns in the glyphs came at almost the same time from a friend of Proskouriakoff, a German-born grocery wholesaler in Mexico City, Heinrich Berlin (a refugee from Hitler's Germany). Berlin discovered that, as might be expected, Mayan inscriptions marked something like place names as well as the dynasties of rulers. Each Maya city state had, generally speaking, its 'emblem glyph', as Berlin called it. Here are eight such glyphs, each of which contains

7. Copán, 8. Quiriguá (see map on page 108). A second pair of signs (marked in 5) stands for Yucatec 'k'ul' (divine). The emblem glyph as a whole therefore stands for 'divine lord of such-and-such a polity'.

One of these polities, Piedras Negras, had already provided a decipherment breakthrough (for Proskouriakoff). The next to do so was Palenque, and this time it would be of a linguistic nature. There, in surely the most dramatic Maya archaeological discovery ever made, the Mexican archaeologist Alberto Ruz Lhuillier had found the first great tomb of a Maya ruler, almost comparable with that of Tutankhamun. He came upon it while investigating the Temple of the Inscriptions at Palenque, after noticing a large stone slab in the floor with a double row of holes provided with removable stone stoppers. Lifting the slab, he saw a vaulted stairway leading down into the interior of the pyramid, but deliberately choked with rubble. It took him four field seasons to clear the stairway and reach a chamber on about the same level as the base of the pyramid, which was also filled with rubble; on its floor he found the skeletons of five or six young adults, probably all sacrifices. At its far end, the way was blocked by a huge triangular slab. When this too was finally removed, on 15 June 1952 Ruz gazed into the great funerary crypt, about 80 feet below the floor of the upper temple. He was the first person to see it for some thirteen centuries.

a pair of phonetic signs now known to stand for 'ahaw' (lord):

The sites are: 1. Tikal, 2. Naranjo, 3. Yaxchilán, 4. Piedras Negras, 5. Palenque, 6. Seibal,

(Above) The Temple of the Inscriptions at Palenque in Mexico, built in the 7th century AD. Its crypt contains the great tomb of Pacal (603–83), ruler of Palenque. His magnificent sarcophagus cover (right), carved with the image of the club-footed Pacal falling into the open jaws of the Otherworld, was discovered in the crypt in 1952. When the cover was lifted, a treasure trove of jade and a life-sized mosaic mask were revealed with the remains of Pacal. (See text for a fuller description of the imagery.)

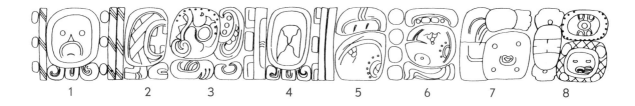

A giant rectangular sarcophagus cover concealed the remains of an ancient Maya king. Inside was a treasure trove of jade with the skeleton: a life-sized mosaic mask of jade lay over the ruler's face, jade and mother-of-pearl discs served as ear spools, several necklaces of tubular jade beads festooned the chest, and the fingers were adorned with jade rings. In each hand and in the mouth was a large jade—a custom documented for the late Yucatec Maya, the Aztecs, and the Chinese. Two jade figures, one representing the sun god, lay beside the ruler.

The carving on the sarcophagus shows the ruler, who is clearly club-footed, falling down the great trunk of the World Tree from the celestial bird (symbolizing heaven) into the open jaws of the Otherworld. As he falls, he is accompanied by the image of a half-skeletal monster carrying a bowl of sacrifice marked with a glyph of the sun. The glyph represents the sun in transition between life and death. Like the sun, the king will rise again in the east after his journey through the Otherworld.

The obvious question was, who was this great Maya lord of Palenque? Eight glyphs carved along one edge of the sarcophagus give a partial explanation. They include various numerals, day names and month names: try working them out for yourself using the information about the numerals and the calendar on pages 111-16.

1. is the date 8 Ahau.
2. is the date 13 Pop.
3. is the glyph signifying birth. So the ruler was born on 8 Ahau 13 Pop, which, when correlated with the 'long count', is 26 March AD 603.
4. is the date 6 Etz'nab.
5. is the date 11 Yax.
6. refers to 4 cycles of 7200 days in the 'long count', i.e. about 80 years.
7. is a glyph signifying death. So the ruler died on 6 Etz'nab 11 Yax, that is 31 August AD 683.
8. is the name of the ruler, nicknamed 'Hand Shield', derived pictographically from the sign at bottom right in the ruler's glyph.

But what was the great Maya ruler's own name for himself, in his Mayan language? A clue came from a glyph in the temple far above the funerary crypt. From its context, the glyph was clearly the name of the ruler buried beneath, yet, confusingly, it was quite different from the glyph on the sarcophagus.

In 1973, epigraphers meeting at Palenque decided to have a go at this problem. By now, a number of syllabic glyphs were securely known, based on Knorozov's method. The experts suddenly twigged the truth—the name glyph on the sarcophagus was *logographic*, while that in the temple was spelt *phonetically*. The glyph in the temple could be transliterated phonetically as:

pa

ca

la

So the Maya 'Tutankhamun' was called Pacal (also spelt Pakal), which indeed means 'shield' in Yucatec Mayan.

Here are three variant spellings of Pacal's name, with the phonetic elements indicated in lower-case letters and the logographic in upper-case letters:

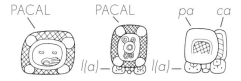

PACAL          PACAL          pa      ca

l(a)—          l(a)—

If the inscription tells the truth—which obviously cannot be taken for granted—Pacal was 80 years old when he died. From other glyphs we can tell that he was only twelve years old when he came to the throne; Pacal therefore ruled for some 68 years—longer than Queen Victoria. We can also identify the names of Pacal's father Kan Mo' Hix and his mother Lady Zac Kuk, and other relatives. Intriguingly, his father never ruled (dying on 1 January AD 643), while his mother did briefly rule, from 612 until her son's accession in 615 (she died on 12 September 640)—because it was she, rather than her husband, who belonged to the royal lineage. We also know (from a glyph at another site) that Pacal's second son, who ruled from 702-11, was captured and eventually sacrificed by another ruler. Historical information of this kind, today available for Palenque and many other Maya sites, was absolutely unknown prior to the decipherment.

Present at Palenque for that fruitful meeting, in addition to Coe and Floyd Lounsbury were two younger novice scholars, Linda Schele, an art teacher, and Peter Mathews, who was still an undergraduate student. Both made vital contributions to the meeting. In the years that followed, they and an international group of young scholars were to pick up from the pioneering work of Knorozov, Proskouriakoff and Berlin, and push the decipherment forward. With the death of Thompson in 1975, the pace became rapid, at times almost frantic, "like a raging prairie fire" (*Breaking the Maya Code*), and remained that way until the 1990s. Schele, in particular, became well known for her rambunctious leadership of the annual Maya Hieroglyphic Workshops at the University of Texas at Austin from 1978, involving hundreds of amateur decipherers from all over the United States and further afield; in the 1990s, these developed into workshops with the Maya themselves in Guatemala, which resulted in some Maya learning how to write like their ancestors after a gap of many centuries.

*Linda Schele (1942-98), the American Mayanist who led the annual Workshop on Maya Hieroglyphic Writing in the United States from the late 1970s. She also taught Maya people how to read their ancestral writing in workshops held in Guatemala.*

What became clear from all this decipherment activity was that the Maya scribes loved to play with their system and use it to spell words in several different and unpredictable mixtures of phoneticism and logography, not just two or three, as in the Egyptian hieroglyphs. Furthermore, the individual glyphs were often 'soldered' together (a feature also found in Chinese characters, though not in Egyptian hieroglyphs)— so intimately that the constituent glyphs could only be discerned by a highly trained eye. The problems encountered by Ventris (and Bennett) in identifying Linear B signs and their allographs were almost as nothing compared to those faced by would-be decipherers of the Mayan glyphs.

Here, for instance, two glyphs spelling 'chum tun' have been 'soldered'/conflated in three different ways, all four spellings of the word being acceptable:

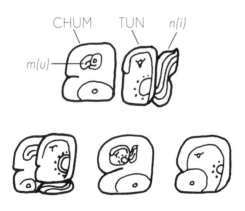

And here are two acceptable Mayan spellings for 'ts'ib' (scribe), the one on the left entirely phonetic, that on the right partly logographic:

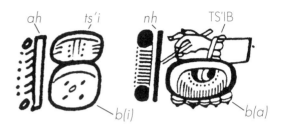

And five acceptable spellings for 'balam' (jaguar) showing differing proportions of phoneticism and logography:

The first is wholly logographic (and pictographic), the last wholly phonetic (and sans pictography).

We can see the mixture of phoneticism and logographic elements in a striking relief sculpture on a stone lintel celebrating a victory of 'Bird-Jaguar' of Yaxchilán. Bird-Jaguar is on the right, wearing a splendid headdress, and grasping his captive 'Jeweled-Skull' by the arm, while on the left Bird-Jaguar's lieutenant Kan Tok Wayib seizes a second captive by the hair. The various glyphs—which are not fully understood— have been labeled.

The date is 7 Imix 14 Tzec (try checking the numerals and the day/month glyphs for yourself),

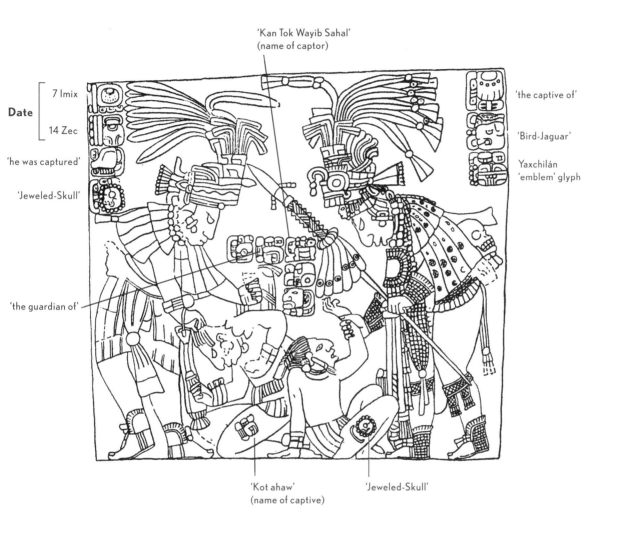

'Kan Tok Wayib Sahal'
(name of captor)

**Date**
7 Imix
14 Zec

'he was captured'

'Jeweled-Skull'

'the guardian of'

'the captive of'

'Bird-Jaguar'

Yaxchilán
'emblem' glyph

'Kot ahaw'
(name of captive)

'Jeweled-Skull'

*Lintel from Yaxchilán in Mexico, showing the city's*
*ruler 'Bird–Jaguar', 8th century AD. (See text.)*

Mayan syllabary. This syllabic 'grid' represents the combined work of many scholars in the 1980s and 90s and is still in the process of change. It allows us to transliterate a large proportion of Mayan glyphs, but of course many other glyphs are not phonetic.

which corresponds to 9 May AD 755. Bird-Jaguar is nicknamed thus, because his glyph combines a bird and a jaguar:

His Maya name may have been Yaxun Balam. The glyph immediately below his name is the 'emblem glyph' of Yaxchilán. The text can therefore be (partially) translated: "On 9 May 755 Jeweled-Skull was captured, the captive of Bird-Jaguar, divine lord of Yaxchilán."

Two of the words on the lintel are spelt purely phonetically:

*chucah(a)*
(he was captured)

| | a | e | i | o | u |
|---|---|---|---|---|---|
| **n** | | | | | |
| **p** | | | | | |
| **s** | | | | | |
| **t** | | | | | |
| **tz** | | | | | |
| **dz** | | | | | |
| **u** | | | | | |
| **x** | | | | | |
| **y** | | | | | |

Of the three syllabic signs, two can be found in Landa's 'alphabet' (page 120):

*ca*  *ha*

And then there is the glyph:

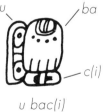

*u bac(i)*
(the captive of)

Hundreds of such decipherments, with their syllabic values cross-checked against each other in as many cases as possible—the work of dozens of scholars—have yielded a syllabic chart for the Mayan script (see previous page). The positions in the chart of every glyph are not universally agreed, but a large proportion is. The complexity of the script is more than evident, even without showing the hundreds of non-syllabic logograms. The chart's most obvious feature is the large number of variant signs for a single phonetic value, for instance nine glyphs for the pure vowel *u* and five for the syllable *nu*. There is nothing comparable in the Linear B syllabary (page 100); without Landa's 'alphabet', no one would have had a chance to create this Mayan equivalent of the Linear B 'grid'. To complicate the picture further, some syllabic signs can act as logograms also, as in Egyptian hieroglyphs.

The degree of *homophony* built into the system is indicated by three different glyphs, all pronounced *can* in Yucatec Mayan (the phonetic elements in the first and third of these are noted):

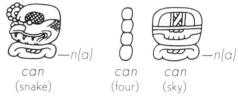

*can*
(snake)

*can*
(four)

*can*
(sky)

The degree of *polyphony*, by contrast, i.e. one sign with different meanings according to its different pronunciations (compare conductor's 'bow' and violinist's 'bow' in English), is shown by the following four glyphs:

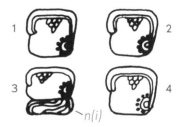

1. is Cauac, a day name; 2. is pronounced *haab*, the word for the 365-day 'vague' year; 3. has the phonetic complement *n(i)* but is pronounced *tun*; 4. is the syllable *cu*.

Lastly, there has been the exceptional help given to the decipherment by weird and wonderful

*"One of the most compelling scenes on codex-style Maya ceramics"*, according to Michael Coe, the first scholar to make a serious study of the glyphs on the ceramics. It shows the aged god Pawahtun (centre right) as a teacher in a scribal school. With a brush pen thrust into his netted headdress, he points at an open codex and lectures his pupils on mathematics. A curlicue 'breath sign' connects his mouth to the text which clearly consists of numerals. No doubt Pawahtun is explaining some intricacy of astrological calculation similar to those found on the Dresden Codex (see page 117). The scene was painted in the 8th century AD.

Maya art, especially by the numerous painted ceramics that include glyphs. This painted writing was largely ignored in Thompson's time, but in the 1980s, assisted by the superb 'roll-out' photography of vases by Justin Kerr, the ceramics have become a key part of the modern decipherment. The chief credit for this goes to Coe, who while organizing a New York exhibition of Maya ceramics in 1971 identified a repeated sequence of glyphs around the rim of many vessels. He termed it the Primary Standard Sequence and hazarded that it referred to known Maya mythical adventures in the Otherworld (like those in the Egyptian Book of the Dead) such as told in the *Popol Vuh*, since these adventures appeared to be the subject matter of much of the art on the ceramics and, in addition, the ceramics were apparently intended as funerary objects, to be placed in tombs.

In fact the sequence turned out to have a somewhat different meaning. One of the Primary Standard Sequence's commonest glyphs occurs in this order:

Phonetic decipherment of the first glyph on the left gives:

In Cholan Mayan, 'uch' means 'to drink', and 'uch'ibl' means 'drinking vessel'. The 'y' prefix is known to signify the third person possessive pronoun (his, her, its, in English). So the glyph 'yuch'ib' probably means, 'his vessel for drink'. "Thompson would have been horrified," says Coe, but it looks as if Maya nobles, like certain people today, wanted their drinking cups name tagged, at least for ceremonial purposes such as burials. Name tagging—a notion first suggested by Peter Mathews in 1979—has subsequently been found to apply to all manner of things Maya, from ear spools to ballcourts.

Further decipherment of the Primary Standard Sequence was even more revealing. It includes the following glyphs, in which phonetic values can be substituted with a little imagination:

Cacao! And when scrapings from Maya pots bearing this glyph were submitted to the Hershey Foods Corporation Technical Center, the answer came back that the residues were indeed the chemical remains of cacao—which remained very important to the later Maya as a prized ingredient of chocolate drinks.

————

Despite all the above achievements, many glyphs cannot yet be read by epigraphers. The decipherment of the Mayan glyphs is a story that is much less advanced than the decipherments of the Egyptian hieroglyphs and Linear B. As Schele made clear in her notes for the 1993 Maya Hieroglyphic Workshop, quoted in the Introduction (page 18), the current picture is complicated: some glyphs can be pronounced and understood as fully as in a dictionary definition; with others no phonetic value but the general meaning or syntactical function of the glyph is known; while with still others, almost everything is still opaque. And of course the continuing flow of new finds periodically produces more unknown glyphs awaiting study and decipherment.

From Thompson onwards, there have been critics, some of them harsh and unforgiving. Many 'dirt' archaeologists of the Maya have resented the decipherment for diverting much of the (North American) public's interest in Maya studies towards writing rather than the sites themselves; for encouraging the looting of inscriptions and other objects from Central America to sell to collectors in the United States and Europe; and for focusing attention on the Maya elite, rather than the common people. Mexican archaeologists, beginning with Ruz, the man who discovered Pacal, have consistently ignored or impugned the decipherment, partly because the Maya have long had low status in Mexican society and also because the work has been done by outsiders, especially from the United States, with almost no Mexican contribution. Among the epigraphers themselves, as well as plenty of productive 'group working', there has been a certain amount of empire building, with individuals rushing to claim priority in deciphering particular glyphs. Surprisingly, and ironically, Knorozov, who started the phonetic decipherment in 1952, was not supportive of the decipherers in later years, himself adopting a basically logographic approach to the glyphs, unchecked by syllabic cross-readings, almost in the manner of his detractor Thompson. After Knorozov's death in 1999, his early champion Coe remarked to me: "I view him as another Einstein—a genius who made all of his important breakthroughs very early in his career, then spent the rest of his life basically off on the wrong track."

What cannot be doubted, though, is that thanks to the Maya decipherment we know that American history does not begin with the arrival of Columbus or the Pilgrim Fathers, four or five hundred years ago, as everyone thought less than half a century ago. In fact, it is two millennia old, and increasingly it can be studied with the same amount of seriousness as the history of ancient Egypt or ancient Greece.

# PART TWO
*Undeciphered Scripts*

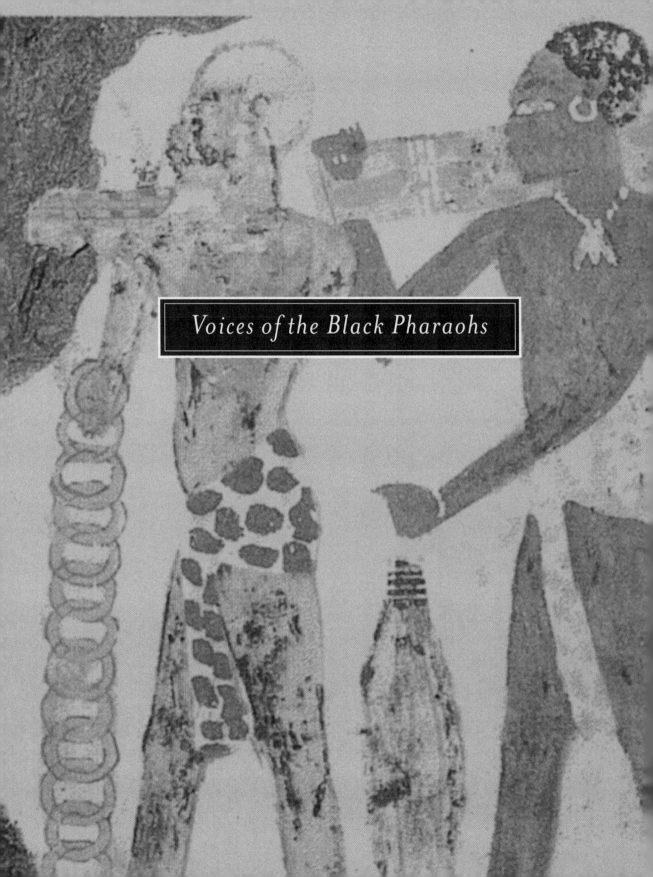

Voices of the Black Pharaohs

*IV*

# THE MEROITIC SCRIPT

L ook at a map of the course of the Nile, and you will see that the river flows in two great bends through six cataracts from Khartoum near the center of Sudan to Lake Nasser and Aswan on the modern border between Sudan and Egypt. This vast area, rivaling in size that of ancient Egypt, is known to archaeologists as Nubia. In ancient times, it was the kingdom of Kush, a word of unknown origin, with its principal city at Meroe on the east bank of the Nile between the 5th and 6th cataracts.

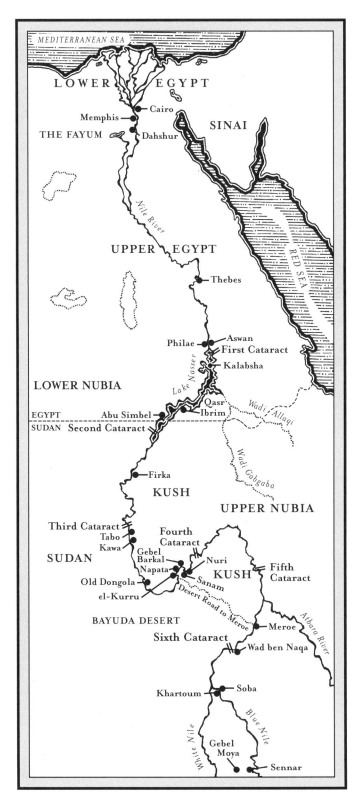

*The Nile Valley and the kingdom of Kush, with its principal city Meroe on the banks of the Nile in today's Sudan. The Meroitic script was used in Kush alongside Egyptian hieroglyphs.*

MEDITERRANEAN SEA

LOWER EGYPT

Cairo

Memphis

SINAI

THE FAYUM

Dahshur

Nile River

UPPER EGYPT

Thebes

RED SEA

Aswan

Philae

First Cataract

Kalabsha

LOWER NUBIA

Lake Nasser

Wadi Allaqi

Qasr Ibrim

EGYPT

Abu Simbel

SUDAN Second Cataract

Wadi Gabgaba

Firka

KUSH

UPPER NUBIA

Third Cataract

Tabo

Kawa

Fourth Cataract

Gebel Barkal

Napata

Nuri

SUDAN

Sanam

KUSH

Fifth Cataract

Old Dongola

el-Kurru

Desert Road to Meroe

BAYUDA DESERT

Albara River

Meroe

Sixth Cataract

Wad ben Naqa

Khartoum

Soba

White Nile

Blue Nile

Gebel Moya

Sennar

*Pyramids in the north cemetery, Meroe: they mark the tombs of the rulers of Kush.*

The Kushite or Meroitic civilization was one of the most important early states of sub-Saharan Africa, despite being regarded until quite recently as an inferior appendage of ancient Egypt. Its archaeological origins go back to the 3rd millennium BC, but it enters history—through references to it in Egyptian hieroglyphic inscriptions—only in the 8th century BC. From 712-656 BC, Kushite kings conquered Egypt and were accepted as its 25th dynasty, 'black pharaohs' ruling an empire stretching from the central Sudan to the borders of Palestine. (Their leader Taharqo receives a passing mention in the Bible, as Tirhakah.) Thereafter, they were forced to withdraw and rule only in Nubia—suffering periodic intrusions from the Egyptians, the Persians and later the Romans (who called the Kushites, confusingly, Ethiopians, meaning 'burnt-faced persons')—until the 4th century AD, when Kush finally disintegrated for reasons unknown into three smaller kingdoms which were converted to Christianity. These were eventually supplanted

*Egypt meets Africa: a complex and controversial relationship. Nubia, the area south of Aswan down to Khartoum, was normally ruled by the Egyptians. Here Nubians are seen presenting exotic gifts to the pharaoh Tuthmosis IV (1419–1386 BC), in a fragment of a wall painting from the Theban tomb chapel of Sobekhotep. However, for a brief period (712–656 BC), the Nubians of the kingdom of Kush conquered and ruled Egypt as the 25th dynasty.*

by the Islamic sultanate of Funj Sennar in the 14th/15th centuries and subsequently other Islamic rulers, who were defeated by British colonial forces at the end of the 19th century.

This thumbnail history of a relatively unfamiliar region is important because it shows how many influences have acted on the area and affected its languages, ancient and modern. And we have not even mentioned the various desert tribes such as those living between Kush and the Red Sea, known to the Greeks as the Blemmyes, to the Arabs as the Beja and to themselves as ti-Bedaawye (hence through Arabic and French the English 'Bedouin', according to some scholars). There is also the possibility—unsubstantiated, but then archaeologists have barely begun to investigate it—that Kush interacted with the rest of Africa, to the west and south as well as to the north and east. However, there is no question that the predominant influence on the kingdom and on its script, generally known as Meroitic, which was used in Kush from the 3rd century BC until the kingdom's disintegration in the 4th century—was Egyptian.

In his book *The Kingdom of Kush*, the British Museum archaeologist Derek Welsby writes that the Kushites took over Egypt in the 25th dynasty "not as conquering barbarians but as champions of the age-old traditions of the Pharaohs." This is abundantly evident from their use of Egyptian hieroglyphs, their worship of Egyptian gods and goddesses and their Egyptian-style mortuary practices, as well as the pyramids they built which still exist at Meroe and other sites—all of which postdate their ousting by the Egyptians after 656 BC. The compliment was not returned, however: Kush is most frequently described in Egyptian inscriptions as "miserable" or "wretched", and the pharaoh

Psammetichus II (595-89 BC) carefully erased all the names of 25th-dynasty Kushite rulers throughout Egypt.

Egyptian hieroglyphs were used in Kush until as late as the 1st century AD. But they increasingly appeared alongside the Meroitic script, or were displaced by it. In the royal cemeteries at Meroe, Egyptian hieroglyphs were employed exclusively in some inscriptions, while in others Meroitic hieroglyphs were used for the royal name and the Egyptian script for the rest of the text, and yet other inscriptions were written entirely in Meroitic hieroglyphs. In due course, a 'cursive' version of Meroitic—compare Egyptian demotic—was used even for the majority of royal texts.

The decipherment of both the Meroitic hieroglyphs and this cursive script—but not their underlying language—was the work of a British Egyptologist at Oxford University, Francis Llewellyn Griffith, with a touch of Champollion's genius (and a wealthy wife, hence today's Griffith Institute in Oxford). Earlier scholars, notably the pioneering German archaeologist Karl Richard Lepsius (who had helped to prove Champollion's decipherment), made a start, but it was Griffith, with access to a mass of newly excavated inscriptions from Meroe and other sites in the Sudan, who 'cracked' the script in the period 1909-11.

It was already clear from the sign analysis undertaken in the 19th century that there were about 23 signs with allographs in the Meroitic hieroglyphs, in other words an 'alphabet' and not a logosyllabic script like Egyptian hieroglyphic. Also clear was that the cursive Meroitic script was written from right to left, like almost all Egyptian cursive script. Somewhat in the manner of Thomas Young, the decipherer of Egyptian demotic, Griffith now undertook a detailed comparison of the cursive and hieroglyphic Meroitic scripts and soon realized that he could draw up equivalences between the cursive and hieroglyphic signs. The key turned out to be a cursive inscription found written around the edges of flat altars or offering tables at Meroe and elsewhere:

Griffith recalled a similar altar from Meroe in Berlin (collected by Lepsius) inscribed in hieroglyphic:

Making a reasonable guess that the two inscriptions might mean the same, he equated them letter for letter. Thus the three signs which are repeated twice in each word appeared to be equivalents:

| Cursive | | Hieroglyphic |
|---------|---|-------------|
| / | = | (sign) |
| 3 | = | (sign) |
| 4 | = | (sign) |

Equivalences could also be made for four more signs:

| | | |
|---|---|---|
| (sign) | = | (sign) |
| ω | = | (sign) |
| (sign) | = | (sign) |
| /// | = | (sign) |

Comparing two other cursive/hieroglyphic pairs, Griffith found that the initial equivalences were confirmed and that equivalences for further signs were suggested (try it for yourself):

In this way, using many more word comparisons, Griffith found 21 equivalences between cursive and hieroglyphic signs:

| Cursive | Hieroglyphic | Cursive | Hieroglyphic |
|---------|-------------|---------|-------------|
| (signs) | (signs) | (signs) | (signs) |

In doing this analysis, Griffith had also proved that the direction of reading of the Meroitic hieroglyphs was the same as that of the cursive script, right to left, like the direction of Egyptian hieroglyphs. For if the Meroitic hieroglyphic reading direction had *not* been the same as the Egyptian, the repeated signs would not have occurred in the same positions in the cursive and hieroglyphic scripts:

However, Meroitic hieroglyphs could be seen to differ from Egyptian hieroglyphs in that they faced in the direction of reading, whereas Egyptian hieroglyphs face in the opposite direction.

The next step was to determine the phonetic values of the Meroitic signs. Here, the key was a bilingual (Meroitic/Egyptian) inscription written in both Meroitic and Egyptian hieroglyphs. Unfortunately, it contained only the names of a Meroitic king and queen, so it was not a substantial bilingual like the Rosetta stone, which contains a long text as well as names. Nevertheless, it was sufficient for Griffith to get a handle on the unknown phonetic values of the Meroitic hieroglyphs by comparing the signs with equivalent Egyptian signs of known phonetic value.

The two royal names were found on the base of a sacred boat from Wad ben Naqa that had been published by Lepsius. The *Egyptian* hieroglyphic cartouches were as follows (first the king's, then the queen's):

ntk-ímn

ímn-try

(Note that we have *not* 'normalized' the cartouches in the manner explained on page 63, because normalization would make them read from left to right, which would here be confusing for the untrained reader.) Griffith was able to read the two cartouches as *ntk-ímn* and *ímn-try*, pronounced Netekamani and Amanitare on the basis of Greek and Coptic clues. You can get a fairly good idea of how he did this by comparing the Egyptian signs with the hieroglyphic 'alphabet' on page 70 and the cartouche of Tutankhamun on page 71, provided that you bear in mind two facts: the sign group for *amun* (*ímn*) 〰𝄐 is placed first in *both* cartouches as a convention of respect for the god—as it is in Tutankhamun's cartouche; and ⌂ in the queen's name is a female determinative, not pronounced.

Sign-for-sign comparison between equivalent cartouches now gave the phonetic values of the signs in the two *Meroitic* cartouches:

ntk-ímn
Netekamani

ímn-try
Amanitare

From this, Griffith derived the following eight phonetic values for Meroitic hieroglyphs:

〰〰 = n      𓀀 = i

𓅓 = m      ⌒ = t

𓅬 = k      ▭ = r

⟋ = t      𝄐 = y

Not surprisingly, given the fact that the Kushites borrowed their script from the Egyptians, these signs have a close resemblance to the Egyptian hieroglyphs of the same phonetic value, such as:

ᗰᗰ = *n*

🦅 = *m*

▭ = *t*

One hieroglyphic (and hence cursive) vowel sign, *i*, had now been identified:

By analyzing initial, medial and terminal sign frequencies of many cursive inscriptions (recall Ventris with Linear B), Griffith identified three more probable cursive vowel signs (and their hieroglyphic equivalents):

(These would turn out to represent *a*, *e* and *o*.)

There were now 12 (that is, 23 less 8 less 3) Meroitic signs still to be assigned phonetic values. Griffith tackled them by subtle contextual analysis, searching for Meroitic words and sign groups that were likely to be equivalent to known Egyptian and Greek place names and other words. Here, the cursive/hieroglyphic equivalences were particularly useful. For example, he identified a repeated cursive sign group:

ϛ/ϡϡϞ

on inscriptions from the temple of Isis at Philae, where the goddess had been worshipped as far back as the time of King Taharqo. Naturally at that time the place would have been called by its Egyptian name, not by its Graeco-Roman name

Philae. The Egyptian name was unknown but was likely to be similar (though not identical) to Pilak, the later name of Philae in the Coptic script (ⲡⲓⲗⲁⲕ).

Written in hieroglyphs instead of cursive, the cursive sign group would look like this:

(You can verify this from the cursive-hieroglyphic equivalents on page 146.)

Griffith already knew that the signs 𓀁 and ϸ were vowels (V), and that 𓀁 represented *i*. The other three signs he compared, as a guess, with equivalent-looking Egyptian hieroglyphs:

▯ = *p*     △ = *ḳ*     🐊 = *l*

This was a reasonable hypothesis, given the close resemblance between the Meroitic and Egyptian hieroglyphs. It produced the following word for the sign group: *pil(V)k(V)*. The resemblance of this to (Coptic) Pilak was patent, and suggested that the early Egyptian name of Philae was Pileke (or Pileqe).

Eventually, Griffith came up with a Meroitic 'alphabet' in hieroglyphic and cursive that most scholars regard as essentially correct, if not absolutely reliable. The modern version is shown opposite.

A comparison with the Egyptian 'alphabet' on page 70 will show that most of the Meroitic hieroglyphic signs have been borrowed from Egyptian. There is, on the other hand, much less resemblance between Meroitic cursive and Egyptian demotic signs; only four are actually the same. The Meroitic 'alphabet' also apparently differs from the Egyptian in having four signs with *syllabic* values: for example, Griffith's two

| Hieroglyph | Cursive | Phonetic value | Hieroglyph | Cursive | Phonetic value |
|---|---|---|---|---|---|
|  |  | initial *a* |  |  | *l* |
|  |  | *e* |  |  | *ḫ* |
|  |  | *i* |  |  | *ẖ* |
|  |  | *o* |  |  | *se* |
|  |  | *y* |  |  | *s* |
|  |  | *w* |  |  | *k* |
|  |  | *b* |  |  | *q* |
|  |  | *p* |  |  | *t* |
|  |  | *m* |  |  | *te* |
|  |  | *n* |  |  | *to* |
|  |  | *ne* |  |  | *d* |
|  |  | *r* | : | : | word divider |

original signs for *t* have been increased by later scholars to three signs, representing *t*, *te*, and *to*. This surprising result suggests that our understanding of the phonetic values of the script and the sounds that it encoded in the Meroitic language may not be as complete as we should like. What is certain is that the Meroitic script is not a simple alphabet.

Following his brilliant detective work, Griffith went on to substitute his phonetic values in all the available inscriptions. But here he came up against what has proved to be the great obstacle to a full decipherment of Meroitic: his readings could not be related to any known language, including of course the ancient Egyptian language; neither did the endless Meroitic personal names yielded by his substitutions resemble known Egyptian or Greek names. Although Griffith could deduce the meanings of a few—perhaps a dozen—Meroitic words from bilinguals and from their contexts, their sounds were quite unfamiliar. One of them was the word for 'beget' or 'begotten of': 'terike' or 'yerike'

in Meroitic, according to Griffith. It bore no resemblance to the word with that meaning in either modern Nubian (as spoken in part of today's Sudan) or the comparable word in Old Nubian, the language believed to have been spoken in the Christian period (following the 4th-century-AD disintegration of Kush) written in the Coptic alphabet, 'unne'. Though there were a few apparent structural resemblances between Meroitic and Nubian, they were in no way conclusive, and Griffith was inclined to dismiss a connection between the two languages, without being able to find evidence for a relationship between Meroitic and any other language. As a consequence, there are only five meager pages on "The Meroitic language" in his immensely detailed 1911 volume on the Meroitic inscriptions. Even so, Griffith commented hopefully (and modestly) in the preface, "If new eyes, whether of trained decipherers or of scholars expert in North African philology, will exert themselves upon it, the secrets of Meroitic should soon be yielded up."

Unfortunately, his optimism was misplaced. Today, we know the meanings of only 26 simple words in Meroitic, all of which have been derived from short Egyptian/Meroitic bilinguals and contextual analysis, not from reconstruction of the Meroitic language based on related languages, as follows:

| English | Meroitic |
|---|---|
| man | abr |
| woman | kdi |
| person | s |
| wife | sem |
| mother | ste |
| brother | wi |
| sister | kdis, kdite |
| ruler | qore |
| king's sister (?) | kdke, ktke, kdwe |
| deity | mk |
| foot/feet | st, stqo (?) |
| lion | tñyi |
| province/land | adb |
| east | yirewke |
| west | tenke |
| north | ḫr |
| south | yireke |
| bread | at |
| water | ato |
| born (by) | edḫe, tedḫe, dḫe |
| begotten of | erike, terike, yerike |
| give | l, el, yel |
| great, big | lḫ |
| small, little | mte |
| good | mlo |
| two | tbo |

In the absence of progress in identifying the language, scholars have devoted themselves to the kinds of internal sign analysis employed by Kober and Ventris in the Linear B decipherment, with the aim of refining Griffith's system of phonetic values. The leading figures have been Fritz Hintze in Berlin and Jean Leclant in Paris. From the late 1960s, there was fresh interest in Nubia as a result of the great UNESCO-sponsored salvage of Nubian monuments threatened by Lake Nasser following the building of the Aswan High Dam. "From this time on, the study of Kush has become an accepted discipline on its own with, as a marked new feature, the participation of scholars without a traditional Egyptological background," says Peter Shinnie, the last British commissioner for archaeology in the Sudan (in the 1950s), and a leading veteran of the subject who dug at Meroe for many years.

In the early 1970s, many hopes and considerable resources were invested in computerizing the corpus of Meroitic inscriptions; even the French secret service, it is said, offered its equipment and expertise in decipherment. But the results were disappointing. Apart from the usual uncertainties in identifying badly written or preserved signs and in distinguishing between allographs, the roman alphabetic letters, needed for the computer at that time, imposed a one-to-one relationship between each Meroitic sign and a roman letter. However, the phonetic values of the Meroitic signs were not necessarily implied by the phonetic values of roman alphabetic letters, and in some cases where the Meroitic signs were thought to have more than one phonetic value or an apparently syllabic value, the simple roman transcription system was misleading.

Computer techniques were eventually abandoned, but the scholarly effort expended was not entirely wasted: it led to the creation of an essential research tool. Compiled in Paris by Leclant and coworkers and known as the Répertoire d'Epigraphie Meroitique, this is a long-running project to publish the Meroitic inscriptions and classify them by 'REM number'. Most current scholars in the field have adopted the system, which means that at least the Meroitic corpus is organized and accessible: a vital requirement for progress in decipherment, as we know.

At the same time, Abdelgadir Abdalla of the University of Khartoum (now at the King Saud University in Riyadh), attempted his own unaided dissection of Meroitic words and analysis of their constituent parts. On the assumption that the unknown Meroitic language is agglutinative, i.e. it builds words by stringing forms together in quite lengthy sequences like Japanese, Abdalla aimed to reverse the process of agglutination and segment Meroitic words into their constituent parts of speech, which could be individually translated and then reunited in order to suggest the meaning of the whole word. (Think of 'Fernsehapparat' in German, literally 'far-see-apparatus,' i.e. a television.) Abdalla's approach has not attracted support from other scholars, however, because his basic assumption is unsubstantiated and his methodology, as presented in many published examples, is dubious and difficult to follow.

But let us return to the question of the Meroitic language and the approach to decipherment advocated by Griffith: the search for relationships between Meroitic words and words of equivalent sound (and if possible equivalent meaning) in known languages, or their reconstructable earlier forms spoken at least 1600 years ago during the kingdom of Kush. We can discard some of the wilder language candidates that have occasionally been proposed: Chinese, Mongolian, Tibetan and Tokharian—this last based simply on an analogy between the name Kush and that of the contemporary Kushan empire of north-west India and Afghanistan! The likely candidates are the languages of the local area—"giving 'local' the meaning of a thousand-mile radius," says Robin Thelwall, an expert on African linguistics who is probably the best-informed commentator on the Meroitic language.

There are two broad language families to which Meroitic might belong (assuming it is not an isolate): the Afro-Asiatic and the Nilo-Saharan, the second of which was defined by Joseph Greenberg only in 1963 and whose membership is still controversial. (Linguists tend to divide into 'lumpers' and 'splitters': those like Greenberg who believe in 'lumping' languages into large hierarchical families like Nilo-Saharan descending from a single proto-language, and those who believe in 'splitting' language families into smaller groups on the grounds that the member languages are not clearly enough related.) The Afro-Asiatic family subdivides into the Semitic languages, which include Egyptian, Coptic and Arabic; the Cushitic languages of the Horn of Africa, including that of the nomadic Beja; the Omotic languages spoken in Ethiopia; the Berber languages of North Africa and the Sahara; and the Chadic languages (belonging to Chad, Cameroun, and Nigeria). The Nilo-Saharan is a family of languages stretching from Lake Turkana in the east to the middle Niger in the west across a belt of north-central Africa which is believed to have supported a cohesive 'aquatic' way of life in the 8th millennium BC or earlier, when the Sahara and Sahel were wetter than today. Nilo-Saharan subdivides into Sudanic languages such as Nubian, Nilotic languages, Saharan languages and Songhai in the far west.

The possibilities for the language(s) of Kush, when viewed against the current linguistic map of Africa, are clearly complex, since its territory incorporates both Afro-Asiatic and Nilo-Saharan languages. Indeed Kush is adjacent to, or coincident with, what has been hypothesized to be the homeland of the Afro-Asiatic languages perhaps 10,000 years ago, according to some scholars. From there the speakers of what would become the individual

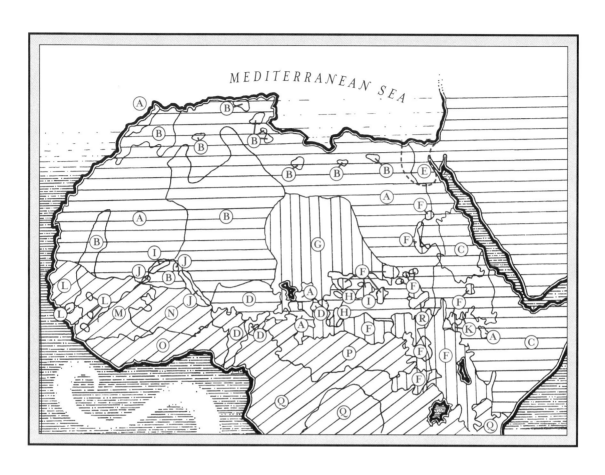

**AFRO-ASIATIC**

A  Semitic
B  Berber
C  Cushitic
D  Chad
E  Ancient Egyptian (Coptic)

**NILO-SAHARAN**

F  Chari-Nile
   (Nilotic, Nubian and other languages)
G  Saharan
M  Maban
I  Fur
J  Songhai
K  Koman

**NIGER-KORDOFANIAN**

L  West Atlantic
M  Mande
N  Voltaic
O  Kwa
P  Adamawa-Eastern
Q  Benue-Kongo (including Bantu)
R  Kordofanian

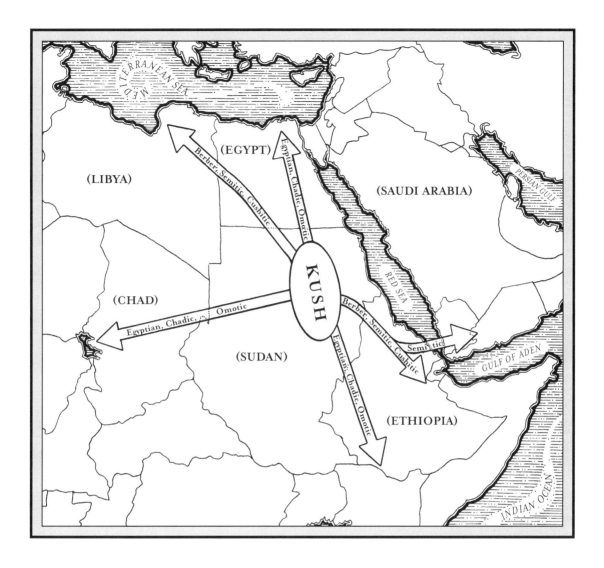

*(Opposite) The three major language families of Saharan and sub-Saharan Africa, as visualized by the linguist Joseph Greenberg. His classification is controversial, especially with regard to the Nilo-Saharan family. Within the Afro-Asiatic family, ancient Egyptian (with its descendant language Coptic) is shown separately rather than being subsumed in the group of Semitic languages, as sometimes done. The map above shows one theory—that of the linguist Lionel Bender—of how the Afro-Asiatic family became dispersed perhaps 10,000 years ago into its present-day constituent language groups, having originated in the area of Sudan occupied some millennia later by the kingdom of Kush. The possible linguistic relationships of the unknown Meroitic language are therefore complex. (See page 151.)*

Afro-Asiatic language groups are believed to have migrated to their present locations. This hypothetical migration must have occurred before the rise of dynastic Egypt and the later kingdom of Kush, but there is, needless to say, a severe dearth of evidence as to the timing and details of the migration.

How then is any progress to be made in identifying the relationship, if any, of Meroitic to this babel of tongues ancient and modern? Essentially, it is a matter of collecting enough accurate data on the vocabulary and structure of all the likeliest African languages 'local' to Kush—many of them little known to philologists—and comparing the data with our meager stock of knowledge of the vocabulary and structure of the Meroitic language given in the list on page 150. In other words, we need to apply the etymological and comparative methods mentioned in the Introduction.

Although efforts have been made in this direction since Griffith's time, and Old Nubian (in the Nilo-Saharan family), the most obvious candidate, has been firmly ruled out as the Meroitic language, linguists like Thelwall are somewhat discouraged by the complexity of the problem and the lack of resources to tackle it thoroughly (not to mention the political turbulence of southern Sudan and the Horn of Africa). What seems clear is that there is no simple linguistic solution waiting in the wings: no sub-Saharan equivalent of Coptic, Greek or the Mayan languages, the keys to the Egyptian hieroglyphs, Linear B and the Mayan glyphs. Greenberg, writing in 1955, was pessimistic about Meroitic: "the language does not appear to be related to any existing language of Africa." More recent experts, such as Chris Ehret and Lionel Bender are locked in disagreement about the nature of the Nilo-Saharan language family, which may contain a language relevant to Meroitic. For the time being, at least, the

*Opening lines written in Meroitic cursive on a sandstone tombstone from Qasr Ibrim in Lower Nubia, c. 300 BC, with a transliteration and suggested translation by Nicholas Millet. Only Meroitic place and personal names, a few divine names and a handful of other words (see page 150) can be certainly identified.*

detailed linguistic data on the relevant languages necessary for a useful comparative analysis of Meroitic, are simply not available.

The best immediate hope for advancing the decipherment started by Griffith is therefore the discovery of a substantial bilingual text, probably in Meroitic and Egyptian. And it is not a forlorn hope, given that short bilinguals exist and there are teams from a dozen countries surveying and excavating in some 20 areas of the Sudan, regularly making new discoveries. In the words of Leclant (the current secretary of the French Academy of Inscriptions), now in his eighties but still actively pursuing the mystery of Meroitic: "we make all our prayers for happy discoveries"–"jusqu'a ce qu'apparaisse enfin le bilingue tant désiré."

As our understanding of Meroitic civilization grows, even without a full decipherment, it may yet turn out, as Griffith speculated in 1909, that it was "nomads from the eastern desert [who] once founded an empire in the valley of the Nile and acquired a veneer of settled civilization"–people like the Beja. Lepsius too favored such a scenario and regretted (in his 1880 grammar of Nubian) his lack of data on the language of the Beja. If this speculation were to be confirmed, would such a truth be more surprising, asked Griffith, than another unlikely but incontestable truth: that the magnificent, highly literate civilization of the pharaohs north of Kush is ancestral to the simple culture of the Egyptian fellahin (peasants) of the 20th century?

:oq     irrtew     : iros     : ileqeniyentew     : sow ←

iwolekiret     ilekiret     : eykerqiy     iwoqeyemt

beletenosos     iwoleḥdet     ileḥdet     : eyertidk

iwoledmtey     eyosek     enḥprh     iwoledmtey

: iwoledmtey     ekiteqes     silbda     : etirep

| 1 Transliteration: | wos : | wetneyineqeli : | sori : | wetrri |
|---|---|---|---|---|
| 2 Gloss: | O Isis | [epithet] | O Osiris | [epithet] |

'O...Isis! O...Osiris!
Here lies the noble Tameye;

| 1 | qo: | tmeye-qowi | | yiqrekye : | terikeli |
|---|---|---|---|---|---|
| 2 | The noble | Tameye-the.noble.one.it.is | | (of) Yiqarekaye | begotten |

Yiqarekaye was his father,
Kaditareye was his mother;

| 1 | terikelowi | kditreye : | tedḥeli | tedḥelowi |
|---|---|---|---|---|
| 2 | begotten.he.was | (of) Kaditareye | born | born.he.was |

he was related to *sosonete*-officers,
to the city governor Keshoye,

| 1 | sosoneteleb | yetmdelowi | ḥrpḥ ne | kesoye |
|---|---|---|---|---|
| 2 | (to) *sosonete*-officers | related.he.was; | (to) the.city.governor | Keshoye |

and to the *adb* agent Seqetike.'

| 1 | yetmdelowi | perite : | adblis | seqetike | yetmdelowi : |
|---|---|---|---|---|---|
| 2 | related.he.was | (to) the.agent | of.the.*adb* | Seqetike | related.he.was |

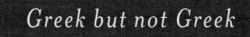

Greek but not Greek

# V

# THE ETRUSCAN ALPHABET

The Etruscans, and their homeland Etruria (modern Tuscany), have exerted a special hold on the imagination of Europeans ever since classical times. During the Renaissance, Cosimo de' Medici, grand duke of Tuscany, was poetically cast (by his celebrated biographer Vasari) as the Etruscan king Lars Porsenna, after the supposed discovery of the ancient ruler's tomb at Chiusi. In the 19th century, many thousands of Etruscan tombs were opened by 'archaeologists' such as Lucien Bonaparte, Napoleon's brother; the plunder was said to have equaled that of Pompeii and Herculaneum. And in the 20th century, D. H. Lawrence imbued much of his final poetry with imagery taken from his descents into Etruscan tombs. "Reach me a gentian, give me a torch!/let me guide myself with the blue, forked torch of this flower/down the darker and darker stairs...even where Persephone goes." Small wonder then, that the classically trained Michael Ventris, too, fell under the Etruscan spell and persisted right up to the moment of decipherment in his mistaken belief that Linear B probably wrote Etruscan or a closely related language.

*Etruscan art: the Sarcophagus of the Married Couple, Cerveteri, late 6th century BC.*

For those who are interested in language and writing, the Etruscans are undoubtedly of crucial importance. As already mentioned, they were the conduit by which the Greek alphabet reached the Romans and hence the rest of Europe. (The Etruscan alphabet may even have directly inspired the runic alphabet of northern Europe, according to some scholars.) But their spoken language became extinct, and so far as we can tell from reconstructions of it based on their inscriptions, Etruscan bore no resemblance to any European language. Simply by comparing the letter forms of the Etruscan and Greek alphabets, scholars can *read* the Etruscan script almost as easily as they can read ancient Greek, but they cannot understand the meaning of most Etruscan words (apart from the numerous proper names), unlike the words of classical Greek.

Herodotus, writing in the 5th century BC, maintained that the Etruscans were a people who had migrated to Italy through the Aegean islands from Lydia in Anatolia. (This was the ancient tradition mentioned on page 91 that encouraged Ventris to think that Linear B wrote Etruscan.) There is no archaeological evidence for such a movement, but there is an intriguing stone stela from the Aegean island of Limnos (not far from Anatolia), found in the 19th century, which contains a short inscription written in an alphabet and language akin to—but not the same as—Etruscan. The inscription is dated to the late 6th century BC, but we have no reliable idea of what it signifies about the history of the Etruscans. In the absence of contrary evidence, most scholars favor the view that the Etruscans were not immigrants to Tuscany.

We are, however, certain about how they came to borrow the Greek alphabet to write their own language. Greek colonists had settled in Italy around 775 BC at Pithekoussai (modern Ischia). Phoenicians, too, established themselves in western Sicily and Sardinia, and became commercially and politically allied with the Etruscans (there are Phoenician/Etruscan bilingual inscriptions, as we shall see); but it was the Greeks who most strongly influenced the Etruscans. "Greek culture first came to Rome by way of Etruria," write Giuliano and Larissa Bonfante in *The Etruscan Language*, the leading book on the subject in English, "for the Etruscans, having learned from the Greeks how to represent divinities in human form, build cities and temples, organize armies, drink wine, and use the alphabet, passed on many of these signs of civilization to their neighbors in Italy."

The Etruscans flourished as a separate people for several centuries until the 1st century BC, when they were effectively absorbed into the expanding Roman empire. Indeed, we owe a considerable amount of our knowledge of the Etruscans to Latin writings. It is clear that there was never an Etruscan empire, more a loose collection of individualistic, independent polities like the Greek city states or the Tuscan cities of the Renaissance. What they had in common was their language and religion and certain customs and costumes that were distinct from other peoples in Italy and the Mediterranean—also the name by which they called themselves, 'rasna'.

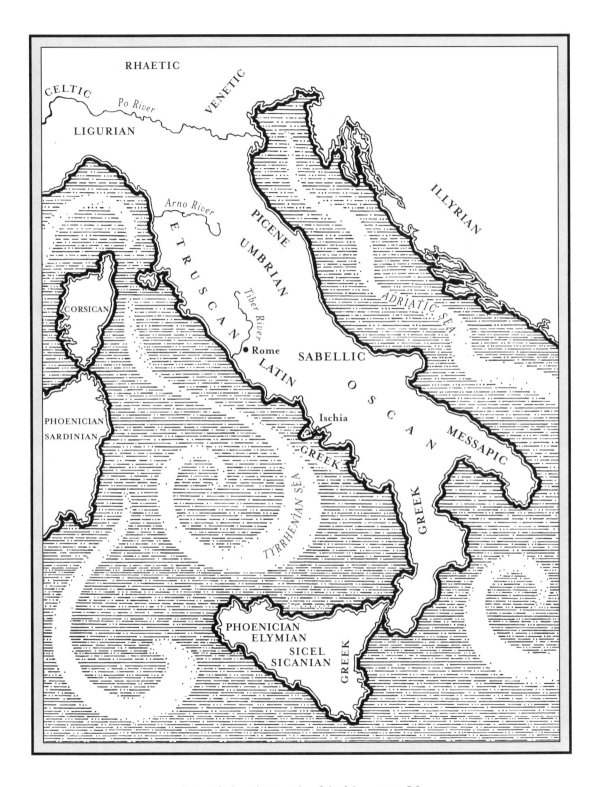

RHAETIC

CELTIC

LIGURIAN

*Po River*

VENETIC

*Arno River*

ETRUSCAN

PICENE

UMBRIAN

*Tiber River*

CORSICAN

• Rome

LATIN

SABELLIC

ILLYRIAN

*ADRIATIC SEA*

PHOENICIAN
SARDINIAN

O S C A N

Ischia

GREEK

MESSAPIC

*TYRRHENIAN SEA*

GREEK

PHOENICIAN
ELYMIAN
SICEL
SICANIAN

GREEK

*Ancient Italy and its peoples, 8th–6th centuries BC.*

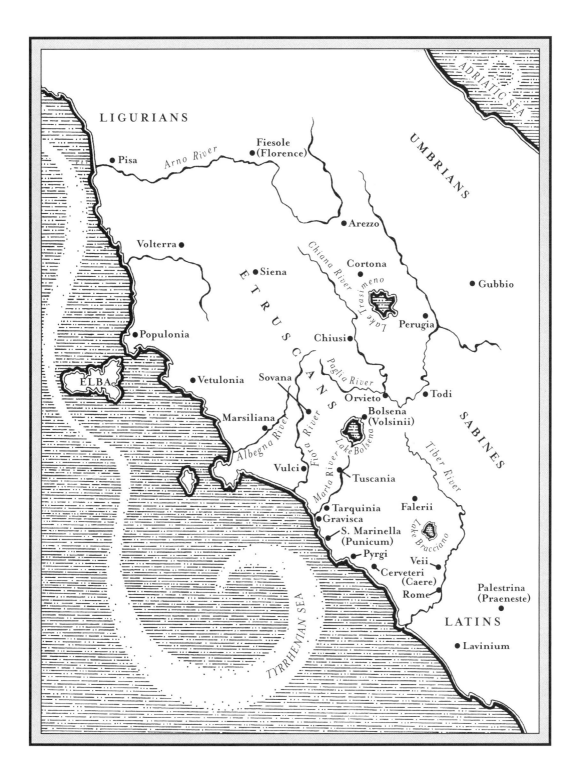

*The Etruscan cities.*

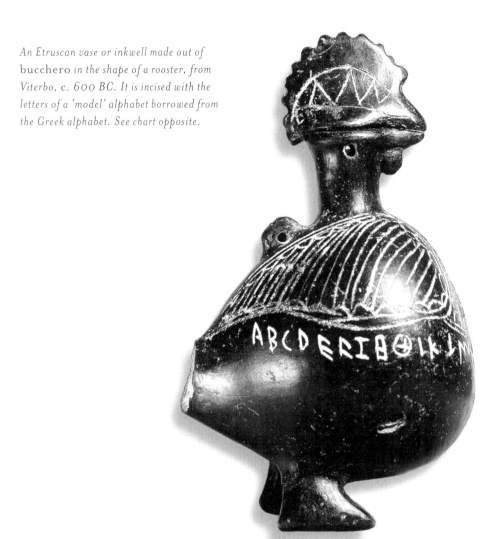

*An Etruscan vase or inkwell made out of* **buccero** *in the shape of a rooster, from Viterbo, c. 600 BC. It is incised with the letters of a 'model' alphabet borrowed from the Greek alphabet. See chart opposite.*

The Romans treated the Etruscans with real respect, at one time sending their sons from Rome to the former centers of Etruscan power such as Caere (modern Cerveteri) where they probably learned the arts of divination, the *disciplina etrusca*, under the tutelage of an Etruscan *haruspex*. It was a *haruspex* in Rome called Spurinna, a known Etruscan name, who warned Julius Caesar against the Ides of March; and even as late as AD 408 Etruscan *haruspices* vainly recited prayers and incantations to save Rome from being sacked by Alaric, king of the Goths.

The Roman writer Seneca remarked of the Etruscans:

❝ The difference between us and [them]... is the following: while we believe that lightning is released as a result of the collision of clouds, they believe that clouds collide so as to cause lightning. For since they attribute everything to the gods' will, they believe, not that things have a meaning insofar as they occur, but rather that they happen because they must have a meaning. ❞

But although the Romans preserved much of Etruscan religious lore, which was useful to them, they showed little interest in Etruscan literature—preferring Greek literature, either in the original or in Latin translation—despite their borrowing of the Etruscan alphabet to write their own language Latin. However they did absorb many Etruscan words into Latin from their ancient neighbor's language. Most were connected with luxurious living and higher culture, including writing, such as 'atrium' (entrance hall), 'histrio' (actor), 'taberna' (inn), 'elementum' (letter of the alphabet), 'litterae' (writing), 'stilus' (writing implement) and 'cera' (wax, as in wax tablets on which to take notes). It is evident from this borrowing and from much of the surviving art of the Etruscans, which depicts writing and reading or includes written texts, the high importance that they placed on literacy.

One of the most charming examples is a vase or inkwell shaped as a rooster, made out of *bucchero*, the shiny, metallic-looking, black or gray ware which is particular to the Etruscans. Written boldly around it in incised letters is a 'model' alphabet, clearly copied from the Greek alphabet. Such 'model' alphabets obviously enjoyed prestige, because they have been found at many sites on objects placed in the graves of aristocratic Etruscans; there are 46 examples known, one of them inscribed on an ivory writing tablet. Try comparing the letter forms in the 'model' alphabet with the same letters as they were normally written by the Etruscans, given in the chart (which also includes the phonetic values of the Etruscan letters, the letters of the early Greek alphabet and the Greek phonetic values). In some cases, there is a difference in direction, for example the two Etruscan letters standing for e and k point towards the right in the 'model' alphabet and towards the left in Etruscan inscriptions.

| Etruscan alphabet | Phonetic value | Greek alphabet | Phonetic value |
|---|---|---|---|
| A | a | A A | a |
|  |  | B | b |
| ) ) | c (=k) | < C | g |
|  |  | D D | d |
| ∃ ∃ ∃ | e | E E | e |
| ⅂ ⅂ | v | F | w |
| I ‡ ⱶ | z (=ts) | I | z |
| ⊟ ⊟ ⊘ | h | ⊟ H | h |
| ⊗ ⊙ ○ | θ (=th) | ⊗ ⊕ ⊙ | th |
| I | i | I | i |
| Χ | k | K | k |
| ⅃ | l | L | l |
| ⋔ ⋔ | m | ⋔ ⋔ M | m |
| Ψ Π | n | Ψ N | n |
| ⊞ | s | Χ | x |
|  |  | O | o |
| ↑ ↑ | p | Γ Γ | p |
| M | ś | M (?) | s |
| Ϙ | q | Ϙ | q |
| ⟨ ⟨ | r | P | r |
| ⟩ ⟩ | s | Ϟ | s |
| Τ ↑ ↑ | t | T | t |
| Y V | u, w | Ρ Y V | u |
| Χ | ṡ |  |  |
| Φ Φ | Φ (= ph) | Φ Φ | ph |
| Ψ ψ | χ (= kh) | Ψ V | kh |
| 8 | f |  |  |

Apart from letter direction, there are some notable differences between the Etruscan alphabet actually used in Etruscan inscriptions and the Greek 'model' alphabet they inscribed on certain objects. First, the Etruscans based their signs on the *early* Greek alphabet (8th century BC), not on the classical Greek alphabet (5th century BC and after), and thus the Etruscan alphabet includes four signs for *s*, ✕, ⊞, ⋔, and ⟩, the last three of which were inherited by the early Greeks from the Phoenician alphabet (where they are called *samekh*, *sade* and *sin*) and which the classical Greeks reduced to the signs ⟩ (*s*) and ⨦ (*ks*). However, only two of the four Etruscan signs for *s* were regularly used at any one time and place.

Second, there were letters in the 'model' alphabet never used by the Etruscans, because their language did not include the particular sounds for which those letters stood in Greek. (A similar situation pertains today in Italy, where school children learn the roman letters 'k', 'j', 'w' and 'y', which never appear in Italian words.) For instance, the Etruscan language apparently had no need of signs for the voiced stops *b*, *d*, *g*, and the vowel *o*, as we can deduce from the fact that Etruscan writers did not use the Greek signs ᛊ, ᚱ, O ; and they gave the Greek gamma (Γ, <, or ⟨ ), the phonetic value *k* (instead of Greek *g*). This means that *three* Etruscan signs were used to write *k* (as in English 'think'): K before *a* (*ka*); < before *e* and *i* (*ce*, *ci*); and ♀ before *u* (*qu*). Latin spelling initially adopted the same system, but since the Latin language (unlike Etruscan) did have the sound *g*, the early Latin letter 'C' could be pronounced either as *k* (as in Caesar pronounced *Kaiser*, from which comes the title Kaisar) or as *g* (as in Caius pronounced *Gaius*); later, the Romans introduced a new letter G, to make this phonetic distinction unambiguous.

These and other nuances of the Etruscan alphabet were settled through comparisons with the Greek and Latin alphabets between the 17th and the early 19th centuries. By 1833, when Lepsius (later famous as an Egyptologist and important in the decipherment of Meroitic) determined the phonetic value *z* of the sign Ɪ , "the cycle of research has been considered closed as far as the alphabet is concerned", wrote the Italian scholar Massimo Pallottino in his definitive study, *The Etruscans*. For two centuries, therefore, scholars have been able to read hundreds, if not thousands of words which must from their contexts in the inscriptions be names, such as Ruma (Rome), Clevsina (Chiusi, a city), Fufluns (the god Dionysos), Seianti Hanunia Tlesnasa (the name of a woman on a sarcophagus) and Laris Celatina Lausa (the name of a man). The problem has been to find the meanings of the many words that are not obviously names—to devise techniques that will give information about the mysterious Etruscan language. Over a long period, it has proved possible to deduce a considerable amount of Etruscan vocabulary and grammar from various clues, as we shall now see.

———

But before considering these techniques, let us take a look at why the Etruscan language is considered to be an isolate. Compare the Etruscan words for family relationships, and also those for numerals, with words of the same meaning in the Indo-European languages Latin, Greek and Sanskrit:

|  | Etruscan | Latin | Greek | Sanskrit |
|---|---|---|---|---|
| father | apa | pater | pater | pita |
| mother | ati | mater | mater, meter | mata |
| son | clan | filius | hyios | sunuh |
| daughter | sech | filia | thygater | duhita |
| wife | puia | mulier, femina, uxor | gyne | gna |
| brother | ruva | frater | (phrater) | bhrata |
| one | thu | oinos, unus | oine | e(kah) |
| two | zal | duo | dyo | dva |
| three | ci | tres | treis | trayah |
| four | sa | quattuor | tettares | catvarah |
| five | mach | quinque | pente | panca |
| six | huth | sex | hex | sat (sas) |
| ten | sar | decem | deka | dasa |

It is obvious that Etruscan does not belong to the Indo-European language family. Neither does it resemble any other European language, including Basque, another intriguing language isolate with which it has sometimes been compared, as one can see simply by comparing the names of some numerals in Etruscan and Basque:

|  | Etruscan | Basque |
|---|---|---|
| 1 | thu | bat |
| 2 | zal | bi or biga |
| 3 | ci | hiru |
| 4 | sa | lau |
| 5 | mach | bost |
| 6 | huth | sei |
| 10 | sar | hamar |
| 20 | zathrum | hogei |

Nevertheless, throughout the 19th and well into the 20th century, scholars and amateurs persisted with often-ludicrous efforts to compare Etruscan vocabulary with that of other languages, i.e. the 'etymological' method mentioned in the Introduction and in the previous chapter on the Meroitic script. (This is naturally much easier to apply in the case of Etruscan, since the vocabulary of Indo-European languages, and their early forms, is well understood, unlike the African languages.) But eventually the method was generally accepted to be leading nowhere.

Subsequent methods of understanding the meaning of Etruscan words have been fundamentally 'cultural', not so much linguistic, since we have no other language with which to compare Etruscan. The ongoing decipherment is therefore intimately dependent on the understanding of Etruscan history, religion and art obtained from non-textual studies, and on clues from Greek and Roman culture which has influenced the Etruscans or been influenced by them.

Although there are about 13,000 known Etruscan inscriptions, some 4000 of these are fragments or graffiti, and the vast majority of the other 9000 inscriptions are short, mainly epitaphs containing only names—the father's name, sometimes the mother's name, the surname of the deceased and, if she was a woman, perhaps the name of her husband and the number of children—maybe an age and a public office held, and formulaic phrases. Dates are not generally included.

One of the most interesting inscriptions, which is also unique in the Etruscan corpus, appears on a set of ivory dice (now in Paris). Clearly the six words that appear on the six faces of each die must be the Etruscan numerals one to six:

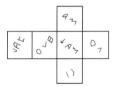

Transliterating these words from the Etruscan alphabet into roman letters (try it for yourself) we get the following six words:

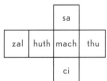

But how do we allot the six words to the numerals 1-6? There is a variety of clues. The most important is that in classical antiquity there was a well-known epigram stating that opposite faces of a die added up to 7. Therefore:

'mach' + 'zal' = 7
'thu' + 'huth' = 7
'ci' + 'sa' = 7

Now, 'ci' without doubt means 'three', because of the way it occurs in the Pyrgi plaques (we shall show this a little later), which implies that 'sa' means 'four'. We can also establish that 'mach' cannot mean 'one', since it appears in the phrase 'husur mach acnanas', in which 'husur' is known to be a plural form. After weighing such evidence with other clues, scholars generally accept the following list: 'thu' = one; 'zal' = two; 'ci' = three; 'sa' = four; 'mach' = five; 'huth' = six (though some other, slighter evidence suggests that 'huth' means four). Higher numbers are often formed in the 'subtractive' manner later borrowed by the Romans, e.g. nineteen is 'thun-em zathrum' (one-minus twenty). The numerical system as a whole is not very well understood, compared say to that of Linear B. For example, we are not sure of the Etruscan signs for 100 and 1000, though it seems clear from various pieces of evidence that both the Etruscan system and the forms of the numerals exerted a major influence on the subsequent Roman numerical system:

| Etruscan | Roman | Arabic |
|---|---|---|
| I | I | 1 |
| ∧ | V | 5 |
| ✕ | X | 10 |
| ↑ | L | 50 |
| ⊂ ✳ | C | 100 |
| ☺ | C or M | 100 or 1000? |
| ⊕ | M or M̄ | 1000 or 10,000? |

Then there is a unique class of short inscription—which runs into thousands (as compared to only one dice inscription)—so-called 'picture bilinguals', because the inscription accompanies a recognizable line drawing, usually of gods, goddesses, heroes and heroines, engraved on the backs of bronze mirrors. About 3000 of these mirrors are known, though not all have inscriptions. Found exclusively in the tombs of women, they seem to have originally been gifts for weddings and other special occasions. Clearly, Etruscan women were literate. Coupled with other inscriptions that refer to women by name, paintings that show Etruscan women attending splendid banquets, and references to the public status of such women by Roman writers, we get a picture of them as much more independent than the relatively invisible domesticated women of ancient Rome.

Helen, the legendary beauty, is a favorite subject on the mirrors who often appears in toilet and adornment scenes. A 4th-century mirror shows her dressing, with the label inscription Malavisch (see opposite left). This may be an Etruscan name or epithet for Helen, meaning something akin to 'the one adorned' and related to 'malstria' and 'malena', words that clearly mean 'mirror' from their context on the objects. (One mirror carries an inscription saying that someone has dedicated the object to his mother.) Around Malavisch are shown four female figures, Turan, Munthuch, Zipu and Hinthial, a word that means 'ghost', 'shade' or 'reflection' and may therefore refer to the 'shade of Helen'.

Another mirror (opposite right), from the 3rd century, shows a group of figures from the story of the Trojan war. The seated male figure on the left is labeled Talmithe, for Palmithe (Palamedes), and the one on the right is Menle (Menelaos). Standing on the left are Clutmsta (Clytemnestra),

*Etruscan bronze mirrors. (See text for explanation.)*

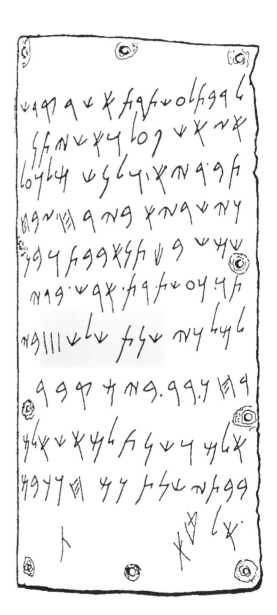

*Two of the three gold plaques from Pyrgi, c. 500 BC. The plaque on the left is written in Etruscan, the one on the right in Phoenician script. See page 170 for an explanation of the drawings.*

**Etruscan**

**Phoenician**

and Uthste (Odysseus); the Greek Δ (d) in Odysseus has been represented in Etruscan by Θ (th). (This is a simplification of the Greek theta Θ; there was no risk of the Etruscans' mistaking it for the vowel o, since this vowel did not exist in Etruscan.) These names are all examples of syncope: the vowels have tended to drop out, as in the English pronunciation of the towns Gloucester and Salisbury. The dates of certain Etruscan inscriptions demonstrate that syncopation occurred after about 500 BC and that it increased over time; an earlier attested Etruscan spelling of Clytemnestra is Cluthumustha.

In addition to 'picture bilinguals', there are a number of more conventional bilinguals of a linguistic nature, written either in Etruscan/Phoenician or in Etruscan/Latin. The most important are the gold plaques discovered in 1964 at ancient Pyrgi, the seaport of Caere, not far from Rome. There are three of these, one written in Phoenician, the other two in Etruscan, of which the longer plaque contains 36 or 37 words. The date is about 500 BC, at which time the Phoenicians were resident in some of the port cities of the Italian peninsula. Hence it was natural for an Etruscan ruler of Caere to write in both Etruscan and Phoenician; alternatively, the bilingual nature of the inscription may attest to a treaty between Caere and its surrounding region and the powerful Phoenician centers at Carthage or on Cyprus. (According to Aristotle, the Etruscans and the Carthaginians were so close as to form almost one people.)

Like most translated texts, the Phoenician and the Etruscan inscriptions are not word-for-word translations. The Pyrgi plaques are more of a 'quasi-bilingual' than a true one. Both record the same event—the dedication by the Etruscan ruler Thefarie Velianas of a cult place and perhaps a statue to the powerful Phoenician goddess of love

and beauty Astarte, or Ishtar, identified here with the Etruscan goddess Uni (Roman Juno, Greek Hera)—but the two plaques express this fact in somewhat different ways. However, both clearly speak of the dedication being carried out in the third year of the ruler's reign. Thus we have the Etruscan-Phoenician equation:

| 'ci avil' | = | 'snt sls III' |
|---|---|---|
| [three years] | | [years three III] |
| **Etruscan** | | **Phoenician** |

The equivalent words are highlighted on page 168, which clearly enables the word 'ci' to be identified as the numeral three. But, exciting as the discovery of the Pyrgi plaques was, 'ci' proved to be the only identifiable new Etruscan word to emerge from it.

The Etruscan-Latin bilinguals referred to above, of which there are about 30, though very short, have provided some useful information, especially about the relationship between the Etruscan cities and Rome in the 2nd and 1st centuries BC, the period when the Etruscans lost their independence and their language gradually died out. During this transition, both languages and both scripts were in use. But sometimes the Etruscan-language version and the Latin-language version were both written in roman script.

An example of the latter is this bilingual inscription marking the grave of two brothers Arnth and Vel, written entirely in roman letters:

| **Etruscan:** | 'arnth spedo thocerual clan' |
|---|---|
| | [Arnth Spedo son of Thocero] |
| **Latin:** | 'Vel Spedo Thoceronia natus' |
| | [Vel Spedo son of Thoceronia] |

The equivalence of 'clan' and 'natus', meaning 'son' in Latin, is obvious. But the important fact here is that this is not a true bilingual, for the Latin and Etruscan inscriptions are plainly not equivalent. Instead, one brother, Arnth, the more conservative, records his name in Etruscan (but using roman letters), while the other brother, Vel, prefers to think of himself in Latin terms, using the word 'natus' instead of the Etruscan 'clan'. Perhaps Arnth was a bit of an Etruscan nationalist, who resented Roman domination of his people, while Vel embraced it and changed his name accordingly, as immigrants often do in a new country. (There are other Etruscan/Latin bilinguals in which the same Etruscan individual records both his original Etruscan name and his adopted name as a Roman citizen, possibly with the addition of a Roman cognomen, i.e. a third 'nickname' added to the ancestral name as in Marcus Tullius *Cicero*. Thus, 'pupli velimna aule cahatial' was known in Latin as Publius Volumnius Auli filius Violens Cafatia natus, meaning Publius Volumnius, son of Aulus, Violens, son of Cafatia—with Violens as his cognomen and 'son of Cafatia' his matronymic, his mother's name, a common feature in Etruscan but not Roman names.)

This historical situation produced a further class of bilingual, which was not actually written on monuments. Certain Etruscan words are explained, or glossed, by Latin authors. The words tend to be drawn from the divination rituals of the *disciplina etrusca*. Examples of such glosses are 'atrium', 'aisar' (god or gods), 'uerse' (fire), 'acale' (June). Sometimes these can be cross-checked with Etruscan inscriptions: 'aisar' and 'acale' are found on one long inscription, for instance, in contexts that suit their glossed meanings in Latin. A particularly interesting example is 'arimos', with the given Latin meaning 'monkey'. According to Virgil, the ancient name for Ischia was Inarime, which must have meant 'monkey island' in Etruscan. The Greek name for Ischia, as mentioned

earlier, was Pithekoussai; and the Greek word for 'monkey' is, neatly, 'pithekos'. It is at least possible that the 'Island of Monkeys' may have been named from a population of monkeys once to be found on it, as in Gibraltar.

This does not quite exhaust the available kinds of bilingual. Scholars have also tried a quasi-bilingual 'cultural' approach. With care and a little intuition, it is possible to compare an Etruscan phrase on an Etruscan object with a phrase from a different language on a similar object from a culture that is broadly similar to the Etruscan. (Imagine comparing epitaphs on, say, Spanish and Italian gravestones, or perhaps the obituary announcements in Spanish and Italian newspapers.) Similar cultural context is the key here, and the obvious cultural comparisons are with the various peoples who were neighbors of the Etruscans, including of course the Romans. For instance, the rituals described on the longest Etruscan inscription of all, the so-called Zagreb mummy, may be compared with rituals described in the Umbrian-language Iguvine tables from Gubbio in Umbria; and the funerary eulogy on the Tarquinia sarcophagus of Laris Pulenas is comparable to the epitaphs written in Latin on the sarcophagi of the noble Roman family of the Scipios.

———

We shall conclude this chapter by looking at the Zagreb mummy and two other lengthy, much-studied Etruscan inscriptions, out of the handful (not even a dozen) of existing long inscriptions. The other two are a curious model of a sheep's liver, used for divination, and a bronze tablet discovered only in the 1990s. Together, these three inscriptions give a good idea of the current state of the Etruscan decipherment.

The inscription on the Zagreb mummy contains some 1200 legible words written in ink. It is a religious text in the form of a linen book, parts of which have survived because they were used to bandage an Egyptian mummy some time between 150 and 100 BC. The mummy was bought in Egypt in the 19th century by a Croatian traveler and given to the National Museum in Zagreb, where it was unwrapped and its Etruscan text discovered. This contains sacrifices and prayers to a variety of gods such as Nethuns (Neptune) in calendrical form. "Though damaged and spotted by the unguents used for mummification, and largely unintelligible because of its technical vocabulary and the repetitions typical of religious texts, it is uniquely precious for our knowledge of the Etruscan language", writes Larissa Bonfante, despite much of the text being obscure in meaning, as is generally true of ritual texts. Here is a representative passage (which includes a numeral): 'celi huthis zathrumis flerchva nethunsl sucri thezri-c'. Translating literally: 'In the month of September [celi] on the twenty-sixth day [huthis zathrumis] the offerings [flerchva] to Neptune [nethunsl] must be made [sucri] and immolated [thezri-c]'.

The Piacenza liver, made of bronze, was found in northern Italy near Piacenza in 1877, though judging from the local variants used in its script and spelling, it was probably made at Chiusi in Etruria. The date is c. 150 BC.

The outer margin of the liver (over page), divided into 16 regions, names sections of the sky; within the liver and on its underside are 24 further regions. A few of the 52 names of divinities, mostly abbreviated, are highlighted on page 175 and transliterated into roman letters with their associated Greek or Roman god (where known):

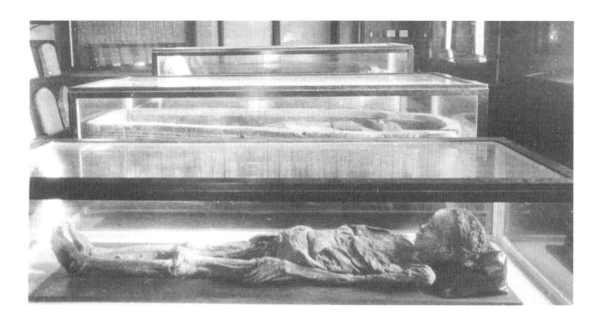

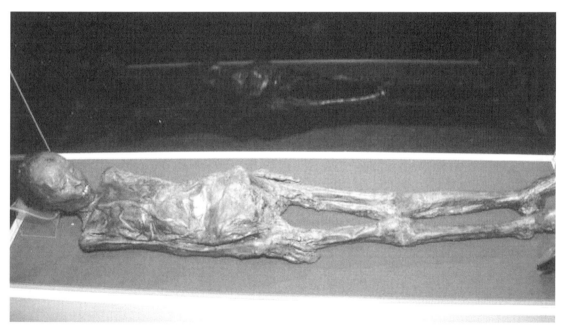

*The Zagreb mummy. The mummy, that of a 30-year old Egyptian woman (above), was wrapped in linen bandages torn from an Etruscan sacred 'book' (opposite), for reasons unknown. This is the longest-known Etruscan inscription.*

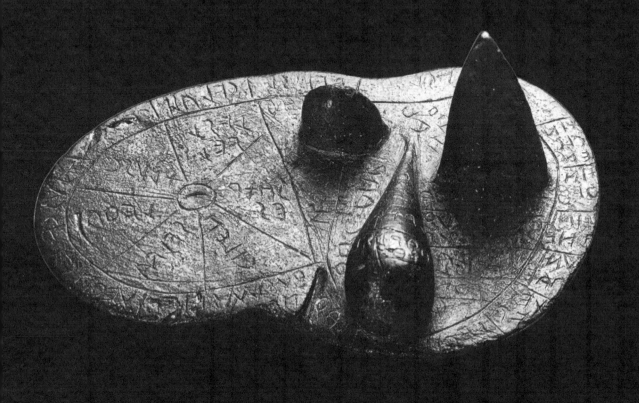

*The Piacenza liver, c. 150 BC. This bronze
model of a sheep's liver was used for divination.
It is inscribed with the names of Etruscan gods
and goddesses, which are labeled in the drawing
opposite with their classical equivalents.*

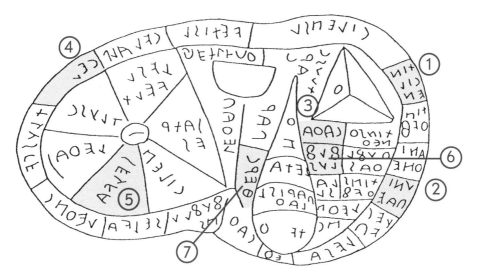

1 **'tin'** (= Jupiter)
2 **'uni'** (=Juno)
3 **'catha'** (= a sun god)
4 **'cel'** (= a mother goddess)
5 **'selvan'** (= Silvanus)
6 **'fufluns'** (= Bacchus)
7 **'hercle'** (= Hercules)
8 **'usil'** (= the sun) ⎫ underside
9 **'tivr'** (= the moon) ⎭ of liver

The discovery of the third inscription produced a ripple of excitement—not just among scholars, but also in the Italian public and in the world press, similar to the excitement created by the three gold plaques found at Pyrgi. In 1999, the Italian authorities revealed that a bronze tablet with about 200 Etruscan words on it—the third-longest known text—had been found in the area of Cortona, near Lake Trasimeno, and named the Tabula Cortonensis. The circumstances of the find, apparently on a building site with other bronze objects, were not entirely clear, and while the local workman who had brought it to the Cortona police in 1992 admitted to having washed the tablet with a toothbrush and running water, traces of a steel brush were found on the surface, suggesting that someone had tried to find out if the metal was gold. An anonymous telephone call warned that the objects were not from the claimed findspot. A piece of the tablet was also missing, but despite the authorities' sifting the earth at the building site, nothing turned up; furthermore, a soil analysis showed that the soil at the site and that inside the bronze objects did not coincide. The 'discoverer' was eventually accused of theft against the state and taken to court; although he was found not guilty, the normal reward was withheld. It was the hope of verifying whether the tablet really was from Cortona and of locating the missing fragment that delayed the public announcement of the find for over six years. (Not even Massimo Pallottino, the dean of Etruscan studies in the 20th century, was told about it before his death in 1995.)

Seven of the eight pieces of the tablet remain, which can be fitted together with only small gaps. That it was broken in antiquity can be proved from a scientific analysis of the lines of fracture; maybe someone intended to melt it down and reuse the bronze. Its size, 28.5 x 45.8 cm (11.2 x 18 in), is roughly that of two sheets of office paper. At the top, there is a handle, so perhaps the tablet once hung in a public place, such as an archive. Its date of manufacture lies between 225 and 150 BC.

A

*The Tabula Cortonensis, 3rd or 2nd century BC. This double-sided bronze tablet probably records a land contract with witnesses. It is the third-longest known Etruscan inscription and was discovered in the 1990s.*

B

Drawing of the Tabula Cortonensis, sides A and B.
Four ancient Etruscan 'insert paragraph' marks
(labeled 1–4) are indicated, as are two occurrences
of the name VELARA (side A) and the phrase
CELTINEITISS TARSIMINASS (side B), which
appears to refer to Lake Trasimeno.

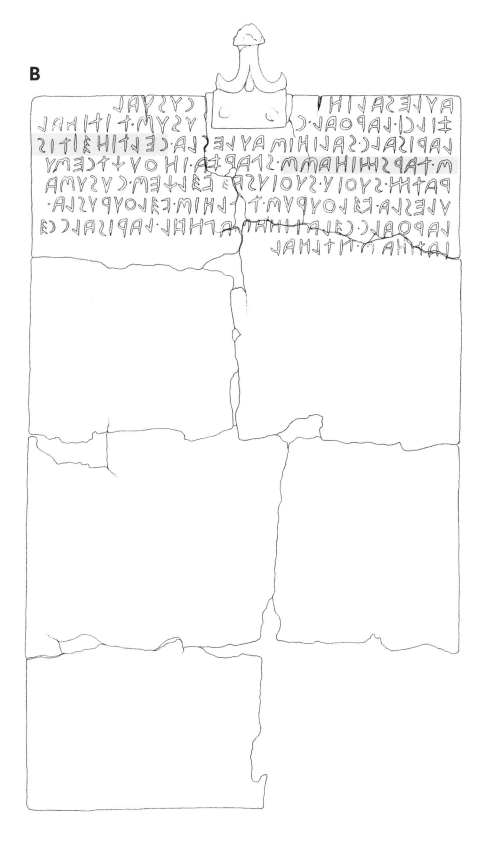

B

The characters, which run from right to left, as usual with Etruscan inscriptions (but of course opposite to the Greek alphabet), have been beautifully inscribed on both sides of the tablet, either from a mould using the *cire perdue* (lost wax) technique or, more probably, by direct engraving on the bronze. They cover all of one side (side A) but only eight lines of the other side (B). Important observations can be made without actually reading the inscription. For a start, it is clear that one scribe wrote both sides of the tablet, except for the last six lines of side A, which are engraved more deeply and therefore with an accentuated curvature. (Why there were two scribes, we can only speculate.) Secondly, there are four unusual marks as in ᛗᛋᒐᚤᛆ on side A, which look remarkably like the 'insert paragraph' marks of a modern proof-reader: which is exactly what their function appears to have been (highlighted). Finally, we can note that the sign standing for *e*, ᛅ, which the Etruscans borrowed from ᛉ, the Greek epsilon, appears in *two* versions in the Tabula Cortonensis, facing in opposite directions: ᛅ and ᛘ. This variant, which is known from other inscriptions to be local to the Cortona area, is virtual proof that the tablet is from Cortona; an inference reinforced by the occurrence of the name Velara, spelt with the local form of the epsilon, twice on the tablet (highlighted):

ᚨᛈᚨᒐᛕᛅ

—Velara is an ancestral (or family) name characteristic of Cortona.

The tablet was quickly read by applying the Etruscan alphabet. Word divisions were easily recognized from the dots inscribed in the bronze and from the familiarity of many of the sign groups as proper names and other known words, such as 'cel' (earth, land), 'vina' (vineyard) [related to 'vinum' (wine)], 'puia' (wife), 'clan' (son), 'rasna' (Etruscans, people) and the numerals 'zal' (2), 'sa' (4) and 'sar' (10). But there were so many names (more than two-thirds of the words) and a relatively high proportion of unknown words among the remaining words, that it was not possible to translate the document, though we can be sure of its general content. According to Luciano Agostiniani of the University of Perugia, who published the Tabula Cortonensis in 2000, what can be stated almost for certain is that the tablet is a record of a contract between the Cusu family, to which Petru Scevas belongs, and 15 other people, witnessed by a third group of names, including some of their children and grandchildren. It relates to a sale, or lease, of land including a vineyard, in the plain of Lake Trasimeno, a place apparently spelt 'celtinêitiss tarsiminass':

ᛗᛗᚨᚺᛁᚺᛃᛋᚤᚨᛏ·ᛗᛉᛏᛁᛏᛁᛃᚺᛁᛏᚤᛅᛃ

The first part of the first word, 'celtinêi' is known to be related to 'cel' (earth, land), so tiss is likely to mean 'lake': a reasonable deduction, which was exciting for Agostiniani since it added a new word to the Etruscan vocabulary.

Thirty-two men are mentioned by name, ten of whom are identified by their mothers' names or matronymics, a characteristic feature of Etruscan society as we know. But only one woman is mentioned, Arntlei, the wife of Petrus ('Arntlei Petrus puia'). These names and their interrelationships were what enabled Agostiniani to make a stab at reconstructing at least part of the tablet's missing section. He noticed that all the names on side B were in the genitive case and that two of the names were apparently repeated on side A. This was a plausible pattern, along the lines of 'X, son of Y.' The two pairs of names (1 and 2) have been highlighted (right) on the two sides of the tablet, which also includes the reconstructed names (3 and 4):

**Side A**
1 Vêlche Cusu Aulesa
2 Laris Cêlatina Lausa

**Side B**
Vêlcheś Cusuś Aulesla
Larisal[c] Cêlatinas Pitlnal

The equation in the second name is not exact but it can be hypothesized on the basis that 'Lausa' is a cognomen and that 'Pitlnal' is a matronymic. (The ending '-c' is the Etruscan for 'and', like '-que' in Latin and the 'currant bun' in Linear B on page 96.)

Agostiniani therefore proposed that the equation would apply to the other two complete names on side B, as follows. The parts in square brackets are reconstructions on side A of the same names as appear on side B:

**Side A**
3 Vêl[thur Titlni Velthur]uś
4 [Lart Cêlatina A]pnal

**Side B**
Vêlthuruś Titlinis Vêlthurusla
Larthalc Cêlatinas Apnal

These reconstructions fit the appropriate gaps in the tablet well, and suggest that the missing section must have consisted of proper names.

As must now be more than apparent, the decipherment of Etruscan is a gradual, evolving project. The Tabula Cortonensis, for all its length and complexity, has so far added mainly to our stock of Etruscan names, apart from giving us the likely word for 'lake'. Our total vocabulary for Etruscan is still only about 250 words, not all of which are of secure meaning; our knowledge of the grammar is extremely patchy, because of the limited nature of the corpus of inscriptions; and we know very little about Etruscan syntax, because no literature has

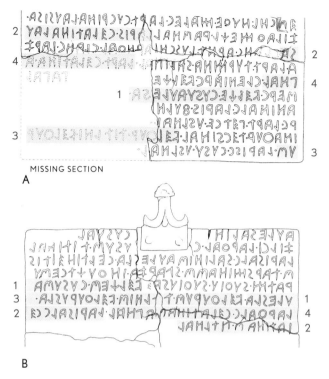

MISSING SECTION

A

B

survived. But we do have a deep and steadily growing knowledge of Etruscan culture that is contributing to what we know of the language. The study of Etruscan is no longer the "favorite playground for cranks, a kind of 'comic' page in the annals of linguistics" bemoaned by Pallottino in his first book on the subject, published in 1936, at a time when the 'etymological' method was still not totally discredited and scholars still hoped to relate Etruscan to another European language. The study of the Etruscan script now feeds upon a large body of reliable knowledge of the Etruscans, with recent major exhibitions about the Etruscan civilization in various countries. There is still much mystery, especially concerning the language, but increasingly the Etruscans are stepping out of the shadows and being recognized as partners of the Phoenicians, Greeks, and Romans.

A Mediterranean Mystery

# LINEAR A

When Sir Arthur Evans began excavating "Linear Script B" a century ago at Knossos, he also discovered, as we know, another script mainly written on clay tablets which strongly resembled it, "Linear Script A"; and in addition a so-called Hieroglyphic script, which was found principally on Cretan seal stones. According to the archaeological record, the Hieroglyphic was the oldest of the three scripts, dating chiefly to 2100-1700 BC; Linear A belonged to the period 1750-1450 BC; while Linear B post-dated Linear A. Evans therefore came to the conclusion that all three scripts wrote the same 'Minoan' language indigenous to Crete, and that Linear B had developed from Linear A which had probably developed from the Hieroglyphic script—on the basis that the later Egyptian scripts such as demotic were derived from Egyptian hieroglyphs and all of them wrote one Egyptian language. This notion was consistent with the prevalent view that writing always evolved over time from pictograms like the Cretan 'hieroglyphs' to comparatively abstract signs like the majority of those in Linear A and B.

Today this simple picture has been abandoned. Linear B has of course been deciphered as Greek; Linear A has been to some degree deciphered but appears to write an unknown language—only possibly Cretan in origin—so that we cannot really read it; while the Hieroglyphic script remains almost wholly mysterious. (Hence we shall mention Hieroglyphic only in passing.) Furthermore, all three scripts have been found outside Crete, and the spans of their dates are now seen to overlap; we can no longer postulate a straightforward line of descent purely within Crete: Linear A and Linear B may be cousin scripts, rather than the first being the parent of the second.

The bulk of the early discoveries of Linear A (about 150 tablets) were made not at Knossos but elsewhere on Crete by excavators other than Evans, most notably at the site of a Minoan palace in the south of the island at Haghia Triada. Some Linear A evidence was published in the 1920s, but the tablets themselves were not made publicly available until 1945 (which was still several years before most of the

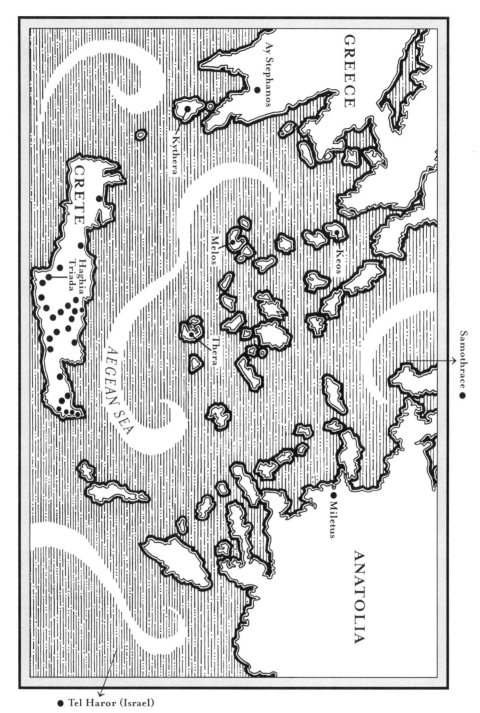

GREECE

Ay Stephanos

Kythera

CRETE

Haghia
Triada

AEGEAN SEA

Melos

Keos

Thera

Samothrace

Miletus

ANATOLIA

● Tel Haror (Israel)

*Findspots of Linear A around the Aegean. Linear A is found mainly in Crete, but also in the Greek islands, on the Greek mainland, at Miletus in Anatolia, at Samothrace (off the map) and even in Israel, though its identification in this location is uncertain.*

Linear B tablets). Fortunately for would-be decipherers of Linear A, the corpus produced by the Italian scholar who published the tablets, Giovanni Pugliese Caratelli, was much better organized than that produced by Evans and his executor Sir John Myres.

Less fortunately—and hence the fact that Linear A has not yet been 'cracked'—there is far less of Linear A than of Linear B: only about 1500 texts, many of them minimal or damaged, containing around 7500 characters. This compares with tens of thousands of Linear B characters (and less than 2000 Hieroglyphic characters). Moreover, almost half of the Linear A corpus has been discovered since 1945, much of it in recent decades. While most of the findspots have been in Crete, inscriptions have also turned up on Greek islands all over the Aegean, at one place on the Greek mainland, on the Turkish mainland (at ancient Miletus), and even, as some scholars maintain, in two places in distant Israel.

The discoveries at Miletus, made in 1994 and 1995 by the archaeologist Wolf-Dietrich Niemeier, though small, made a considerable impact on archaeologists (and were even reported in *Scientific American*). Not only were they the first Linear A signs to be discovered in Anatolia—where Cretans were said (by Herodotus) to have settled after a quarrel between Minos and his brother Sarpedon over who should be king of Crete—the signs could be shown to have been written on a pot *before* it was fired. This suggested that Minoan speakers were actually living in Anatolia, rather than simply trading with the area, at this time (the potsherd has been dated to the 15th century BC, probably to 1490/70 BC). According to Niemeier, supported by the classicist Tom Palaima, there seems to have been a Minoan colony at Miletus.

*Potsherd from ancient Miletus in western Turkey bearing three Linear A signs (the first of which is damaged), early 15th century BC. They are the signs AB 56—AB 41—AB 47, according to the chart on page 193. The meaning of the signs is unknown.*

The first major steps in deciphering Linear A were taken in 1950, before Ventris's breakthrough with Linear B. They concerned the numerical system. It was not difficult to identify which Linear A characters were numerals: they stood out from the other characters just as they did in Linear B. Evans had already established that the numerical system of Linear A was basically the same as that of Linear B, plus an alternative sign for 10–a heavy dot (page 78). But in addition to the familiar signs which count units, tens, hundreds and thousands, in Linear A there are a series of numerical signs not found in Linear B, which in some places occur singly, in other places in combination. In 1950, Emmett Bennett Jr., the scholar who compiled the sign list of Linear B, was able to prove that these undeciphered signs were fractional numerals, as already mentioned in the Linear B chapter. Let us now see how he did this.

First, Bennett counted the number of occurrences (frequency) of each of these numeral signs in the Linear A corpus, as indicated here:

| $L$ | $7$ | $\lambda$ | $7$ | $T$ | $+$ | $\ddagger$ | $Z$ | $\frac{z}{2}$ | $\diamondsuit$ |
|---|---|---|---|---|---|---|---|---|---|
| 59 | 26 | 14 | 7 | 8 | 8 | 9 | 9 | 9 | 6 |

| $\frac{L}{7}$ | $L\lambda$ | $\frac{L}{7}$ | $\frac{L}{T}$ | $\frac{L}{+}$ | $\frac{L}{\ddagger}$ | | $L\diamondsuit$ |
|---|---|---|---|---|---|---|---|
| 17 | 1 | 1 | 1 | 1 | 1 | | 1 |

| $77$ | $\pi$ | $\frac{L}{7+}$ | $77$ | | $\frac{zz}{zz}$ | $\diamondsuit$ |
|---|---|---|---|---|---|---|
| 5 | 1 | 1 | 1 | | 1 | 1 |

Making the reasonable assumption that they must be signs for fractions–for what other kind of numbers could such a large set of numeral signs with their various combinations represent?–Bennett commented:

" To assign the proper values... is most difficult. There are very few well-preserved tablets in which appear both fractional signs and their summation. The study of the values [starts] from these few tablets, and from the apparent similarity of the Egyptian [fractional] signs which we may suppose to have been the models. Unfortunately the schemes deriving from these two sources do not agree. "

The sign $L$ has the highest frequency, and is also the most frequent sign in combination. This suggests that it has a value of $1/2$. The next most frequent signs are $7$ and $\lambda$, which suggests they may stand for either $1/3$ and $1/4$, or vice versa. In order to decide which way round the values were, Bennett introduced an idea, following Egyptian precedent, that there should be a sign for $2/3$. This latter sign could not occur in combination with $L$ (since $1/2 + 2/3 > 1$), and it would be, he considered, of moderate frequency. He also postulated a sign for $1/6$ which again could not occur with the sign $L$, since $1/2 + 1/6 = 2/3$, and $2/3$ was already assumed to have its own sign. On the basis of the above sign list, this logic threw up two candidates, $Z$ and $\frac{z}{2}$, for $1/6$ and $2/3$, or vice versa.

Bennett arbitrarily assigned the following values of these two signs as a working hypothesis:

$$\frac{z}{2} = 1/6 \qquad Z = 2/3$$

Assuming the (unproven) values:

$$7 = 1/3 \qquad \lambda = 1/4$$

then generated the following table of fractions with their frequencies (to understand the argument you need to check each sign and combination-sign frequency with the table of data above):

| z̄/z̄ | 𝍐 | 𝍑 | 𝍒 | 𝍓 | 𝍔 | 𝍕 |
|---|---|---|---|---|---|---|
| ¹/₆ | ¹/₄ | ¹/₃ | ¹/₂ | ²/₃ | ³/₄ (¹/₂ + ¹/₄) | ⁵/₆ (¹/₂ + ¹/₃) |
| 9 | 14 | 26 | 59 | 9 | 1 | 17 |

If instead we reverse the assumed values ¹/₃ and ¹/₄ of the above two signs, we obtain a second table of fractions and frequencies:

| z̄/z̄ | 𝍑 | 𝍐 | 𝍒 | 𝍓 | 𝍕 | 𝍔 |
|---|---|---|---|---|---|---|
| ¹/₆ | ¹/₄ | ¹/₃ | ¹/₂ | ²/₃ | ³/₄ | ⁵/₆ |
| 9 | 26 | 14 | 59 | 9 | 17 | 1 |

This second set of frequencies is more in accordance with the expected frequency of fractional quantities in general, since it shows higher frequencies of occurrence for ¹/₄ and ³/₄ than for ¹/₃ and ⁵/₆.

New discoveries of Linear A since 1950 have not affected Bennett's basic picture. But his assigning of fractional values is not entirely secure, even today, because there is insufficient evidence of calculations and summations available in the Linear A tablets to confirm or deny the Bennett values beyond any doubt; indeed there are significant inconsistencies.

We shall now have a look at some of the tablets from Haghia Triada: both those that include fractions and those that do not but which instead illustrate other interesting aspects of Linear A. Consider the tablet drawing on the right:

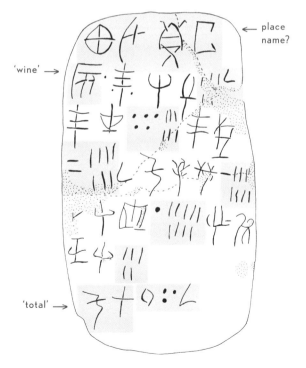

place name? →

'wine' →

'total' →

Working from the top down, we can pick out a series of numbers (highlighted): 5 ½, 56, 27 ½, 17 ½ [unclear], 19, 5, and, at the bottom, 130 ½–which is the correct total of the preceding six numbers. The two signs that appear to the left of the total probably signify 'total', as in Linear B (page 79). We can also identify a logogram 𐂏 (highlighted), which means 'wine' in Linear B. (It may picture a vine growing on a trellis.) If we postulate a general analogy between Linear A and Linear B tablets, this tablet is likely to concern amounts of wine given to or given by various named individuals at a certain place, which is thought to be named in the first line of the tablet.

A second tablet, without fractions, appears to count people, because it contains what appears (from various other lists in the tablets) to be the logogram for 'man':

The numerals here are 12, 12, 6, 24, 5, 3, 4, and the total is 66, which is correct. The seven separate entries may be, as John Chadwick suggests, "place names or descriptive titles, or even persons to whom the groups of men are assigned", though of course no one can be sure of this.

Linear A calculations are seldom so clear, however. The next Haghia Triada text (drawing first, standardized transcription second) appears to list pigs, judging from the pictogram at the top left-hand corner:

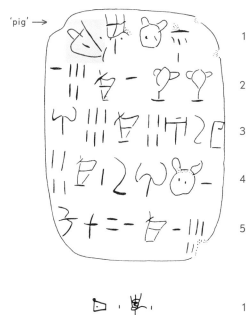

'pig' →

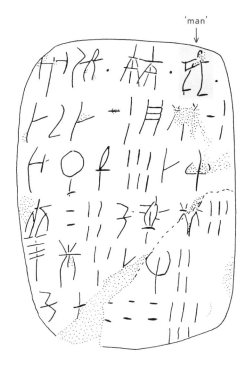

'man'

| | | | | |
|---|---|---|---|---|
| | | 𐝥 . 𐂚 . | | 1 |
| 𐘇 𐀮 | 15 | | 𐀳 10 | 1-2 |
| 𐀠 𐀠 𐀝 | 6 | | 𐀳 4 | 2-3 |
| 𐀳 𐘃 𐘖 | 4 | | 𐀳 1 | 3-4 |
| 𐘃 𐀝 𐘇 | 10 | | | 4 |
| 𐘖 𐘄 | 30 | | 𐀳 15[ | 5 |

Note that the Linear A scribe felt no necessity to write the numerals on the same line as the signs to which they refer. The signs and their accompanying numerals are separated, for example, between lines 1 and 2, and between lines 3 and 4, but not between lines 2 and 3 and lines 4 and 5—as you can see by comparing the tablet drawing with its standardized transcription (this splitting being evidence, incidentally, that the direction of Linear A writing is from left to right like Linear B, given that the breaks occur at the right-hand end of each line). Linear B scribes were more particular in this matter of splitting: they kept a sign group and its associated numeral on the same line of a tablet. Such untidiness, both in the grouping and in the draughtsmanship of the signs themselves, is typical of Linear A relative to Linear B. But we do not know what, if anything, this difference implies about the purposes for which the two scripts were used.

The column on the right of the transcription adds up to 15, but the column on the left does not add up to 30, indeed the 'total', 30, does not appear to relate to either column, unless one takes it to be the result of subtracting 10 from the sum of 15 + 6 + 4 + 10 + 4 + 1 = 40. Maurice Pope, who studied Linear A extensively after the decipherment of Linear B, has suggested one possible interpretation (along with Jacques Raison): that the column on the left refers to adult pigs and the one on the right to young ones. The numbers might then refer to 10 pigs withdrawn from the adult category as part of, say, a tax levy, leaving 30 pigs in total, of which 15 are young ones. But this would leave an inconsistency, as Pope and Raison themselves point out. It would mean that the sign 日 is used in two different ways: as part of an addition sum ('and 10//4//1 young ones'), and as an explanation ('including 15 young ones'). Perhaps scribal error is a better explanation of this tablet; such error is attested in the Linear B tablets.

A fourth, double-sided Haghia Triada tablet is interesting both for its totals and for the rest of its signs:

A

B

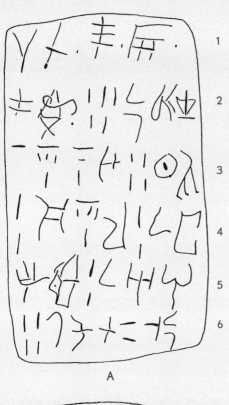

A

B

Here are the standardized tablet transcriptions:

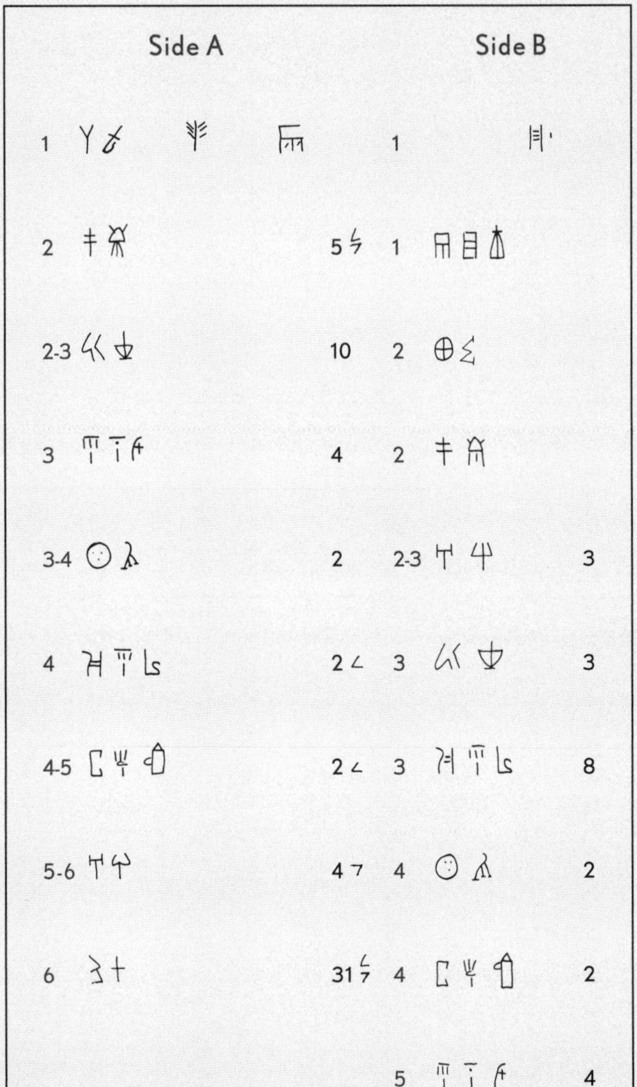

| | Side A | | | | Side B | |
|---|---|---|---|---|---|---|
| 1 | Y𝔶 | ⚘ | 𝌅 | 1 | | 𝌆· |
| 2 | ‡⚹ | | | 5𝌮 1 | | 𝌂𝌇𝌐 |
| 2-3 | ⟨⟨⚘ | | | 10 2 | | ⊕𝌟 |
| 3 | 𝌃𝌄𝆑 | | | 4 2 | | ‡𝌇 |
| 3-4 | ⊙𝆏 | | | 2 2-3 | | ⼦ ⚘ |
| 4 | 𝌅𝌃𝆑 | | | 2𝌮 3 | | ⟨⟨⚘ 3 |
| 4-5 | 𝌑⚹𝆑 | | | 2𝌮 3 | | 𝌅𝌃𝆑 8 |
| 5-6 | 𝌇⚘ | | | 4𝌰 4 | | ⊙𝆏 2 |
| 6 | 𝌾𝌴 | | | 31𝌮 4 | | 𝌑⚹𝆑 2 |
| | | | | 5 | | 𝌃𝌄𝆑 4 |
| | | | | 6 | | 𝌾𝌴 24 |

*Drawings and transcription of double-sided Haghia Triada tablet shown on page 189.*

The numerals on side A are 5 3/4, 10, 4, 2, 2 1/2, 2 1/2, 4 1/4, and the total is 31 3/4, which does not exactly match the given sum 31. The numerals on side B, on the other hand, 3, 3, 8, 2, 2, 2, 4, do exactly match the total 24—but it has to be admitted that these are partly conjectural, since side B is damaged. We do not know the reason for the inconsistency in side A. (Another scribal error, perhaps?)

If we compare all the signs on sides A and B, we find that seven sign groups are repeated:

This suggests that the two sides of the tablet refer to the same set of individuals but to different products, though as before we cannot be certain. The logogram at the top right of side A ⊞ is once again the sign that probably denotes 'wine', while that on side B ⊟· appears on other tablets but is of uncertain meaning.

Comparison of all the characters on sides A and B—or indeed on any of the Linear A tablets—with the sign list of Linear B (page 88) yields an important conclusion: the vast majority of the phonetic Linear A signs (if that is what they are) resemble those of Linear B. For example, the two Linear A signs ⊤ ⊬ closely resemble the Linear B signs for *a* and *ru*, and the three signs ⊓ ⊺ resemble the Linear B signs for *di, na, u*. In this way—equating unknown Linear A values with known Linear B values purely on the basis of the resemblance in *shape* of A and B signs—we can 'transliterate' (i.e. give phonetic values to) most, but not all, of the signs on sides A and B as shown in the drawing which appears in the next column:

| Side A | | | | | Side B | | | |
|---|---|---|---|---|---|---|---|---|
| sa | te | ⊞ | | | | | ⊟· | |
| pa de | | | 5 3/4 | | wa | ja | pi | |
| tu | | | 10 | | ka | | | |
| di na u | | | 4 | | pa de | | | |
| qe pu | | | 2 | | a ru | | | 3 |
| di ra | | | 2 1/2 | | tu | | | 3 |
| ta i | | | 2 1/2 | | di ra | | | 8 |
| a ru | | | 4 1/4 | | qe pu | | | 2 |
| ku ro | | | 31 3/4 | | ta i | | | 2 |
| | | | | | di na u | | | 4 |
| | | | | | ku ro | | | 24 |

Note carefully that the Linear A sign group denoting 'total' reads *ku-ro*; we shall return to this later.

If we count up the 'transliterated' signs, 20 out of 23 signs on side A appear in both Linear A and Linear B; only three signs are unique to Linear A. On side B, 22 out of 25 signs appear in both Linear

<table>
<tr><th colspan="2">Side A</th><th colspan="2">Side B</th></tr>
</table>

| Side A | | Side B | |
|---|---|---|---|
| 31  315  04  131a | | 56 | |
| 03  45 | 5 | 54  37  39 | |
| 306  69 | 10 | 77  305 | |
| 07  06  10 | 4 | 03  45 | |
| 78  50 | 2 | 08  26 | 3 |
| 324  07  60 | 2 | 306  69 | 3 |
| 59  28  123 | 2 | 324  07  60 | 8 |
| 08  26 | 4 | 78  50 | 2 |
| 81  02 | 31 | 59  28  123 | 2 |
| | | 07  06  10 | 4 |
| | | 81  02 | 24 |

A and B; again, only three are unique to Linear A. This proportion (80–90 per cent) is typical of the Linear A corpus. According to Bennett, about 50 out of the 60 'phonetic' Linear A signs (assuming that they are phonetic) resemble the syllabic signs of Linear B, and about 40 of the 60 Linear A logograms (e.g. 'wine') resemble Linear B logograms. Pope reckons that the two syllabaries, Linear A and B, differ "in about the same degree as the English and French alphabets in the 18th century—that is to say a difference of between 10% and 15% each way, English not having written accents and French not having the letters 'k' and 'w'."

But having noted these sign resemblances we must ask, is a comparison between the signs of Linear A and Linear B valid? Epigraphers generally treat sign resemblances between different scripts with great caution, because there is a high probability of coincidence and wishful thinking; Ventris, as we know, was reluctant to use the Cypriot script 'clue' in deciphering Linear B for precisely this reason, but eventually yielded to the temptation because there were good *historical* grounds for thinking that Cypriot had borrowed its signs from the Cretan script. Such a comparison is even better grounded, historically and culturally, in the case of the Etruscan and Greek alphabets. With Linear A and Linear B, given their similar dates of use and locations of discovery, sometimes even in the same excavation, there undoubtedly exist strong historical and cultural grounds for postulating similar sound values for similar-looking signs. But we must always bear in mind that this *is* an assumption; and that even if the assumption is correct, there may be certain Linear A and B signs that are 'false friends': they appear to be the same but in fact they have different values. As a reminder of this possibility, consider the Cyrillic alphabet used in Russia today, which obviously resembles the roman alphabet (because Cyrillic was derived from the Greek alphabet in the 9th century AD)—and yet the Cyrillic letters 'B', 'C', 'P' and 'X' stand for the sounds *v*, *s*, *r* and *h*.

So compelling is the Linear A/B sign resemblance that Linear A signs are labeled 'AB' and 'A' in the most widely used sign list of Linear A. The suggestion to introduce the AB label, originally made by Myres, has been followed by Louis Godart and Jean-Pierre Olivier, editors of the five-volume collection of Linear A inscriptions, *Recueil des Inscriptions en Linéaire A* (known familiarly as *GORILA*), who published the sign list in their fifth and final volume in 1985 (below). If we go back to the tablet just considered, and apply the *GORILA* sign list, we can now number a sign group such as ⟨sign⟩ as 08-26 (*a-ru* in Linear B) and a sign group such as ⟨sign⟩ as 07-06-10 (*di-na-u* in Linear B). The 'wine' logogram ⟨sign⟩ takes the number 131a, and is naturally an AB sign, since it is found in Linear B too. Every sign in the tablet may be labeled AB according to *GORILA*'s sign list, except for the few signs that appear only in Linear

| | | | | | | | | | | | |
|---|---|---|---|---|---|---|---|---|---|---|---|
| AB 01 | AB 21 | AB 31 | AB 54 | AB 76 | AB 123 | A 307 | A 318 | A 333 | A 348 cum 303 | A 363 | A 406 VAS |
| AB 02 | AB 21f | AB 34 | AB 55 | AB 77 | AB 131a | A 308 | A 319 | A 334 | A 349 | A 364 | A 407 VAS |
| AB 03 | AB 21m | AB 37 | AB 56 | AB 78 | AB 131b | A 309a | A 320 | A 335 | A 350 | A 365 | A 408 VAS |
| AB 04 | AB 22 | AB 38 | AB 57 | AB 79 | AB 131c | A 309b | A 321 | A 336 | A 351 cum 301 | A 366 | A 409 VAS |
| AB 05 | AB 22f | AB 39 | AB 58 | AB 80 | AB 164 | A 309c | A 322 | A 337 cum 188 | A 352 | A 367 | A 410 VAS |
| AB 06 | AB 22m | AB 40 | AB 59 | AB 81 | AB 171 | A 310 | A 323 | A 338 | A 353 | A 368 | A 411 VAS |
| AB 07 | AB 23 | AB 41 | AB 60 | AB 82 | AB 180 | A 311 cum 301 | A 324 | A 339 | A 354 | A 369 | A 412 VAS |
| AB 08 | AB 23m | AB 44 | AB 61 | AB 85 | AB 188 | A 312 | A 325 | A 340 | A 355 | A 370 | A 413 VAS |
| AB 09 | AB 24 | AB 45 | AB 65 | AB 86 | AB 191 | A 313a cum 100/102 | A 326 | A 341 cum 39 | A 356 | A 371 | A 414 VAS |
| AB 10 | AB 26 | AB 46 | AB 66 | AB 87 | A 301 | A 313b cum 100/102 | A 327 | A 342 | A 357 | A 400 VAS | A 415 VAS |
| AB 11 | AB 27 | AB 47 | AB 67 | A 100/102 | A 302 | A 313c cum 100/102 | A 328 | A 343 | A 358 | A 401 VAS | A 416 VAS |
| AB 13 | AB 28 | AB 49 | AB 69 | A 118 | A 303 | A 314 | A 329 | A 344 | A 359 | A 402 VAS | A 417 VAS |
| AB 16 | AB 28b | AB 50 | AB 70 | AB 120 | A 304 | A 315 | A 330 cum 01 and 31 | A 345 | A 360 | A 403 VAS | A 418 VAS |
| AB 17 | A 29 | AB 51 | AB 73 | A 120b | A 305 | A 316 | A 331 | A 346 | A 361 | A 404 VAS | |
| AB 20 | AB 30 | AB 53 | AB 74 | AB 122 | A 306 | A 317 | A 332 | A 347 | A 362 | A 405 VAS | |

'Simple' signs in Linear A, drawn by Louis Godart and Jean-Pierre Olivier (in GORILA). Signs labeled with A are found only in Linear A, while those labeled with AB are found in both Linear A and B; compare these with the Linear B sign list on page 88. (The precise forms of many signs are disputed by scholars, and some oppose the AB classification.)

A, which are. numbered as follows:

A305    A306    A315    A324

If we examine the list of so-called 'simple' signs in *GORILA*, just reproduced, we notice that most of the signs in the left-hand portion are AB signs, and these are numbered in the same way as Linear B signs—hence the gaps between, for example, signs 13 and 16 or 70 and 73: there are no Linear A signs that resemble signs 14, 15, 71 and 72 of Linear B. Of the total number of signs, 178, nearly half of them, that is 80 signs, have been labeled AB, of which 69 function as syllabic signs in Linear B and 11 as logograms. Thus Godart/Olivier (some of whose work has been criticized by other experts) detect more resemblance between Linear A and B *phonetic* signs than does Bennett (page 192), and less resemblance between the A and B *logograms*. The discrepancy arises because the judgement of whether or not an A and a B sign are equivalent is based partly on shape, which involves a subjective element, and partly on similarity of context of the sign in the inscriptions (and hence its hypothesized function), in which scholarly judgements naturally may differ too.

Let us now take a look at some of the other evidence for the correctness of the idea that Linear B values may be applied to Linear A signs. The methods used by Ventris in deciphering Linear B are relevant here. For instance, we can search the corpus for Linear A words of some length differing only in one or perhaps two signs, which may be evidence of variant spellings of the same word, and also of inflection. Alas, there is not nearly enough material to set up the kind of inflectional parallels used by Kober (the Linear B 'triplets' on page 90), but there are several good

examples, the most suggestive of which takes the form of three Linear A words:

*a-sa-sa-ra-me*
*ja-sa-sa-ra-me*
*ja-sa-sa-ra-ma-na*

Here the same word seems to be spelled either with an initial *a-* or an initial *ja-*, pronounced *ya* as in German 'ja'. "Not only are the sounds very much alike, but we have a similar alternation in Linear B", Chadwick observed. Other examples include *pi-ta-ka-si* / *pi-ta-ke-si* and *ku-do-ni* / *ka-u-do-ni*.

What is more, when Linear A sign groups transliterated with Linear B values are compared with sign groups of known value in Linear B (rather than with other Linear A sign groups as done above), we find a remarkable number of 'doublets' or alternations, such as the following (there are many others):

| Linear A | Linear B |
|----------|----------|
| *ka-sa-ru* | *ka-sa-ro* |
| *di-de-ru* | *di-de-ro* |
| *qa-qa-ru* | *qa-qa-ro* |
| *pa-ja-re* | *pa-ja-ro* |
| *te-ja-re* | *te-ja-ro* |
| *sa-ma-ro* | *sa-ma-ra, sa-ma-ri-jo* |
| *da-mi-nu* | *da-mi-ni-jo, da-mi-ni-ja* |
| *ku-do-ni* | *ku-do-ni-jo, ku-do-ni-ja* |

The last forms, ending in *-jo* and *-ja*, recall those discovered by Ventris (page 99) in the proper names written in Linear B on the Knossos tablets. Proper names (of places or of persons) are precisely where one might anticipate overlaps between languages (e.g. the English town Chester/Roman 'castra', English Henry/French Henri). In the Linear A/B case, it is likely that some of the names used in Minoan Crete (which were presumably recorded in Linear A) would have continued in use after the Greek conquest of

Crete and the invention of Linear B. For instance, it is significant that many of the Linear A ('Minoan') words ending in -u appear in Linear B (Greek) with an -o ending, as if the Minoan name was changed to fit a common archaic Greek declensional type ending in -o (compare classical Greek ending -os). Analysis of the Linear A corpus shows that the frequency of the vowel u is much higher than in Linear B, and the frequency of the vowel o is much lower. (Vowel frequency analysis shows also significant differences between the spelling of Linear B proper names at Knossos and at mainland Pylos, a pattern we might expect from the likelihood of 'Minoan' influence on the Knossos names but not on the Pylos names.)

Coincidence was not excluded here, however, and so in the late 1960s a young Harvard University doctoral student with an interest in classics and computing, David Packard (son of the cofounder of Hewlett-Packard) decided to conduct as rigorous a statistical analysis as possible of the Linear A inscriptions then available. Following the tradition of Kober and Bennett in the Linear B story, Packard wanted to discover in a scientific manner if the Ventris/Chadwick phonetic values alone, and no other set of values, when substituted in Linear A, would produce the patterns seen in Linear A/Linear B 'doublets'. He therefore constructed nine so-called 'false decipherments' in which no Linear A sign took the same value in any two of the 'false decipherments', and which allowed for the fact that the frequency of Linear A signs differed and was also position dependent (as could be ascertained by counting occurrences in the corpus, regardless of the signs' phonetic values). The details of Packard's technique are too complex to explain briefly, but its importance is that when he used a computer to apply his nine 'decipherments' to the Linear A corpus, the results were statistically significant. Although Packard was careful to note in his published study that "my conclusions do not possess any special validity simply because a computer was involved", it was clear that the Ventris/Chadwick values produced 'doublets' much more frequently than any of his other 'decipherments'. Moreover, only these values produced strong evidence for the overlap in place names and personal names (mentioned above) being confined to Crete. Therefore it was reasonable to assume that Linear B values were generally applicable to Linear A. (Packard's work on Linear A was fruitful in other ways too, but his key finding is the applicability of Linear B values to the undeciphered script.)

Subsequent work on deciphering Linear A has proceeded on this assumption. Attention and debate have concentrated on two disputed tablets from Haghia Triada, HT 86 and HT 31. The signs on side A of HT 86, as drawn and transcribed in *GORILA*, are shown below and over page:

The sign (120 in the *GORILA* sign list) has been taken to be the logogram for 'grain' in Linear B, although the resemblance is not exact. The three-sign group that precedes it (highlighted), 81-30-58, may be read as *ku-ni-su*. Now to revert for a moment to Linear B, in a Linear B tablet from Mycenae the 'grain' logogram appears, following two syllabic signs and before a numeral:

These Linear B signs are pronounced *si-to*, a word which must mean 'grain' ('sitos' in classical Greek). Thus, by analogy with the Linear B inscription—so the argument goes—the Linear A sign group must mean 'grain', too. What makes this identification especially enticing is that there is a word 'kun(n)isu' in a Semitic language (Akkadian) of the right period which means 'emmer wheat'. Some scholars have therefore jumped to the conclusion that the language of Linear A must be of a Semitic type—a hypothesis we shall return to.

Critics of this analogy with Linear B have been numerous, leave aside altogether the Semitic 'identification'. For a start, we have no independent evidence for the Linear A values *ni* and *su*; the values rely entirely on the assumption that Linear B values apply to Linear A. More important, the sequence, syllabic signs + logogram + numeral, common in Linear B (e.g. the tablet with four-handled cups on page 101), is completely *unknown* in Linear A, where one finds only the coupling, syllabic signs + numeral, and the logogram (e.g. 'man', 'wine', 'pig') is written separately, often at or near the top of the tablet. Most damaging of all to the theory, the three-sign group 81-30-58 occurs elsewhere in the Linear A corpus in contexts that make it probable that it does *not* mean 'grain'. For example, the following tablet from Haghia Triada, in which the repeated sign group is highlighted:

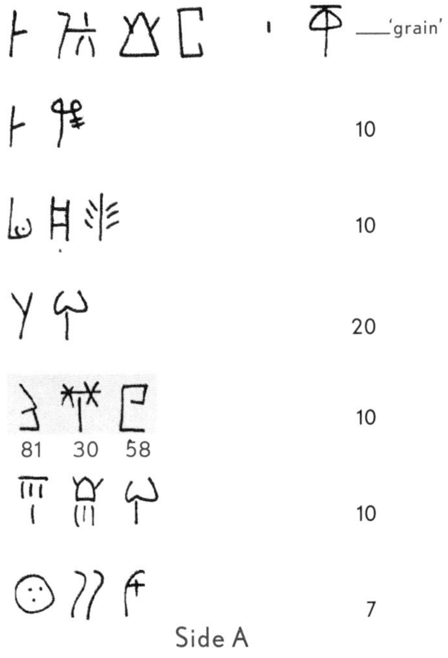

10

[ ]

10

20

81 30 58
10

10

7

**Side B**

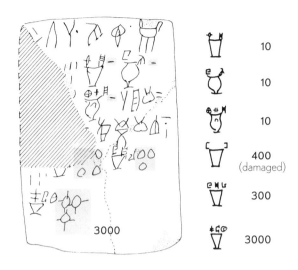

10

10

10

400
(damaged)

300

3000

3000

Although we cannot be sure, this tablet, which also appears to concern grain judging from the logogram in the top right-hand corner of side A, is believed to be a list of names (some of which appear on other tablets also). If they are *names*, they clearly cannot be commodities too, such as grain. If on the other hand they are commodities, then it seems strange that the tablet is headed by a sign referring to 'grain'. It is conceivable that the various words on the tablet refer to different *types* of grain, but this does not seem a likely explanation.

The second important disputed Linear A tablet, HT 31 (above right), shows what is unquestionably a series of vessels with numerals (highlighted) written beside them that count as high as 3000. Crucially, five of the vessels have small words written above them (see transcription with numerals to the right of the next tablet):

Let Chadwick describe the controversy:

" Much debate has raged over the question whether these words describe the vessels or their contents—no other choice appears open. I believe that they are the names of the vessels, for two reasons: the numerals with each vessel are ranged in ascending order, the last being no less than 3000; this suggests that the vessels are in descending order of size. Yet all the pictograms are of roughly equal size—hence descriptive terms are needed to prevent a beaker being confused with a bucket. Secondly, Linear B parallels exist where pictograms of vessels are accompanied by their descriptions in words; none has notes of contents—in such cases it is made plain that the container is a mere measure. "

The words can be read with Linear B values in the usual way, but not without difficulty, because the sign ᛄ, which occurs in three of the words, is very rare in Linear B and thus has an insecure phonetic value, perhaps resembling *pa*. Substituting values for the rest of the signs gives:

qa-Ħ

su-pu

ka-ro-Ħ

su-Ħ-ra

pa-ta-qe

Supplying the reasonably conjectured value *pa* for Ħ, a few scholars, beginning with Cyrus Gordon, have produced words which supposedly conform to known Semitic names for vessels, such as 'supu' and 'supala' ('r' and 'l' are not distinguished in Linear B and thus arguably not in Linear A) and 'karopa'—compare our 'beaker', 'tumbler', 'bucket' and so on. Most scholars remain unconvinced that this is anything more than a coincidence, however. James Hooker, a University of London classicist spoke for the consensus when he said: "Resemblances [in vocabulary] can always be found, but their existence proves nothing unless they can be shown to conform to a system—and a system which is compatible with one language or linguistic group and with no other. It was a demonstration of this order which Ventris carried out for the Linear B script".

Turning finally to the language of Linear A, it is a fact that well over a dozen candidate languages have been pressed into service by would-be decipherers of 'Minoan'; and of course the very notion of a related language excludes the possibility that 'Minoan', like Etruscan, may have been an isolate. The most seriously pursued comparisons have

been the following three languages or language groups: Semitic, Greek (i.e. the language of Linear B) and Anatolian (Indo-European). They are all possible to the extent that these languages, or their archaic dialects, were spoken around the eastern Mediterranean in the 2nd millennium BC when Linear A was in use. The difficulty is, there is insufficient evidence from the Linear A inscriptions to rule any of these languages in or out conclusively. Let us briefly consider the probability for each relationship in turn.

The chief evidence for the Semitic hypothesis is the observation that the common Linear A sign pair that apparently signifies 'total', Ⴢ †, may be read as *ku-ro* (or *ku-lo*) with Linear B values (remember that *r* and *l* are not distinguished in Linear B). The Semitic root for 'all' is *kl*, with vowels unrepresented in the Semitic script as usual (Semitic *kl* is actually pronounced like English 'col'). Is there a genuine link between *ku-ro/ku-lo* ('total') and *kl* ('all')? Specialists in Semitic are impressed, but as Yves Duhoux, a Belgian scholar of Linear A, points out, there is no Semitic word comparable to *po-to-ku-ro*, which appears to mean 'grand total' in certain Linear A tablets: "This...shows how quickly an interpretation may reveal its limits." Furthermore, the lack of vowels in Semitic scripts, in *contrast* with Linear A/B, means that the Semitic spelling rules are rather flexible, and the scope for ingenious comparison of Semitic words with Linear A words is proportionately greater. Since the (often extravagant) claims of Semitic supporters rest almost entirely on a handful of words, apart from 'kuro', that are supposedly equivalent in Linear A and various Semitic languages (such as Akkadian)—i.e. the familiar 'etymological' approach to decipherment without any evidence of *structural* similarity—the Semitic hypothesis has been nearly universally rejected.

Greek has been seriously advanced in the past by several scholars, notably Gregory Nagy of Harvard University, in a detailed article entitled "Greek-like elements in Linear A", written in 1963. But the hypothesis stumbles badly on *ku-ro*, one of the few relatively certain identifications of a Linear A word. This reading is totally different from the Linear B (early Greek) word for 'total', *to-so* (page 191)–an observation first made by Kober in the 1940s; and *ku-ro* cannot be reconstructed as any Greek word of suitable meaning similar to 'total' without doing violence to common sense and logic. For instance, Nagy tries to relate *ku-ro* to the root of Greek 'kolōne' and 'kolōnos', meaning 'peak' (and hence inferred 'total') by suggesting that *ku-ro* is an abbreviation and that there is a "*u = o/u* ambivalence" in Linear A (i.e. 'o' and 'u' are interchangeable as in an English spelling variant like 'ae/e' in the words encyclopaedia/encyclopedia), to account for the Linear A > Greek vowel change k*u* > k*o*. But no one has ever suggested that Linear B *to-so* is an abbreviation–for the obvious reason that it makes perfect sense (in relation to classical Greek 'tosos') just as it is. According to Chadwick, who specialized in early Greek, "there is one deduction which is immediately possible: the language [of Linear A] cannot be Greek." Only a few scholars, including a determined Pope, would disagree with this statement.

The Anatolian hypothesis is reasonable on historical and archaeological grounds. Herodotus, in the 5th century BC, noted that "The Lycians [of south-west Anatolia] are in good truth anciently from Crete." And as we know, Linear A was recently found in Anatolia (at the site of ancient Miletus). Of the half-dozen or so ancient Anatolian languages, Lycian is the currently favored candidate for the Linear A language. According to Margalit Finkelberg of Tel Aviv University, who bases her view on comparisons between the structure of Anatolian languages and apparently related structures in Linear A inscriptions, the Linear A language shows an agglutinative structure with chains of 'particles' peculiar to Anatolian languages, and to Lycian more than any other Anatolian language. While her argument has received some support from the Anatolian philologist Craig Melchert, the fact remains that it rests on a very small number of Linear A inscriptions, and that the structure of Lycian is not well understood, unlike the Semitic languages (and of course Greek). The case for Anatolian must remain therefore unproven, if much more probable than that for Semitic and Greek.

Overall, the decipherment of Linear A remains hamstrung by lack of inscriptions. There is enough evidence of various kinds to be reasonably confident that Linear B phonetic values are applicable to the majority of Linear A inscriptions. Beyond this, scholars can only continue to subject the inscriptions we have to further study with the expectation of "minimal results"–to quote a pessimistic Olivier, one of the editors of *GORILA*. But given the discoveries in the field during the past few decades, one can reasonably hope for new discoveries of inscriptions. As a more positive Tom Palaima remarked in the 1980s in a review of *GORILA*, the very existence of its five volumes of tablets and analysis, and the recent publication of other Linear A research tools, "invite Aegean prehistorians to continue in the directions taken by Linear B studies and Mycenaean archaeology... It may no longer even be too optimistic to look forward to the publication of *Linear A and Minoan Prehistory: A 2016 Survey*."

# Secrets of the Ancient Ledgers

# VII

# THE PROTO-ELAMITE SCRIPT

P roto-Elamite is the world's oldest undeciphered script, assuming that it is a fully developed writing system—which is by no means certain. If it could be deciphered, it is therefore likely to tell us more about the origin(s) of writing than any of the other undeciphered scripts in this book, just as the even older, largely deciphered proto-cuneiform script found at Uruk in neighboring Sumer has done (pages 24-26).

The proto-Elamite script was used for a brief period 5000 years ago, *c.* 3050-2900 BC, in Elam, the biblical name for the province of Persia and the area known to the classical geographers as Susiana from the name of its ancient capital Susa; Elam corresponds very roughly to the region of today's oil fields in western Iran. The script, however, seems to have been used over a much wider area than Elam, because it has been found as far east as the Iranian border with Afghanistan. Little is known from archaeology or other written sources about the people who wrote the script.

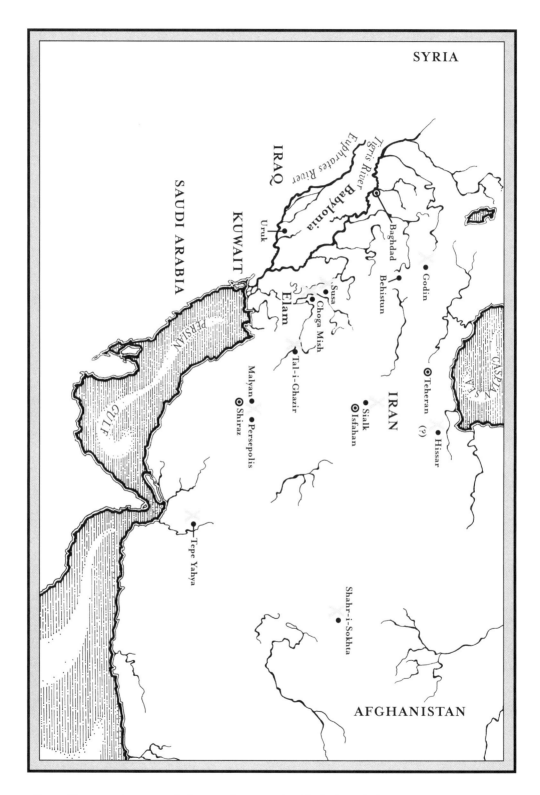

*Proto-Elamite settlements on the Iranian plateau, with tablet finds marked.*

**Obverse**

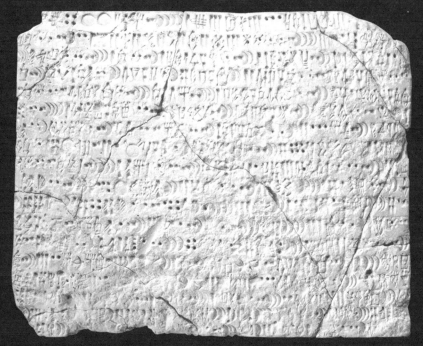

**Reverse**

*Proto-Elamite account text, obverse and reverse, from Susa, c. 3000 BC. It was found by French excavators in the early 20th century and is now in the Louvre in Paris. Much of the proto-Elamite numerical system is understood, but the language is totally unknown. The reverse shows the impression of a cylinder seal, made by rolling the seal over the wet clay.*

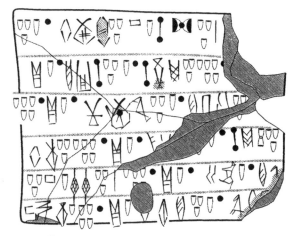

Proto-Elamite

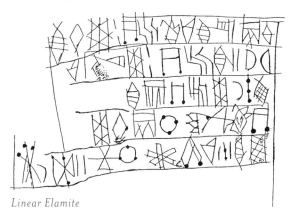

Linear Elamite

Elamite cuneiform

*The scripts of Elam. From top to bottom: proto-Elamite, linear Elamite and Elamite cuneiform. Proto-Elamite was used from c. 3050–2900 BC, Linear Elamite only around 2150 BC and Elamite cuneiform from the 13th century BC onwards; the cuneiform inscription is from the palace of Darius at Persepolis, c. 500 BC. Scholars formerly assumed that there was a linguistic relationship, perhaps even the same language, connecting the three scripts— particularly the earliest two scripts—but today this theory seems unlikely, especially given the large chronological gaps in the written record.*

brief period, c. 2150 BC. Linear Elamite in turn preceded Elamite cuneiform, which the Elamites used from the 13th century BC for many centuries; it was one of the three cuneiform scripts (the other two being Babylonian and Old Persian) inscribed by Darius c. 500 BC at Persepolis and on the famous cliff at Behistun north-west of Elam: the trilingual inscription that proved vital to the decipherment of Babylonian cuneiform in the 19th century. Hence there are three 'Elamite' scripts, each separated by about 800 years with no textual evidence pertaining to the time gaps.

The proto-Elamite corpus is a substantial one (much bigger than the Linear A corpus, for example): almost 1500 texts, containing some 100,000 characters, even if many of them are so badly damaged they are known only from reconstructions. Linear Elamite, by contrast, can boast only 22 documents. Yet ironically, Linear Elamite is somewhat better understood than proto-Elamite, since some of its few inscriptions are bilinguals (the second, known, language/script being Akkadian cuneiform). The proto-Elamite script, on the other hand, lacks bilinguals, and its language is totally unknown.

The prefix proto- is used by scholars because the script preceded a much later script known as Linear (Old) Elamite, also found at Susa, which was used by the ruler Puzur-Insusinak, again for a

*A bilingual dedication in Akkadian cuneiform (top) and Linear Elamite (bottom) from Susa, c. 2150 BC. The cuneiform identifies the dedicator as Puzur–Insusinak. The well–understood Akkadian inscription has enabled scholars partially to decipher the Linear Elamite inscription. There are no equivalent bilinguals for the older proto–Elamite script, a lack that has hindered its decipherment in comparison with Linear Elamite.*

The relationship between proto-Elamite and Linear Elamite is controversial. The French excavator of proto-Elamite in the early 20th century, Vincent Scheil, was convinced that they shared the same Elamite language and that the later script had developed from the earlier. Subsequent scholars agreed, which is why the term proto-Elamite was first introduced in 1949. But since the 1980s, two leading specialists in Elam, the archaeologist Dan Potts (of the University of Sydney) and the epigrapher Robert Englund (a Berlin scholar now at the University of California), have become increasingly persuaded that there is no evidence for a shared language and culture.

Although one must be careful in drawing conclusions about two cultures from the nature of their respective writing systems–after all, Egyptian demotic and Meroitic cursive differ radically but there are strong similarities in underlying culture–it is nevertheless noteworthy that there are perhaps 1000 signs in proto-Elamite (the latest estimate), while there are only about 80 signs (most of them presumably syllabic) in Linear Elamite. There are also few convincing graphic similarities between the two scripts, despite claims of up to 35 signs in common which rest on the usual doubtful premises in comparing sign shapes. A much more important piece of evidence is that attempts to substitute Linear Elamite phonetic values for graphically similar proto-Elamite signs (on the Linear B/A model), in the hope of producing recognizable names in proto-Elamite inscriptions, have failed: which suggests that the two languages are different. Potts therefore emphatically rejects the "so-called" proto-Elamite script and prefers instead to speak neutrally of "Susa III" texts (i.e. texts from level III at Susa), without implying any connection between these texts and the later texts of Elam. In *The Archaeology of Elam* (1999), he writes:

> ❝ No one would ever argue that the prehistoric vestiges of the Susa I settlement were in any sense ancestral to the palace built there by the Achaemenid Persian king Darius or that the latter was ancestral to the château constructed by the late-19th-century French excavators. Why, then, should we assume that the Susa III texts have anything to do with the later Elamite language or people? In fact, nothing suggests that either the writing system or language of the Old [Linear] Elamite texts was lineally descended from those of Susa III. ❞

Even so, responded the Harvard University archaeologist, Carl Lamberg-Karlovsky (who excavated some proto-Elamite tablets at Tepe Yahya in the 1970s), "One wonders what language other than Elamite the proto-Elamite texts could refer to in light of the fact that they are distributed over precisely the same geographical region in which Elamite was later spoken."

If the connection with Linear Elamite is contested, and on balance probably implausible, proto-Elamite's link with the proto-cuneiform script of Mesopotamia (which was used to write Sumerian), is highly probable. The tablets from Uruk, generally thought to show the beginning of 'full' writing, as we know, date from 3300 BC or soon after, and are therefore a century or two older than those from Susa. In general appearance, the two sets of tablets undoubtedly resemble each other: both seem to consist of lists of objects and people with numerical calculations and to use similar symbols. There are differences in layout, notably the fact that lines are used for entries in proto-Elamite but not in proto-cuneiform, which makes the proto-Elamite script more linear than the earlier script; but even a brief examination suggests that both sets of tablets are forms of archaic book-keeping.

The characters look more abstract in proto-Elamite, however, as one might expect from the fact that it developed after proto-cuneiform. Thus one does not find in proto-Elamite the kind of clearly pictographic representation seen in the two proto-cuneiform tablets opposite. The tablet at the top deals with barley, and the one at the bottom with the disbursement of rations, pictured as 'head' + 'rationing vessel' = 'disbursement'.

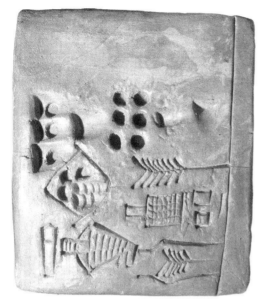

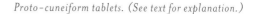

*Proto-cuneiform tablets. (See text for explanation.)*

Yet there are a few clear resemblances between proto-Elamite signs and the more abstract of the proto-cuneiform signs:

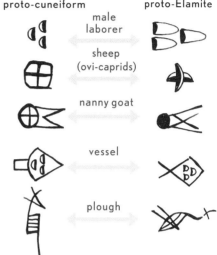

The proto-Elamite meanings, deduced from the context of these signs on the tablets as well as from their graphic similarity to proto-cuneiform signs, are not definite. But even if they and others are correct, Englund estimates that only about 1 per cent of the proto-Elamite signs can be definitely related to signs in proto-cuneiform. (A few other signs are pictorially unrecognizable but may be the result of defective borrowing from the Mesopotamian script.)

Proto-Elamite tablets were written from right to left and from top to bottom, and both sides of a tablet were used (as in proto-cuneiform). At the bottom of the obverse, the tablet was rotated about its horizontal axis, and inscribing continued along the top edge of the reverse. But if it was a summation of the obverse that was to be entered on the reverse, the tablet would instead be rotated about its vertical axis, as in the diagram over page. (This fact helps decipherers to distinguish summations.)

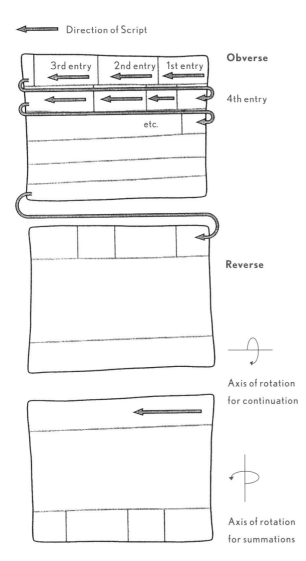

Direction of Script

**Obverse**

3rd entry | 2nd entry | 1st entry

4th entry

etc.

**Reverse**

Axis of rotation
for continuation

Axis of rotation
for summations

*The direction of reading of a proto–Elamite tablet.*

Decipherment of proto-Elamite has been hampered by various factors. As already remarked, there is effectively no help available from the underlying language since we know nothing about it (unlike that of proto-cuneiform); neither are there any bilinguals. Then there is the content of the tablets—self-evidently lists and calculations as in proto-cuneiform—which warns us that the correlation between the script and the spoken language may not be an exact one (how much could we learn of a modern spoken language working only from a series of supermarket till receipts?). Furthermore, there are no lexical lists, only lists of people and objects, so far as we can tell. In Mesopotamia, there was a lexicographical tradition of copying lists of words, as in a dictionary, adhering to the same sequence of words over periods of up to 1000 years and more; these lexical lists were of much assistance in identifying in the proto-cuneiform corpus scribal variants, which are of course valuable in decipherment.

The various attempts at compiling a proto-Elamite sign list have therefore relied mainly on internal analysis of the characters. One compiled in 1949 contained as many as 5500 signs, a few of which are shown opposite.

The high number of signs, 5500, did not by itself mean that some of them must be allographs—the Chinese and Japanese scripts have even more signs than this—but careful inspection reveals that many of the signs are highly similar and some are mirror images (highlighted). The Italian scholar Piero Meriggi, in the 1970s, managed to reduce the total number to the 1000 or so proto-Elamite signs already mentioned, but only by making a number of untenable assumptions as to how signs were to be interpreted; he was also seriously in error about the numerical system. Although Englund and his collaborators have been working on an improved sign list since the 1980s, it is far from completion.

In the absence of the usual aids to decipherment, it is the numerals that have enabled real progress to be made with proto-Elamite in the

*Part of a sign list of proto–Elamite compiled in 1949 (now superseded).*

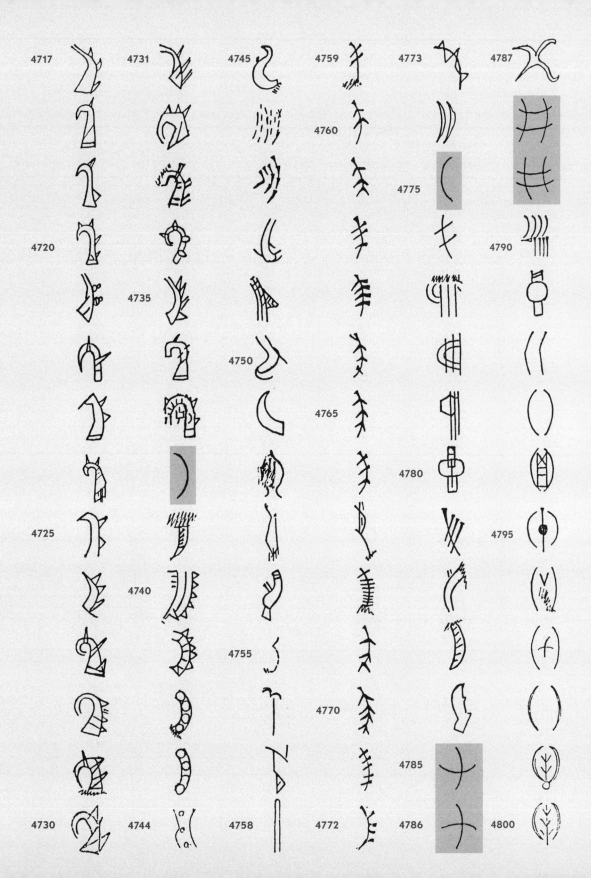

1980s and 90s. Once the subtleties of the various proto-Elamite counting systems could be established, relationships between various logographic signs standing for objects and people being counted became clear (or at least clearer), and reasonable guesses could sometimes be made about their meaning. Unlike epigraphic analysis of every other undeciphered script, the proto-Elamite decipherment has therefore turned into a minor branch of the history of mathematics. While this is of no help to those who want to know what the underlying language is, it does make sense of much in the tablets and is therefore a valid type of decipherment. It may seem arcane, but it need not be dull, as Englund and his Berlin colleagues Hans Nissen and Peter Damerow proved in their fascinating unraveling of the proto-cuneiform and proto-Elamite texts, published as *Archaic Bookkeeping*– perhaps the most important book on the origins of writing yet written.

The French excavator Scheil was the first to tackle the numerals, in the early decades of the 20th century. Unfortunately, he made a major mistake: he tried to combine what were in fact a variety of numerical notations in use in Mesopotamia and Elam into a single 'decimal' system. His model was the ancient Egyptian system, as opposed to the sexagesimal system favored in ancient Babylon, which one might think was a more likely candidate on historical and geographical grounds. "His projection into the archaic period of a modern abstract conception of number, and thus of a unified numerical sign system, is understandable in an age which had yet little experience with a comparative ethnology of early arithmetical technologies," write Damerow and Englund. The regrettable effect, though, was to stymie understanding of proto-Elamite numerals for about half a century.

Scheil's basic error was to assume that the sign ● had the same decimal value when representing grain measures as when representing numbers of discrete objects:

$$● = 10 \times \triangleright$$

whereas in fact, the grain measurement system was sexagesimal:

$$● = 6 \times \triangleright$$

The truth was discovered by the Swedish mathematician Jöran Friberg, who explained the essentials of the proto-Elamite system of measuring capacity in a report in 1978. Writing about it later in *Scientific American*, he mentioned a second discovery he had made, which was just as significant: "the proto-Elamites (but not the proto-Sumerians) used the sexagesimal number system only when they were counting people or inanimate objects such as loaves of bread or clay vessels. When they were counting animals, they worked with a decimal number system!" So Scheil was not wholly in error.

Friberg was right about the use of both a sexagesimal and a decimal system in the proto-Elamite script but not in proto-cuneiform. However he himself was incorrect in saying that the decimal system was used only for counting animals. This has been demonstrated by the detailed studies of Damerow and Englund, who have shown that proto-Elamite laborers too were counted in the decimal system. Gaps and inconsistencies remain in the Damerow/Englund scheme, but many of the proto-Elamite summations have been accounted for in a consistent way.

Consider the tablet opposite from Susa, which was inscribed on the obverse, then turned about its vertical axis and inscribed on the reverse with its summation.

|  | Obverse | Reverse |
|---|---|---|

"heading" (function
of the tablet)

designation of the
foremen:

number of subordinate
workers:

male
laborers:

total of the
laborers:

94  +  69  +  147  +  44  +  50  +  112  +  75  =  591

---

The calculation appears to concern a work gang of male laborers, who are symbolized by the sign:

It is based on a decimal system of numerals:

| sign | | value |
|---|---|---|
|  | = | 1 |
|  | = | 10 |
|  | = | 100 |
|  | = | 1000 |
|  | = | 10,000 |

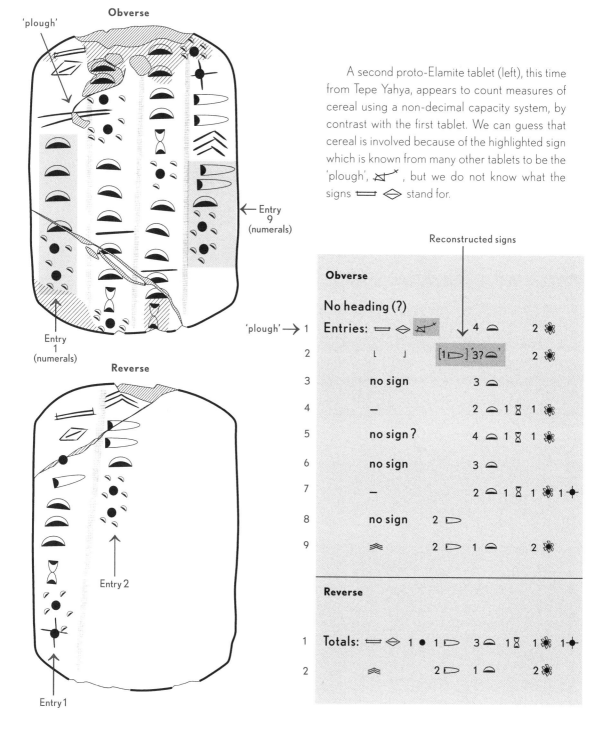

**Obverse**

'plough'

Entry 9 (numerals)

Entry 1 (numerals)

**Reverse**

Entry 2

Entry 1

A second proto-Elamite tablet (left), this time from Tepe Yahya, appears to count measures of cereal using a non-decimal capacity system, by contrast with the first tablet. We can guess that cereal is involved because of the highlighted sign which is known from many other tablets to be the 'plough', , but we do not know what the signs stand for.

Reconstructed signs

**Obverse**

No heading (?)

| | | | | |
|---|---|---|---|---|
| 'plough' → 1 | Entries: | | 4 | 2 |
| 2 | | [1 ] 3? | | 2 |
| 3 | no sign | | 3 | |
| 4 | – | | 2 1 1 | |
| 5 | no sign? | | 4 1 1 | |
| 6 | no sign | | 3 | |
| 7 | – | | 2 1 1 1 | |
| 8 | no sign | 2 | | |
| 9 | | | 2 1 | 2 |

**Reverse**

| | | | | |
|---|---|---|---|---|
| 1 | Totals: | 1 1 3 1 1 1 | | |
| 2 | | 2 1 | 2 | |

For some unknown reason, there are *two* totals on the reverse. Total 2 applies to entry 9 on the obverse and is straightforward to understand by simply comparing the entries. Total 1 is more complex. It is the summation of entries 1-8. You can work this out as follows. First add up each sign in entries 1-8 and you get:

3 ▷    21 ⌒    3 ⧗    7 ✻    1 ◆

Then convert this total using the following non-decimal system:

● $\overset{6}{\longleftarrow}$ ▷ $\overset{5}{\longleftarrow}$ ⌒ $\overset{2}{\longleftarrow}$ ⧗ $\overset{3}{\longleftarrow}$ ✻

(It may help to think of ✻ = X, therefore ⧗ = **3**X, ⌒ = **6**X, ▷ = **30**X, ● = **180**X. Thus the above total equals:

|  |  |  |
|---|---|---|
| 3 times 30X | = | 90X |
| 21 times 6X | = | 126X |
| 3 times 3X | = | 9X |
| 7 times X | = | 7X |
| | **TOTAL** | **232X** |

Now calculate the total on the reverse:

1 ●    1 ▷    3 ⌒    1 ⧗    1 ✻    1 ◆

in the same way, and you should get 232, which equals the total on the obverse.)

The weakness here is that two of the signs in obverse entry 2 have been reconstructed. To check whether the reconstruction is right, "requires a collation of the original in the Teheran museum", say Damerow and Englund. (Unsurprisingly, excavation and scholarly work on this subject in Iran came to a halt with the Islamic revolution in 1979.)

A third tablet, from Susa (see next page), which has been reconstructed by Nissen, Damerow and Englund (the drawings show their reconstruction,

not the actual tablet obverse and reverse), concerns two labor gangs' grain rations, which are probably symbolized by ▷◫ .

Here, the laborers are counted in the *decimal* system and the rations are measured in the *sexagesimal* system, in which ● = 6 ▷. The tablet "reveals with a certain degree of clarity the hierarchical structure of the labor gangs," explain the authors of *Archaic Bookkeeping*:

    ❝ Two individuals stood at the top of the hierarchy attested by this text. Both probably functioned as chief supervisors of the registered laborers. Of special interest are the people under the control of the first supervisor, since it seems that they actually formed together a full force of laborers, whereas the second supervisor only administered the remainder of the listed workmen. The first labor force can be qualified as a century, since it consisted of ten gangs, of ten laborers each plus one foreman, thus forming together eleven individuals per gang. That number was recorded after the name of every foreman. The reverse side of the tablet with the totals accordingly records a sum of 111 laborers for the first chief supervisor, that is, the total of all gangs together with their respective foreman and the chief supervisor himself. ❞

As for the rations, two labor gangs, consisting of 22 individuals in all, are shown to receive a measure of 1● + 5 ▷ (= 11 ▷); all ten gangs receive a measure of 9 ● +1 ▷ ( = 55 ▷). In other words, every laborer received half of the measure represented by ▷ . If the capacity units were the same in the proto-Elamite system as in proto-cuneiform, this amount would be about 12 litres (per month?—we do not know)—which is half of what a laborer seems to have received in

Mesopotamia, judging from proto-cuneiform tablets. In other words, it seems to have been an underfed life as a laborer in ancient Elam. But in fact there are indications that the units of capacity in Mesopotamia and Elam differed, despite the structural identity of their capacity systems, so the laborer in Elam may perhaps have had more to eat than first implied.

*The hierarchy of work in ancient Elam. (See previous page for explanation.)*

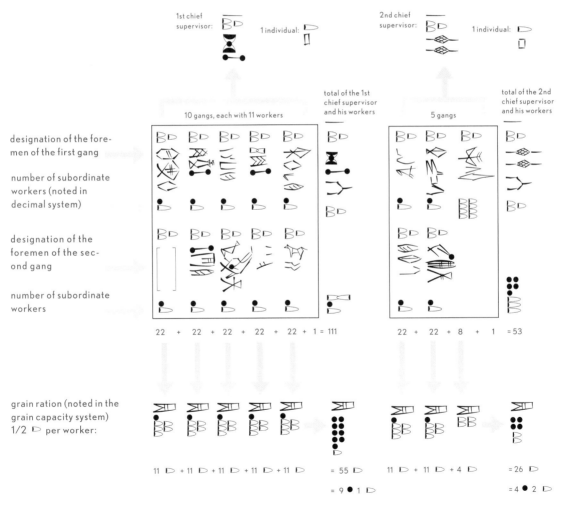

The full picture of the numerical systems in proto-Elamite worked out by Friberg, Damerow and Englund is actually even more diverse than indicated above. There is no need to give further examples from the tablets, but it is worth summarizing the different systems to give an idea of the current state of the proto-Elamite 'decipherment'. If we omit the familiar decimal system used to count discrete animate objects, especially domesticated animals and human laborers, as we have seen, there were the four other systems as follows:

1. a sexagesimal system used to count discrete inanimate objects:

2. a bisexagesimal system used to count discrete grain products, such as rations (a variant of which was used to count quantities of an unclear nature):

3. a capacity system (with variants) used to count measures of grain, especially barley, in which the smaller units designate bisexagesimally counted cereal products (as we saw in the second and third tablets discussed above):

4. an area system used to note area measures:

Unfortunately, the working out of the numerical systems is of very limited help in identifying the meaning of *non*-numerical signs on many, more complex proto-Elamite tablets. To understand how little we know, consider two tablets from Tepe Yahya (11 and 13)—shown on the next page in their standardized transcriptions. The first, TY 11, almost certainly concerns a list of laborers responsible for keeping or delivering sheep because each entry except the top one contains the signs and (one example is highlighted in entry 18), accompanied by numerals recorded in what appears to be a random order. The sign at the top:

known as 'the hairy triangle', is common in proto-Elamite tablets and seems to record an institutional affiliation, but we do not know exactly what. All the other signs are probably the names of the persons, which are completely unknown. What is interesting is that many of these unknown signs recur in the second tablet, TY 13 (highlighted), but this time there are *no* signs (e.g. and ) that are common to all the entries; confusingly, the sign appears against one entry only. We can only presume that some of the persons are common to both TY 11 and TY 13, but we have no idea what role—laborer, shepherd, slave and so on—they may have shared in life. Again, the numerals cannot help us.

For reasons which must be fairly obvious by now, the difficult proto-Elamite tablets, though relatively plentiful for an undeciphered script, have not been subjected to anything like the intensity of study directed at the much fuller, older and more prestigious proto-cuneiform corpus.

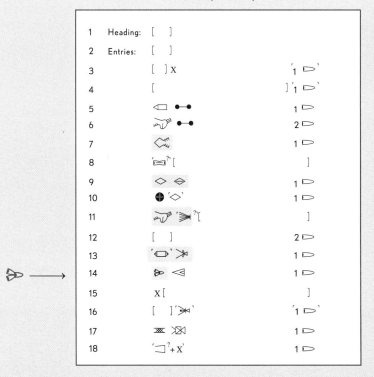

## TY11 (obverse)

'hairy triangle' ⟶

| | | | |
|---|---|---|---|
| 1 | Heading: | ⟶⊞ ◢ | |
| 2 | Entries: | ▷ ⊝ ⟩? ⧫ | 2● 7▷ |
| 3 | | ▷ X X ⧫ | 5▷ |
| 4 | | ▷ ◇ ◈ ⧫ | 3● 2▷ |
| 5 | | '▷'[ ⧫ | 1● |
| 6 | | ▷ ⩘ ⊡ ⊞ ⧫ | 8▷ |
| 7 | | ▷ ◿ X [⧫ | ] |
| 8 | | [▷]'⩘ ⊸ ▤ ⧫ | 2▷ |
| 9 | | ▷ ☞ ⩚ ⧫ | '2▷'[ ] |
| 10 | | [▷]'⊕? X ⧫ | 3▷ |
| 11 | | ▷ ⊞ ●—● ⧫ | 7▷ |
| 12 | | ▷ ◈ ⧫ | 4▷ |
| 13 | | ▷ ⬖ ◇ ⧫ | 2▷ |
| 14 | | ▷ ⊏⊐ ⩚ ⧫ | 6▷ |
| 15 | | ▷ ⊥ '⊞'? ⧫ | 6▷ |
| 16 | | ▷ ◿ ●—● ⧫ | 6▷ |
| 17 | | '▷' ◁ ⩚ ⧫ | 1● |
| 18 | | ▷ ◁ ▷ ⊸ ⧫ | 1● 2▷ |

'laborer' ⟶                                              ⟵ 'sheep'

## TY13 (obverse)

| | | | |
|---|---|---|---|
| 1 | Heading: | [ ] | |
| 2 | Entries: | [ ] | |
| 3 | | [ ] X | '1▷' |
| 4 | | [ | ]'1▷' |
| 5 | | ◁ ●—● | 1▷ |
| 6 | | ☞ ●—● | 2▷ |
| 7 | | ◿ | 1▷ |
| 8 | | '▭'?[ | ] |
| 9 | | ◇ ◇ | 1▷ |
| 10 | | ● '◇' | 1▷ |
| 11 | | ☞ '⩚'?[ | ] |
| 12 | | [ ] | 2▷ |
| 13 | | '⊏⊐'⩚ | 1▷ |
| 14 | | ▷ ◁ | 1▷ |
| 15 | | X [ | ] |
| 16 | | [ ]'⩚' | '1▷' |
| 17 | | ▥ ⬚ | 1▷ |
| 18 | | '⊐'?+X' | 1▷ |

▷ ⟶

Indeed, the only in-depth study concerns the 26 tablets found at Tepe Yahya by Lamberg-Karlovsky, which were analyzed in the late 1980s by Damerow and Englund. Although these have yielded useful insights into the numerical system, they tell us very little that is new about the people that made them, because the logographic signs stubbornly resist interpretation, being mostly more abstract than their counterparts in proto-cuneiform. "In all likelihood [they] represent professional titles or personal names. One might, for example, hope to find in such designations references to stone cutters, to smiths, even to trade agents", write Damerow and Englund. This was exactly the kind of information that was discovered in the Linear B accounting tablets—but in that case, of course, the truth was revealed because the Linear B signs were phonetic symbols and Ventris discovered the underlying Greek language.

The proto-Elamite language, alas, offers no hope of decipherment at present, since it does not appear to be related to the later languages of Elam and we do not know what other languages to compare it to. Nevertheless, much remains to be done in analyzing the signs; and Englund is actively working on this. This very early script clearly evolved for the purpose of record keeping. But for the time being, the question of whether the proto-Elamite script was a real writing system with phonetic symbols or merely a complex system of logograms for noting economic records, remains unresolved.

# Birdmen of Rapanui

# VIII

# RONGO-
# RONGO

**M**eroitic, Etruscan, Linear A and proto-Elamite—the four undeciphered scripts so far considered—are essentially known scripts that write unknown languages. With *rongorongo*, the script of Easter Island—a word meaning 'chants' or 'recitations'—we face an undeciphered script that writes what is almost certainly a Polynesian language closely similar to various modern languages of Oceania.

So exotic and enigmatic is it, that *rongorongo* has proved to be a permanent magnet for would-be decipherers. In late 1999, the German weekly *Der Spiegel* carried the following item in its online news service in English under the heading of 'ethnology':

*The* rongorongo *script, as inscribed on the wooden tablet known as Aruku Kurenga. The undeciphered signs were probably inscribed using a shark's tooth or obsidian flake. Only two facts about* rongorongo *reading are generally accepted: the direction of reading is reverse-boustrophedon; and a small part of one inscription records a type of lunar 'calendar'.*

" They were cannibals who could write, they celebrated sexual rituals and put up huge statues made of tuff—the inhabitants of Easter Island established a bizarre advanced civilization. Now an attempt has been made at deciphering their mysterious writing. A people who lived in dreamy cultural backwaters and whose culture was as screened as if it had been under a glass dome, developed an independent system of writing all on their own, known as *rongorongo*—the only such case in all of Oceania. While missionaries learnt the language of the Easter Islanders fairly quickly, all attempts at deciphering their writing have so far failed. According to Egbert Richter, a Bremen expert in linguistic and religious studies and translator of old Indian writings, the texts—half Bible, half *Kamasutra*—deal with the most secret cult of Easter Island. 'The slabs contain details of deflorations and sexual rituals,' says the codebreaker, 'all the texts revolve around the sphere of the sacred'. "

Elsewhere on the internet, another decipherer was offering "an Easter Island zodiac", with a drawing of the *rongorongo* tablet—carved in wood, like all *rongorongo* tablets—known to scholars as Honolulu 3622 (below). According to him, "the key to decipherment of this tablet is in the recognition that it is neither alphabetic, syllabic nor purely hieroglyphic—but that like signs simply belong together as 'one sign' viz. one concept": the zodiac. (Readers may recall a similar explanation of the Egyptian hieroglyphs by Horapollo and Athanasius Kircher on page 53.) Thus, goat's horns (Capricorn), fishes (Pisces), the

three stars in the belt of Orion, twins (Gemini), grabbing claws (Cancer) and so on—"ALL in the correct order"—are apparently identifiable in the Honolulu tablet. Finally, "The two [separate] symbols of the bird and the fish mean 'zodiac' and read ZIB.BU(tnis) deriving from Latvian ZIV (fish) and PUtnis (bird)," the decipherer helpfully explains, before referring the interested surfer to volume IV of his own study of the subject published in 1981.

It is easy to mistrust the first 'decipherment' without further investigation and to ridicule the second one—but be warned: the borderline between the lunatic and the intelligent, the 'cracked' and the creative, in *rongorongo* studies, is often far less obvious than in these two cases. Perhaps the best example dates back to 1932, when a Hungarian engineer living in Paris, Guillaume de Hevesy, claimed that there was a relationship between the *rongorongo* characters and the similarly undeciphered characters of the Indus Valley civilization which had just been discovered (see chapter X), on the basis of a strong resemblance between the two sets of signs. The periods in which both sets had been used were known to differ by at least 2000 years, probably more like 3500 years; and no one could deny that Easter Island and the Indus Valley were separated by half a planet (13,000 miles of ocean) and shared few other similarities of any kind. Still, the sign parallels were undoubtedly thought provoking: de Hevesy drew attention to nearly a hundred of them, the most striking of which are shown on the next page. He claimed that coincidence must be ruled out, and that the two undeciphered scripts were related through a common ancestor, the older—and of course undeciphered—proto-Elamite script (which

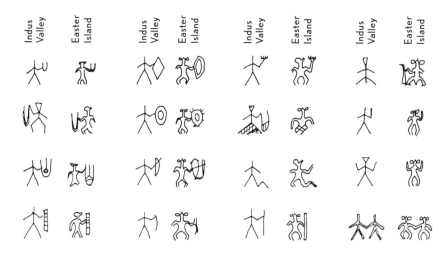

Indus Valley / Easter Island sign comparisons

shares virtually no graphic resemblance with either 'successor' script!). The conduit for transmission of the Indus signs to Easter Island was said to be through South-east Asia.

This extraordinary hypothesis, rather than being treated as a curiosity, was presented by a senior French scholar to the Academy of Inscriptions (as Champollion's had been in 1822), and then picked up by the French press; while a senior British Orientalist in London quickly published a letter of support in *The Times*, which was followed by respectful reports in *Nature* and the *Journal of the Polynesian Society*. Interest in the idea snowballed to such an extent that in 1934-35 a Franco-Belgian expedition was sent to the Pacific, with a principal aim of testing de Hevesy's idea. Skepticism was naturally rife too. In the late 1930s, the differences between 'pro-' and 'anti'-de Hevesy scholars turned into open warfare, the 'anti' group being headed, ironically, by the former leader of the expedition, Alfred Métraux. To cut a longish battle very short, Métraux eventually triumphed, but it took until the 1950s for specialists to reach general agreement that de Hevesy's hypothesis really was too far-fetched to have any validity.

For well over a century, dozens of scholars have tried their hands at deciphering the writing of Easter Island, as recorded at length in Steven Roger Fischer's survey *Rongorongo: The Easter Island Script* (1997); and many of them have resorted to arguments as fantastic as de Hevesy's. Indeed, Fischer's own proposed decipherment in the mid-1990s has sparked off a debate with some uncanny resemblances to the debate over de Hevesy, as we shall see. Both the unique geography and the strange history of Easter Island—especially the fate of its huge, deliberately toppled stone statues, the *moai*—have encouraged uninformed speculation about its writing system. But enough for now: let us turn to some undisputed facts about the place and its history, before considering how one might decipher *rongorongo* rationally.

For a start, Easter Island is among the most isolated inhabited spots on earth: some 2350 miles west of Chile and about 1400 miles east-southeast of Pitcairn Island, its nearest inhabited neighbor. It is also small as islands go, only 64 square miles, roughly triangular in shape, with a maximum length of 15 miles. The land surface is volcanic in origin, consisting of lava from the remains of three small volcanoes; there are no permanent watercourses, and until very recently no large trees either. Scientific evidence suggests that it was originally forested but was denuded by its inhabitants, leading to a conflict over natural resources that may have destroyed its society.

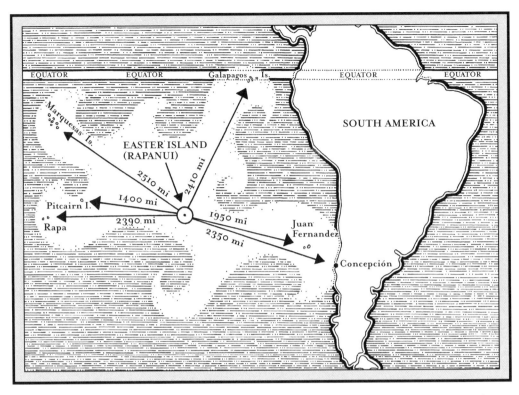

*Easter Island or Rapanui. Despite its exceptional geographical isolation, it appears to have had the only writing system in pre-colonial Oceania, but no one knows how this arose.*

Where did its inhabitants (who have called the island Rapanui since colonial times) come from? The most publicized theory is Thor Heyerdahl's, backed by his 1947 *Kon-Tiki* expedition and other attempts to prove that Polynesia, including Easter Island, was settled from the east, in other words South America, first in the early centuries AD (again around 1100 AD), and only subsequently, in the 15th or 16th centuries, from the west. Unfortunately for Heyerdahl, the scientific evidence—archaeological, ethnological, linguistic and genetic—overwhelmingly supports the opposite theory: that Easter Island was settled from the west, i.e. from Polynesia, probably from the Marquesas Islands (north-east of Tahiti) in the early centuries AD; there was no migration from South America. For example, a 1990s analysis of the DNA in early skeletons from Easter Island (predating the colonial contacts of the 18th century) revealed no trace of genetic contact with South America. More controversial, but nevertheless predominant, is the view that the island was settled only *once*: there was no second wave of Polynesian settlement.

The Rapanui language belongs to the Polynesian family. It has, however, been heavily influenced by Tahitian since colonial times—to the extent that the name Rapanui is Tahitian and today's Rapanui word for 'hello', 'iorana', is Tahitian ('ia ora na'). Almost all the Polynesian languages are mutually intelligible, a bit like standard Dutch and standard German; thus in the 1770s, Captain Cook could make himself understood on Hawaii, using an interpreter who spoke only Tahitian. In Europe, Italians and Spaniards can communicate with each other in their own languages. Today's Rapanui language and the Maori language of New Zealand "are like Italian and Spanish," says the linguist and would-be *rongorongo* decipherer Jacques Guy.

Few seriously doubt that the *rongorongo* inscriptions are written in a Polynesian language related to today's Rapanui language. The problem is to determine how the *rongorongo* language has changed since the time when the inscriptions were written. The nature of the Mayan language written in the Classic Mayan glyphs is a subject of debate, as we know; it is thought to be substantially different from any present-day Mayan language and may be an extinct 'literary' language. "Perhaps the language of the *rongorongo* is a priestly language very different from that of the plebs," wonders Guy. "Just like you have High Balinese and Common Balinese—for instance 'dog' in Common Balinese is 'anjing', while in High Balinese it is 'asu'."

But this raises the fascinating, and contentious, question of the age of *rongorongo* inscriptions (not a problem, of course, with the extensively dated Mayan inscriptions). None of the *rongorongo* inscriptions is dated. Was the script brought to the island from Polynesia perhaps a millennium and a half ago, or invented on the island unaided by outside influences, or was it a product of contacts with European visitors in the 18th century? There is

some evidence—none of it satisfactory—for all three possibilities. If the second of them, independent invention on the island, were to be proved, it would constitute exceptionally strong support for the idea that there were origins, as opposed to one origin, of writing, as already noted in the Introduction.

Oral tradition on Easter Island, recorded in the 19th century, has it that the first settler, the legendary Hotu Matu'a, brought 67 tablets with him from his homeland in Polynesia. But of course writing may have been invented centuries after the settlement and then attributed to Hotu Matu'a to make it more respectable. The most serious difficulty with invention outside the island, however, is that we know of no writing systems in Oceania (except conceivably *rongorongo*) prior to the colonial period. If *rongorongo*, or least the concept of writing, came from the islands to the west, why is there no trace of ancient writing there?

If writing was invented on the island, we might expect *rongorongo* signs to be found carved in stone on, for example, the *moai* statues and on the walls of caves. There is no evidence of this, but there are petroglyphs with a distinct resemblance to *rongorongo* signs—though not as a rule on the *moai*. For example, this petroglyph in cave Ana O Keke resembles a certain *rongorongo* sign:

Here is a series of petroglyphs that resemble *rongorongo* signs, as suggested by Guy and the archaeologist Georgia Lee:

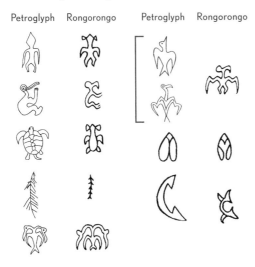

Petroglyph    Rongorongo        Petroglyph    Rongorongo

On the reasonable, though unproven assumption that these petroglyphs predate European contact, Lee concludes: "Certain designs in the rock art were established as *rongorongo* glyphs, allowing us to postulate that the carved wood tablets antedated contact with the western world." Most scholars have taken the same view.

Yet it is perfectly possible that the petroglyphs existed pre-contact, but no one on the island had figured out how to use them to represent phonetic speech. This was the situation in North America among Native Americans. Then, in 1821, the Cherokee chief Sequoya, stimulated by contact with white settlers and their writing, sat down and produced a Cherokee 'alphabet' (actually a syllabary) with his own symbols, which was then used to print newspapers and books in Cherokee. Sequoya, however, had a long period of contact with the white man's "talking leaves", which was definitely not the situation on Easter Island.

The first European visitors to Easter Island (who named it) were sailors from a Dutch fleet under the command of Jacob Roggeveen which briefly landed in 1722; the party saw no evidence of writing among the islanders, though it did see plenty of impressive *moai*. Then, in 1770, two Spanish ships called in and claimed the island for the king of Spain with a military ceremony, before quickly sailing away. Some islanders who looked like chiefs were drafted in by the Spanish to mark the 'treaty'. They drew the following characters:

—at least two of which, the 'vulva' and the 'bird', resemble common petroglyphs but which are certainly *not* recognizable as *rongorongo*.

This is not conclusive evidence, though, that in 1770 the islanders were unable to write *rongorongo*. For the circumstances of the 'signing' were scarcely propitious: the islanders must have been frightened and confused by their first contact with the armed Spanish, and they were being asked to sign on paper with pen and ink, instead of inscribing their characters on wood with a shark's tooth or obsidian flake. Moreover, perhaps the drafted individuals were not the Rapanui who were literate in *rongorongo*; it is quite likely that scribal activity was the province of specialists rather than chiefs.

Nevertheless, when James Cook landed in 1774, he and his party saw no sign of writing. The first definite sighting of *rongorongo* does not occur until nearly a century later, recorded by a French missionary, Joseph-Eugène Eyraud, in 1864, immediately after labor raids on the island by entrepreneurs operating out of Peru, who carried away much of the population and infected the remainder with often-fatal diseases. (In the 1860s, about 94 per cent of Easter Islanders either emigrated or died.) According to Eyraud, knowledge of the meaning of the signs was already dying out. Thus, one could argue that *rongorongo* was invented some time after contact with European visitors in the 1770s, brought to a fine pitch and more or less abandoned, all within less than 90 years. While possible, this scenario—which is much favored by Fischer—is not altogether plausible and is certainly not proven, though it does accord with the young age of the wood in all surviving *rongorongo* inscriptions.

There are 25 of these, scattered from Honolulu and Santiago to European capitals, in particular Rome; not a single one remains on Easter Island itself. Most are named after their current locations, for example the Large St Petersburg tablet, but a few have names in the Rapanui language, such as Mamari ('egg'), from the object's egg-like shape, or in one case a French name Echancrée ('notched'), again because of the tablet's appearance. The total corpus lies somewhere between 14,000 and 17,000 characters, depending on how one chooses to count the more complex characters. Many of the inscriptions are very short, but the largest and longest, the Santiago staff, has some 2300 characters on a wooden staff that measures 126 x 6.5 cm (49 x 2.5 in), and a second inscription,

Tahua, a wooden tablet made out of a European or American oar, contains about 1825 characters; it is the longest tablet inscription.

The first step in understanding *rongorongo* was taken by a cleric, Florentin Etienne 'Tepano' Jaussen, bishop of Tahiti. In 1869-70, missionaries working on Easter Island did their best to rescue tablets from destruction and concealment by the islanders; they were able to send Jaussen four tablets (including Mamari and Echancrée). Eventually, he located a laborer from Easter Island, Metoro Tau'a Ure, then working in Tahiti, who was thought to be able to read the tablets. While Metoro chanted the content of the tablet, Jaussen planned that he would note down phonetically what was said and ask Metoro what it meant in the Rapanui language (the bishop knew only Tahitian).

At the outset, Jaussen learnt one crucial fact. To read a *rongorongo* tablet, one started at the bottom left-hand corner and read along line 1 to the right-hand corner. Then one turned the tablet through 180 degrees and began reading line 2 from left to right again. At the end of line 2, one repeated the 180-degree turn so that the tablet was in the same orientation as at the beginning, and read line 3 from left to right, and so on. This direction of writing is known as reverse-boustrophedon, with every even-numbered line written back-to-front and upside-down in relation to an ordinary English text. You can see how it works if you compare the photograph of tablet Mamari with the transcription of lines 6-9 (which are of course all printed the right way up) on the next two pages.

Less successful was Metoro's attempt to explain the meaning. He told Jaussen: "this is how the priests used to read. I'm reading like them, but without knowing what I am saying." And his interpretations made little sense: "He is pierced. It is the king. He went to the water. The man is sleeping against

←9
←8
←7
←6

←2

*The direction of reading of the tablet Mamari, known as reverse-boustrophedon. Even-numbered lines are upside-down. Four lines are printed right side up on the opposite page.*

blossoming fruit. The posts are set up..." Jaussen was disconcerted but, like Diego de Landa in 16th-century Yucatan in the Maya decipherment, he persisted, and made a copious transcription of each tablet. In the end, he compiled a list of signs with their pronunciation in the Rapanui language and their meaning in French, of which the chart on page 228 is a part.

The general impression is that Metoro was simply guessing and making up meanings on the basis that the *rongorongo* signs were pictographic. A few of these identifications – 'bouche' (mouth), 'soleil' (sun), 'cancrelat' (cockroach), 'frégate' (frigate bird) – are obvious; the rest are not. Nevertheless, some of the Metoro values have proved suggestive clues in 20th-century decipherment efforts.

It is not at all clear from this encounter whether Metoro was *unable* to read *rongorongo* (either because he had forgotten how or because he

6

7

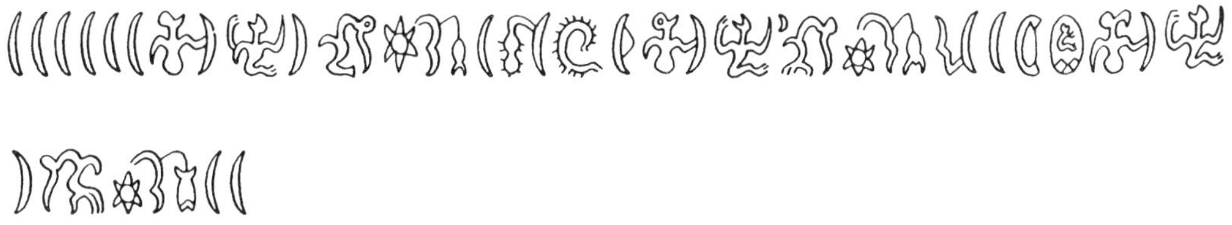

8

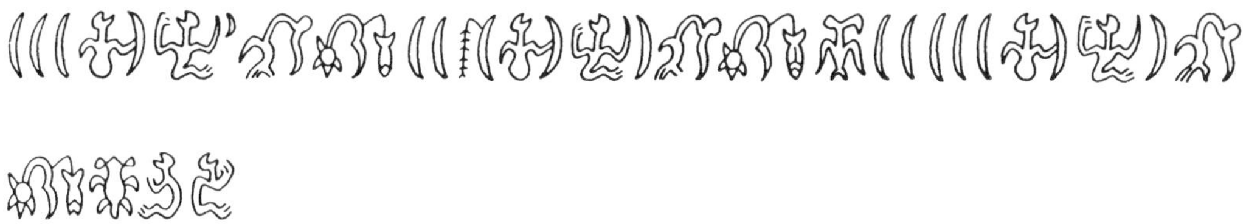

9

was never taught how in the first place), or whether *rongorongo* was intended not to be read in the sense of, say, Egyptian hieroglyphs, but was, rather, a series of mnemonic signs designed to prompt the chanter who would have committed their meaning to memory. The scientist T. H. Huxley, at this time, having examined *rongorongo* in England, refused to believe the characters were writing and suggested they might have been used for stamping cloth. At any rate, the experiment with Metoro was a disappointment for Jaussen, who did not publish his notes. Only after his death did an edited version appear with his list of signs, some of which were then promptly borrowed by the painter Paul Gauguin to decorate a portrait of his Tongan mistress (next page): the symbols in the background are clearly *rongorongo*, but Gauguin has arranged the signs without any regard for their meaning (and they are almost all the right way up, unlike in a reverse-boustrophedon script).

DIEUX (GODS)

Atua reroreroa
Dieu fardé

Atua hiko rega
Dieu peint en jaune

Atua hiko kura
Dieu peint en rouge

Atua hiko tea
Dieu peint en blanc

Atua mata viri
Dieu aux yeux
contournes

Atua mago
Dieu requin

HOMMES (HUMANS)

Te ariki
Le roi

Toru ariki tuhuga
Trois rois savants

Tagata
Hommes

Koia
Lui, il, elle

Te hua rae
Les enfants

Te poki
L'enfant

Tamaiti
Enfant

Te atariki
Le fils aine

Te teina
Le cadet

Vie poko pono
Femme coiffée

Nuku
Assemblée

Nuku
Troupe

Vaha
Bouche

Vae
Jambe

Rima
Main

Mata
Yeux

CIEL (THE HEAVENS)

Ragi
Ciel

Raa
Soleil

Hetu
Etoile

Rua hetu
Deux etoiles

Matariki
Pleiades

Marama
Lune

Te Goe
Voie lactée

TERRE (THE EARTH)

Henua
Terre

Rotia henua
Terre coupée

Vere henua
Culture

Henua puku
Terre soulevée

Henua tupu
Terre en production

Pito o te henua
Nombril de la terre

Mauga
Mont

Mata no te henua
Les yeux de la terre

Mauga pu
Montagne percée

Matagi
Vent

Ua
Pluie

Vai tahe
Eau courante

Kotokotona
Route

Te pa
Enclos

Ahi
Feu

Te hupe
Rhume,
air froid

MER (THE SEA)

Tai
Mer

Tai vave
Mer soulevée

Garu Flot

Haga
Baie

Vai
Eau

ANIMAUX TERRESTRES
(GROUND ANIMALS)

Kiore
Rat

Moko
Lézard

Moko matea
Lézard mort

Ravareva
Geophile

Pepe
Papillon

Takaure
Mouche

Makere
Cancrelat noir

Mea no te henua
Ver de terre

Veveke
Libellule

OISEAUX (BIRDS)

Taha
Frégate

Kukurutou
Mouette

Moa
Poule

Moa tagi
Coq qui chante

Moa rere
Poule qui vole

Moa rikiriki
La poule et
ses petits

*Part of Bishop 'Tepano' Jaussen's list of rongorongo signs, compiled in the 1870s. The meaning of each sign in the Rapanui language according to Jaussen's informant Metoro was translated into French by Jaussen. Most of Metoro's 'meanings' seem to have been guesswork, based purely on the appearance of the sign rather than any knowledge of the script: five obvious examples of this are highlighted.*

*(opposite)* Merahi Metua no Tehamana *(The Ancestors of Tehamana) by Paul Gauguin, 1893. Rongorongo signs appear at the top of the painting in a recognizable, if distorted form, though not written reverse–boustrophedon.*

In 1886, an American naval officer, William Judah Thomson, with a keen personal interest in rongorongo, made the second—and what turned out to be the last—productive attempt to have the characters read by a knowledgeable native of Easter Island. He had a bare two weeks to spend on the island, but he managed to locate and purchase two new tablets (the Washington tablets, now in the Smithsonian Museum) and persuade an 83-year-old man Ure Va'e Iko to 'read'—not from real tablets but from photographs of Bishop Jaussen's tablets. The old man apparently balked at chanting from the real objects because it would be breaking a taboo, but a photograph, which was something he had never seen before, especially if it belonged to Bishop 'Tepano', was acceptable; even so, he had to be loosened up with alcohol to persuade him to chant anything, during an all-night session in his shack.

The resulting readings, noted down by Thomson with a rough translation, are an important source of knowledge about rongorongo. But they contain multiple obscurities—there is no 'agreed' reading—and unfortunately they cannot be correlated with particular tablets, unlike Jaussen's notes; again, the problem seems to have been that Ure Va'e Iko did not so much 'read' as employ the tablet photographs as aide memoires in the retelling of Rapanui legends. The most significant recitation, "Atua-Mata-Riri" (God Angry Eyes), consists of 48 verses, 41 of which tell of such-and-such a god copulating with such-and-such a goddess, who gives birth to such-and-such an animal, plant, or natural phenomenon. This is verse 1: "Atua-matariri ki ai ki roto ki a te Poro, ka pu te poporo" (God-of-the-angry-look by copulating with ?Roundness [goddess Teporo] produced the poporo [Solanum nigrum]).

By 1915, when two British anthropologists, Katherine and Scoresby Routledge, spent a long period on Easter Island, the old knowledge of rongorongo was dead. Some local informants obligingly 'read' tablets for them from photographs, but it was clear that these readings had nothing to do with the content of the tablets. One of the informants commented that "the words were new, but the letters were old", which scholars take to be an indication that there had been a major change in the system, perhaps under Tahitian influence, such that the iconicity of a sign no longer matched the reader's interpretation of it. Routledge herself claimed that rongorongo had always been merely a system of mnemonics, like a knot tied in a handkerchief designed to trigger a memory which has nothing to do with the shape of the knot. And this view was broadly endorsed by Métraux following the Franco-Belgian expedition of the 1930s: "The magical or ornamental character of the signs superseded their pictographic value." Later however, under the impact of Russian ideas, Métraux changed his mind and decided that rongorongo might be a real, logosyllabic script after all.

––––––––

New approaches to rongorongo came from two directions in the 1950s. In Russia, scholars working in St Petersburg (then Leningrad), including Yuri Knorozov, began to analyze the characters to identify regularities in them and to speculate as to how these might represent phonetic patterns in the underlying Polynesian language, with the help of the Jaussen/Metoro readings. In Germany, a former Wehrmacht cryptographer, Thomas Barthel, analyzed the characters and compiled a detailed sign list, to which he then attempted to assign logographic meanings based mainly on the Jaussen/Metoro sign list and readings. Neither the Russians nor Barthel had much time for each other's work—which was perhaps not surprising in the immediate aftermath of the second world war. Indeed, there is a definite parallel here with the Maya decipherment, in which the German scholar was also interested: Barthel was friendly with Sir Eric Thompson and hostile to Knorozov for intellectual and personal reasons similar to those of Thompson.

The Russian 'school' began with the work of the young Boris Kudryavtsev, who identified several parallel passages in four different tablets where the same, or very similar sequences of characters were clearly repeated. Here is one example:

![Tahua script]
*Tahua*

![Large St Petersburg script]
*Large St Petersburg*

![Large Santiago script]
*Large Santiago*

![Small St Petersburg script]
*Small St Petersburg*

Kudryavtsev's notes were published after his death in the war by his academic mentor, D. A. Ol'derogge, who went on to compare *rongorongo* to Egyptian hieroglyphic script at an early stage of its development, in which the pictograms were open to various interpretations

and were combined with a number of phonetic signs, i.e. a strong but not exclusively mnemonic principle was at work.

Knorozov and his collaborator Nikolai Butinov agreed, and took the analysis somewhat further, claiming to identify four categories of sign: logograms; logograms combined with determinatives; phonetic signs combined with determinatives; and purely phonetic spellings such as the rebus combination:

'sun'      'rain'

which they 'read', using the Jaussen list, as:

'raa' ('sun') + 'ua' ('rain') = 'raua' (Polynesian 'they').

All their readings are open to doubt and some, based on their own, idiosyncratic 'identifications' of objects depicted by Jaussen with the words for those objects in the Rapanui language, are frankly far-fetched. Knorozov's brilliant cross-substitution of syllabic Mayan glyphs that yielded a series of known Mayan words in the Dresden Codex (pages 123–25) did not appear to work for *rongorongo* and its language.

The most influential suggestion by Butinov and Knorozov concerned a sequence of characters on two lines of the Small Santiago tablet, which they divided into groups. Six of these groups are shown here:

| 1 | 2 | 3 | 4 | 5 | 6 |
|---|---|---|---|---|---|

![rongorongo glyph sequence]

The 'man' is the first sign in each of these groups. To quote the two Russians (writing in 1957):

> This gives us reason to believe that we have to do with a list of names... In the third group the sign of man is followed by the signs of a seated man with raised hands and a tortoise; in the fourth group the signs of the tortoise and the shark; in the fifth the signs of the shark and an octopus; in the sixth group we have only the sign of the octopus... This position of signs shows that we have to do not simply with a list of names but with a genealogy which ascends from descendants to ancestors. The second sign in each group gives the name of the father. "

In other words, groups 3-6 might read as follows:

A, son of B//B, son of C//C, son of D//D.

The regular occurrence of such patterns in Rapanui names recorded by Jaussen, such as father Pito//son Roto-Pito and father Vai-a-nuhe//son Ure-a-vai-a-nuhe, supported the two Russians' suggestion of a genealogy.

The German Barthel's approach is probably best summarized by his own statement in an article, "Talking boards of Easter Island", that he published in *Scientific American* in 1958, the same year in which appeared the most important of his several dozen publications on *rongorongo*, *Grundlagen zur Entzifferung der Osterinselschrift* (Foundations for Deciphering the Easter Island

Script). He wrote in *Scientific American*:

> I'll never forget the moment when the first textual fragment began to make sense. In one row of an inscription I found that geometrical symbols evidently representing the sun and the moon were preceded by an abstract sign combining two sticks. Now the sun and the moon are commonly depicted in mythologies as twins, and I recalled that a Maori (i.e., Polynesian) proverb actually refers to these celestial twins with the metaphorical expression 'two sticks'. Thus the sign became my first clue to decipherment of the Easter Island script. "

Clearly, Barthel's definition of 'decipherment' was that of Thompson, rather than that of Knorozov. Does it not recall Thompson's explanation of the 'dog' glyph on page 19?

The decipherments in the *Grundlagen* follow the same pattern. To take but one example, in his chapter on "Nature", Barthel took a common sign 𓏲 and identified it as 'sky, heaven', following Jaussen's list, which he translated as 'rangi'. Finding this sign combined in the texts with other signs whose meaning he had also deduced from Jaussen, Barthel went on to interpret the combined signs as "heavenly child", "heavenly woman" and "heavenly warrior", supporting these interpretations with copious analogies taken from east Polynesia.

Another combination of sign 𓏲 with the sign 𓏲 occurred frequently, for instance on the Tahua tablet:

Metoro/Jaussen gave ⸙ the meaning 'hau tea' (hibiscus tendril). Barthel decided to read this as simply 'tea' (bright, white), which led him to interpret ⸙ as 'rangi tea' (white sky, bright sky). He even went on to equate this phrase with the place name Ra'iatea, an important center of culture in the western Society Islands. But as Steven Roger Fischer claims: "Ra'iatea is composed of Tahitian 'ra'i' (sky) and 'atea' (serene, clear), not Tahitian 'tea' (white)."

All Barthel's interpretations suffered from assumptions and flaws like this, and it is now generally recognized, even by sympathetic critics such as Fischer, that Barthel's 'decipherment' of *rongorongo* in the 1950s is nothing of the kind. As Barthel himself admitted in 1993, a few years before his death: "The Metoro Chants are in fact no 'Rosetta Stone'; but they remain of heuristic value

and... ought not to be neglected by future investigations."

Nevertheless, Barthel's extensive sign list, published in his *Grundlagen*, is widely used. It is based on the kind of internal analysis of the inscriptions—the frequencies, contexts and recurrent patterns of the characters—employed by scholars such as Bennett in Linear B and Godart/Olivier in Linear A, supplemented by Barthel's interpretations. The sign numbers go up to 699, but there are fewer signs than this in total, because not all the numbers 1-699 are allotted to signs. The main organizing principle, never properly explained by Barthel but apparently an intuitive one based on shape, such that signs with the same main element begin with the same numeral (9, 90, 91, 92 and so on, for example)—is fairly clear from the chart of signs 1-99:

*Part of the sign list of* rongorongo, *devised by the epigrapher Thomas Barthel. It is based mainly on similarity of shape, not on contextual analysis of the signs, and is therefore seriously flawed.*

However this principle gives rise to many shortcomings: "many holes, many irregularities, and internal inconsistencies", to quote Jacques Guy. An example cited by him is sign 200:

If we break this down into its component elements—the head and the various limbs—and consider just the 'head' element, we can see that this element is found in the top of sign 5, in sign 95a, the top half of signs 90-93 and 99, the bottom half of sign 94 and in the top and bottom of sign 96. So would it not be better to number the 'head' element as 9? But 9 is taken by the sign that looks like a Viking helmet.

Compound signs (ligatures) are even more problematic. Signs 400 and 405 are as follows:

400       405

It would therefore seem logical to number this ligature:

as 400.405. But Barthel chose to give it the new number 415.

Again, signs 8 and 513a look like this:

8        513a

So we might expect this ligature:

to be 513a:8, but in fact it has a new number 518.

The trouble is that to devise a better system is immensely time consuming, as Guy is keenly aware after making several failed attempts at analyzing the sign elements and their combinations. He tried, for instance, to use the ASCII signs familiar in computing, such that each sign looked like the *rongorongo* element it symbolized. But he soon ran out of ASCII signs with a sufficiently intuitive resemblance. Yet without a reliable system of transliterating the inscriptions, one cannot compile a concordance, in which (as explained in the Introduction) under the heading of each numbered sign—that is 1-699 in Barthel's system—every occurrence of the sign in the corpus of inscriptions would be listed, so that one could quickly compare and analyze the entire range of contexts in which the sign appeared. Guy says: "If we had an efficient transliteration system, a concordance would be a piece of cake. But to elaborate such a system, we need to carry out those analyses, discover those rules... a vicious circle."

Born and educated in France—he nicknames himself 'Frogguy' in all correspondence—from which he emigrated to Australia in the 1960s, Guy is a linguist (a fluent speaker of Chinese, Japanese, Tahitian and other Pacific languages, as well as several European languages) who did research at the Australian National University on Pacific languages before turning to computing and its application to natural language understanding while working at the national telecommunications company Telstra. He is one of three *rongorongo* specialists who have tried to build on the better aspects of Barthel's work in the last decade or so. The other two are Fischer, who was born and educated in the United States (he studied languages at the University of California) but is now based in New Zealand where he is something of a loner, and Konstantin Pozdniakov, a specialist in west African languages until recently at the museum of ethnography in St Petersburg (Knorozov's old academic home).

Guy's work, though limited in scope, has been appreciated by both Fischer and Pozdniakov. They, on the other hand, have made radical (and quite different) claims amounting to a decipherment, which have attracted derision from Guy in the case of Fischer, and tentative, if critical endorsement in the case of Pozdniakov (most of whose work is as yet unpublished). Fischer's work has, however, been welcomed by many non-specialists who have been inclined to accept his claims at face value—despite the near-total scholarly rejection of his earlier, 1980s 'decipherment' of the Phaistos disc (see chapter XI). We shall now look at the three scholars' approaches in turn, starting with that of Guy.

————

Guy's determination to avoid exaggerated claims reminds one a little of Alice Kober's approach to undeciphered Linear B in the 1940s, though he is undoubtedly a bolder thinker than Kober. At the outset of his study of *rongorongo*, in the 1980s, comparing the texts common to four tablets Guy stated:

  ❝ No attempt at translation is to be made, any hypotheses about the possible functions and meanings of the glyphs are to be carefully avoided, and no use is to be made in this analysis of the data obtained by various authors from [Rapanui] informants (e.g., Metoro... Ure Va'e Iko) or to studies of [Rapanui] and Polynesian culture and traditions [by Métraux, Barthel etc.], for it is felt that, given the justifiably low level of acceptance with which any hypotheses about the Easter Island tablets are likely to be met, resorting to such external evidence could only weaken whatever conclusions might be drawn from the analysis of these four parallel texts. ❞

Later, he relaxed this rigid restriction, but he has remained sharply critical of all the sources of evidence about the script, especially Metoro's chants.

Though Guy has made many contributions to the subject, his most significant one concerns the Mamari tablet, which was read by Metoro in the 1870s. Here, once again, are a little more than two lines of Mamari as transcribed by Barthel:

Beginning of 'calendar' ↓

End of 'calendar'

Barthel realized, as was fairly obvious from the repeated symbols ◖ and ◗, that this portion of the tablet was some kind of lunar calendar. But it was Guy who put Barthel's initial interpretation on a firm footing in 1990 by comparing the characters with the names for each day in the lunar month as recorded by William Judah Thomson in 1886, by Alfred Métraux in the mid-1930s and by Father Sebastian Englert, a Capuchin priest who lived on Easter Island from 1935 until his death in 1969 and who compiled a valuable dictionary of Rapanui words. (Guy ignored the dubious interpretation of Metoro, who hardly recognized the crescent as a moon.) This is Guy's analysis:

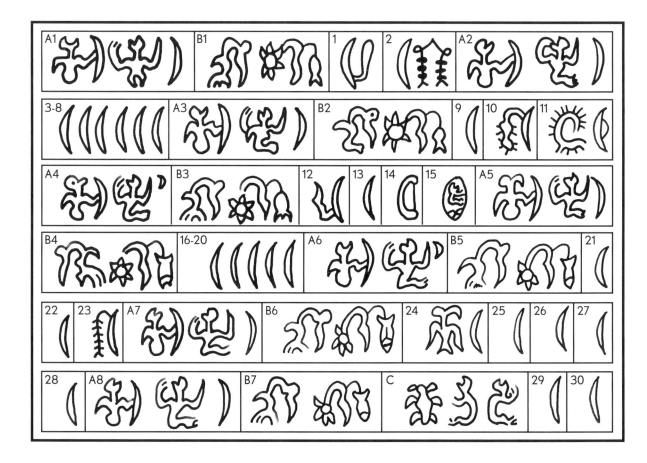

*The lunar 'calendar' in the tablet Mamari, analyzed by the linguist Jacques Guy.*

The characters numbered 1-30 represent the nights of the traditional Rapanui lunar calendar, totaling 30, of which the last two (29 and 30) appear to be intercalary nights, named Hotu and Hiro. These must have been inserted as needed—one shortly before the full moon, the other immediately before the new moon—in order to maintain the accuracy of the lunar calendar, which alternated 29-day and 30-day months (a lunar month is actually 29.52 days long). The inscription is therefore not a calendar strictly speaking, but rather a list of instructions, an "astronomical canon for telling in advance when to insert two intercalary nights", says Guy.

Number 2 for the first night after the new moon was called 'ari', according to Métraux. The sign accompanying the crescent looks something like a string with barbs. The anthropologist Katherine Routledge recorded gatherings of "rongorongo men" at the time of the new moon, who brought with them strings of white feathers tied to sticks. This sign could be a representation of these. Number 15, the full moon, is a picture of the 'Cook-in-the-Moon' (a homunculus with cooking stones as oven), common to Polynesian and most Melanesian mythologies. Number 24, accompanied by a picture of a frigate bird, was known as 'orongo taane' (Thomson and Englert) or 'rongo tane' (Métraux). Since the Rapanui word for frigate is 'taha', the first syllable may be used here phonetically for *ta*[ne].

The rest of the characters are of unknown meaning. Still, certain plausible hypotheses have been put forward by Guy. For example, the 'moon' symbols facing to the left are labeled A 1-8 to distinguish them from the right-facing 'moon' symbols: presumably the left-facing crescent means 'moon', while the right-facing crescent means 'night'. The signs that accompany the left-facing crescents may be instructions to observe and note the apparent diameter of the moon. The characters labeled B1-7 appear to refer to the waxing and waning of the moon, since the fish sign depicted in B1, B2 and B3, before the full moon, points upwards , while its equivalent in B4, B5, B6 and B7, after the full moon, points downwards . The remaining characters, labeled C, which accompany the intercalary nights, look like a turtle followed by two back-to-back figures. The Rapanui word for turtle is 'honu' and the word for two is 'he rua', so these characters may be phonetic approximations for Hotu and Hiro, the names of these two nights. Although not all of these suggestions have met with general acceptance, Guy's basic interpretation of the above section of the Mamari tablet is accepted by every *rongorongo* scholar.

Moving on to Fischer, his work as a decipherer also rests on a suggestion first made by Barthel, arising from one of Metoro's readings for Bishop Jaussen. On the Aruku Kurenga tablet there appears the line shown below:

'ure'

Metoro read the marked sign as 'te tangata ure huki' (the man with an erect penis). That 'ure' means penis or phallus is confirmed by Englert's dictionary. Barthel therefore wrote this sign as 430.76, a combination of:

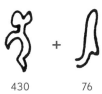

Note that Barthel has casually equated two signs— the one in Aruku Kurenga with the protuberance on the left 🐚, and the second one, sign 76, with the protuberance on the right; we shall return to this point.

Adopting Barthel's 'identification', Fischer observed that a phallus-like appendage appears on certain tablets (but not others). We have already seen (page 231) an example in the proposed genealogy of Butinov and Knorozov on the Small Santiago tablet, however the two Russians were interested in the repeated main signs, not in the 'phallus' (which they did not even mention). Fischer, rejecting their putative genealogy, concentrated instead on an analysis of the occurrence of Barthel's sign 76, especially in the long inscription on the Santiago staff, as transcribed opposite (in part) by Fischer, with sign 76 highlighted.

It is clear that sign 76 occurs, often but by no means always, in the following pattern: immediately after each word divider (as the vertical line is taken to be) and then every three characters (1, 4, 7, 10, 13, etc.) within each sequence between word dividers. (Try it for yourself to see how regular or irregular the pattern really is.) Fischer went on to detect the same pattern, as he thought, in the Small Santiago tablet and the Honolulu 3629 tablet. He called this pattern a

"triad structure" consisting of the basic unit, X.76 + Y + Z.

Then he took an interpretive leap in the dark. He knew that the chant "Atua-Mata-Riri", recorded by William Judah Thomson, consisted of a repetitive structure, "God X by copulating with Goddess Y produced Z". Fischer decided, simply from intuition, that the 'triad structure' of the tablets recorded a creation chant, his so-called "Rapanui Genesis", similar to but not the same as "Atua-Mata-Riri", with the 'phallus' of course representing the idea of copulation—and he thereby proceeded to 'translate' the tablets, interpreting the signs à la Barthel. Thus the triad:

highlighted on the Santiago staff, Fischer translated as: "All the birds copulated with the fish: there issued forth the sun." (The 'hand' shape is a plural form according to Fischer.) A second Santiago staff triad:

was said to mean: "All the birds copulated with the sea: there issued forth the shellfish." And a triad from the Small Santiago tablet:

The beginning of the rongorongo Santiago staff, analyzed by the linguist Steven Roger Fischer.

was translated as: "The shark copulated with the male deity: there issued forth the shark."

But even if this hypothesis were correct, it left Fischer with a serious scholarly headache: how to account for the many tablets in which the 'phallus', sign 76, did *not*, as he put it, "flaunt" itself? The telltale sign is altogether absent from the major tablets Tahua, Mamari, Echancrée and Aruku Kurenga which were presented to Jaussen, and either absent or very infrequent on a majority of the other tablets. How was Fischer to solve what one might term 'the mystery of the missing phallus' (other than by assuming that all the 'non-phallic' tablets did not record creation chants)? After spotting what he took to be the same 'triad' (the first one above) as on the Santiago staff also inscribed on Echancrée, but now *sans* 'phallus', Fischer came up with an ingenious answer: "the phallus was dropped on later *rongorongo* inscriptions… It was apparently dispensed with as superfluous by later Rapanui scribes." In other words, the scribes came to assume that chanters would know that a phallus was intended, and so they stopped inscribing it (somewhat as we do not bother to write 'born' and 'died' with a person's dates).

When Fischer announced these deductions and a few translations in 1995, it is no exaggeration to say that he was soon greeted as the long-awaited decipherer of *rongorongo*. Barthel offered "unlimited endorsement" of the basic triad and the idea that sign 76 was a phallus meaning 'copulated with'. The archaeologist Paul Bahn, who has a special interest in Easter Island, endorsed all Fischer's findings in *Nature* and even more enthusiastically in the popular magazine *New Scientist*, which was then reported in *The Times*. Sir David Attenborough, the naturalist who has an interest in Polynesia, congratulated

Fischer on solving a problem "that has baffled so many able minds for so long." Most extraordinary of all, Oxford University Press published a 700-page monograph on *rongorongo* by Fischer, in which he declared that following his discovery of the triad structure, "The complete translation of the *rongorongo* inscriptions is only a question of time and dedication."

But apart from Barthel (who never published his endorsement), no other person who has studied *rongorongo* in depth has declared in favor of Fischer's 'decipherment'. For a start, there is no proof that sign 76 , the lynchpin of the decipherment, represents 'ure' (phallus). Not only does it look significantly different from the relevant part of the sign that was read as 'ure' by Metoro:

it is also the case that Metoro read it as 'ure' only once; with seven other instances of the sign, he did *not* read 'ure'. Furthermore, Metoro read *none* of the many instances of sign 76 as 'ure'; indeed his only other reading of 'ure' refers to a completely different sign:

Also, it is worth noting that the tablet containing (Metoro's 'phallus') does not contain a single example of sign 76 (Barthel's and Fischer's 'phallus').

Second, Fischer's analysis of the tablets is fatally flawed. Close inspection of the Santiago staff reveals that only 63 out of 113 sequences on the staff fully obey the 'triad' structure (and 63 is the maximum figure, giving every Fischer attribution of a 'phallus' the benefit of the doubt). In other words it is not true, as he claims, that "nearly every" sequence obeys the rule; in fact there is *no* reliable 'triad structure' in the Santiago staff. Moreover, there are many examples of adjacent 'phalluses', which are forbidden by the Fischer interpretation (what would X.76 + Y.76 + Z mean?), and some examples of identical signs 'copulating' (X.76 + X.76 + Z), which do not appear to make much sense either. There are also examples of 'phalluses' either as the final sign or as the penultimate sign of sequences, which again are forbidden by the interpretation. Examination of the 'phallus' sign on other tablets (when it is actually visible) reinforces the deduction that the so-called 'triad structure' is illusory.

Third, Fischer's 'dropped phallus' theory is ludicrous—a classic example of decipherer's disease: because the text does not fit one's preconception, one manipulates the text rather than dropping one's preconception as being wrong. Guy comments aptly: "whenever [Fischer] did not see a phallus, he supplied one."

Leaving aside such internal analysis, Guy has ridiculed Fischer's approach on other grounds. What is the evidence for equating the Santiago staff with the type of chant found in "Atua-Mata-Riri?" Nothing direct, as Fischer admits, only that both staff and chant were produced by the same culture, presumably at the same time, which he defends as a good enough reason for the analogy to hold. But this is to commit what is known in logic as the fallacy of the excluded middle, says Guy: "dogs have four legs, tables have four legs, therefore tables, like

dogs, wag their tails and pee against trees." And if one is going to link the 'triad structure' with a creation chant like "Atua-Mata-Riri," then one would expect that the translations would yield copulations between gods and goddesses, rather than between mere creatures like birds and fish. Anyway, how much sense does it make to speak of a shark copulating with a god to produce another shark? We must not take the ancient Polynesians for cretins, says a sarcastic Guy.

While Fischer has responded to some of these criticisms, the chief weaknesses in his 'decipherment' outlined above remain unanswered. It is highly significant that in his huge 1997 study of *rongorongo*, which attempts comprehensiveness (and which is certainly valuable in bringing together hitherto-scattered materials), *there is no sign list*: the basic tool required for a convincing decipherment. In a reply to Guy, Fischer concluded by stating that "*rongorongo* does not resemble any other known script in the world." This, of course, was the line taken by Sir Eric Thompson (with more conviction and subtlety) against Knorozov and other proponents of the Mayan script as a logosyllabic script. We now know that Thompson was hopelessly wrong. Unless Fischer can come up with stronger arguments for his theory, his 'decipherment' will go the same way as Barthel's, not to speak of de Hevesy's much-publicized 1930s theory of a link between *rongorongo* and the Indus script.

The third of our trio of *rongorongo* decipherers, Pozdniakov, holds a view not dissimilar to that of Knorozov in his early work on the Mayan script. Unfortunately, he has yet to develop his ideas thoroughly in print, but it is clear from his single accessible published paper in French that he has evidence for a small set of basic signs, perhaps 55 in all, which has led him

to propose that *rongorongo* may be fundamentally syllabic. Barthel's hundreds of signs—some of which are clearly unnecessary combinations as indicated above—could be reduced much further, if they could be shown to consist of syllabic elements, arranged to look like people, animals and objects in the same way in which the letters of the Korean script are strung together not in sequences like alphabetic letters but rather arranged within notional squares to look like Chinese characters. Thus, according to Pozdniakov, *rongorongo* has gulled us moderns into thinking it is much more pictographic in underlying conception than it really is. (Recall Sir Arthur Evans's pictographic fallacy about Linear B, as discussed on page 80.)

Pozdniakov has reached this conclusion from two basic lines of evidence. First, by analyzing the texts, he has isolated a range of sign elements. For instance, the element that looks like a 'hand' on many signs, such as 🖐, 🖐 and 🖐, alternates freely, even in combination with *non*-anthropomorphic signs such as 56 🖐 and 57 🖐. This suggests that it is not being used pictographically, as it superficially appears to be, but phonetically. In other words, the same sign can look sometimes like a hand and sometimes like an abstract shape—but in both cases it functions as a phonetic sign.

Second, Pozdniakov has compared the frequencies of a range of the 'elements' he has distinguished in the inscriptions with the frequencies of actual syllables in a Rapanui recitation recorded by William Judah Thomson in 1886 (not "Atua-Mata-Riri", another one). Although Pozdniakov cannot directly compare the 'songsheet' with the sung version (since we do not know the actual inscription from which Thomson's informant chanted), there appears to be enough general similarity between the two frequency distributions to equate the 'elements' with the syllables; but

Pozdniakov has so far been unable to identify particular 'elements' with particular syllables in the Rapanui language. As Guy points out, such comparisons could stumble on two problems: the likelihood that the Rapanui language changed in the period between the inscribing of the tablets (which predated the 1770 Spanish visit, in Guy's view) and the recitation to Thomson in 1886; and even more, on the possibility that the inscriptions record *lists*, not the tales known to be in the 1886 recitation (in which case the syllable frequencies in the inscriptions and in the recitation might differ as much as those of Linear B tablets do from Homer).

It is early days yet for the Pozdniakov interpretation. Nevertheless, Guy suspects that the Russian linguist has hit upon a fruitful line of inquiry. But he remains pessimistic—and most other scholars would agree—about the prospects for a full decipherment of *rongorongo*, because there is virtually no chance of finding any more tablets; being made of wood, they will have rotted away in a warm and moist climate. Eventually we may establish the general meaning of some tablets, but a translation of them will probably always elude us. Guy likes to quote the prophecy placed in the mouth of Hotu Matu'a, the first settler of Easter Island, by Father Sebastian Englert:

> 66 Our *ko hau rongorongo* are lost! Future events will destroy these sacred tablets which we bring with us and those which we will make in our new land. Men of other races will guard a few that remain as priceless objects, and their *maori* will study them in vain without being able to read them. Our *ko hau motu mo rongorongo* will be lost forever. *Aue! Aue!* 99

*Moai on Easter Island. Did their sculptors know how to write* rongorongo*? No one knows for sure.*

The New World Begins to Write

# IX

# THE ZAPOTEC AND ISTHMIAN SCRIPTS

**N**ow that the Mayan glyphs have been to a large extent deciphered, attention has begun to focus on the puzzle of their origin. Although the earliest Mayan inscription dates from the 3rd century AD, it is almost inconceivable that such a complex script would not have had a period of gestation and development during the preceding few centuries. From various lines of evidence, it seems that the Maya took the idea of writing–though not their particular signs–from the earlier scripts of Mesoamerica. There are several of these, as shown in the map on the next page, but the only ones with enough text to offer any hope of decipherment are the Zapotec script and the Isthmian script. As is clear from the map, the area of the Isthmian script was contiguous with that of the Mayan script, while the Zapotec script was a close geographical neighbor of the Isthmian. Diffusion of writing across the Isthmus of Tehuantepec into the Maya area is therefore a reasonable (if entirely unproven) hypothesis.

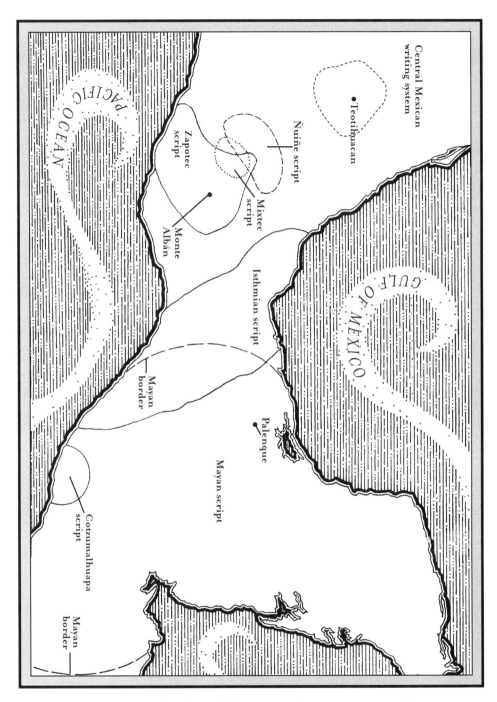

Mesoamerican writing systems. Apart from the Mayan script, the two most important Mesoamerican scripts are the Zapotec script found in the Mexican state of Oaxaca and the Isthmian script found in the Isthmus of Tehuantepec, both of which are undeciphered. The other scripts marked on this map, such as the script found at the great capital city of Teotihuacan, which are also undeciphered, have too scanty a corpus of inscriptions for any worthwhile analysis to be possible.

One might have expected the most ancient civilization of all in Mesoamerica—that of the Olmecs who flourished on the Veracruz coast of the Gulf of Mexico from about 1500-400 BC and created some of the greatest works of art in the region—to have used a writing system. But the evidence for this is weak and disputed. The earliest undoubted writing in the New World seems to belong to the Zapotecs, who inhabited the modern state of Oaxaca, bordering the Pacific coast, and who still live there, speaking their own languages and with a lively artistic tradition, especially in the modern city of Oaxaca and surrounding valleys. The first use of the Zapotec script has been dated to somewhere between 600 and 400 BC (though some scholars are not convinced that the date is as early as this). Since this period predates the appearance of the Isthmian script by several centuries, we shall look at the Zapotec inscriptions first.

They do not form a big corpus (especially when compared to the Mayan one). Javier Urcid, a Mexican-born scholar working in the United States who is now the leading authority on the Zapotec script, estimates some 1200 inscribed objects, ranging from stelae, lintels and painted walls to ceramic vessels, bones and shells. Only half of these (570) include glyphs that are clearly 'writing'; the rest are, in a loose sense, 'pictographic' and of a bewildering diversity. There are no long inscriptions and many are fragmentary with only a few incomplete glyphs. "Assuming that each object has at least one glyph (a very conservative assumption)," says Urcid, "then the Zapotec corpus would have at least 1200 glyphs."

The majority of the inscriptions—and the most significant ones—come from the Zapotec capital city built on the tremendous hill-top site of Monte Albán outside the modern city of Oaxaca. This is principally known for its great plaza, surrounding structures and tombs built during its Classic period of prosperity (after about AD 300), but it has earlier structures, dating from perhaps 500-300 BC,

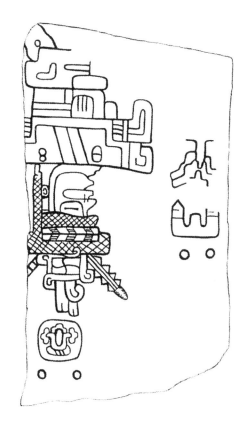

which carry Pre-Classic inscriptions. The Zapotec script thus appears to have flourished in the valley of Oaxaca and region (including the Pacific coast) for more than a thousand years until perhaps 800 AD, by which time Monte Albán had been mostly abandoned. When the Spanish arrived in the 16th century, the Zapotec language was still being spoken and there was still writing in Oaxaca, but it does not appear to have resembled the ancient Zapotec writing.

The Monte Albán inscriptions include the above detail in the wall of a building, which probably records the capture of a town (whose ruler has been inverted) on a certain date (unreadable). There is also writing on stone stelae. The one on the next page, shown disassembled for ease of interpretation, apparently depicts a prisoner (far right) being presented by a shaman (who has been transformed into a bird) to the governor of Monte Albán (reclining):

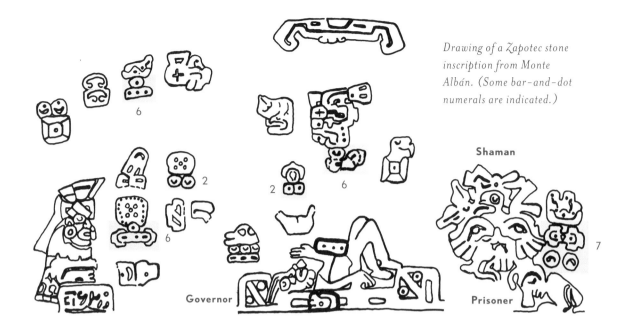

*Drawing of a Zapotec stone inscription from Monte Albán. (Some bar-and-dot numerals are indicated.)*

**Shaman**

6

2

2

6

6

**Governor**

**Prisoner**

7

An early excavator of Monte Albán, Leopoldo Batres, drew an important conclusion from a series of such inscriptions. He compared them to glyphs from other parts of Mesoamerica, including those in various codices, and concluded that Zapotec writing was aesthetically quite distinct from Mixtec, Aztec and Mayan writing. A century later, the Mayanist Michael Coe, strongly agrees:

❝ In either their Pre-Classic or Classic form, the blocky, somewhat crude texts of the Zapotec bear no resemblance to the highly calligraphic, grid-regulated, painted or carved texts of the Classic Maya; even if the two systems shared common roots, which they almost surely did not, they progressed along increasingly divergent paths. ❞

A second early investigator, Nicolas Léon, of the Mexican National Museum, made another crucial observation: the inscriptions included glyphs accompanied by bar-and-dot combinations. (These have been highlighted in the above inscription.) If the values of these bars and dots were the same as those used by the Maya and the Aztecs (page 111), i.e. each bar counted five and each dot one, then it looked as if the calendrical system used throughout Mesoamerica was a Zapotec invention.

The Mexican archaeologist Alfonso Caso took up the challenge of proving this, and began the first systematic study of the Zapotec inscriptions in 1928. He soon realized that none of the bar-and-dot numerals exceeded thirteen: strong evidence that the system was like that of the Maya and Aztecs, if we recall the fact that the Maya used a system of 13 numerals combined with 20 named days to create a 260-day count. The glyphs accompanying the bar-and-dot numerals should therefore represent the Zapotec names for the days. Caso could easily compile a list of these glyphs, which turned out to number more than 20—presumably because some were variants (as in the Mayan script).

Caso knew that a Dominican priest in Oaxaca in the 16th century, Fray Juan de Córdova, had published a Spanish-Zapotec dictionary in 1578, which included the names of the 20 days in Zapotec.

Unlike Diego de Landa who wrote down a Mayan 'alphabet' based on the actual glyphs, Córdova did not work with the Zapotec script itself, which had died out, but with locally available codices probably in Mixtec style (we cannot be sure, as Córdova does not show these images). We must assume that, by pointing to the codex glyphs and asking a Zapotec informant to pronounce the name of each day in Zapotec, Córdova recorded his published list of 20 day names:

| | Zapotec | Spanish | (English) |
|---|---|---|---|
| 1 | Chilla | Lagarto | Crocodile |
| 2 | Laa | Relámpago | Lightning |
| 3 | Laala | ? | ? |
| 4 | Lachi | Juego de pelota? | Ballgame? |
| 5 | Zee | Miseria | Misfortune |
| 6 | Lana | Flecha, Tizne | Arrow, Soot |
| 7 | China | Venado | Deer |
| 8 | Lapa | ? | ? |
| 9 | Nica | Agua | Water |
| 10 | Tella | Nudo | Knot |
| 11 | Loo | Mona, Mono | Monkey |
| 12 | Pija | Planta jabonera | Soap plant |
| 13 | Laa | ? | ? |
| 14 | Lache | Corazón | Heart |
| 15 | Naa | Milpa | Corn field |
| 16 | Loo | Ojo | Eye |
| 17 | Xoo | Temblor | Earthquake |
| 18 | Lopa | ? | ? |
| 19 | Lape | Gota | Drop |
| 20 | Loo | Principal | Ruler, Lord |

How was a scholar working in the 20th century to correlate the 16th-century Spanish words for the day names with their ancient Zapotec glyphs? The main method had to be by matching the apparent iconic meaning of the glyphs, however tricky this was to discern, with the Spanish meanings of the day names as recorded by Córdova (four of which he did not provide). Thus, eleven glyphs that accompany bar-and-dot numerals have been linked by scholars with Córdova's day names on the basis that they 'look like' the meanings of the Spanish words: crocodile, lightning, deer, water, knot, monkey, soap plant, corn field, eye, earthquake, ruler, in English. Three other correlations were plausible on the basis of the metaphorical/iconographic associations of the object depicted in the Zapotec glyph: 'snake' = misfortune, 'skull' = soot (death), 'jaguar' = heart. The meaning of two of the remaining six glyphs has been determined by comparative analysis with other Mesoamerican calendrical, iconographic and linguistic conventions. This is the current list of day names, as refined by Urcid, now with the ancient Zapotec glyphs added:

| | English | Zapotec sign(s) |
|---|---|---|
| 1 | Crocodile | |
| 2 | Lightning | |
| 3 | ? | |
| 4 | Ballgame? | |
| 5 | Misfortune | |
| 6 | Arrow, Soot | |
| 7 | Deer | |
| 8 | ? | |
| 9 | Water | |
| 10 | Knot | |
| 11 | Monkey | |
| 12 | Soap plant | |
| 13 | ? | |
| 14 | Heart | |
| 15 | Corn field | |
| 16 | Eye | |
| 17 | Earthquake | |
| 18 | ? | |
| 19 | Drop | |
| 20 | Ruler, Lord | |

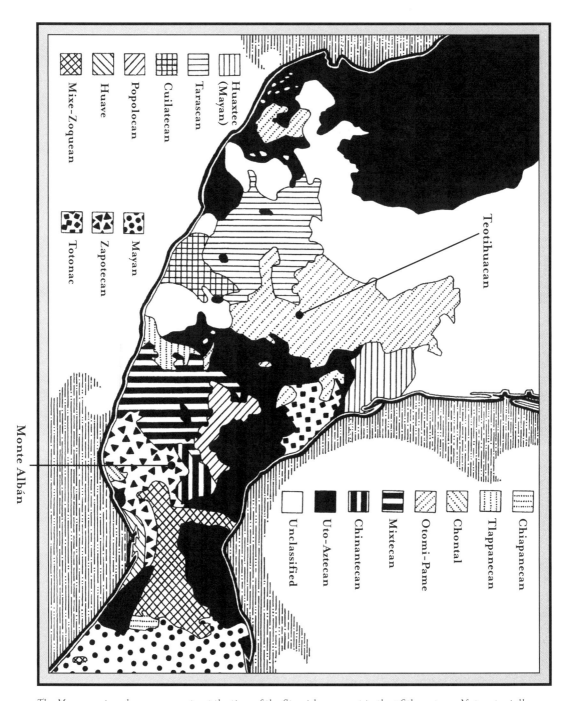

Legend (left):
Mixe-Zoquean
Huave
Popolocan
Cuilatecan
Tarascan
Huaxtec (Mayan)

Totonac
Zapotecan
Mayan

Teotihuacan

Monte Albán

Legend (right):
Unclassified
Uto-Aztecan
Chinantecan
Mixtecan
Otomi-Pame
Chontal
Tlappanecan
Chiapanecan

*The Mesoamerican language groups at the time of the Spanish conquest in the 16th century. Note especially the area of Zapotecan speakers and Mixe-Zoquean speakers; their languages may relate to the languages of the ancient Zapotec and Isthmian scripts respectively, if in a complex way given the large time gap.*

From this understanding of the numerals and the day names, the rest of the Zapotec calendrical system, with its 52-year 'calendar round' like that of the Maya, has been more or less worked out by scholars. But it has not, alas, enabled them to date the Zapotec inscriptions. The reason is that unlike the Maya (and the Aztecs), the Zapotecs never adopted the 'long count' (page 116). In other words, Zapotec dates float, unanchored to any fixed point in time, or at least one known to epigraphers. Presumably the 'long count' was an innovation added to the Zapotec calendar by those who adopted their system, such as the Maya.

Vital though it is, the understanding of the calendrical glyphs started by Caso and improved by others, has not brought deep understanding of the *non*-calendrical Zapotec glyphs, in the way that it did in the Maya decipherment with the construction of genealogies of rulers and other chronologies. Instead it has been only somewhat helpful. For example, since the Zapotecs named people after the day on which they were born, day-name glyphs appear in non-calendrical contexts too, referring to individuals, and this enabled Urcid (with Marcus Winter) to propose a partial list of rulers of Monte Albán and to name, say, the shaman on the Monte Albán stela (page 248) as '7 Soap Plant'; indeed Urcid believes that "most of the glyphs accompanied by numbers are undoubtedly names of people (i.e. historical figures)"–not calendrical glyphs. But the difficulties impeding a fuller decipherment are formidable. First, there is the small corpus of texts, though this is gradually increasing as a result of extended surveys in Oaxaca state, new excavations and searches in museum storerooms, not to mention the brevity of all these inscriptions.

Then there is the lack of provenance for many inscriptions: we have no idea where they came from, which deprives us of crucial contextual information. Furthermore, no bilinguals have been found. Finally, studies aimed at reconstructing the ancient Zapotec language assumed to have been spoken in the period 500 BC - AD 800, have not yet proceeded far.

The overlap between the current speech area of Zapotec and the distribution of the ancient script makes it reasonable to assume a link between the language and the script. Compare the map opposite of the languages spoken in Mexico at the time of the Spanish conquest (and of Córdova's dictionary) with the map of the ancient Mesoamerican scripts on page 246. The area of the ancient Zapotec script and the area of the spoken language do not match exactly, but the overlap is still substantial.

Yet if geography is broadly in favor of a connection between the language of the ancient script and modern Zapotec, the linguistics of this link are likely to be tangled. Modern Zapotec belongs to the Otomanguean family which contains eight other branches including Mixtecan, the evolution of which is poorly understood. Not only is there the issue of language change over some 2000 years to consider, the Zapotecan language group itself is highly diversified, with three major branches and several mutually unintelligible variants. One linguist has compared the diversity of speech among the perhaps 450,000 Zapotecan speakers spread over half the state of Oaxaca with the linguistic diversity among a few hundred million Romance-language speakers spread over parts of Europe and a large part of the New World. To make the situation more intractable still, we know the names of only a few ancient locations—which might be expected to appear in the inscriptions—in Zapotec, because many locations in Oaxaca have long been known by their names in Nahuatl, the language of the Aztecs (the main language of the Uto-Aztecan family shown in the above linguistic map), which intruded into what is now Oaxaca state well before the Spanish conquest.

Nevertheless, useful work is being done in analyzing the glyphs, chiefly by Urcid. After a wide-ranging check of the original inscriptions that have been published and the documentation of well over 100 unpublished ones in the late 1980s and 90s, he has concluded that the Zapotec script contains at least 100 signs; it is not possible to put an exact figure on the signary because there is no reason to assume that in a small corpus, all the available signs have been used. So far we have no clue as to what proportion of the signs are purely phonetic and how these signs combine with logographic signs. But we can be sure that 100 is a figure too high for Zapotec to be a purely syllabic script and too low for it to be a logosyllabic one like the Mayan. In Coe's opinion, the Zapotec scribes may never have tried to develop the phonetic/syllabic side of their system to the same degree as the Mayan scribes, although he cautions that unlike in the Maya case, "no pre-conquest Zapotec codices survive at all, and what little of the script appears on monuments may gave only a very truncated view of the whole." On this view, even if epigraphers were to develop a good grasp of the ancient Zapotec language, they might find that it was not fully represented by the script, as we suspect to be the case with the proto-Elamite script and perhaps *rongorongo* too.

———

The Isthmian script presents an intriguing contrast to the Zapotec script. There is considerably less of it—a mere 500-600 characters *in toto*—yet it is concentrated in one long inscription and we are somewhat more confident and informed about its underlying language. As a result, two respected scholars claim to have deciphered Isthmian as a logosyllabic script, providing phonetic values for most (80 per cent) of its syllabary and the meanings of dozens of logograms—a situation comparable with the Maya decipherment. Their claim is strongly contested, but if it were to be proved right, theirs would be an achievement with far-reaching implications for other undeciphered scripts, given the small amount of Isthmian text available.

The Isthmian story begins in 1902, when a strange little statuette made of jade was ploughed up in a field in the Olmec area, southern Veracruz, supposedly in the Tuxtla Mountains near San Andrés Tuxtla. It depicted a man dressed as duck, and was inscribed with about 70 characters of unknown writing. Deposited in the Smithsonian Institution in Washington DC, the Tuxtla statuette acquired a kind of cult status over the decades—like the Phaistos disc found a few years later—because no other examples of the script turned up; a well-known Mayanist of the time at Harvard University used to give replicas of the statuette to favored students when they got married.

*The Tuxtla statuette (opposite) and the La Mojarra stela (see pages 255–56). Both objects are inscribed with the same undeciphered script, known variously as the La Mojarra script, the epi-Olmec script and (as here) the Isthmian script.*

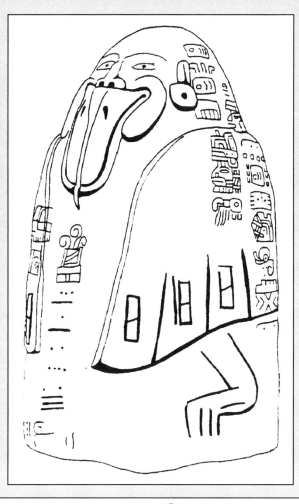

Then, in late 1986, bare-footed fishermen at La Mojarra, a small ranching and fishing settlement on the Acula River not far from Tuxtla, stumbled upon a large stone underwater, while laying log pilings for a small dock. Stone of any kind is unusual in that swampy, alluvial area. When the locals hauled this one out, it was obviously unique for the area: a 4-ton basalt stela, 2.34 metres high and 1.42 metres broad (7.68 x 4.66 ft)—twice the dimensions of the Rosetta stone and five times its weight, polished on one face and incised with a drawing of a princely looking figure and a long inscription, mostly on one side of the stela flanking the figure. When epigraphers were able to examine this, after a certain amount of local politicking, they were excited enough to call it perhaps the most important inscription ever discovered in Mesoamerica.

There were now two major samples of the mysterious Isthmian script, as well as nine other inscriptions from the Isthmus of Tehuantepec, such as a celt, a carved monkey mask and a potsherd, which were however too fragmentary to be of much use in decipherment. That the writing on the La Mojarra stela and on the Tuxtla statuette was of the same kind, even though only some 25 signs were shared, was clear from both visual and epigraphic evidence. The two scripts definitely looked similar, allowing for the fact that one was monumental and the other was written on a small object; and both contained dates written in the bar-and-dot notation of the Mesoamerican calendar, using the 'long count' (unlike the Zapotec dates). There was one date on the statuette and two on the stela. You can work them out for yourself (the last part is the corresponding day in the 260-day count with the Mayan day name):

**Tuxtla statuette**

8.6.2.4.17  8 Kaban (14 March AD 162)

**La Mojarra stela**

8.5.3.3.5  13 Chikchan (21 May AD 143)

8.5.16.9.7  [5] Manik (13 July AD 156)

The fact that the dates were so close in time strongly supported the visual evidence that the two inscriptions were written in one script.

Choosing a name for it has proved somewhat problematic. The compilers of the sign list and concordance, Martha Macri and Laura Stark (of the University of California), refer to the La Mojarra script. John Justeson (of the State University of New York) and Terrence Kaufman (of the University of Pittsburgh), its would-be collaborative decipherers, prefer the name epi-Olmec script, after its supposed Olmec origin. Others, such as the Mayanists Stephen Houston (of Brigham Young University) and Michael Coe, prefer the more general and neutral name Isthmian script, in recognition of the script's occurrence at several places in the isthmus and its possible links with both the Olmecs, the Maya and perhaps the Zapotec script.

Although the Tuxtla statuette remains important, the discovery of the La Mojarra stela has eclipsed it because its inscription is much longer: 400-500 characters, depending on how one counts the symbols. These are referred to by column letters A-U and numbered from top to bottom, as indicated over page:

*Part of the La Mojarra stela.*

*Drawing of the La Mojarra stela.*

The reading order is known to be from top to bottom and from the center to the outer edges. The first is clear from the direction of reading of the two dates (highlighted) which must be from top to bottom so that the 260-day count comes last, while the second order arises from the positions of the dates, which would be expected to begin (not end) each half of the inscription, and also from the fact that the same signs on opposite sides, e.g. F5/R39, (highlighted), face towards the center, i.e. they are mirror images. Careful examination reveals a few scribal errors in this latter respect, for example sign D1 on the left of the stela and signs O25 and R23 on the right of the stela :

D1          O25          R23

in which the scribe has failed to reverse the circle/dot inside the small rounded box as expected.

The Macri/Stark sign list for the script, covering all known Isthmian inscriptions not just the La Mojarra stela, numbers the signs as MS 1-185; it contains 166 non-numerical signs and 14 numeral signs (there are unattested numeral signs, hence gaps in the numbering 1-19). Of the 166 signs, 143 occur on the stela. Of these 143 signs, 58—that is about 40 per cent—occur only once, while 27 signs occur fairly frequently (three or four times), 15 signs occur frequently (between five and nine times), and 5 signs are very frequent (ten or more occurrences): a reasonable distribution for a mixture of logograms and syllables in a logosyllabic script. However, Macri and Stark warn: "Given the rudimentary understanding of the text which we have at this time, the numbers for each of the signs are assigned according to form, and not according to function. No phonetic and little semantic information is assumed." They also make no attempt to segment the text into 'words', since there is no graphical indication of word boundaries (unlike the proto-Elamite script and some of the *rongorongo* writing).

Thus far, there is a good measure of agreement among scholars, and the MS (Macri-Stark) numbers have been used by Justeson and Kaufman in their much fuller analysis of the script. There is also general agreement that the most likely candidate for the Isthmian language is an early form of Zoquean, a branch of the Mixe-Zoquean language family spoken in the isthmus and adjacent areas today (see map on page 250); seven Mixe-Zoquean languages are spoken by some 100,000 to 150,000 people. (Mixe-Zoquean is *not* part of the Otomanguean family that includes Mixtec and Zapotec.) Kaufman has made a special study of these languages over many years and has reconstructed a proto-Zoquean language spoken about 1400 years ago. Those who lived in the area before that date, i.e. the writers of the Isthmian script (and of course the much older Olmecs), would, Kaufman proposes, have spoken pre-proto-Zoquean. The existence of such a language receives support from the fact that dozens of the key words spread far and wide in Mesoamerican culture—such as those for cacao, tortilla, incense and turkey—can be shown to be loan words from Mixe-Zoquean languages. To account for these words' geographical spread and high significance, the languages must have roots going back to the beginning of civilization in the area. The Olmecs were Mixe-Zoqueans, say Justeson and Kaufman; hence their belief that Isthmian is an 'epi-Olmec' script.

Apart from pre-proto-Zoquean, the only other serious candidate for the Isthmian language might be a Mayan language. While this has been pursued by one writer, Lloyd Anderson, there has been no support for the idea from professional epigraphers, including (unsurprisingly) Justeson, who is a Mayanist by training. The resemblance between the Isthmian and Mayan scripts, though present, is superficial and weak to the trained eye (unlike, say, the clear resemblance between Linear A and B). Anyway, it seems unlikely–though not inconceivable–that two different scripts would have developed at around the same period to write the same or a similar Mayan language.

However, once we start to examine the attempt of Justeson and Kaufman to apply Mixe-Zoquean to the La Mojarra stela and other Isthmian inscriptions, there is no longer much agreement between all the experts. Having collaborated on the problem since the beginning of 1991, Justeson and Kaufman startled their colleagues by announcing a decipherment in a detailed article in 1993, published as a cover story in *Science*, followed by a second shorter piece in *Science* four years later and some other articles. However they have yet to produce a substantial publication on the subject, and say that they are unlikely to do so for some time to come.

Their first article begins with the following statement:

" The keys to our decipherment were (i) the discovery of a lengthy text in the script; (ii) the assumption that the texts were in Mixe-Zoquean languages; (iii) our analysis of the grammatical structures of available texts; (iv) an account of these structures in terms of the previously reconstructed grammar of proto-Mixe-Zoquean; and (v) clues to

word meaning, from calendrical constraints and from comparison with similar Mayan signs, that enabled us to correlate spelled-out words with reconstructed proto-Zoquean and proto-Mixe-Zoquean vocabulary. "

Given the lack of sufficient Isthmian texts for a purely internal analysis like that applied to Linear B, or the availability of a bilingual clue such as Landa's 'alphabet' in the Maya case, the above is a reasonable approach. The danger is that the analysis of the grammatical structure, which is necessarily highly speculative with so little text, and the separate reconstruction of the grammar of pre-proto-Zoquean, which is also speculative, will reinforce each other and produce apparent 'matches' between script and language almost as misleading as 'Chinese whispers'. (This is the children's game where a sentence whispered once only into the ear of the first person in a chain emerges at the other end, after multiple whisperings, as something completely and comically different, because each person has attempted to match the indistinct sounds they thought they heard with their mental conception of the language being spoken.)

For instance, Justeson and Kaufman state that their structural analysis of the text on the stela and the statuette allowed them "to recognize two signs as representing frequent grammatical prefixes, which often appear at the beginning of words, and two other signs as representing frequent grammatical suffixes, which often appear at the ends of words." But nowhere do they properly explain how they determined what they take to be the beginning and end of words. Apparently they deduced the existence of words by identifying recurring sign sequences–which they do not show–and then assuming these sequences to be words, and also by assuming that the end of a column on the stela generally coincides with the end of a word. Both deductions are questionable, especially the second one: texts written in other scripts frequently run over from line to line or column to column without a word break. (This seems to be true of the script in the last chapter, *rongorongo*, and also of the Indus script in the next chapter.)

The most frequent Isthmian sign is MS 20, ⌒⌣⌐, which occurs 36 times on the La Mojarra stela (and 10 times on the Tuxtla statuette), and which ends 7 out of the 21 columns on the stela. Justeson and Kaufman, to some extent supported by other scholars, claim that MS 20 is "word-final". They immediately jump to the conclusion: "It can hardly be other than a syllabogram for *wʉ*"–the most frequent verb suffix in Mixe-Zoquean, and which they expect to be the most frequent of the six tense-aspect-mood verb suffixes reconstructed for pre-proto-Mixe-Zoquean. (In English, change of tense is expressed in 'I run' versus 'I will run, I ran'; change of aspect in 'I run' versus 'I am running'; change of mood in 'I run' versus subjunctive 'I may run' or imperative 'run!'– without of course using suffixes.) In making this equation between MS 20 and *wʉ*, Justeson and Kaufman have clearly assumed that MS 20 is often the final sign of Isthmian verbs, but they offer no solid internal evidence for *why* they think that these particular sign sequences represent verbs.

In support of the equation, they now inform the reader that *wʉ* sometimes has a *second* grammatical function in Mixe-Zoquean (and hence in the reconstructed language hypothesized for the script). This function is unconnected with verbs, but is instead a suffix to nouns–designations for titles or offices in references to the ruler–and conveys the meaning '**he who is** TITLE'. Again, they find a parallel with the Isthmian script,

such as the sequence in column P (33-39) of the stela:

But Justeson and Kaufman offer no internal evidence as to how they distinguish when MS 20 is acting as a noun suffix from when it is acting as a verb suffix. Instead they simply claim: "This twin usage of MS 20 not only confirms the reading but is also a signature of the Mixe-Zoquean grammar, confirming the hypothesized language identification." And they translate the above seven signs as:

1  BLOODLETTING
2  PENIS-
3  INSIDE
4  *mʉ*
5  *k(ʉ)*
6  TITLE
7  *wʉ*

–"he who is TITLE [underwent] his bloodletting from within the penis", with the first two signs (reading from the top down) being interpreted 'iconically' as logograms for 'bloodletting' and 'penis' (this being a familiar ritual among the Maya and other Mesoamerican rulers), and the other two syllabic values, *mʉ* and *kʉ*, meaning 'from', being derived from other grammatical comparisons between language and script.

Tempting though such iconic 'decipherments' are—as with the day names in Zapotec—Justeson and Kaufman are at pains to state that they made very few inferences based on iconicity, and none that was crucial to the decipherment as a whole. The reason for their wariness is, of course, that there is much scope for disagreement about the iconic nature of any given sign, i.e. what it 'looks like'. Very little reliable evidence exists, for example, to support the iconic identification of 'penis' above—as with Fischer's identification of the 'phallus' sign in *rongorongo* (page 240)—especially given our ignorance of Isthmian culture and the necessarily small number of signs in the Isthmian corpus that can be compared with any particular sign as a check on wrong identifications. (The 'penis' sign occurs only twice in Isthmian inscriptions.) As an example of their caution, Justeson and Kaufman cite the signs MS 31 and 32—Venus as evening star and as morning star, according to Macri—which they treat as one sign:

They explain that many Mayanists had identified this sign from its close visual parallel to the Mayan logogram for 'star'. They, however, did not make this assumption, because nothing in the immediate context of the sign supported the identification. Instead they noticed that the sign was immediately preceded by a sign which they had already read as *ma*, which is the opening syllable of the proto-Zoquean word 'matzaʔ' (star). Furthermore, once they had worked out the chronology of the text, they found the two occurrences of this sign to be separated by 9 x 584 days—exactly 9 Venus cycles. (Their chronology, too, is controversial.)

Iconography (rather than iconicity) is called in to support Justeson and Kaufman's grammatically based identification of MS 44, , as a pronominal prefix with the phonetic value *na*. The sign resembles iconography found at two contemporaneous Mesoamerican sites, where it is clearly associated with the concept of earth. The proto-Zoquean word for 'earth' is 'nas'. The phonetic value *na* is therefore said to be derived from 'nas', on the 'A as in Apple' model (the so-called 'acrophonic' principle).

By hundreds of (often intricate) arguments such as those outlined above, Justeson and Kaufman have compiled a 'grid' containing 52 syllabic signs out of the expected 66 Isthmian syllabic signs (there are 6 vowels and 11 consonants in Mixe-Zoquean); they have produced a list of meanings of many logograms; and they have published a translation of a small part of the La Mojarra stela inscription. This reads: "Behold, there/he was for 12 years a [title]. And then a garment got folded. He [uttered]—the stones that he set in order were thus symbols, ?kingly ones: 'What I chopped is a planting and a good harvest'. [A] shape-shifter(s) appeared divinely in his body." Despite the doubtfulness of this last contribution, Justeson and Kaufman clearly regard the Isthmian script as fundamentally deciphered, even asserting that, "it is difficult to imagine that this model would yield a complete, coherent, and grammatical text if these portions of the decipherment—language structure, sign values, and spelling conventions—were not essentially correct."

Since 1993, the two scholars have invested much effort in trying to persuade other epigraphers that they have 'cracked' the script. Besides its prominent publication in *Science*, the leading science journal of the United States, the decipherment has received unqualified support from David

## PHONETIC READINGS

| | | | |
|---|---|---|---|
| | 104 | ''ʔips' | 'twenty' (this sign is also used for 'moon') |
| | 172 | 'jama' | 'day', 'animal spirit companion' |
| | 164 | 'jama' | 'animal spirit companion' |
| | 23 | 'juʔtz' | 'to pierce' |
| | 24 | 'juʔtzi' | 'how, when, as' (relative) |
| | 171 | 'kiʔm' | 'to accede' (this sign is also used for 'rule' and other words derived from 'kiʔm' |
| | 57 | 'komi' | 'boss', 'lord' |
| | 10 | 'mak' | 'ten' (in deity name Ten Sky) |
| | 31/32 | 'matzaʔ | 'star', 'planet' |
| | 137 | 'poyʔa' | "month" of 20 days |
| | 50 | 'tokoy' | 'to get lost or ruined' |
| | 158 | 'tuki' | 'turtle' |
| | 136/144 | 'tzap' | 'sky' |
| | 150 | 'wik' | 'to sprinkle' |

## RITUAL-RELATED

| | | |
|---|---|---|
| | 91 | 'to perform (ritual)' |
| | 22 | 'blood' |
| | 132 | 'to let blood' |
| | 107 | 'penis' |
| | 115 | 'to chop' |
| | 147 | 'to cast/scatter' |
| | 58 | 'droplets' or 'grains' |
| | 99 | 'liquid', 'drops' |

## CALENDRICAL

| | | |
|---|---|---|
| | 72 | 'year' (presumably 'ʔame'), 'drum' (presumably 'kowa') |
| | 104 | 'moon' (presumably 'poyʔa') |
| | 89 | day count indicator |
| | 106 | month name/patron XIII |
| | 110 | month name/patron XVI |
| | 156 | month name/patron XVIII |
| | 154 | day name Deer |
| | 131 | day name Earthquake |
| | 155 | day name Snake |

## ROYAL

| | | |
|---|---|---|
| | 181-84 | royal title determiner |
| | 129 | royal accession |
| | 60 | title/office |
| | 61 | title/office |
| | 62 | title/office |
| | 76 + 78 | title/office |
| | 51 | 'split conch shell' (so-called "knuckle dusters") |
| | 68 | symbol-bearing object (possibly 'kipsi') |
| | 75 | 'hallowed' |
| | 83 | symbol of status/role |
| | 111 | 'throne' |

## MISCELLANEOUS

| | | |
|---|---|---|
| | 134 + 44 | geographic location (town?) |
| | 119 | 'mountain' |
| | 40-41 | 'to get pounded' |
| | 120 | 'inside' (possibly 'joj') |
| | 33 | 'hide', 'skin' (presumably 'naka') |
| | 36 + 44 | 'sunset' |

*A chart of Isthmian logograms, according to the epigrapher John Justeson and the linguist Terrence Kaufman, who together claim to have deciphered much of the Isthmian script. It was published in* Science *in 1993. Few scholars accept these phonetic readings and semantic interpretations and almost all regard the script as essentially undeciphered, although many agree with Justeson and Kaufman that the Isthmian language is likely to be an early form of Mixe-Zoquean. (All numbers next to the signs refer to Macri-Stark (MS) numbers, as described in the text.)*

Kelley, one of the pioneers of the Maya decipherment. Other specialists are said by Justeson and Kaufman to be convinced, but none has yet said so in print. On the other hand, skeptics, notably Stephen Houston, have taken time to publish a detailed refutation of the claims. Since both Justeson and Kaufman have strong reputations in their respective fields—Mayan epigraphy and the historical linguistics of the Americas—an effective critique would require both deep and wide-ranging knowledge, and this may be a brake on potential critics.

Some basic criticisms of their methodology are possible, however, without going into the nuances of Mixe-Zoquean. At the beginning of their 1993 announcement in *Science*, Justeson and Kaufman state revealingly: "Decipherment is a process of accounting for the patterns of sign use in texts"—a definition that would not have satisfied, say, Michael Ventris, because it omits to mention *language*. More accurate would be: "Decipherment is a process of deducing from texts a known or plausibly reconstructed language that accounts for the patterns of sign use in texts." Later in the article, the authors state: "Our decipherment of epi-Olmec hieroglyphic writing has allowed us to *identify* the epi-Olmec language... We have *shown* that the grammatical structure of epi-Olmec texts is Mixe-Zoquean [my italics]." But as they themselves candidly admit above (page 258), they *assumed* that the language was Mixe-Zoquean as one of the "keys" to their decipherment. In reality, their technique consists of using the grammar of their assumed language, pre-proto-Mixe-Zoquean, as a tool to impose (*not* "show") grammatical structure and then, having created this supposed structure, using the structure in reverse as evidence for the correctness of

their language hypothesis! Put like this, their argument is obviously circular, though in practice this is often difficult to discern. To take only one more example, proto-Zoquean 'nas' is used, as we saw, to support the reading of a sign as *na*; but two pages later in their 1993 article, the fact that the sign now read as *na* agrees with 'nas' becomes a small piece of evidence *in support of* the language being proto-Zoquean. Thus, first Justeson and Kaufman assume the Isthmian language is pre-proto-Mixe-Zoquean, then they proceed to "identify" it as such.

What is lacking is any clear account of how they analyzed the sign patterns in the texts (*à la* Kober and Ventris in Linear B) *before* looking for parallels with their chosen language. In effect, they say: this undeciphered script must write pre-proto-Mixe-Zoquean, now let's have a look for some patterns in the signs that support this assumption. The internal analysis done by scholars with Linear B long before the language was known to be Greek (and when Ventris suspected an Etruscan-related language), not to speak of Knorozov's analysis of the Mayan glyphs and even Fischer's search for patterns in *rongorongo*, is not at all evident in the published work of Justeson and Kaufman. The supposed dual function of MS 20—as a verb suffix and as a noun suffix (both with value *wʉ*) is never demonstrated by them in the texts, by showing that particular sign groups containing MS 20 are likely to be verbs and nouns. Indeed, according to Macri and several other epigraphers, MS 20 is really a *punctuation* sign, not a verb or noun suffix at all, which Macri maintains has no phonetic value. Without broad agreement on such a basic issue concerning the most frequent Isthmian sign, how can the much more elaborate Justeson/Kaufman interpretations be trusted?

Considering how little Isthmian text there is, especially when compared with the large corpus of Mayan texts, the degree of Isthmian decipherment claimed by Justeson and Kaufman is really not credible. Besides the large number of syllabic signs and logograms, they claim also to have identified in the La Mojarra text *all six* tense-aspect-mood suffixes—a variety never displayed in a single Mayan text. Indeed, their very claim that the text is "complete, coherent, and grammatical" arouses suspicion, since this has not been the case in other successful decipherments, where individual large texts always contain inconsistencies and obscurities. *A priori*, why should the La Mojarra stela be different?

It is also difficult to know how much reliance should be placed upon arguments based on comparisons of the Isthmian signs with the Mayan glyphs, which are frequent in the Justeson/Kaufman work, because there is insufficient evidence to resolve the relationship between the Mayan script and the Olmecs. On the one hand, Justeson and Kaufman are keen to relate the Isthmian script to Olmec iconographic traditions, on the other they maintain that the "closest relative of epi-Olmec [Isthmian] writing is Mayan writing" and that "some epi-Olmec signs and their values were adopted by the Maya, and vice versa." But Coe, an Olmec as well as a Maya expert, in *The Art of the Maya Scribe*, comments that the Isthmian script resembles *Zapotec* writing much more than Mayan in its visible structure—the way that the glyphs are arranged—and that aesthetically the resemblance with Mayan is even weaker: "Perhaps, like runic, the Isthmian script was first developed on wood rather than stone; in its aesthetic 'feel' it is totally non-calligraphic, and certainly not influenced by use of the brush pen so apparent in the Maya style. The art of Mayan writing most assuredly did not have Isthmian roots."

Overall, then, the case for the Justeson/Kaufman 'decipherment' of Isthmian is decidedly unproven and currently rests on shaky foundations, apart from its reasonable assumption of an early form of Mixe-Zoquean for the Isthmian language. What it needs, more urgently than some other 'decipherments' given its evident linguistic sophistication, is the discovery of a new text or texts as substantial as the one found at La Mojarra in 1986. Then, like the virgin tablet that confirmed Ventris's decipherment of Linear B in 1953, the Justeson/Kaufman 'decipherment' could be fairly tested, preferably by others, to see if their phonetic and logographic values would produce meaningful readings consistent with what is known of the history, culture and languages of the Isthmian region.

At the Sign of the Unicorn

# X

# THE INDUS SCRIPT

We now come to the biggest challenge of all in archaeological decipherment, that of the Indus script. If it were to be 'cracked', the silence of a great ancient civilization would be broken. Not only that: a decipherment might shed important new light on the true identity of the proto-Indo-Europeans, ancestors of the modern West, whose language gave birth to most of the modern languages of Europe as well as Sanskrit.

The Indus Valley civilization was lost even at the time of Alexander the Great. When his emissary Aristoboulos visited the area in 326 BC, he found "an abandoned country, with more than a thousand towns and villages deserted after the Indus had changed its course". It was not mentioned again in historical records for over 2000 years. In the early 1920s, an Indian archaeologist out searching for non-existent victory pillars put up by

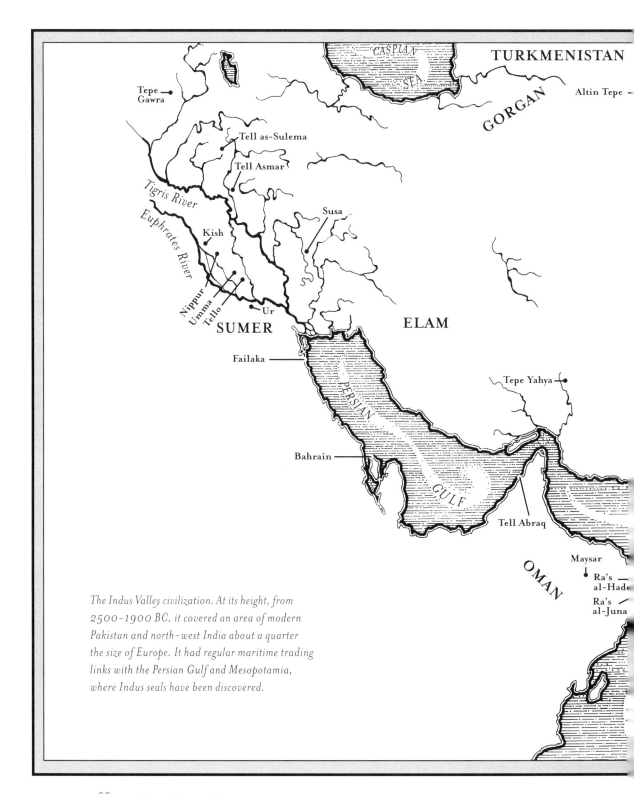

TURKMENISTAN

CASPIAN SEA

GORGAN

Altin Tepe

Tepe Gawra

Tell as-Sulema

Tell Asmar

*Tigris River*

*Euphrates River*

Susa

Kish

Nippur

Umma

Tello

Ur

SUMER

ELAM

Failaka

PERSIAN

Tepe Yahya

Bahrain

GULF

Tell Abraq

OMAN

Maysar

Ra's al-Had

Ra's al-Juna

*The Indus Valley civilization. At its height, from
2500–1900 BC, it covered an area of modern
Pakistan and north-west India about a quarter
the size of Europe. It had regular maritime trading
links with the Persian Gulf and Mesopotamia,
where Indus seals have been discovered.*

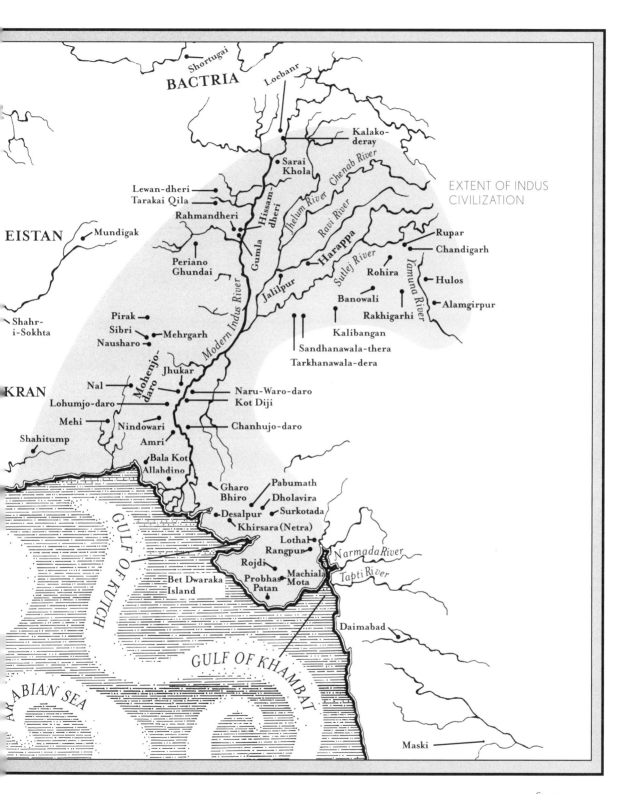

BACTRIA

Shortugai

Loebanr

Kalako-
deray

Sarai
Khola

*Chenab River*

*Jhelum River*

EISTAN

Mundigak

Lewan-dheri
Tarakai Qila

Rahmandheri

Hissam-
dheri

*Ravi River*

Harappa

Rupar

Chandigarh

EXTENT OF INDUS
CIVILIZATION

Periano
Ghundai

Gumla

*Modern Indus River*

Jalilpur

*Sutlej River*

Rohira

*Yamuna River*

Hulos

Shahr-
i-Sokhta

Pirak

Sibri

Nausharo

Mehrgarh

Banowali

Rakhigarhi

Alamgirpur

Kalibangan

Sandhanawala-thera

Tarkhanawala-dera

KRAN

Jhukar

Nal

Mohenjo-
daro

Naru-Waro-daro

Kot Diji

Lohumjo-daro

Mehi

Nindowari

Chanhujo-daro

Shahitump

Amri

Bala Kot

Allahdino

Gharo
Bhiro

Pabumath

Dholavira

Desalpur

Surkotada

Khirsara (Netra)

Lothal

Rangpur

Rojdi

Machiala
Mota

Probhas
Patan

*Narmada River*

*Tapti River*

Bet Dwaraka
Island

GULF
OF
KUTCH

Daimabad

GULF OF KHAMBAT

ARABIAN SEA

Maski

Alexander on his retreat from India, stumbled across the true significance of the ruin mound at Mohenjo-daro (now in Sind province of Pakistan). His discovery, and a similar discovery 350 miles away at Harappa (also in Pakistan), would double the recorded age of civilization in the Indian subcontinent at one stroke—shifting it from the imperial inscriptions of Ashoka in 250 BC back to about 2500 BC. Immediately, a team under Sir John Marshall, director general of the Archaeological Survey of India, began excavating at both sites.

Over the past eight decades, they and their successors have revealed some 1500 sites belonging to the Indus Valley civilization in Pakistan and north-west India, covering an area approximately a quarter the size of Europe, larger than either the ancient Egyptian or the Mesopotamian empires of the 3rd millennium BC. Most were villages, but five were major cities. At its peak, between 2500 and 1900 BC (the precise limits are debatable), Mohenjo-daro and Harappa were comparable with cities like Memphis and Ur. They could not boast great pyramids, palaces, statues, graves and hordes of gold, but their well-planned streets and advanced drainage put to shame all but the town planning of the 20th century AD, and some of their ornaments—such as the long, drilled carnelian beads found as far afield as the royal cemetery of Ur—rival the treasures of the pharaohs for loveliness and technical sophistication. Indus Valley archaeology has come a long way in 80 years, as a recent Asia Society exhibition proved to Americans; the civilization it studies can no longer be regarded as the dowdy poor cousin of ancient Egypt, Mesopotamia and China.

But this advance in understanding how the Indus Valley dwellers lived has served to highlight the embarrassing fact that we can only speculate about how they thought—because their writing remains undeciphered.

Unlike Mayan and Egyptian hieroglyphs, Mesopotamian cuneiform and Linear B, the Indus script appears not on walls, tombs, statues, stelae, clay tablets, papyri and codices, but on seal stones, pottery, copper tablets, bronze implements and ivory and bone rods, found scattered in the buildings and streets of Mohenjo-daro, Harappa and other urban settlements. (No doubt it was written too on perishable materials, such as the palm fronds traditionally used for writing in India.) The seal stones are the most numerous of the inscriptions and are justly celebrated for their exquisiteness and unique style of carving. "At their best, it would be no exaggeration to describe them as little masterpieces of controlled realism, with a monumental strength in one sense out of all proportion to their size and in another entirely related to it", wrote the archaeologist Sir Mortimer Wheeler. Once seen, they are never forgotten.

About 3700 inscribed objects are known, 60 per cent of them on seals, but some 40 per cent of these are duplicate inscriptions, so the useful total for the decipherer is not as large as it seems. More have been found in the 1990s, but it is not an abundant corpus, especially as the inscriptions are tantalizingly brief: the average has less than four characters in a line and five in a text, the longest only 26 characters divided among the three sides of a triangular terracotta prism. In addition to the characters, many seal stones are engraved with an often-detailed intaglio of animals. These are generally recognizable—rhinoceroses, elephants, tigers, buffaloes, zebus, for instance (though curiously no monkeys, peacocks or cobras)—but some are fantastic or chimerical, including a one-horned animal

*Bird's-eye view of part of Mohenjo-daro, one of the two principal cities of the Indus Valley civilization.*

which the early excavators promptly dubbed a 'unicorn' (a creature legendarily originating in India). Unidentified anthropomorphic figures, sometimes seated in yogic postures, also feature and may be gods and goddesses. Various schol-ars, beginning with Marshall, have therefore suggested that some of these figures are precursors of the Hindu deities first mentioned two millennia later in Sanskrit texts; one in particular Marshall dubbed "proto-Shiva".

*Terracotta miniature mask of a bearded, horned deity, from Mohenjo-daro. Two holes on either side allow the mask to be attached to a puppet or worn as an amulet.*

*"Proto-Shiva", an Indus seal from Mohenjo-daro, so-called by the archaeologist John Marshall, its excavator in the 1920s, because the 'yogic' figure wearing a horned headdress surrounded by animals (tiger, elephant, water buffalo, rhinoceros) reminded Marshall of classical Indian depictions of the Hindu god Shiva. There is, however, no evidence for this identification, although there is considerable evidence for other kinds of continuity between the Indus Valley civilization and classical Indian civilization. If we could decipher the Indus inscription written at the top of the seal, we might learn whether Marshall was right or not.*

Such a corpus reminds Emmett Bennett, the Linear B scholar, of the problem of the undeciphered Cretan Hieroglyphic script—most of which appears on seal stones with a picture and a few characters. Another comparison, made by several would-be decipherers, is with the decipherment of the Mayan script, since both scripts involve a large, complex and partly iconographic set of signs, and neither the names of places nor rulers are independently known (in contrast to the Egyptian hieroglyphs, where Young and Champollion could turn to Greek and Roman sources). But there are clear-cut differences, as Michael Coe points out. Maya mathematics and calendrics, "in which the

Classic and codical texts are embedded," were well understood long before Knorozov's breakthrough. Mayan inscriptions are "numerous, often lengthy, and encode complete sentences." Mayan languages are well known. "The cultural context is rich and detailed, and many aspects of it survived the Spanish conquest." Lastly, and crucially, a bilingual is available (in the form of Landa's 'alphabet'). None of these advantages applies to the Indus script. Apart from the brevity of the inscriptions, which may well contain mostly names and titles, we know virtually nothing of the Indus calendrical system, are uncertain about the numerical signs, can only make informed conjectures about the language and culture, and lack anything resembling a bilingual. Above all, the Indus Valley civilization disappeared more than 2500 years before that of the Classic Maya, which is a long time, speaking either archaeologically or linguistically.

The vacuum of knowledge has been filled by some bizarre theories, as well as serious scholarship. We came across one of these in the *rongorongo* chapter: de Hevesy's idea that Easter Island and Indus Valley writing might share a common (proto-Elamite) origin. We also met there, in passing, a German investigator who had found *rongorongo* to record secret sexual deflorations; he was described by *Der Spiegel* as a "translator of old Indian writings". I remember him well, a determined bearded figure at a conference of South Asian archaeologists I attended in Paris in 1989, who tried to buttonhole a reluctant Asko Parpola, the leading scholar of the Indus script, in order to discuss his own decipherment. I have kept the booklet I obtained from him, *The Symbolic Conception of the Indus Script* by Egbert Richter-Ushanas. My favorite part is the author's reading of the Indus sign ⋃ as 'thala', which he derives by comparing the two graphic elements in it to the signs for *tha* and *la* in the Brahmi script used (at the time of Ashoka) to write Sanskrit—for Brahmi is supposed by Richter-Ushanas (and a few others) to be a descendant of the Indus signs, despite a 1500-year gap in the written record. The decipherment of 'thala' leads him to conclude that the 6th-century-BC Greek philosopher, mathematician and astronomer Thales of Miletus (one of the Seven Sages listed by Plato) derived his name from the Indus civilization, because Thales was said to have been a Phoenician and, according to our author, the Phoenician letters, which to some extent resemble the Brahmi letters, must therefore also be derived from the Indus signs: "The Phoenicians were only the first who brought them to the West." Now comes his punchline: "The legend tells, furthermore, that Thales had fallen into a well, when looking at the stars during the night. The compound ⋃ may also symbolize a well with something having sunk or fallen down into it, i.e. a bucket or somebody, who has fallen into the well." Or might it be, perhaps, an ancient Indus Valley swizzle-stick?

The archaeologist Gregory Possehl (of the University of Pennsylvania), who has recently surveyed with dry humor most of the attempts at Indus script decipherment in his book *Indus Age: The Writing System*, knows of over 60 "serious claims". Iravatham Mahadevan, a retired civil servant living in south India who has made himself the leading Indian scholar of the script, is aware of more than 100 such claims. Asko Parpola, who is professor of Indology at the University of Helsinki, in his essential study *Deciphering the Indus Script*, published in 1994, does not put a figure on the total but lists some of the wilder links advanced by serious scholars since the first claim in 1925:

" Connections have been sought with the manuscripts of the Lolos living in southern China and in Southeast Asia, dating back to the 16th century AD; with proto-Elamite accounting tablets; with ideograms carved some two centuries ago on Easter Island in the southeastern Pacific Ocean; with Etruscan pot marks ["More Seven League Boots!" comments Possehl]; with the numerical system of Primitive Indonesian; with Egyptian, Minoan and Hittite hieroglyphs; with the auspicious symbols carved on a 'footprint of the Buddha' in the Maldivian archipelago; and with the glyphs of ancient Central America. "

Let us examine fairly briefly four of the more serious claims, all by respected scholars. Although none has been accepted—in fact, they have been almost universally rejected—each has something worthwhile to teach us about how to tackle this difficult problem; and how not to. Note in what follows that all the inscriptions are read from right to left (we shall come to the evidence for this later).

The first of these 'decipherments', published in 1932, treated the Indus script as if it functioned like Egyptian hieroglyphs. Its author, the celebrated Egyptologist Sir Flinders Petrie, did not postulate any connection between the Indus and Egyptian *languages*, but he did suggest that the pictographic quality of some Indus signs, their variants and their syntax might indicate their meanings on the Egyptian model, assuming that the seals belonged to officials and contained their titles. Thus he read the Indus sign:

which is by far the most common sign, frequently found at the end of inscriptions, as a title meaning 'agent' ('wakil', in Petrie's terminology).

The sign:

he took to be a tree with lopped branches, and the sign:

was said to be a writing tablet with a handle, a kind of hornbook. The sequence:

was therefore said to mean (reading from right to left) "wakil [agent] of the registrar of timber".

On a similar basis, judging that the Indus sign:

looked like the Egyptian hieroglyphic symbol for 'irrigated field', Petrie translated the following sequence:

as "wakil of irrigated land".

He also noted another very common sign and its apparent allographs:

These signs are often found doubled:

Petrie decided that the first of the five variants (on the far left) might indicate a title, inspector or intendant, while in combination the signs might indicate various grades of inspector, such as sub-inspector and deputy inspector: "a most imaginative explanation" for the doubling, notes Possehl.

To be fair to Petrie, he stressed the speculative nature of his 'decipherment', warning that "for 'is' read 'may possibly be' in all instances"—a sound caution, not often heeded by subsequent Indus script decipherers. For even if he were right, there was no way of proving it, since his methodology was largely intuitive. But his suggestions did have one definite merit: they reminded everyone of the likely bureaucratic subject matter of the inscriptions. That is, unless one took the view, as some scholars have, that the Indus Valley civilization is fundamentally different from Egypt, and indeed Mesopotamia, in its use of writing, and that the seals therefore probably contain esoteric ideas.

The second 'decipherment', proposed by an Assyriologist, J. V. Kinnier Wilson (of Cambridge University), in his book *Indo-Sumerian* (1974), links the Indus Valley civilization with the Sumerians. They are said to have sprung from one stock, probably in India, and to have separated into two branches, with the smaller branch settling in Sumer and the larger in the Indus Valley; thus according to the theory, the Sumerian and Indus languages are related to each other, which allows their inscriptions to be compared. While there is no epigraphical evidence for any common ancestry at inland sites lying between the Indus Valley and Mesopotamia (for example, in Elam), there was undoubtedly sea trade between Sumer and the Indus valley in the 3rd millennium BC: Indus seals have been found in Mesopotamia and in the Persian Gulf area, and so have Indus Valley products, such as the drilled carnelian beads. (Puzzlingly, the trade seems to have been one way, because no cuneiform or Mesopotamian products have been found in the Indus Valley.) The Akkadian ruler Sargon (2334-2279 BC) boasts in a cuneiform inscription of ships from Dilmun, Magan and Meluhha that are docked at his capital Akkad. Most scholars equate Dilmun with the Gulf islands of Failaka and Bahrein, Magan with the Makran and Oman, and Meluhha with the Indo-Iranian borderlands and the Indus Valley.

Kinnier Wilson's approach, influenced by the clay tablets of Sumer, assumes that the Indus seals concern economics: he calls it "the case for accountancy". The sign which Petrie read as 'inspector', 𝕏, is read straightforwardly by Kinnier Wilson as 'fish', and its variant 𝕏 is read, also pictographically, as 'carp', a common freshwater fish throughout Asia which has thread-like filaments (known as barbels) hanging from its mouth. (This idea was first proposed by Knorozov, who was interested in the Indus script as well as the Mayan glyphs and *rongorongo,* as we shall see later.) The Sumerian word for carp is 'suhur'.

The next step was to equate Sumerian tablets from Uruk known to concern fish rations (left) with Indus 'fish' inscriptions from three different sources (right):

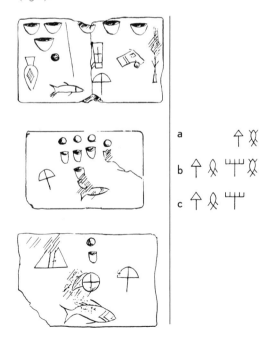

The key, for Kinnier Wilson, is that the Sumerian sign 𐎟, *ba*, meaning 'rations', looks like the final sign of the Indus inscriptions. In 1974, he had regarded it as a word divider, but during the 1980s he changed his mind and allotted it (without other evidence) the meaning 'rations'. By further equating the Indus sign with the Sumerian sign of similar shape, which means 'great' or large', he went on to offer the following interpretations of the above three Indus inscriptions:

   **a.** carp rations ('suhur-ba');
   **b.** giant carp rations;
   **c.** similar to b.—either this was an abbreviation, or the carp was sometimes known simply as the 'giant' fish, without 'carp' being specified pictographically.

The weaknesses in the 'Indo-Sumerian' approach are manifest—why, for a start, does the 'fish' sign occur in b. *as well as* the 'carp' sign?—not the least of its flaws being the gross mismatch between the high artistic quality of the seals and the notion that they were intended as receipts for fish. But Kinnier Wilson's attempt, like Petrie's, also has one definite virtue: it reminds us of the risks of comparing sign shapes across cultures and our duty, if we do, not to manipulate the evidence to fit our preconceptions.

The third 'decipherment' comes from S. R. Rao, an archaeologist well known in India who excavated various Indus sites and became a director of the Archaeological Survey. He proposed it in a large and detailed book, boldly titled *The Decipherment of the Indus Script*, in 1982. It involves at least three radical assumptions. The first is that the Indus signs are mostly compounds (ligatures) of a smaller set of signs—a proposal reminiscent of Pozdniakov's attempt to 'reduce' the sign list of *rongorongo* (pages 241-42). Thus Rao analyzes a series of

signs as follows into ligatures of the common simple sign and other simple signs:

He concludes that there are 62 Indus signs—a figure far lower than that of the sign list proposed by almost all scholars.

By studying graffiti from Indus sites, which appear to post-date the 'mature' phase of the Indus script—i.e. to belong to the centuries after its disappearance c. 1900 BC—Rao postulates the eventual development of an even smaller set of signs, about 20 in all. Indeed, he assumes that the Indus script became alphabetic, and that it was the Indus Valley civilization (or at least its successor culture) which invented the alphabet. Rao believes it was then transmitted to Palestine in the mid 2nd millennium BC, though he does not say how: his second assumption. This then enables him to compare the signs used in the earliest Semitic inscriptions with the mature ('Harappan') signs and the signs on the graffiti ('Late Harappan'):

| S. NO. | PHONETIC VALUE | OLD NORTH SEMITIC SIGNS 16th–13th c.B.C. | HARAPPAN SIGNS | LATE HARAPPAN SIGNS |
|---|---|---|---|---|
| 1 | b | ☐ ʕ | ☐ | ☐ |
| 2 | g | ∧ ↑ | ∧ ∧ | ∧ |
| 3 | d | ◖ △ | ◖ ◗ | ◖ ◗ |
| 4 | h | 𐤄 | 𐤄 E | 𐤄 |
| 5 | w | Y Y | Y | Y |
| 6 | ḥ | ⊟ ⊟ | ⊟ ⧻ | ⊟ |
| 7 | th | ⊖ ⊕ | ◌ ⊙ | ⊘ |
| 8 | k | ⋁ ↓ | ↓ ↓ | ⟟ |
| 9 | n | 5 ʅ | ʃ ʃ | ʅ |
| 10 | s | ‡ | ‡ | ‡ |
| 11 | ᶜ (ay) | ○ ○ | ○ | ○ |
| 12 | p | ⟩○·◇· | ○◇⟩◖ | ○ ◇ |
| 13 | r | ٩ ٩ | ▷ | ▷ |
| 14 | sh | ⩗ ⩗ | ⩗ | ⩗ |
| 15 | t | + × ⅄ | × ⅄ ⊗ | ⅄ |
| 16 | ś | ⊓ · | ⊓ ↑ | ↑ |
| 17 | ḥ | ⊎ · | ⊎ 8 | ⊎ |
| 18 | m | ⟩ · | ✕ Ⅸ | ✕ |
| 19 | ạ | K K K | ∪ | ∪ |
| 20 | ṛ | | ⚥ | ⚥ |
| 21 | ś | | ⚲ | ⚲ |

Note that Semitic equivalents for the common Indus signs ⚥ and ⚲ are missing.

Now—this is the third assumption—Rao applies the phonetic values of the Semitic letters to his Indus 'alphabet': which permits him to read the Indus inscriptions. The words produced by his readings suggest to him that the Indus language is closely related to Vedic Sanskrit—that is, the form of Sanskrit used in the *Vedas*, the earliest-known Indian literature, which are thought to have been composed during the 2nd millennium BC. (He therefore derives the 'missing' phonetic values for the two signs just mentioned, from Vedic Sanskrit, not from the disobliging Semitic signs.) The content of the inscriptions turns out to be names, titles, and other epithets.

There is no independent archaeological, cultural or linguistic support for any of Rao's assumptions—especially his belief that Semitic sound values are applicable to an Indo-European language, Sanskrit. It is hard to avoid the conclusion that Rao, for nationalistic reasons, was determined to prove that the Indus language was the ancestor of Sanskrit, the root language of most of the modern languages of north India, and that Sanskrit was therefore *not* the product of the so-called Indo-Aryan (Indo-European) 'invasions' of India from the west via central Asia but was instead the expression of indigenous Indian (Indus) genius. But almost every other current major scholar (including Mahadevan) rejects early Sanskrit as the Indus language and favors an early form of Dravidian, the family of languages currently spoken in south India, which were probably once spoken in the north, including the Indus Valley area, prior to the influx from the west. The debate is somewhat like that over the language of Linear B, between 'Minoan' supporters (led by Evans) and the supporters of Greek, with the linguistic positions now reversed, so that the Dravidian (read Minoan) hypothesis has the upper hand over the Sanskrit (read Greek) hypothesis.

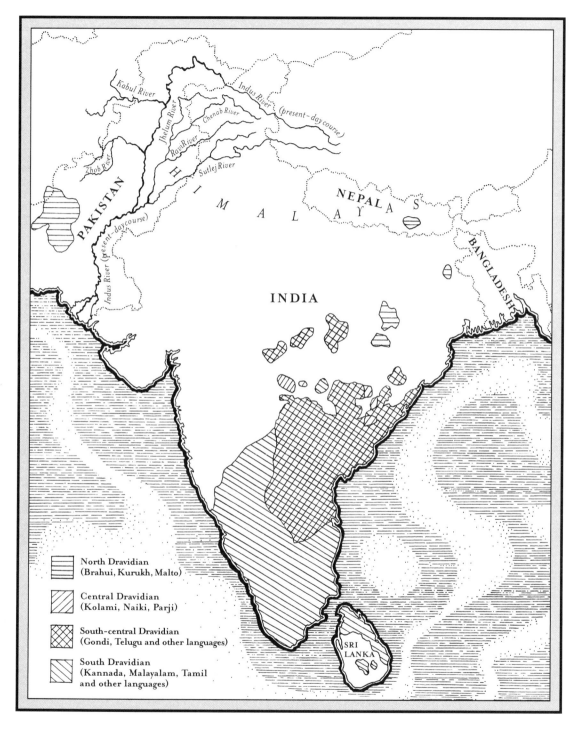

The two chief language families of the Indian subcontinent, Indo-Aryan (white) and Dravidian (shaded), and the subdivisions of the Dravidian family. Note the pockets of Dravidian speakers within the northern Indo-Aryan area, especially Brahui near the Indus Valley. The unknown language of the Indus script, if it is not an isolate, could belong to the Indo-Aryan, Dravidian or Munda families, but the most likely candidate seems to be Dravidian.

We shall return to the evidence for Dravidian as the Indus language later.

The fourth, and final, 'decipherment' is by an American archaeologist, Walter Fairservis Jr., who spent decades digging in the Indus Valley and surrounding areas (as well as in Egypt), partly sponsored by the American Museum of Natural History. In 1983, he published a long article on the Indus script in *Scientific American*, which eventually became a book, *The Harappan Civilization and Its Writing: A Model for the Decipherment of the Indus Script* (1992). Although the title sounds fairly cautious, there is no doubt that the author thinks he has 'cracked' the problem. (I recall the amused disbelief of a British Museum curator of Indus seals, who had just had them all 'read' for him by a visiting Fairservis.)

Fairservis's method is both simple and complex. It is simple because it boils down to three steps. First, decide what an Indus sign 'looks like' iconically or iconographically. Second, chose a word from a Dravidian language that fits the chosen visual meaning. Third, determine the range of possible Indus meanings of the sign, arising from its definition in Dravidian, based on archaeological, cultural and linguistic evidence. The complexity, of course, comes from the ambiguity introduced at each stage. Signs resemble different things to different people (first step); there are usually several different words that fit any selected 'icon' (second step); finally, different scholars derive very different conclusions from the same pieces of evidence, especially when these conflict (third step). And this is not to mention the important fact that, if the Indus language really is Dravidian, it must be a proto-Dravidian language 2000 years older than the oldest attested Dravidian words in the Old Tamil

inscriptions of the state of Tamil Nadu in south India (probably 3rd century BC). How reliable a guide to its earlier form is any language at so great a temporal remove?

Perhaps the best example of these difficulties is the sign ⚲. Most scholars regard it as a 'fish', while differing as to its significance. But Fairservis prefers to see a twist, loop or part of a knot. Some of his reasons give pause for thought, such as the fact that the scribes seem always to have drawn the sign with an under-over technique as one would a loop (but perhaps not a fish); the fact that many variants of the sign have small 'bodies' and enormous 'tails'; and the fact that all known Indus Valley fishes have several fins, not just one pair. Following his intuition, Fairservis goes on to identify various Dravidian words for 'twist', 'loop', 'net', and settles on 'piri'. This he now connects to another Dravidian word 'pir' meaning 'chief'. Hence he 'translates' the 'fish' sign and its variants (including the so-called 'carp' sign) as follows:

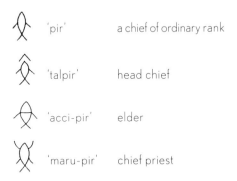

| | | |
|---|---|---|
| | 'pir' | a chief of ordinary rank |
| | 'talpir' | head chief |
| | 'acci-pir' | elder |
| | 'maru-pir' | chief priest |

No one has agreed with this, for the very good reason that it is highly subjective (and Fairservis had no training as a linguist, certainly not in the Dravidian languages). Even Possehl, a devoted student of Fairservis, summing up his review of all the significant 'decipherments', felt compelled to write:

 **"** Since there is little basic research on the script and so little sharing of programmatic visions, it is scarcely a wonder that the writing system has not yet been understood. With everyone reaching directly for The Grail, based on his or her own genius, it seems highly unlikely that the work could be used in a productive, additive program of research, since it is all so idiosyncratic. There is little reason to agree with Fairservis when he says: 'I believe that the [Indus] script is now well on its way to final decipherment because of these [i.e. his] efforts.' In fact, just the opposite seems to be the case. **"**

The comment about lack of basic research underestimates the efforts of several researchers, especially Parpola and Mahadevan, as we shall now see. But the rest of the criticism, that each Indus script scholar strives to 'go it alone'—a criticism that cannot be leveled at the Maya decipherment (or that of Linear B), has considerable point. But then, one might counter that the Indus script problem is so intractable that only someone with a high degree of confidence in his own intuition, would think of trying to solve it.

––––––––

Having scrutinized four putative decipherments, we shall now turn to some more cautious and logical approaches to the Indus script. How far is it possible to advance purely by internal analysis of the inscriptions, without taking a stab at guessing the Indus language? The answer is: we can settle the matter of the direction of writing and reading; we can establish an approximate number of signs and a sign list on which there is considerable agreement; we can agree on some of the numerals; and we can show that certain texts are likely to be segmentable into words. Let us take a look at each of these deductions in turn.

To begin, it is necessary to establish that it was the seal *impression* that was intended to be read, not the intaglio of the seal, in which the characters are naturally reversed. (There is room for some doubt here, as seals far outnumber seal impressions, and many of the seals are hardly worn, suggesting that they were not used but carried, perhaps as identity 'cards' or even charms.) Fortunately, the correct orientation is easy to establish, because we can compare the sign sequences and sign orientations of seal impressions with the same sequences in inscriptions clearly meant to be read directly on, for example, pottery graffiti and metal implements. Generally, they match. All the images in this chapter, and all references to inscriptions appearing on seals, are to seal impressions.

As for the direction of writing, we might expect to obtain a clue from the direction in which directed pictograms such as face. (Remember that in Egyptian hieroglyphic the pictograms face in the direction opposite to that in which the writing should be read.) But it turns out that while the main image on the seal impressions (e.g. the 'unicorn') generally, but not invariably, faces to the right, the direction in which the Indus script characters face is inconsistent.

The most dependable evidence for the direction of reading comes from the spacing of the inscriptions. If a short text starts from the right-hand edge and leaves a space on the left, it may be assumed to run from right to left. And if it shows cramping of symbols on the left-hand edge as over page, the same conclusion may be drawn.

As observed by Parpola, in the seal at the bottom of the page opposite, the sequence ⋎⌂ is found nowhere else in the inscriptions in the furthest left position, whereas ʊ⋎⌂ is found there 76 times. This suggests that the scribe was forced by lack of space to put the last sign on the second line, and that the inscription should be read from right to left. (The alternative, left to right, would produce the pairing ⋓ ⋔, which is found only *once* elsewhere, in the middle of an inscription.)

More striking still is the following seal impression from Harappa:

Plainly, the reader started at the top right-hand corner, turned the seal clockwise through 90 degrees twice, and part of the third edge and all of the fourth edge were blank.

Other decisive evidence comes from another simple seal impression:

In the 1970s, Mahadevan established from a detailed analysis of the corpus of inscriptions that ∥ ◯ is the most frequent pair combination in the Indus script. Out of 291 instances, the combination occurs 245 times at the right-hand end of a line. ∪ is, as already mentioned, the most frequent Indus sign. Out of 1395 occurrences, it is found at the left-hand end of lines 931 times. This must of course mean that there are some seals in which the above two orientations are not obeyed—but they are relatively uncommon. Statistically speaking, it is very unlikely that when the pair combination and the single sign appear together on one seal, as here, *both* will be written untypically (i.e. that the pair combination will appear *not* at the right-hand end of a line and the single sign will appear *not* at the left-hand end of a line), so we can conclude that the normal direction of the Indus script is from right to left. However, there is a significant number of left-to-right examples of the script (6.6 per cent of the corpus, according to Mahadevan), and nine undeniable examples of boustrophedon writing.

As we have seen with earlier scripts, a sharp photographic corpus with drawings (if the photographs are insufficient to see details), a reliable sign list and a concordance showing the occurrence of each sign in the corpus, are some of the basic tools in any decipherment. (They are still lacking for *rongorongo*.) For the Indus script, these have been the work of Parpola and Mahadevan from the 1970s onwards, though they have worked separately, if amicably. Parpola's two volumes of photographs covering the collections in India and in Pakistan, which appeared in 1987 and 1991 (with the support of UNESCO), have revolutionized the study of the script, and his 1994 sign list, containing 386 signs with 12 more unnumbered signs (as against Mahadevan's 419 signs), are generally recognized as fine achievements, not least by Mahadevan, who says that Parpola's sign list replaces all other sign lists including his own. Allowing a margin for allographs and undiscovered signs, Mahadevan reckons that "the present best estimate for the total number is 425 ± 25 signs."

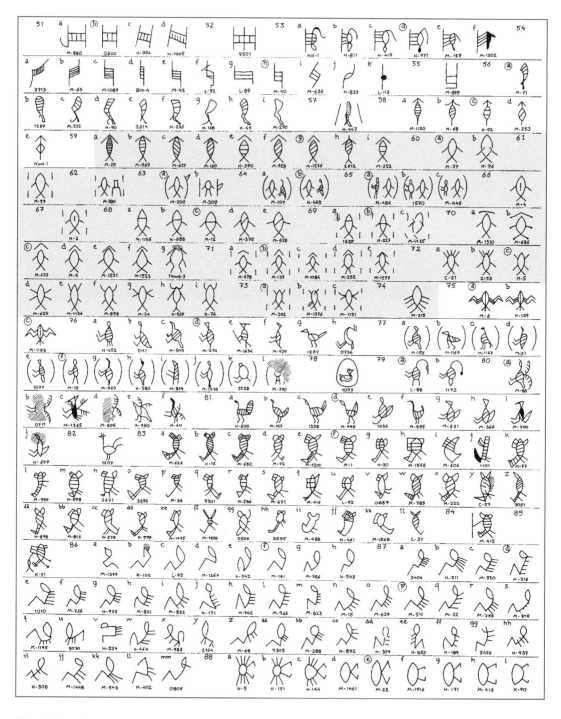

(Above) Part of a sign list for the Indus script, as proposed by the Indologist Asko Parpola, and (right) part of his concordance. In each case the 'fish' sign ⟨𝄐⟩ is highlighted.

This is a significant figure. It is too high for a syllabary like Linear B (or an alphabet, like that proposed by Rao), and too low for a highly logographic script like Chinese. The nearest comparisons (as listed in the chart on page 42 of the Introduction) are probably the Hittite hieroglyphs with about 500 signs and Sumerian cuneiform with perhaps 600+ signs (the corresponding Mayan figure is about 800 signs, though many of these are hardly used). Most scholars therefore agree that the Indus script is likely to be a logosyllabic script like its west Asian contemporaries—although there has been little progress in identifying the signs for phonetic syllables (as we shall see).

Parpola has also, with his collaborators, standardized and thereby computerized the signs to make a concordance, but this has met with somewhat less enthusiasm. The reason is already familiar, especially if we recall Barthel's sign list for *rongorongo*, and Guy's criticism of it (page 234). Computerized analysis is a good idea in principle, but it is potentially misleading if based on a doubtful sign list. We certainly cannot rely on a computer to make judgements about which signs are allographs (variants of the same sign) and which are ligatures (combinations of two or more simple signs). Rao, at one extreme, favors the reduction of the sign list to 62 signs, by ruthlessly eliminating allographs and ligatures, while at the other, Bryan Wells, a linguist now at Harvard University, has recently proposed 584 signs: a step that Parpola regards as retrograde. While no one (except Rao) favors such a drastic loss of potential information, it is much less clear where to draw the line at the higher end of the sign spectrum: in other words how many potential allographs and ligatures to keep as separate signs, so as to err on the side of disambiguity. Like *rongorongo* and the Isthmian script (but unlike Linear A), since we do not have marked Indus word boundaries, in compiling an Indus sign list there is rather little to go on except the external forms of the signs, "and any

such procedure is bound to be arbitrary and subjective", admits Mahadevan.

Nevertheless, a few techniques are available. We know that the signs Ⴤ and ⵧ are allographs, because they are each found paired with more or less the same two dozen signs, and they occur interchangeably in the common sequence:

$$\text{ᘮ Ⴤ ᗜ : ᘮ Ⴤ ᗜ}$$

And we know from positional frequency analysis that the three signs: ᘮ ᘮ and ᘮ

are probably *not* allographs of the simple sign:

$$\text{ᘮ}$$

(The small strokes might, for example, be allographs like the various accents on a vowel in French, é, è and ê.) For though this very frequent simple sign occurs often at the end of inscriptions, as we know, at the beginning of inscriptions it occurs only *once* out of 1395 total occurrences. The relevant figures for the other three signs are:

ᘮ   20 initial out of 177 total occurrences

ᘮ   4  initial out of 35 total occurrences

ᘮ   25 initial out of 51 total occurrences.

"It seems likely that ᘮ, ᘮ, and ᘮ are indeed related to ᘮ, but that they are to be regarded as distinct signs, in a distinct functional subclass of their own, and not as mere allographs", writes Steven Bonta, a linguistics student (then at Brigham Young University), who has attempted to analyze the Indus signs without making any assumptions about their language. But as Parpola—who distinguishes four distinct signs in this particular case—notes: "Application of the context criterion can be very convincing if the signs have a high frequency, but when they occur a few times only, the conclusion is bound to remain open to doubt."

Distinguishing the Indus numerals has proved a special challenge, unlike the numerals in the Mayan script or Linear A/B. Groups of short strokes of varying number (1-10 and 12, but no 11) occur in the inscriptions, for instance with the 'fish' sign, as do groups of long strokes (1-7). Do these groups represent numerals, and if so, what is the difference between the short and the long strokes? Complicating the situation is that there is frequent use of single and double short strokes in an obviously *non*-numerical way: the single short strokes often surround a sign like a sort of cartouche (an example is highlighted below), and both single and double short strokes appear in the same texts as groups of long strokes. (The short strokes look as if they might be word dividers, but other evidence we shall discuss in a moment suggests that they are not.) Of course, single and double short strokes could be capable of acting both numerically and non-numerically, depending on their context—compare the roman numerals V, X, C, M, which are also letters of the roman alphabet. Here are some examples of potential numerals:

The occurrence of the group of 12 short strokes also seems inconsistent with its being a numeral. Therefore, ignoring the groups of 1, 2 and 12 short strokes, Mahadevan did a frequency count of the remaining groups of short strokes (3-9) and revealed the following numbers of occurrences in the corpus of inscriptions:

| | | Frequency |
|---|---|---|
| 3 | III | 151 |
| 4 | IIII | 70 |
| 5 | III I | 38 |
| 6 | III III | 38 |
| 7 | IIII II | 70 |
| 8 | IIII IIII | 7 |
| 9 | IIII IIIII | 2 |

The abrupt drop in frequency after 7, and the fact that there are no groups of long strokes greater than 7, suggested to Fairservis that the Indus Valley civilization counted in base 8—a possibility enhanced by the fact that there is evidence for a Dravidian base-8 system. But this contradicts considerable other evidence that the Indus numerical system used base 10, with the following signs representing 10, 20, 30 etc:

10    20    30

Perhaps, therefore, more than one system was used, for different purposes (e.g. counting and weighing), as in ancient Elam. At least one researcher, Bonta, believes that the various 'fish' signs—which regularly occur with groups of short strokes—were actually for counting; according to him they represented quantities in a measuring system.

The current uncertainty around the numerical system is well brought out in this comment by Parpola:

> **❝** Numbers seem to be represented by repeated long vertical strokes only in the early inscriptions (the miniature tablets of Harappa). In the mature script, the smaller numbers (ones) are written exclusively with short strokes (in one or two tiers), while the long strokes have some other meaning. This can be concluded from the fact that the number of short strokes varies in front of specific pictograms (especially ⚹, Υ and ∪), while the number of long strokes does not (to any significant degree), except in the early texts. Moreover, the long strokes in the later inscriptions do not cover all the numbers represented by the short strokes, and they occur much less often, mainly in a few predictable sequences. **❞**

Obviously—and everyone agrees about this— the numerical system needs much further study, of the kind brought to bear on the Sumerian and proto-Elamite tablets by the authors of *Archaic Bookkeeping* (page 215). However, since the Indus inscriptions are almost certainly not primarily economic, they are unlikely to yield straightforward answers to questions about counting. For the time being, therefore, both Parpola and Mahadevan have retained separate sign numbers in their respective sign lists for the groups of long and short strokes.

Which brings us at last to the question of word dividers and how the Indus texts may be segmented. One of the most convincing techniques involves choosing a long text and searching for its constituent sequences within the corpus. It is highly likely, for example, that there is a word boundary after the first two signs of this seven-sign seal impression:

because we know of two other seal impressions which together make up the sequence in the above impression:

We may even postulate a second boundary within the seven-sign text—perhaps a phrase rather than a word?—by examining a fourth seal (opposite) which contains the final three signs of the above seven-sign text:

At first sight, the single and double short strokes on the inscriptions, such as the seven-sign inscription just considered, appear to be word dividers. This is certainly a plausible interpretation of the double and single short strokes in the following two comparisons taken from five different inscriptions:

But the theory is challenged by inscriptions in which the double and single short strokes occur one after the other:

Also, they occur most frequently after the very first sign of an inscription, an odd position for a word divider; and at the end of inscriptions, where a word divider is least needed. And, as Parpola remarks, "If the sign ❜ is really a word divider, it is difficult to understand why the sign should be so frequent in a very limited number of

contexts", for example:

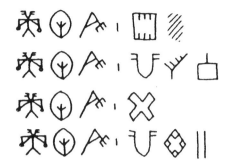

—rather than its occurring regularly throughout the corpus.

A more reliable method of segmenting words is by the use of pairwise frequencies, that is the total number of occurrences of a sign pair in the corpus. A high pairwise frequency indicates a high affinity between the two signs and hence that the pair may be part of a word, while a low frequency indicates a weak junction, probably a word boundary. Thus, in a six-sign Indus text, ABCDEF, such as the following text segmented by Mahadevan, we may compare the frequencies of the adjacent pairs of signs AB, BC, CD, DE and EF:

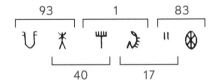

Word boundaries appear to correspond to the low pairwise frequencies 1 and 17, so we segment the text as follows (with the double short stroke sign falling next to a word boundary but now *not* thought to be a word divider):

"By this method almost all the long texts can be segmented into constituent phrases and words", writes Mahadevan. There is, however, room for doubt in cases where the pairwise frequencies do not differ substantially.

———

So far, in the preceding two sections, we have presented a consensus view of the Indus script, with clear signposts towards minority opinions. From here on, we shall be dealing in speculation, like the four scholars whose 'decipherments' we considered earlier. But some speculation is much better informed than other speculation. To avoid total confusion—an all-too-present prospect in Indus script decipherment—we shall stick with ideas that are taken seriously by more than one scholar.

Apart from word boundaries, a lot of effort has gone into the analysis of affixes (i.e. prefixes and suffixes), which, if they could be proved to exist, would tend to suggest the presence of grammatical inflection, which would in turn tell us something important about the Indus language (as Kober's 'triplets' did about Linear B). The most likely candidates are the signs:

which seem to represent suffixes. To quote Parpola: "These signs usually occur at the end of inscriptions, are very frequent, and can be postfixed to a large number of different signs; they are mutually exclusive (one never being found before or after the other), and seem to alternate after many recurring sequences"—for example:

$$\text{ᚒ ⚛ ‖ vs ↑ ⚛ ‖}$$

$$\text{ᚒ ⚞ ⯅ vs ↑ ⚞ ⯅}$$

In the late 1960s, the young Parpola and his Finnish collaborators noticed another fairly frequent example of apparent suffixing, involving three signs:

These three signs occurred mainly at the end of inscriptions too, and when one did occur in the middle of an inscription, segmentation could usually show that it belonged to the preceding sequence, i.e. it was still a 'word-final' sign.

Intriguingly, two of the signs appeared to be ligatures, formed in the following manner:

$$\text{⚔ + ᚒ = ⚕}$$

$$\text{⚔ + ↑ = ⚖}$$

Parpola now jumped to a conclusion. He decided that ⚔ was the plural marker, and that ⚕ and ⚖ were case markers (probably genitive and dative, since accusative would imply the existence of verbs in the texts, which is unlikely if they contain only names and titles). Recall here Alice Kober's speculations about the 'triplets' in Linear B. Parpola expressed his hypothesis as a table (see over):

| Case | Singular | Plural |
|---|---|---|
| nominative | null | 𝍖 |
| genitive? | ⪫F | 𝍖 |
| dative? | ↑ | 𝍖 |

The new idea attracted much attention, including cautious praise from John Chadwick, as well as strong criticism. Parpola eventually abandoned it, though, because there are a few texts which do not follow the expected rules, for instance:

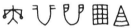

in which the genitive plural ligature is not used and the case sign, against expectation, precedes the plural sign. And, more damagingly:

where the ↑ sign (supposedly in ligature form) is adjacent to the ⪫F sign—a 'forbidden' combination. Nevertheless, Parpola and other scholars continue to believe that these two signs are inflectional markers of some kind. The latest theory, tentatively advanced by Mahadevan, concerns gender marking: ⪫F is a masculine singular suffix, and ↑ is a non-masculine (female and neutral) singular suffix, as found in certain early Dravidian languages. It too is open to criticism.

Other informed speculations about the script depend on the assumption that the Indus language is Dravidian, so we shall now briefly review the evidence concerning the complex issue of what the language may be. In doing so, we must discount the possibility that the language has completely died out, if we are to make any progress—an assumption for which there is some rationale, given the exceptional cultural continuities of Indian civilization as a whole. (For example, there is the 'swastika' symbol, first seen on Indus Valley objects, and still used as a good luck symbol on the walls of Indian homes—not to mention the system of Indus Valley weights still used by some Indian jewelers today.) We shall also discard a second possibility, that the Indus language is related to the Munda languages of central and (mainly) eastern India, a part of the Austro-Asiatic family which covers most of the languages of south-east Asia, because this theory receives little support from linguistic evidence and no support from archaeology. That leaves us with the Indo-Aryan (Sanskrit) and the Dravidian hypotheses.

Geographically, Sanskrit has the edge over Dravidian as the descendant of the Indus language, since it was the classical language of northern India (like Latin in Europe), while today's Dravidian speakers belong almost exclusively to south India, far away from the Indus Valley region. But that said, there exist pockets—"pools left by the receding tide" in Chadwick's evocative phrase—of Dravidian languages in northern India, such as Kurukh and Malto, and one of these languages, Brahui, spoken by around 300,000 nomadic people in Baluchistan (west Pakistan), is significantly close to the Indus Valley. These Dravidian speakers are presumably remnants of a once-widespread Dravidian culture submerged by encroaching Indo-Aryans in the 2nd millennium BC, though it is conceivable that they could have migrated to their present locations from the south. There is disagreement about this, but in general it seems improbable that a people would migrate from the relatively clement plains of India into the rugged and hostile mountains of Baluchistan. "If the Brahuis were not the indigenous inhabitants of Baluchistan, who were?" asks Parpola reasonably enough. "Certainly not the Baluch, who came from northern Iran in the 10th century AD or later."

The rest of the evidence for the Dravidian hypothesis may be said to be from 'silence'; it suggests that the Indus language is probably *not* Indo-Aryan, rather than it *is* Dravidian. The Indo-Aryan hymns, the *Vedas* (eventually written down in Sanskrit), which appear to post-date the mature period of the Indus Valley civilization, recount tales of conquest of the forts of the dark-skinned Dasa or Dasyu, who were possibly (though this is unclear) an indigenous people. Sir Mortimer Wheeler decided that skeletons he found on the mound at Mohenjo-daro in the 1940s were Dasa victims of Indo-Aryan invaders, but his theory is no longer tenable: the people seem actually to have died of disease, and the forts described in the *Vedas* do not conform to the layout of Indus cities. On the other hand, the *Vedas* repeatedly mention the horse in their descriptions of warfare and sacrifice, and this animal was clearly a vital part of Indo-Aryan society, as it was of all early Indo-European societies. But there is no horse imagery at all in the Indus Valley civilization and virtually no horse remains have been found by archaeologists. Hence the Indus civilization is unlikely to have been Indo-Aryan.

As for the evidence for the Indus language of the script itself, there has been some effort, especially by Knorozov and his collaborators in Russia, to show by internal analysis that the structure was of a suffixing, agglutinative type, more typical of a Dravidian language than of an Indo-European one (such as Sanskrit). But the Russian group's claims are highly suspect, as we have just seen from the uncertainty surrounding even the most solid example of Indus suffixing; and so, unlike with the Mayan glyphs, Knorozov cannot be said to have made any solid contribution to the study of the Indus script. The truth is, we know nothing reliable about the syntax and grammar of the Indus language.

The Dravidian hypothesis is therefore the best one we have, though in no sense proven. On the working assumption that it is right, we can try to look for sensible links between the meanings of words in early Dravidian languages such as Old Tamil, Telugu, Malayalam and Kannada, and the iconic and iconographic signs and images on the Indus seals and other inscribed objects, taking help from cultural evidence about Dravidian civilization and its religious beliefs and archaeological evidence about the Indus Valley civilization. This is what scholars, such as Fairservis, Knorozov, Mahadevan, Parpola and many others have done. The disadvantage is, of course, that as with Eric Thompson's interpretations of Mayan glyphs, no one can be sure if their interpretations are correct.

The simplest example was first suggested by the Jesuit Father Henry Heras (who lived in India) in the 1950s. The word for fish in almost all Dravidian languages is 'mīn'. In many Dravidian languages 'mīn' also means 'star'. Could the very common 'fish' sign on the Indus seals have been pronounced *mīn* but have had the dual meaning 'fish' and 'star', which, as Parpola demonstrates, is an emblem of divinity and can thus stand for 'god'? The 'fish' sign could then be a rebus forming part of a theophoric name—a very common occurrence in Indian culture, where people are often named after gods and goddesses (e.g. Rama, Krishna, Ganesh, Indira, Lakshmi, Arundhati).

*Combined 'fish' and 'star' motifs on pottery from Amri belonging to the mature period of the Indus Valley civilization, may support the theory that similar-looking 'fish' and 'star' signs in the Indus script are linguistically related.*

One could object to this: why is the star not represented pictorially too, like the fish? We are used to representing a star with a few short lines crossing at a point ('twinkling', so to speak), but this is just our particular convention, which happens to distinguish all the other stars from our sun, which we generally represent with a small circle with 'rays' sticking out of it. It is quite conceivable that the Indus Valley writers could have chosen a different and more subtle approach based on a homophony in their language between the Indus word for fish and star that English does not possess. (An English parallel might be 'son' and 'sun'.) As Robert Caldwell, the bishop of south India who first identified the Dravidian language family, beautifully observed:

> **❝** Who that has seen the phosphorescence flashing from every movement of the fish in tropical seas or lagoons at night, can doubt the appropriateness of denoting the fish that dart and sparkle through the waters, as well as the stars that sparkle in the midnight sky, by one and the same word—viz., a word signifying that which glows or sparkles? **❞**

Parpola has extended Heras's small 'decipherment' and given an interpretation of a series

of symbols on the seals, in which a 'fish' sign appears alongside a number of strokes that appear to be numbers. Above is one such seal.

Parpola reads 'fish with three strokes' as 'mum mīn', 'three stars', that is the asterism (i.e. the small constellation) Mrigasirsa; 'fish with six strokes' as 'aru mīn', 'six stars', the Pleiades; and 'fish with seven strokes' as 'elu mīn', 'seven stars', Ursa Major. Mahadevan comments cautiously:

**"** It is interesting to note that the numerical names for the three asterisms are actually attested in Old Tamil. There is however no proof that these interpretations are the only correct ones. There are, in the Indus texts, several sets of 'number + sign' sequences. The interpretation of 'number + fish' signs as asterisms would make this set unique among such sequences. **"**

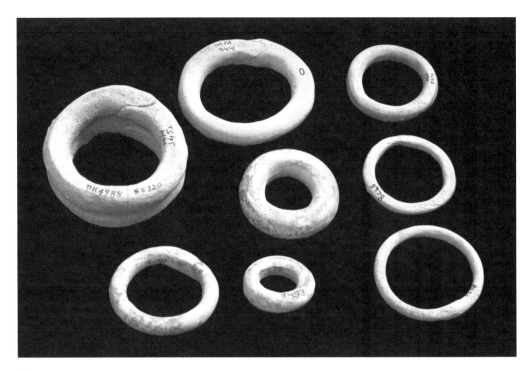

*Terracotta bangles from Mohenjo-daro bearing signs from the Indus script.*

Another of Parpola's several readings concerns the fairly common Indus sign depicting a pair of intersecting circles:

He identifies this as "ear/nose rings" or "bangles". (Fairservis takes it to mean the number 8!) There are substantial numbers of fine stoneware bangles from the excavations in the Indus Valley, many of them inscribed with signs; and as Parpola points out, the 'intersecting circles' sign occurs in these bangle inscriptions with a frequency disproportionate to its occurrence in non-bangle inscriptions—suggesting that its meaning may be related to bangles. Other, more complex and disputable evidence, based on the occurrence of ⬭ in various seal inscriptions, suggests that it might express the name of a deity. A Dravidian word for bangles is

'muruku', which is nearly homophonous with Murukan, the principal deity of the early Tamils, youthful god of war and love. Therefore, says Parpola, the sign showing intersecting circles may represent Murukan; and he supports this proposition with references to ear-rings and bangles in a variety of Indian religious and folk traditions.

Again Mahadevan, who feels that Parpola is over-inclined towards religious explanations of the Indus script, is attracted but skeptical:

❝ It is very likely that the interlocking circles do pictorially represent a pair of bangles. But when you try to give a phonetic value for it, this becomes very difficult. Parpola has chosen a word which means twisted wire bangle, or twisted wire amulet or a twisted wire ear-ring or nose ring—where the operative word is twisting: the root is 'murugu', which means in

Old Dravidian 'to twist'. But the polished vitrified stoneware bangles have no twists in them, so that is very unlikely. There are other words for bangles but [Parpola] does not choose them because they are not homophonous with the word for Murukan that he is looking for. I personally believe that if the Indus Valley people were Dravidians, one of their gods was called Murukan. But he is hiding in still some other sign. **"**

To sum up, whatever the linguistic nuances of the Indus language issue, there can be no doubt of the general uncertainty inherent in interpreting the Indus signs. Let us conclude with one final, cautionary example. As we know, virtually every scholar except Fairservis thinks that ⚵ depicts a fish. But consider the disagreement about ⊐F, the most common Indus sign of all. To Parpola, it shows the head of a horned cow seen from the front; to Fairservis, a pot with handles; and to Knorozov a pipal tree. Each has his reasons. As Parpola was obliged to confess in the final words of his massively erudite *Deciphering the Indus Script*:

**"** Many of the signs... are so simplified and schematic that it is very difficult to understand their pictorial meaning unambiguously and objectively. Another drawback is the scantiness of the material... It looks most unlikely that the Indus script will ever be deciphered fully, unless radically different source material becomes available. That, however, must not deter us from trying. **"**

This assessment is honest, scientific and true, if unsensational. Yet there are signs of hope in tackling the fascinating enigma of the Indus script. Major,

innovative archaeological projects continue at Mohenjo-daro (supported by UNESCO) and Harappa (supported by Harvard University), and new samples of the script appear from time to time, both from these places and from other sites, such as a substantial inscription found at Dholavira near the coast of Kutch in 1990, which appears to have been a kind of sign board for the city. The director of the Harappa excavations, Mark Kenoyer (of the University of Wisconsin) is currently engaged in a reanalysis of the seals and other inscriptions on the basis of their chronological and spatial distribution, so as to compensate for the poor contextual information given by the early excavators in the 1920s and 30s. This, if combined with a more intensive and rigorous internal analysis of the signs and their patterns, the input of 'cultural' experts like Parpola and Mahadevan, and the linguistic 'control' provided by professional Dravidianists, may in due course yield solid results. Collaboration seems to be the name of the game here, since no *one* scholar can hope to command sufficient knowledge of ancient writing systems, Indus Valley and Indian archaeology, South Asian civilizations ancient and modern, and the relevant languages (Dravidian, Sanskrit and others). After all, it took well over a century to 'crack' the Mayan script, with several false starts and hiatuses, and would-be decipherers have been on the barer and more ancient Indus trail for less than 80 years.

Anyway, one thing is beyond dispute: people will continue to try to decipher the Indus script. The mysterious and vibrant little seals get a grip on a certain kind of mind that cannot be broken. Assuming that excavations in Pakistan and India continue in the new century, I think there is a real prospect of a widely accepted, if inevitably partial Indus script decipherment.

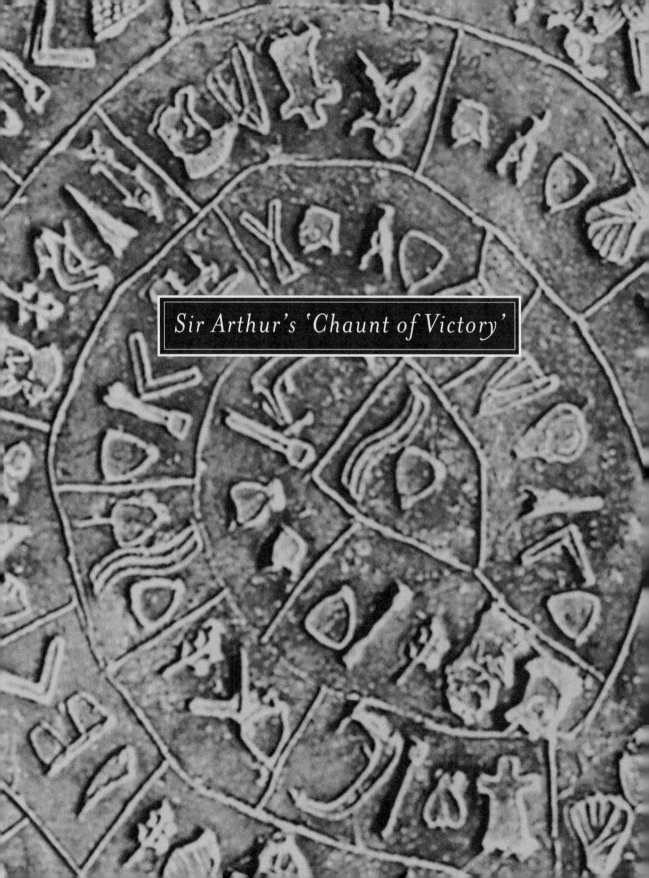

Sir Arthur's 'Chaunt of Victory'

# THE PHAISTOS DISC

The Phaistos disc is the only undeciphered script that may fairly be described as notorious. "THAT Disc" is the way one classical scholar I know generally refers to it. Emmett Bennett Jr., the Linear A and B scholar, once remarked that any book-jacket emblazoned with the Phaistos disc— and there have been many—was for him "the equivalent of the skull and crossbones on the bottle of poison".

In 1999, *The Economist*—a somewhat unlikely source for 'Discology', one might think—published two short letters that show why Bennett was only half joking. The first was from a woman living in New Jersey:

" I enjoyed your article on 'messages over millennia'. However, your use of the Phaistos disc as an example of the 'difficulty of long-range messaging' is not correct.

Steven Roger Fischer translated the message of the disc and identified its language as Minoan Greek of the 2nd millennium BC, a language closely related to Mycenaean Greek. The 'message' was a call to arms to various ethnic groups in Crete to repel the piratical Carians (from Anatolia) at Naxos in the Cyclades. Sometimes, if the audience is receptive, the message does get through. "

The second letter came from the editor of an art and archaeology magazine based in New York:

" In my opinion, having studied the Phaistos disc at length some 30 years ago, the reason it has not been deciphered and that its symbols do not relate in any way whatsoever to any other known script is simple: it is a forgery. It is a joke perpetrated by a clever archaeologist from the Italian mission to Crete upon his fellow excavators.

Taking a thermoluminescence test, which should date the firing of the clay at about 100 years ago, can solve the mystery of the disc. It is hoped the Greeks will take this simple step to clear up this vexing problem; until now they have been unwilling to do so. "

It is unlikely the Greek authorities ever will. In nearly a century, no Greek scholar has contributed to the debate about the disc, observes Yves Duhoux, the Linear A expert at the University of Louvain in Belgium, who is the author of *Le Disque de Phaestos*,

a small compendium of photographs, drawings, facts and careful deductions about the disc that is the most reliable publication on the subject. And it is not hard to understand why. For a Greek to suggest that this emblem of high Minoan civilization is really a modern artifact would be a bit like joining the international chorus of allegations that Schliemann faked some of his discoveries at Troy and Mycenae, or supporting the right of the British Museum to keep the Elgin marbles. At the Heraklion Museum in Crete, where the Phaistos disc is kept, the eager crowds are firmly told by the guides that the disc is about 3600 years old and that it cannot yet be read. No one is going to thank the person who proves the disc to be a fake. "For who would want to look at an *ex-enigma*, or buy a Phaistos disc postcard, or any souvenir, if the disc had already been deciphered?" asks Bennett.

*(Pages 299-302) The Phaistos disc. First discovered in Crete in 1908, and believed to be the world's first 'printed' document dating to 1850-1600 BC, the disc has resisted dozens of ingenious attempts to 'crack' its mysterious signs. It is about 16 cm (6.5 in) in diameter and about 1.9 cm (0.75 in) thick. There is a total of 242 characters (one of which is defaced) either stamped or punched on the two faces, arranged into 61 groups demarcated into sections by lines. It appears that the characters were written from the outer edge, and spiral inwards in a clockwise direction. No other examples of the script have been discovered. The language it records, assuming the disc is not a hoax, is totally unknown, despite many claims to the contrary.*

**A**

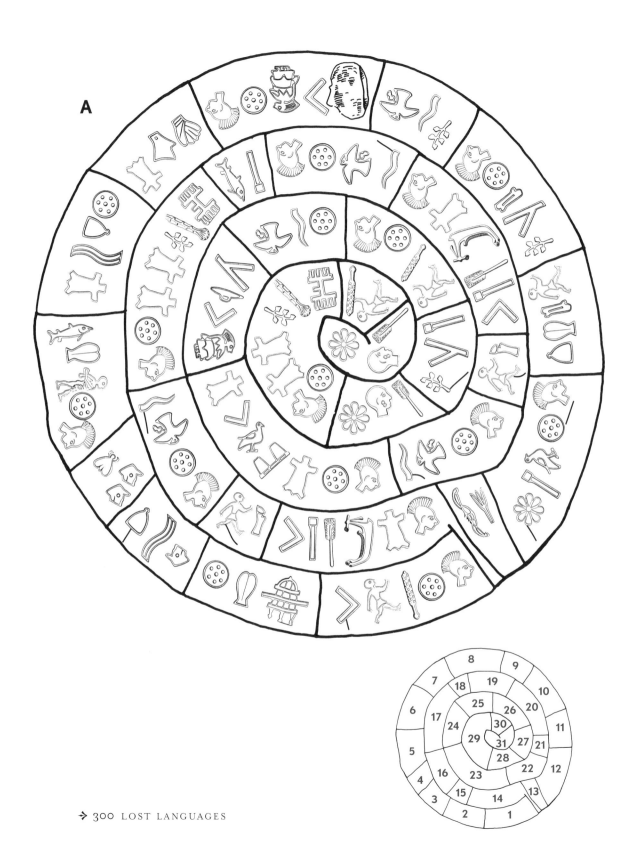

**A**

**B**

**B**

In fairness, it must be said that the hoax theory is very much a minority opinion. Neither Duhoux, nor Bennett, nor John Chadwick, nor Maurice Pope, nor Tom Palaima, nor any other current scholar of the Cretan scripts except Jean-Pierre Olivier—nor for that matter Sir Arthur Evans, who first wrote about the disc in detail—have supported the theory. For a start, the disc appeared in an official excavation report written by a reputable archaeologist. Secondly, it was found close to a Linear A tablet of incontestable authenticity. Lastly, and most important of all, one can detect a substantial number of scribal corrections on both sides of the disc, such as those in the roughened clay of sections 4 and 5 of side A, where the original dividing line between the sections has been erased (it is faintly visible) to make way for two extra signs:

which were then added in a cramped fashion in section 5 of the disc before the scribe redrew the dividing line at an angle that is uncharacteristic of the other dividing lines on the disc:

It would have been an ingenious hoaxer indeed who would have bothered to introduce bogus 'corrections' in a bogus disc, but some hoaxers are indeed ingenious. So puzzling is the Phaistos disc that we cannot entirely rule out some archaeologist's prank.

As for the claim by Fischer (of *rongorongo* decipherment fame) to have deciphered the disc, mentioned in the first *Economist* letter, we shall come to it later, along with a few others of the dozens of disc 'decipherments' that are published decade after decade. But first, let us take a careful look at the disc itself and establish some basic facts about it.

It was discovered in 1908 by the archaeologist Luigi Pernier in the ruins of a palace at Phaistos in southern Crete. The archaeological context suggests that the date of the disc is 1850-1600 BC—in other words contemporary with Linear A and Evans's Cretan Hieroglyphic. The disc is roughly 16 cm (6.5 in) in diameter and 1.9 cm (0.75 in) thick, and is made of fine clay. On both sides (A and B) is an inscription, which consists of characters impressed on the wet clay with a punch or stamp before it was fired. There are 241 or 242 characters (one is damaged), consisting of 45 signs, divided by lines into short sections (31 on side A and 30 on side B). They are arranged in a spiral around the center of each side. Here is the sign list numbered by Evans:

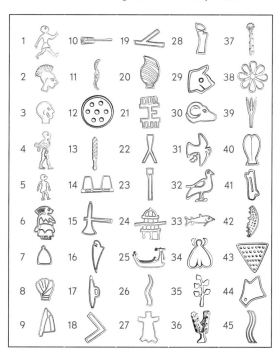

The fact that the characters are undoubtedly impressed, not incised, into the clay (unlike the characters of Linear A and B), means that the disc is, so to speak, "the world's first typewritten document" (Chadwick), created 2500 years before printing began in China, and more than 3000 years before Gutenberg's Bible. But why should anyone have bothered to produce a punch/stamp, rather than inscribing each character afresh as in Linear A and B? If it was to 'print' many copies of documents, then why has not a single other document in this script been found in over 90 years of intensive excavations? And why do the signs on the Phaistos disc fail to resemble, more than coincidentally, the signs of the Hieroglyphic script, Linear A or Linear B? Could the disc have been imported into Crete?

The last question is obviously highly significant for would-be decipherers, since an unknown foreign origin for the disc would render problematic any meaningful comparison between the disc and other objects and inscriptions known to be indigenous to Crete and the Minoan civilization (including Linear A), besides making it much more difficult to guess the likely language recorded in the disc, of which we currently have not the foggiest idea. Not surprisingly, therefore, the issue of foreign origin has generated controversy. Chadwick and Duhoux, for example, have disagreed over it, with Chadwick convinced of foreign provenance and Duhoux favoring Cretan origin, as does Fischer.

Evans—a Minoan imperialist if ever there was one—nevertheless was *not* convinced that the disc was indigenous. (Perhaps he would have been more sympathetic to its Minoanness, had he, rather than the Italian Pernier, found it!) In his long section on the disc in *The Palace of Minos*, Evans wrote:

> ❝ In default of the strongest evidence to the contrary, the inference would be almost obligatory that the clay disc, found thus on a Cretan site and in purely Minoan associations, was itself an indigenous product. But there are serious objections of a negative character to this conclusion as well as positive indications pointing to a geographical area outside Crete. ❞

The most obvious of the objections is the lack of any more discs, disc fragments or other samples of the script, which is particularly surprising given the 'printed' nature of the disc. But we have to be a little cautious about an argument 'from silence'. After all, the Tuxtla statuette, found in Mexico in 1902, remained essentially the only sample of the Isthmian script until the fortuitous discovery of the La Mojarra stela in 1986. (See page 252.) For decades, there was much uncertainty about the origin of the statuette, but the inscription on the stela proved beyond reasonable doubt that the statuette was indigenous to the area in which it was found.

Negatively again, the lack of resemblance between the disc and the Minoan scripts and Minoan art is striking. One might especially expect some resemblance between the Phaistos disc signs and the Hieroglyphic signs which are often found engraved on gemstones (such as carnelian), because of the similarity in technique of production: cutting with punches/stamps versus gem engraving. But the artistic styles are notably dissimilar. As for similarity with Linear A signs, consider this list of comparisons made by Fischer:

|  | Phaistos disc | Linear A |
|---|---|---|
| 12 | ⊙ | ⊙ |
| 35 | ⚹ | ⚹ |
| 19 | � | Ⴤ |
| 18 | ▷ | ∧ |
| 38 | ✿ | ⊕ |
| 10 | ♈ | Ψ |
| 34 | ⚐ | ⚐ |
| 1 | 🏃 | 🏃 |
| 37 | ⸙ | ⸙ |
| 15 | ⵟ | ⵛ |
| 36 | Ⴘ | Ⴘ |
| 24 | ⛩ | ⛩ |
| 20 | ◊ | ⿳ |
| 14 | Ⴀ | ⿲ |
| 26 | ⸮ | ⵜ |
| 29 | ◌ | ⊕ |
| 25 | ⌣ | Ⴙ |
| 22 | ⛏ | Ⴘ |

*Some signs of the Phaistos disc and Linear A, compared by the linguist Steven Roger Fischer. (The numbers refer to Evans's sign list on page 303.)*

Only 18 out of the 45 Phaistos disc signs are compared, and the similarities are hardly convincing, if we discount mere coincidence of the kind to be expected with simple pictograms—with the possible exception of the 'pagoda' (Evans's sign 24):

Evans himself said that this sign bore no resemblance to Cretan imagery but was remarkably similar to the rock tombs later built by the Lycians in Anatolia (and hence a "positive indication" that the disc was not Cretan). Here is his Anatolian comparison:

Apart from this sign, some of the really distinctive, 'complex' Phaistos disc signs, such as:

are ignored in Fischer's list. Evans's sign 6, the bare-breasted woman, depicts a style of female dress very different from any depicted in Minoan art. Evans's sign 2, a 'Mohican' profile—which is actually the commonest sign on the disc—was compared by Evans, rather fancifully, with a plumed Viking cap; while Chadwick preferred to relate it to a crested helmet of a type used at a later date by the Philistines. Neither scholar saw any relationship with Minoan art. But in fact there is a notable resemblance to some symbols showing a 'crested' head seen from the front and in profile on a contemporary Cretan object, an axe found in a cave at Arkalochori:

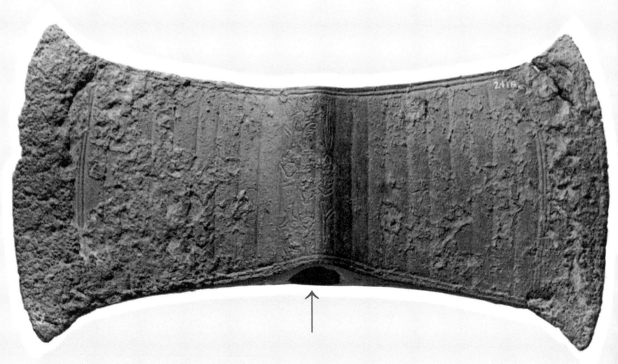

*The Arkalochori axe. Are the signs on its haft (shown opposite) related to signs on the Phaistos disc, in particular the sign* ？ *If so, the disc may share a Cretan origin with the axe.*

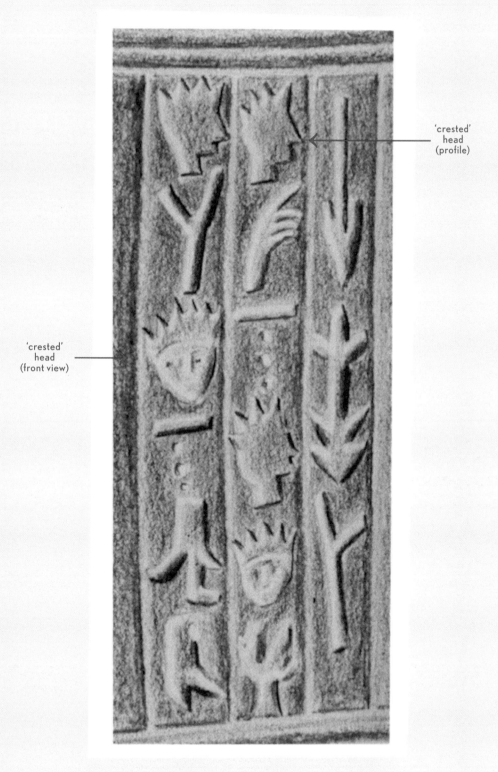

'crested'
head
(profile)

'crested'
head
(front view)

*Detail from the haft of the Arkalochori axe.*

Less significant—because the sign is not so distinctive—is the similarity of the 'shield' (Evans's sign 12):

to some symbols impressed on a vase from Knossos:

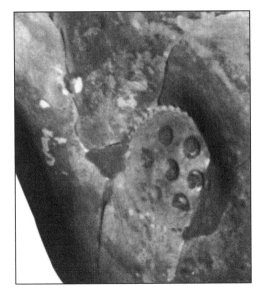

Duhoux attaches much weight to these two comparisons, along with a few other 'simple' sign resemblances, in support of his thesis that the Phaistos disc is of Cretan manufacture.

Thus the evidence, for and against non-Cretan origin, is patchy and inconclusive. One can only assume, as a reasonable working hypothesis supported by a majority of scholars, that the disc is of Cretan (Minoan) origin, and see where the idea leads.

Of course certain deductions can be made by internal analysis regardless of an external factor such as the origin of the disc, as always in decipherment. We already know the character count (241 or 242) and the number of signs (45), which present none of the usual difficulties of sign lists, since there seem, purely on the visual evidence, to be no allographs and ligatures (itself slightly suspicious, particularly when one considers the complications of the Linear A sign list). These two numbers immediately tell us two things. Assuming that the writing on the disc is 'full' writing representing a spoken language, and not some specialized notation, the low ratio of characters in the corpus to number of signs means that we do not have enough text on its own (i.e. without any help from other clues, such as archaeological context or underlying language), for a decipherment. Secondly—and this is more hopeful—the script is probably a syllabary: 45 signs is too large a number for any known alphabet and far too small for a logosyllabic script, as already discussed with other undeciphered scripts.

There are two possible objections to this second conclusion. First, how do we know that the text of the Phaistos disc is typical of the script as a whole? If it is a specialized type of text (for example a list, rather than a narrative), containing an untypical number of logograms, for example, or the repetition of certain unusual words, it will contain a distorted sign list and sign frequencies. The answer is that we do not know; we have simply made an assumption that the inscription is typical. Second, even assuming it is typical, is 242 characters of text enough to be representative of the writing system? Will all the signs in the signary be included in the disc? Here, statistical analysis of scripts in general comes to our aid.

There is an empirical formula for working out the probable number of signs in an alphabet or

A vase from Knossos. Are the signs related to signs on the Phaistos disc? Again, like the Arkalochori axe, if the signs are related, then a Cretan origin of the Phaistos disc is implied.

syllabary from a small sample of the alphabetic or syllabic writing. It has been shown to work well, not only with modern languages and scripts such as English, Arabic and Japanese *kana*, but also with Linear B. (For those with a taste for a little arithmetic, the formula is as follows: "In a small sample of an alphabetic or syllabic writing system consisting of L characters of M different kinds, the probable number of symbols in the alphabet or syllabary is, subject to various restrictions..., given approximately by (L x L)/(L-M) - L." Thus, in the preceding quoted sentence, there are 189 characters (L = 189) if we ignore the symbols L and M, and 24 kinds of character (M = 24) since the symbols q and z do not occur in the sample. This gives a probable number of symbols in the English alphabet of (189 x 189)/(189 - 24) - 189 = 27.5, i.e. between 27 and 28 symbols in the alphabet. With a somewhat bigger sample, the probable number of symbols would

be 26, as expected.) When the formula is applied to the Phaistos disc, it predicts a syllabary of 56-57 signs. In other words, there are probably 11 or 12 syllabic signs in the script that are not found in the text of the disc. This would seem to be a manageable number if the signs were actually used for 'printing' (as opposed to, say, hundreds of logograms).

A syllabary makes sense too in relation to the lengths of the section sequences which are typically 3, 4 or 5 characters long, if we assume that the sequences are mainly words; such lengths for character strings are typical of words in syllabic scripts (recall the word lengths in Linear A and B). This fact allowed Chadwick to make an interesting speculative deduction. There is a stroke sign which occurs at the left-hand end of certain sign groups ('words') on both side A and side B of the disc. Here is an example from side B:

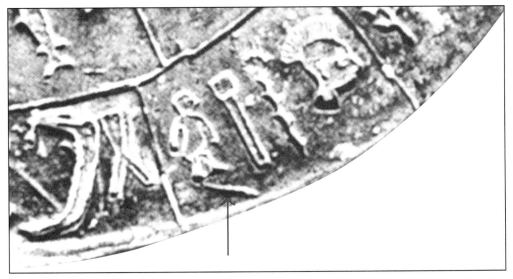

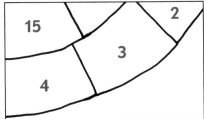

Could the stroke be a device for canceling the vowel in the final syllable of the 'word' it marks, so as to convey that the 'word' ends with a consonant (C[V], instead of the normal consonant + vowel, CV)? "No script of the Minoan family... has such a device," admitted Chadwick, "but the Devanagari script used for Sanskrit has a similar mark which is used in this way." He was not of course suggesting any link between the Phaistos disc's language and Sanskrit—he could safely leave such suggestions to would-be decipherers—only that such a method of final consonant marking was credible.

If the marked symbols are indeed word-final, it means that the Phaistos disc must be read spirally from the rim to the center, not from the center to the rim—because only then will the stroke mark fall at the end of the 'words', rather than at the beginning. (Try checking this for yourself.) But the strongest evidence for the direction of reading is actually quite different, and not linguistic but physical. Careful examination of the characters impressed in the clay has shown that in some cases a character very slightly overlaps the character to its right. This can only mean that the scribe wrote the characters from right to left (while revolving the disc for convenience, one imagines). A right-to-left direction is feasible, given the order of the characters on the disc, only if the disc was inscribed from the rim to the center. Presumably, it was also meant to be *read* in the same direction it was written. This rim-to-center direction of writing and reading is one of the very few matters that (almost) all Phaistos disc decipherers agree on. (It means, incidentally, that the directed pictograms such as  face away from the direction of reading, like the Egyptian hieroglyphs; but as we saw with the Indus script, there is no fixed rule about such orientations.)

If the characters of the script represent syllables, and the sample on the disc is representative, then there is clearly little point in interpreting the characters logographically, by trying to guess their meanings from their iconicity. For example the signs

are *not* logograms meaning 'shield', 'prisoner', 'manacles', 'boat' and 'skin' or related concepts (to cite Evans's identifications); they are syllabic signs, though their sounds may perhaps be linked in some way to their iconic meanings. But this fact has not deterred many 'decipherers' from precisely such futile pursuits. Such is the power of the Disc.

Over the years, scholars such as Chadwick, Bennett and Duhoux have attracted quite a collection of weird and occasionally wonderful contributions to 'Discology'. To spend a day at Cambridge University dipping into Chadwick's Phaistos disc correspondence files—one of the three boxes helpfully marked with a large 'π' (for 'potty')—as I did while researching this chapter, is to be reminded forcibly, if sometimes entertainingly, of the passion and imagination with which human beings can hold irrational ideas. "Dear Dr Chadwick", writes someone from California, "I would like to solicit your opinion on a suggestion I would like to make in regard to the Phaistos disc. I believe that the disc is a playing board for a snake game of/or like Egyptian 'mhn' but in a different language. I am not making a suggestion as to which one." "Dear Sir, It's really the truth and no April joke at all. Yesterday I cracked the code... In a few days I shall be able to understand the whole sermon of three and half thousand years ago. And it sounds just like yesterday. How little the minds of people have changed. Still the same mixture of angel and killer ape", writes someone else from Germany. One correspondent seriously suggests that the disc is a chart for interplanetary navigation. *The Bronze Age Computer Disc*, a hardback published in Britain in 1999, reveals the disc to be a highly sophisticated calendar; the division of the two sides into 30 and 31 sections naturally reflects the numbers of days in the months. Decipherment reveals, among other things, that in 2000 BC Bronze Age man "knew that the world was round", was able to measure the equator "accurate to 1 kilometre" and "used telescopes to study the heavens at night"!

It hardly needs to be said that none of these disc 'decipherers' agrees with any other. "The Phaistos disc has been a millstone round my neck for decades, since every enthusiast thinks I shall be delighted to hear their latest decipherment", Chadwick complained to me in 1998. Perhaps, rather than trying to reply to them seriously as he generally did, he should have taken his own joking advice and put each would-be decipherer in touch with another one.

While it is true that no widely respected epigrapher or archaeologist has deluded himself into offering a full decipherment of the disc (unlike the Indus script), Sir Arthur Evans came perilously close. Evans pointed out the, undeniably intriguing, repetition of certain groups and sequences on side A:

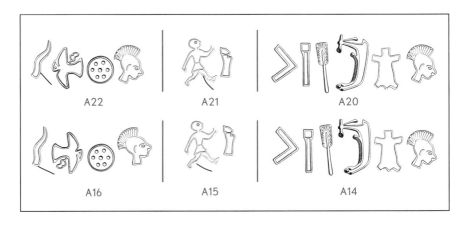

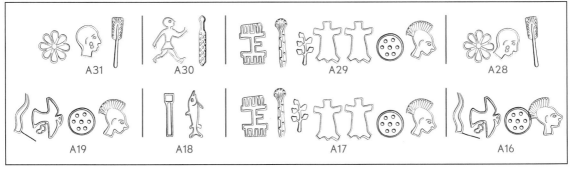

Then he suggested they might be "refrains", and that the disc inscription as a whole "follows the laws of primitive music, and... may well represent a chaunt of Victory." After this he added, wholly misleadingly:

> ❝ The ideographic element in the inscription is so patent that its principal theme can hardly be a matter of doubt. The preponderance of pictorial characters belonging to a certain group of allied subjects strongly suggests that it is mainly concerned with some maritime expedition, probably of a warlike kind, in which case we may see its material results in the form of spoils, captives, as well as the manacles with which they were secured. The plumed head recurs nineteen times, in fourteen cases followed by the round shield, which itself appears in seventeen places; the ship with its armed prow is found seven times, the fish, which at least has a marine significance, six, the arrow four times. It seems probable that the marching figure, which occurs eleven times, should be taken in the same connection. ❞

Evans's view seems to have influenced Fischer's 1980s 'decipherment' of the disc (though Fischer does not explicitly say so), which translates the inscription as a Minoan proclamation in a "Hellenic" language related to but not identical with archaic Greek, that urges everyone in the empire (including the Libyans) to sail to Naxos and fight off a great threat from the Carians of Anatolia. This is side A of the disc in Fischer's translation:

> ❝ Hear ye, Cretans and Greeks: my great, my quick! Hear ye, Danaidans, the great, the worthy! Hear ye, all blacks, and hear ye, Pudaan and Libyan immigrants! Hear ye, waters, yea earth: Hellas faces battle with the Carians. Hear ye all! Hear ye, Gods of the Fleet, aye hear ye all: faces battle with the Carians. Hear ye all! Hear ye, the multitudes of black people and all! Hear ye, lords, yea freeman: To Naxos! Hear ye, Lords of the Fleet: To Naxos! ❞

As Fischer himself tells us at one point in *Glyph-Breaker*, his simplified account of his remarkable achievement: "Approaching each word of the text through its Indo-European root, I compared it with some twenty other sister languages, and bit by bit, like soft clay slapped onto the murmuring potter's wheel, the entire terrible message of the Phaistos disc took shape."

Fischer's work on the disc is misguided from beginning to end (unlike his later work on *rongorongo*): it is a grotesque parody of Michael Ventris's methods in deciphering Linear B, complete with Fischer's own 'grids' and 'work notes'. It would not be worth discussing at all, were it not for the fact that the author has published two books on it, one heavily footnoted, the second (quoted above) for the general reader; that its claim of a decipherment has attracted considerable attention (as witness *The Economist* reader on page 298) which very nearly tipped the *National Geographic* magazine into publishing a full endorsement of the claim in 1984; and finally, that Fischer's 'decipherment' perfectly illustrates the pitfalls beckoning the unwary. Only the spirited debunking of it by Chadwick, aided by Emmett Bennett and another scholar, saved the *National Geographic* editors from making "utter fools of themselves", in Chadwick's words. The whole episode became almost a textbook example of the thin line which divides sense from nonsense in archaeological decipherment.

We shall not go into the tangled details of Fischer's method. A quick outline is sufficient to understand its defects. First, he tries an internal analysis of the characters, discovers certain patterns and comes up with the conclusions that: a) the language of the Phaistos disc may be inflecting like Greek (reasoned, if impossible to prove with such a short inscription), and b) that side A may be some sort of invocation or proclamation (purely intuitive). How to go further and introduce phonetic values? Mostly, he does so by comparing and equating the shapes of the disc's signs with the shapes of Linear B and Cypriot signs of known phonetic value (while glancing at the shapes of Linear A signs and the Hieroglyphic script), and then equating the established value with the unknown value. This, as we know, is a dubious method at best; in this case, there is no secure rationale for the comparisons, since we know nothing definite of the disc's origin and nothing at all about the underlying language; anyway, the comparisons are graphically unconvincing, as already shown (page 305). Having assigned values to three-quarters of the signs, Fischer next resorts to the even more dubious acrophonic 'A as in Apple' principle: he guesses the iconic meaning of a sign (e.g. ⊙ = 'shield'), assigns this meaning a word in some flexible kind of Greek, and then takes the first syllable of the chosen word to be the syllabic value of the sign. Having now filled his 'grid' with signs and sounds, he proceeds to 'translate' the disc into words, which he can torture into some semblance of a coherent 'unknown' Hellenic dialect by showing that the 'translated' words resemble words in (as he says above) 20! other languages. Lo and behold, known Cretan (Minoan) names come tumbling out of the disc, and so does a word "Libu" apparently meaning 'Libyans', a people known to have had contact with Crete at this time. Yet as Fischer himself admits: "Perhaps I subconsciously put together these imagined 'Minoan' names myself, though I consciously believed that I was proceeding objectively. I might have been deceiving myself all along, in other words."

It was the proper names that so greatly impressed the *National Geographic* editors. The 'decipherment' even seemed to make good sense of some Linear A inscriptions (on the basis that both Linear A and the Phaistos disc were written in the same kind of 'Minoan' Greek). How could it produce so many names, known from independent sources, as had happened before to Ventris with the names of Cretan towns, Amnisos, Knossos, Phaistos and so on—and yet still be wrong?

But as Chadwick sternly told the magazine's editors in a ping-pong correspondence across the Atlantic lasting several months:

> **❝** There is only one valid test of sense: can it be shown to agree with what is deducible about the text in advance? In the case of the disc, this is virtually nothing… In the case of Linear B, [the decipherment produced] a recognizable early form of Greek for which no special [sound] rules had to be posited. And the meaning of the documents was exactly what we should expect for palace archives, being instantly seen to be parallel to similar documents in known languages such as Akkadian.
>
> Fischer's decipherments of the new Linear A tablets he has given are totally unexpected, for the very good reason that he has deliberately selected the ones the contents of which are not immediately obvious. He has ignored the one word of certain meaning ('ku-ro' = 'total') and those for which we can make at least good guesses. Instead he operates in an area where no check is possible. **❞**

This was the argument that finally carried the day and scuppered the publication of the Fischer decipherment by the *National Geographic*. There is only *one* Phaistos disc, so there is no 'control' on a claimed decipherment; no way of telling from fresh material in the same script whether the decipherment is capable of producing meanings that fit an agreed body of knowledge. You can happily claim to have discovered any 'unknown' language you like in the signs—and no one can gainsay you. The fact is, disappointing though it may be, that until more material turns up (or maybe the Greeks agree to that thermoluminescence test), the Phaistos disc riddle will remain unsolved—we can be certain of it. In the amusing words of Chadwick, touched with exasperation: "We must curb our impatience, and admit that if King Minos himself were to reveal to someone in a dream the true interpretation, it would be quite impossible for him to convince anyone else that his was the one and only possible solution."

The Urge to Decipher

# CONCLUSION

"I have not made up my mind that he is right, nor have I made up my mind that he is wrong. Of course, as a purveyor of popular culture, I wish very much for him to be right; it would make such a good story! But I am aware my wishing does not make it so." This comes from the final letter about Fischer's 'decipherment' of the Phaistos disc written by the *National Geographic* editor to John Chadwick.

Why do decipherments of ancient scripts interest many people so much? What makes them headline news? And what causes a highly intelligent and gifted man like Michael Ventris to become obsessed with ancient squiggles written on clay tablets, and hundreds of enthusiastic amateurs to descend every year on the Maya Hieroglyphic Workshops in Austin, Texas—not to speak of what drives the scholars and other specialists who have labored over the undeciphered scripts in this book ever since they were discovered? A Harvard University professor in zoology, Barry Fell, was convinced he had deciphered *rongorongo* and the Phaistos disc before he died a few years ago, though his extensive published papers were very far from scientific in their method. The Czech Orientalist Bedřich Hrozný, who played a key role in the decipherment of Hittite cuneiform, bizarrely claimed to have deciphered most of the world's undeciphered scripts towards the end of his life. ("From this occupational disease of decoders we may all wish to be preserved", wrote Ventris.) Is the urge to decipher only an esoteric branch of crossword puzzling, but without the prizes? Speaking as someone who has

*(Opposite) "Each character is full of life"*
*—Japanese inscription by Shinagawa Tetsuzan.*

never wanted to solve crossword puzzles, I think decipherment's appeal is rather different. Crossword puzzling appeals chiefly to the intellect, albeit at a fairly trivial level. Decipherment answers to both the intellect and the emotions at a deep level, the level of questions like 'What is it that makes us human?', 'What is it that makes us civilized?'

I began this book with the claim that the great decipherments, such as that of Egyptian hieroglyphs, are on a par with the 'cracking' of the genetic code in 1953. By coincidence, I finish writing it at the very time that the human genome has finally been decoded. Newspapers, radio and television are agog with the announcement and its potentially wonderful implications for the treatment of certain diseases—not to speak of the awkward ethical challenges during the coming century. While the achievement is certainly a dramatic step forward, especially for those who have personal experience of one of the terrible medical conditions caused by genetic defects, I am much less persuaded by further, excitable claims that 'transliterating' the letters of the genetic alphabet will help us to understand what it is that makes us human. For a start, decoding the letters and sign groups of a script is a far cry from fully deciphering it, as we know from Meroitic, Etruscan and Linear A. But then, even when scientists have learnt how to 'translate' the letters into meaning—in other words how to link particular gene sequences with particular aspects of the body's development—how will this tell us anything relevant about human consciousness and creativity? A geneticist such as Luigi Cavalli-Sforza, the author of *Genes, Peoples and Languages*, who has devoted decades to studying the idea that the evolution of languages may resemble genetic evolution, will undoubtedly disagree with me, but I suggest that archaeological decipherment is far more informative and illuminating about these great cultural questions than genetic science will ever be.

In purely intellectual terms—i.e. looking at them as achievements independent of the civilizations they reveal—the great archaeological decipherments rank with great scientific achievements, as I hope this book has made clear. Champollion, Ventris and Knorozov are certainly to be compared with Crick and Watson—even with Einstein, if you believe Michael Coe. Like the scientists, the great decipherers took a bewildering mass of incomprehensible information, a hodge-podge of other people's ideas, some right some wrong, and by perseverance, logic and some lateral thinking based on wide knowledge, revealed a beautiful order. "It is this quality, the power of seeing order in apparent confusion, that has marked the work of all great men," Chadwick accurately observed about Ventris in *The Decipherment of Linear B*.

Listen now to the physicist Richard Feynman, who was passingly mentioned in the Introduction, on the subject of the Mayan glyphs, which he first tried to decipher while on honeymoon in Central America in June 1952 (curiously, the very month Ventris 'cracked' Linear B, and the year Knorozov announced his Mayan breakthrough). Feynman had first come across the glyphs as a boy when his father took him to the New York World's Fair and showed him a reconstructed Maya temple. Now, in some small Guatemalan town he ran across a Spanish edition of the Dresden Codex. He admitted (if reluctantly) that other people had already figured out the numerical system, but he thought he would have a go for himself, just for the mental challenge:

" I love puzzles and codes, so when I saw the bars and dots, I thought 'I'm gonna have some fun!' I covered up the Spanish with a piece of yellow paper and began playing this game of deciphering the Mayan bars and dots, sitting in the hotel room, while my wife climbed up and down the pyramids all day.

I quickly figured out that a bar was equal to five dots, what the symbol for zero was, and so on. It took me a while longer to figure out that the bars and dots always carried at 20 the first time, but they carried at 18 the second time (making cycles of 360) [i.e. the 20 named days and 18 named months on pages 113-14]. I also worked out all kinds of things about various faces: they had surely meant certain days and weeks.

After we got back home I continued to work on it. Altogether, it's a lot of fun to try to decipher something like that, because when you start out you don't know anything—you have no clue to go by. But then you notice certain numbers that appear often, and add up to other numbers, and so on.

There was one place in the codex where the number 584 was very prominent. This 584 was divided into periods of 236, 90, 250, and 8. Another prominent number was 2920, or 584 x 5 (also 365 x 8). There was a table of multiples of 2920 up to 13 x 2920, then there were multiples of 13 x 2920 for a while, and then—*funny numbers*! They were errors, as far as I could tell. Only many years later did I figure out what they were. "

At last, having supposedly worked out for himself most of the complicated astronomical tables in the codex (beginning with the period of Venus seen from Earth, 583.92 days), Feynman gave a lecture on the subject in the 1970s. "I got a big kick out of giving my talk 'Deciphering Mayan hieroglyphics'. There I was, being something I'm not, again."

Clever stuff by a brilliant Nobel laureate, which gives a partial picture of why people become fascinated by undeciphered scripts: what one might call decipherment's detective appeal. But when writing here about decipherment—in an article with the ironic title "Bringing culture to the physicists"—Feynman showed not the faintest awareness of how the much harder (and more interesting) problem of reading the *glyphs*, not merely the numbers, had been solved by Knorozov and others. To 'crack' this problem would require powers of scientific analysis *and* linguistic/archaeological/cultural knowledge: the kind of personal combination that in general Feynman, who was notoriously arrogant about the humanities, did not value. Taken as a whole his account implies, quite wrongly, that archaeological decipherment is basically a branch of science.

Although much of the work of physicists, even a theoretician like Feynman, has a direct practical impact on our lives—through atom bombs, computers, lasers and the like—the same obviously cannot be said for successful decipherers. It makes little difference to the everyday lives of the vast majority of people whether the Egyptian hieroglyphs, Babylonian cuneiform tablets and Maya stelae can be read or not. But imagine for a moment if the huge crowds attending the glittering Tutankhamun exhibitions in the 1960s and 70s had been told by the experts: sorry, we have no idea what the hieroglyphs in the tomb and on the treasures mean—perhaps they are hymns to the ancient gods or curses against tomb robbers? Or suppose that the crowds of tourists who now visit Pacal's tomb at Palenque in Mexico were to be told (as a visitor would certainly have been told in the 1960s): we do not know who this ruler was, when he lived or what he did. You see, the writing is not deciphered.

Two centuries ago, before Champollion, "the oldest known languages were Greek, Latin and Hebrew; and no records which had been written down earlier than about 600 BC could be read or understood," Ventris remarked in his BBC announcement of his decipherment in 1952. "All that was known of the earlier civilizations of the Near East was limited to those parts of the Old Testament which seemed historical, and to the garbled accounts of Greek and Roman writers." A mere quarter of a century ago, the oldest readable records in the Americas post-dated Columbus. The great decipherments, by rescuing the 'cradle of civilization' in Mesopotamia, the Egyptian pharaohs, the Mycenaean Greeks and the Mayan rulers from myth and obscurity, have altered our view of modern civilization. They have not only have put the Greek and Roman classics in their proper perspective so that they are no longer the fountainhead of all western wisdom, have given the Old Testament new meaning (challenging to creationists), and have redefined the much-debated issue of the origin of the alphabet and the origin of writing itself—they have also made the New World no longer so new. The discovery that the Maya had an amazing civilization at the time of Rome's glory, many centuries before the rise of European colonialism, is yet a further blow to racist beliefs. It has certainly generated new respect for the surviving Maya—not least in Central America itself—and new self-respect among the Maya themselves. (For one thing, they have started to argue with foreign scholars about the correct interpretation of their glyphs!)

If we could read and understand the undeciphered script of Linear A, we could learn something of life and thought in Europe's very earliest civilization—not perhaps the true story of Minos and the Minotaur, but in what way the Minoans resembled and differed from the ancient Egyptians and Mycenaean Greeks. If we could work out the language behind the Meroitic script, we might well learn something important about the black African elements in ancient Egyptian civilization—a hot topic in today's world, as Martin Bernal's related theories in *Black Athena: The Afroasiatic Roots of Classical Civilization* have shown. And if we could decipher the Indus script, we would perhaps learn if the roots of Indian civilization really did possess some special genius, different from the other ancient civilizations, as suggested by the material artifacts at Mohenjo-daro and Harappa and the spiritual emphasis of subsequent Indian culture—Buddha instead of Alexander, so to speak. It is most extraordinary that in 80 years of excavation in the Indus Valley no solid evidence of militarism has turned up, either in the buildings or in the art (including the seal imagery). The contrast with the ancient Middle East, Egypt, Greece, Central America and China, is stark. Maybe—many archaeologists cannot help but wonder—the Indus Valley dwellers were the spiritual forebears of the non-violent tradition epitomized in modern times by Mahatma Gandhi, who was born in the region (near Kutch)?

Not long ago, I watched a television program devoted, yet again, to the mystery of the Easter Island *moai*. Why were these giant stone statues constructed and how on earth were they moved around? Evidence is scanty, so the archaeologists in the program could really only speculate with varying degrees of credibility. Wouldn't it be exciting if the *rongorongo* could be read, and the Rapanui sculptors themselves were able to tell us through their enigmatic signs something of their shadowy motives?

There is a more direct contemporary significance in decipherment too. Ancient scripts have helped us to understand how our modern writing systems function, and the profound processes involved in speaking, reading and writing, as well as the nature and significance of literacy. It is a thought-provoking fact that the ancient Egyptians possessed a basic phonetic 'alphabet' (the first part of the script to fall to Young and Champollion); but they chose not to limit themselves to it and instead added to this alphabet hundreds, even thousands, of non-phonetic logograms. The Japanese, by contrast, went in the opposite direction and having borrowed thousands of Chinese characters (logograms), invented their syllabic *kana*; but again, like the ancient Egyptians, the Japanese did not replace the Chinese *kanji* with Japanese *kana*, they kept both types of sign in one, complex writing system, in use to this day. Japan, as we know, has one of the highest literacy rates in the world.

The success of Japanese industry, the growth of air travel and the explosion in personal computing and use of the internet—not to speak of the long-running debate about whether to teach children to read through letters or words—have fuelled a renewed interest in pictography and logograms. We urgently require more visual means of international and instant communication. Perhaps the ancient logosyllabic scripts with their strong iconic elements, including most of the undeciphered scripts, have something to teach us in this area? Although some fashionable nonsense has recently been written about how to design more usable computer icons and 'visual language' using the principles of Egyptian hieroglyphs and Mayan glyphs, the basic idea that we might learn from the graphic composition of these scripts (and the Chinese script) is worthy of serious study.

Finally, there is the sheer aesthetic pleasure of scripts, deciphered and undeciphered, from all ages. Calligraphy is still considered to be one of the highest arts in China; even Mao Zedong practiced it. The finest examples of Egyptian hieroglyphs, whether monumental or encrusted on a box belonging to a pharaoh; some of the Mayan glyphs carved rococo in stone and painted in gorgeous colors on ceramics; and the most refined of the miniature, engraved Indus seal stones—are artistic marvels of world importance. Even the simply engraved *rongorongo* script, with its exquisite 'birdman' figures, sharks and octopuses—is often a delight to the eye. When we can read what these works of art say, too, they become even more marvelous.

Archaeological decipherment therefore bridges both the sciences and the arts (hence probably the lack of any departments of decipherment and professors of decipherment in our over-specialized modern world). It involves a range of scientific techniques, from chemical analysis of written materials to sign frequency analysis and comparative linguistics, which are applicable to every undeciphered script—but at the same time the decipherer needs also to involve, subtly, the entire archaeological, historical and cultural evidence, which is unique to a particular script. Each undeciphered script therefore constitutes a genuinely different problem; there are no universal principles of archaeological decipherment. Thus it is not like deciphering the genome or, for that matter, climbing

Mount Everest, where the skills needed for one gene sequence or mountain peak can be applied to the next sequence or peak, and the one after that. "It is more like inventing," says Maurice Pope. If you have invented the internet, it does not mean you are well placed to invent the worldwide web. Perhaps even the reverse. This realization seems to have been the chief reason why Ventris never tackled any undeciphered script but Linear B.

So, the decipherment of ancient scripts is a compelling intellectual and imaginative challenge; it makes history; it changes our perceptions of our place in the world; it casts new light on how we read and write; and it is sometimes the handmaiden and interpreter of fine art. The urge to decipher is our vital response to our species' urge to express its thoughts and feelings through writing in all its unique diversity and incredible ingenuity over five millennia. This, surely, is what most makes us human.

**"The worm thinks it strange and foolish that man does not eat his books."**

– Rabindranath Tagore, *Fireflies*

# NOTES AND REFERENCES

## I INTRODUCTION

**p.11** *"The Decipherment of Linear B"* Chadwick,
1958: 4.

*"Nature"* The first Crick and Watson paper
appeared on 25 April 1953, the second,
more speculative paper, outlining the genetic
implications of their discovery, on 30 May.

**p.12** "London *Times*" 25 June 1953.

"Everest of Greek archaeology" Chadwick,
1958: 80.

"there can be no question" Pope: 9.

**p.13** "speaking with the dead" Parkinson: 195.

**p.14** "Feynman" Sykes: 230. See also Feynman:
313-17.

"scribe for King Minos" Alice Kober to Sir
John Myres, 8 July 1948, in Palaima, Pope
and Reilly: 10.

"a magnificent beaker" Homer, *The Iliad*: 214.

**p.15** "Hunter told me a story" This was in 1989.
Hunter was quite sure that Ventris first
encountered Linear B informally, not
through a formal lecture by Evans as implied
in *The Decipherment of Linear B* (p. 1) and subsequently repeated by most scholars.

"BBC...broadcast" The text appears in Ventris,
1952.

**p.16** "Rivalry" See Parkinson, Adkins, Solé and
Valbelle, and Robinson, 2006, for the story of
Champollion versus Young; Larsen (esp. pp.
293-305) for Rawlinson versus Hincks; and Coe,
1999, for Knorozov versus Thompson. Ventris
gave due credit to Kober in his chief account of
the decipherment (Chadwick, 1973: 15-17), but
his first announcement on the BBC did not

mention her, while mentioning some other less
important contributors. One must add that
Kober herself had been sharply critical of Ventris
(see, for example, Ventris, 1988: 37).

"Franklin" See Anne Sayre, *Rosalind Franklin
and DNA*, New York, 2nd edn, 2000.

"Schele remarked" Drew: 170.

**p.18** "glyph for 'dog'" Thompson, 1950: 78-79.

**p.19** "It...cannot help us make sense" Knorozov,
1958: 288.

**p.20** "codes and ciphers" See Singh for an
introduction to cryptanalysis, which also
refers (not always accurately) to archaeological
decipherment.

"Diffie" Parkinson: 190, 191.

"cryptanalysts-turned-scholars" A second
contributor to the decipherment of Linear B,
Emmett Bennett Jr., also had wartime experience as a cryptanalyst. However, none of the
scholars in the Maya decipherment was trained
as a cryptanalyst. Among the key decipherers in
general, the only ones with cryptanalytical experience seem to be Edouard Dhorme and Hans
Bauer, who 'cracked' Ugaritic cuneiform with
Charles Virolleaud; Dhorme was even decorat-
ed by the French government for his cryptanalytical work in the first world war. See Gordon:
106, 108, and Doblhofer: 220.

**p.21** "Socrates" The story, from Plato's *Phaedrus*,
appears in Harris: 19.

**p.22** *"Short History of the World"* Wells: 53.

**p.23** "The earliest writing of all" See Nissen,
Damerow and Englund.

**p.24** "perishable materials" See Postgate, Wang
and Wilkinson.

"clay 'tokens'" The theory has been developed by Denise Schmandt-Besserat in many articles and books.

**p.25** "even earlier in China" See Boltz. Some Chinese archaeologists have claimed to find writing on pottery dated to the 5th millennium BC. Boltz, and most other scholars, see no relationship between these cryptic early marks and what is undoubtedly the 'full' writing of the Shang culture, *c.* 1200 BC.

**p.27** "writing diffusing across the oceans" For discussion of the controversial subject of transoceanic contact between early civilizations, see *Pre-Columbiana: A Journal of Long-Distance Contacts*, started by the Early Sites Research Society in 1998.

**p.29** "to quote...DeFrancis" DeFrancis: 4.

**p.31** "fellows of the Royal Society" Maurice Pope, "Ventris's decipherment—first causes", in Duhoux, Palaima and Bennet: 27-28.

**p.32** "Saussure...said" Saussure: 111.

**p.33** "Herbert" Maurice Pope, "Ventris's decipherment—first causes", in Duhoux, Palaima and Bennet:26.

"Ventris summarized the process" Ventris, 1953:200.

**p.34** "Guy...declares" Personal communication.

"'pseudo-hieroglyphs' found at Byblos" Daniels and Bright: 29-30.

**p.37** "comments...Barber" Personal communication.

**p.39** "regrets...Guy" Personal communication. Guy observes that the photographs in Fischer, 1997b, are neither complete nor clear.

**p.41** "broad system of classifying scripts" This was first noted by A. H. Sayce in May 1876. See Maurice Pope, "Ventris's decipherment—first causes", in Duhoux, Palaima and Bennet: 29.

**p.44** "Chadwick, echoing Ventris" Chadwick, 1975b: 918.

"right to be very skeptical" Chadwick to Joseph Judge, November 1984. The letter is part of a long correspondence with the *National Geographic* about a claimed decipherment of the Phaistos disc (see pages 313-17). The tablet is discussed in Chadwick, 1976: 88-89, and Chadwick, 1973: 311-12.

**p.46** "Carian" See Pope for a brief treatment and Ray, 1998, for a fuller one.

"runic alphabet" See Page.

"ancient Chinese inscriptions" See Moore.

"websites" See Further Reading.

**p.47** "two still earlier fragments" These were found by John Coleman Darnell, an Egyptologist at Yale University, and his wife Deborah, while they were surveying ancient travel routes in the southern Egyptian desert. See Man: 69-90.

"Tangut script" Daniels and Bright: 228-30. Their edited book discusses almost all the undeciphered scripts, major and minor. See also the encyclopedia of writing systems by Coulmas.

"Voynich manuscript" See D'Imperio, and also Gerry Kennedy and Rob Churchill, *The Voynich Manuscript*, London, 2004.

# I EGYPTIAN HIEROGLYPHS

**p.52** "Diodorus Siculus" Boas: 101.

"Horapollo" See Boas, Iversen, and Pope.

"dog" Boas: 63.

**p.53** "vulture" Boas: 49-50.

"The protection of Osiris" Pope: 31-32.

**p.56** "Napoleon's army was so awestruck" Quoted in Claiborne: 24.

"the most popular single object" Parkinson: 12.

"the Stone's iconic status" Ibid: 25.

**p.60** "a decree issued at Memphis" Translations of the Rosetta stone appear in Andrews: 25-28 (Greek section) and Parkinson: 198-200 (demotic section).

**p.61** "Young" The best discussion of Young's role in deciphering Egyptian hieroglyphs is in Robinson, 2006.

**p.62** "dictionary of scientific biography" Porter and Ogilvie: 1000-01. Walter Moore (*Schrödinger: Life and Thought*, Cambridge, 1992, p. 122) calls Young's three-color theory of vision "the most prescient work in all of psychophysics".

"striking resemblance" Hooker *et al*: 123.

**p.64** "decipherer of demotic" See Ray, 2007.

**p.65** "letter...from de Sacy" Parkinson: 33.

"Pope...Ray" Pope (pp. 66-68), for example, is sharply critical of Young for claiming more credit than was his due, while Ray, 2007, is broadly supportive of Young's claims.

**p.68** "Ingrained preconceptions" Coe, 1999: 13.

**p.69** "[Champollion] was naturally more concerned" Pope: 75.

"The most contradictory objects" Pope: 75.

**p.72** "I recognize that [he] was the first" Parkinson: 40.

"[Champollion] knew" Andrews: 15.

"Young discovered" Parkinson: 40.

**p.73** "like any act of reading" Ibid: 195. There are numerous beginner's guides to reading Egyptian hieroglyphs, such as Davies and Zauzich.

## II LINEAR B

**p.75** "There is a land called Crete" Homer, *The Odyssey*: 232.

"In 1900...Evans" See Brown, and MacGillivray.

"a Mainland branch" Chadwick, 1973: 10.

**p.76** "clay tablets...[Evans] had discovered" Evans saw his first Linear B tablet in 1895, before he began digging Knossos. It was found in 1877 by Minos Kalokairinos. See Chadwick, 1973: 8, and MacGillivray.

"a suspense account" Palaima, 1999.

**p.78** "Evans...did take some...steps" Evans's principal discussions of Linear B are in *Scripta Minoa*, Vol. I, and *The Palace of Minos*, Vol. IVb.

**p.84** "Ventris...was invited to help" See correspondence in Myres papers at Ashmolean Museum, Oxford.

"Blegen" See Alsop for a description of Blegen's work at Pylos.

**p.87** "Bennett proved" Bennett, 1950.

"Bennett's...sign list" Bennett, 1947 and 1951.

"How difficult the task is" Chadwick, 1958: 39.

**p.89** "PYLOS TABLETS" Personal communication.

"Kober's career" For a detailed account, see Bennett, 1971.

"consuming interest" Bennett, 1971: 345.

"Kober's triplets" Ventris, 1953: 203.

**p.91** "There is enough evidence" Kober, 1948: 98-99.

"One other result by Kober" Kober, 1949; Chadwick, 1973: 17.

"When we have the facts" Kober, 1948: 103.

"a rather pessimistic note" Ventris to Myres, 28 January 1948.

"prim but necessary" Chadwick, 1973: 15.

"Ventris's background" See Robinson, 2002, a short biography of Ventris (especially chapters 1-3), and also Tetlow *et al.*, a booklet about Ventris prepared by Stowe school.

**p.92** "Palaima...emphasizes" Personal communication.

"There are three golden rules" Ventris, 1948: 17.

"Introducing the Minoan language" This article was entirely ignored by Kober in her published work on Linear B.

"The theory that Minoan could be Greek" Ventris, 1940: 494.

"correspond...closely to Etruscan" Ibid: 517.

"no Champollion" Ventris to Myres, 16 November 1942.

"I have good hopes" Ventris, 1988: 108.

**p.95** "The problem of decipherment" Ventris and Chadwick: 88.

"summary of [Ventris's] basic techniques" My treatment relies chiefly on Ventris's own account in Chadwick, 1973: 17-20, supplemented by Chadwick's two accounts in Chadwick, 1958 and in Ventris, 1988: 369-96 (reprint of a 1973 article).

**p.98** "only a little adjustment" Ventris to Myres, 28 February 1952.

"To wait for a *bilingual*" Ventris, 1988: 294.

"a leap in the dark" Preface to Tetlow *et al*: 5.

**p.99** "though it runs completely counter" Ventris to Myres, 17? June 1952.

**p.101** "a difficult and archaic Greek" Ventris, 1952: 58.

"The most interesting fact" Chadwick, 1975b.

"he rarely showed signs of emotion" Chadwick, 1958:81.

**p.103** "Not quite the Greek you taught me" Tetlow *et al*: 38.

## III MAYAN GLYPHS

**p.105** "Dresden Codex" The best reproduction is still the one published by Ernst Förstemann

in 1880 (see Codex Dresden in
Bibliography).

p.107 "Maya writing is not syllabic" Thompson,
1972: 28.

"Their ideal...consideration for others."
Thompson, 1963: 81, 93 and 137.

"The highest goal" Coe, 1993: 199.

"*Breaking the Maya Code*" My account of the
decipherment relies mainly on this book,
Coe (1993), Coe and Kerr, and Knorozov
(1958).

p.109 "If a like discovery" Stephens, Vol. II: 296.

"No Champollion" Stephens, Vol. I: 160.

p.111 "precise nature of the earlier Mayan
language" Houston, 2000: 157-64.

p.112 "complicated Maya calendar" For a detailed
explanation of the calendar, see Sharer:
chapter 12 and Appendix.

p.119 "Fray Diego de Landa" See Clendinnen for
a fascinating study of this period, including
the life of de Landa.

p.122 "Rosetta Stone" Coe and Kerr: 53.

p.123 "any writing system made by a man"
Knorozov, 1998 (first part of interview).

p.124 "phraseology obligatory for a Soviet scholar"
Quoted in Coe and Coe.

p.125 "the Russian Knorozov" Coe, 1999:
162.

p.126 "the idea that Maya texts record history"
Proskouriakoff, 1961: 16.

"well nigh inconceivable" Thompson, 1950:155.

"It is not at all certain" Proskouriakoff,
1961: 21.

p.131 "prairie fire" Coe, 1999: 214.

p.136 "the work of dozens of scholars" See, for
example, Stuart, 1987, Houston, 1989 and
2000, Schele and Mathews, and Martin and
Grube.

p.138 "Thompson would have been horrified" Ibid: 245.

"Cacao" See Stuart, 1988.

## IV   THE MEROITIC SCRIPT

p.143 "Meroitic civilization" See Shinnie, 1967 and
1996, and Welsby.

p.145 "Bedouin" Dalby: 81.

"not as conquering barbarians" Welsby: 19.

"miserable or wretched" Ibid: 7.

"Griffith" The decipherment appears in
Griffith, 1909 and 1911. See also Shinnie,
1967: 132-40, for a summary.

p.149 "terike or yerike" Griffith, 1911: 22-23.

"If new eyes" Ibid: vi.

p.150 "26 simple words in Meroitic" This list is
taken from Török: 63.

"Hintze...and Leclant" For a list of their
publications, see Török.

"the study of Kush has become an accepted
discipline" Shinnie, 2000.

"computerizing the corpus" See Jean
Leclant, "The present position in the
deciphering of Meroitic script" in
UNESCO: 112-16.

"Répertoire d'Epigraphie Meroitique" The
corpus is being published in the *Meroitic
Newsletter: Bulletin d'Informations Meroitiques*, edited
by Leclant.

p.151 "Abdalla's approach" See the representative
article by Abdalla in the Bibliography. For a
sounder analytical approach, see Rilly.

"says Robin Thelwall" Personal communication.
See Thelwall's article in the Bibliography, to
which I am indebted for his analysis of the
potential languages written in the Meroitic script.

p.154 "Greenberg, writing in 1955" Shinnie,
1967: 133.

"Ehret and...Bender" See Thelwall for a
list of their earlier publications, and
Bender (1997) for their more recent
arguments.

"bilinguals exist" See Millet: 311-12.

"In the words of Leclant" Preface to
*Meroitic Newsletter*, 26, 1999.

"nomads from the eastern desert" Griffith,
1909: 54.

"Lepsius" Ibid: 45.

## V   THE ETRUSCAN ALPHABET

p.157 "Lawrence" Spivey: 193.

p.159 "Greek culture" Bonfante and Bonfante: 43.

"*The Etruscan Language*" I have drawn extensively
on this book.

p.162 "Seneca" *Naturales Quaestiones*, 32: 2.

p.164 "the cycle of research" Pallottino: 209.

"Etruscan words for family relationships"
The comparative chart appears in Bonfante
and Bonfante: 140.

**p.165** "Etruscan [numerical] system" See Keyser, and Wilkins.

**p.166** "mirrors" See Bonfante, 1997, for some beautiful examples of these mirrors.

**p.172** "Though damaged and spotted" Hooker *et al*: 345.

**p.175** "Tabula Cortonensis" See Agostiniani and Nicosia; and Becattini for the story of the tablet's discovery.
"Pallottino" Bonfante, 2000: 22.

**p.181** "favorite playground for cranks" Pallottino: 189.

## VI LINEAR A

**p.185** "Linear A...Linear B...Hieroglyphic" See Duhoux, 1998, for a comparison of the three corpuses.
"even in...Israel" The discoveries are described in Finkelberg, Uchitel and Ussishkin.
"discoveries at Miletus" See Schneider, and Niemeier.

**p.186** "numerical system of Linear A" Bennett, 1950.

**p.188** "Chadwick suggests" Hooker *et al*: 181.

**p.189** "Pope...suggested" Pope and Raison: 47.

**p.192** "According to Bennett" Daniels and Bright: 132.
"Pope reckons" Pope and Raison: 38.

**p.194** "Chadwick observed" Hooker *et al*: 180.

**p.195** "Vowel frequency analysis" Pope and Raison: 29.
"Packard" There is an accessible analysis of Packard's rather technical work (published as *Minoan Linear A*) in Pope and Raison: 23-31.
"my conclusions do not possess any special validity" Packard: 7.

**p.196** "Critics of this analogy with Linear B" See, for example, Hooker (esp. pp. 169-70).

**p.197** "Much debate has raged" Chadwick, 1975a: 145.

**p.198** "words which supposedly conform to Semitic names" Gordon: 140-41.
"Resemblances can always be found" Hooker: 172.
"Duhoux...points out" Duhoux, 1998: 33. See also Pope and Raison: 43.

**p.199** "Nagy tries to relate *ku-ro*" Nagy: 202-03.
"According to Chadwick" Hooker *et al*: 181.
"Herodotus...noted" Herodotus, I: 173.

"According to Margalit Finkelberg" See Finkelberg. The first part of her article discusses why the language of Linear A is not Greek or Semitic, the second part attempts to show that it is Anatolian.
"some support from Melchert" Personal communication from Margalit Finkelberg. As useful background, see Melchert's article on Anatolian hieroglyphs in Daniels and Bright: 120-24.
"to quote... Olivier" Personal communication.
"Palaima remarked" Palaima, 1987: 337.

## VII THE PROTO-ELAMITE SCRIPT

**p.204** "the famous cliff at Behistun" For its role in the decipherment of Mesopotamian cuneiform, see Pope: chapter 4, and Walker.
"Linear Elamite" See Salvini.

**p.205** "relationship between proto-Elamite and Linear Elamite" See Potts: 71-79.
"first introduced in 1949" Lamberg-Karlovsky, 1978: 114.

**p.206** "claims of up to 35 signs in common" M.-J. Steve cited in Potts: 79.
"'so-called' proto-Elamite script" Potts: 84.
"No one would ever argue" Ibid: 75, 79.
"One wonders what language other than Elamite" Lamberg-Karlovsky, 1999.

**p.207** "Englund estimates" Personal communication.

**p.208** "Meriggi" Damerow and Englund: 5-6.

**p.210** *Archaic Bookkeeping* Most of this book is concerned with the early Mesopotamian tablets as a whole, but see pp. 75-79 and 93-95 for the proto-Elamite script. The fullest discussion of proto-Elamite appears in Damerow and Englund, which analyzes only the tablets from Tepe Yahya.
"His projection into the archaic period" Damerow and Englund: 18.
"Writing about it...in *Scientific American*" Friberg: 118.

**p.213** "the original in the Teheran museum" Damerow and Englund: 36.
"Two individuals stood at the top" Nissen, Damerow and Englund: 77.

**p.217** "In all likelihood [they] represent" Damerow and Englund: 63.

## VIII  RONGORONGO

**p.220** "They were cannibals" "Message from
Fantasia", *Der Spiegel* (English summary), 30
October 1999. See page 272 for Richter's
Indus script 'decipherment'.

"de Hevesy" See Possehl, 1996: 90-100,
and Fischer, 1997b: 147-53. A linguistic
link between India and Easter Island was
first suggested in the 1880s.

**p.221** *"Times"* 21 September 1932 (letter from Sir E.
Denison Ross).

*"Nature"* Skinner, 1932a.

*"Journal of the Polynesian Society"* Skinner, 1932b.

"Dozens of scholars" See Fischer 1997b, who
discusses almost every attempt at deciphering *rongorongo*. For lack of space, chapter 8
does not deal with notable work by Irina
Fedorova, José Imbelloni and Sergei
Ryabchikov. Fischer's summaries are useful
but are not entirely objective, especially in
relation to Sebastian Englert, whom Fischer
misrepresents.

**p.222** "Heyerdahl" See Bahn and Flenley for a
detailed discussion of Heyerdahl's
theories.

"analysis of the DNA" E. Hagelberg *et al.*,
"DNA from ancient Easter Islanders",
*Nature*, 369, 1994: 25-26.

**p.223** "says...Jacques Guy" Personal communication.

**p.224** "Lee concludes" Lee: 204.

"Sequoya" See DeFrancis: 129-30 and 234-35.

**p.225** "this is how the priests used to read"
Fischer, 1997b: 50.

**p.230** "Atua-Mata-Riri" Thomson: 520.
Thomson's readings were subsequently
'corrected' by Métraux and, independently,
by Fischer. This reading is from Métraux:
320.

"the words were new" Fischer, 1997b: 136.

"The magical or ornamental character"
Guy, 1985: 385.

"Métraux changed his mind" Fischer,
1997b: 164-65.

**p.231** "Russian...parallel passages" Ibid: 192.

"Knorozov and...Butinov agreed" Butinov
and Knorozov: 13-14.

**p.232** "This gives us reason to believe" Ibid: 15.
This paper contains the only evidence ever

given by Butinov and Knorozov for their
theory. Guy, 1998b, suggests a different
interpretation of the same pattern.

"I'll never forget the moment" Barthel,
1958b: 65.

"Barthel went on to interpret the combined
signs" Fischer, 1997b: 231.

**p.233** "even by sympathetic critics such as Fischer"
Fischer, 1997b: 229-33.

"The Metoro chants" Barthel, 1993: 175.
This article is more or less an admission of
Barthel's failure to make headway with deci-
phering *rongorongo*.

**p.234** "many holes...vicious circle" Personal
communication.

"Guy's work...appreciated by both Fischer
and Pozdniakov" Fischer, 1997b:250-59;
Pozdniakov, 1996. Most of Guy's later work
on *rongorongo* can be found at
http://www.rongorongo.org

**p.235** "No attempt at translation is to be made"
Guy, 1985: 373.

**p.236** "Barthel realized" Barthel, 1958a: 242-47.

"Guy's analysis" Guy, 1990.

**p.238** "Fischer went on to detect the same pattern"
See Fischer, 1997a: 187-222.

"Rapanui Genesis" Ibid: 212.

**p.240** "flaunt" Ibid: 193. The 'phallus' is
substantially present on the Small Santiago
tablet, the Santiago staff and Honolulu
3629, and very occasionally occurs on Keiti,
and the Large Santiago, Large Washington,
Small St Petersburg, Large St Peterburg,
Small Vienna and Large Vienna tablets.

"the phallus was dropped" Ibid: 207.

"Barthel offered" Ibid: 222.

"Bahn" See Bahn, 1996a, 1996b and 1998.
However, in 1998 Bahn admitted (p. 45)
that he was "a nonlinguist who does not
know a grapheme from a glyph".

*"Times"* Nuttall. The 'decipherment' was also
hailed in the French, Italian and other press.

"Attenborough" Fischer, 1997a: 222. But
Attenborough later wrote: "I found Steven
Roger Fischer's interpretation of *rongorongo*
convincing not from any knowledge of scripts
and codes but simply because it coincided
with what I know about Polynesian society and
their great concern for genealogies.... I am

not a cryptographer and would not presume
to comment on the technical aspects of his
work." (Letter to author, 29 March 2000)

"The complete translation of…*rongorongo*"
Fischer, 1997b: 557.

"no other person who has studied *rongorongo*"
For scholarly reactions to Fischer's work, see
Pozdniakov, Guy (1998a, 2000), Coe
(1998) and Macri.

"no proof that sign 76…represents 'ure'"
Guy, 1999a.

**p.241** "whenever [Fischer] did not see a phallus"
Personal communication.

"dogs have four legs" Guy, 1998b: 554.

"says a sarcastic Guy" Guy, 1999b.

"Fischer has responded" Fischer,
1998: 234.

"[Pozdniakov's] single…published paper"
Pozdniakov, 1996.

**p.242** "enough…similarity between the two
frequency distributions" Ibid: 302. Macri
too supports the syllabic theory in Daniels
and Bright: 185-86.

"Our *ko hau rongorongo*" Englert: 76.

## IX   THE ZAPOTEC AND
## ISTHMIAN SCRIPTS

**p.247** "says Urcid" Personal communication.

"[stone stela]…shown disassembled"
Urcid, 1997: 49.

**p.248** "Batres" For the history of attempts to
decipher the Zapotec script, see Urcid,
1992: chapter 2 and Urcid, 2001.

"Michael Coe strongly agrees" Coe and
Kerr: 64.

"Córdova" See Urcid, 1992: 90, 218-20
and 338, for a discussion of Córdova's work.

**p.251** "Zapotecs named people" Urcid, 1998: 9.

"glyphs accompanied by numbers" Personal
communication.

"the linguistics of this link" See Urcid,
1992: 16-21.

"One linguist has compared" Morris
Swadesh, quoted in Urcid, 1992: 18.

"names of…ancient locations" Joyce Marcus
and, separately, Gordon Whittaker have
attempted to identify ancient place names in
the Zapotec glyphs, as discussed in Urcid,
1992: 60-68.

**p.252** "at least 100 signs" Ibid: 325-26.

"In Coe's opinion" Coe and Kerr: 64.

"a well-known Mayanist" A. M. Tozzer,
mentioned in Kelley: 30.

**p.254** "Then, in late 1986" For details of the
discovery, see George Stuart.

**p.257** "a few scribal errors" Macri and Stark: viii.

"Given the rudimentary understanding"
Ibid: vi.

"cacao, tortilla, incense and turkey"
Campbell: 365-66.

"The Olmecs were Mixe-Zoqueans"
Justeson and Kaufman, 2004: 1071.

**p.258** "The keys to our decipherment" Justeson
and Kaufman, 1993: 1703.

"Justeson and Kaufman state" 1992: 18.

**p.259** "It can hardly be other than a syllabogram"
Justeson and Kaufman, 1993: 1708.

"This twin usage of MS 20" Ibid: 1708. The
translation is discussed on pp. 1706 and
1709.

**p.260** "identification of MS 44" Justeson and
Kaufman, 1993: 1708.

"It is difficult to imagine" Justeson and
Kaufman, 1997: 210.

"support from David Kelley" See Kelley.

**p.262** "skeptics [such as] Houston" See Houston,
2000: 130-31, for a brief critique, and
Houston and Coe, for a detailed critique
that analyzes a new inscription.

"Decipherment is a process of accounting"
Justeson and Kaufman, 1993: 1703.

"Our decipherment of epi-Olmec…
writing" Ibid: 1709.

"reading of a sign as *na*" Ibid: 1708 and 1710.

"According to Macri" Macri and Stark: 3.

**p.263** "all six tense-aspect-mood suffixes" Justeson
and Kaufman, 2004: 1075.

"relationship between the Mayan script and the
Olmecs" For a brief discussion of the evidence, see Coe and Kerr: 66-67.

"Justeson and Kaufman are keen to relate"
Justeson and Kaufman, 2004: 1075.

"Perhaps, like runic" Coe and Kerr: 66.

"discovery of a new text or texts" In 1995,
the National Geographic Society supported
a project to survey the area around La
Mojarra with a magnetometer, but no further monuments showed up.

## X   THE INDUS SCRIPT

**p.265** "an abandoned country" Strabo, quoted in Parpola, 1994: 5.

"the Indus Valley civilization" For recent surveys, see Jansen *et al.*, Kenoyer, McIntosh, Parpola, 1994, and Possehl, 1999; also, http://www.harappa.com

**p.268** "little masterpieces" Wheeler: 101.

**p.269** "unicorn" See Kenoyer: 83-88. The great film director Satyajit Ray wrote a science-fantasy story, "The Unicorn Expedition", inspired by the seals of Mohenjo-daro. His explorer-scientist hero Professor Shonku comments at the beginning: "In addition to…familiar animals, there are representations of a beast unknown to us. It is shown as a bull-like creature with a single curved horn growing out of its forehead. Archaeologists have taken it to be a creature of fantasy, although I see no point in depicting an imaginary creature when all the others shown are real."
(Satyajit Ray, *Stories*, London, 1987: 156)

**p.271** "Bennett" Bennett, 1994-95: 386.

"Coe points out" Coe, 1995: 394-95.

**p.272** "My favorite part" Richter-Ushanas: vii.

"serious claims" Possehl, 1996: 22. Possehl's book is a valuable survey, but the reader should be warned that it contains some serious factual errors and many misprints.

**p.273** "Connections have been sought" Parpola, 1994: 57.

"More Seven League Boots!" Possehl, 1996: 101.

"Petrie" Ibid: 88-90.

**p.274** "unless one took the view" Both Possehl (1996:13-14) and Kenoyer (p. 15) are sympathetic to the view that the Indus Valley civilization is fundamentally different. It is puzzling, however, that it shows no clear remains of religious buildings and ceremonies.

"sea trade [with Mesopotamia]" See Kenoyer: 96-98, Ratnagar, and Crawford and Rice's book on Bahrain (Dilmun).

"Kinnier Wilson's approach" My account is based on Kinnier Wilson, 1987.

**p.276** "He therefore derives the 'missing'…values" Rao: 83 and 90. The derivation is, frankly, a fudge.

"nationalistic reasons" Nevertheless, it should be noted that Rao is not a north Indian (as pointed out in Mahadevan, 1995: 10). For an unashamedly nationalistic 'decipherment' by a north Indian, see Jha.

"Indo-Aryan…'invasions'" See Parpola (1994), Trautmann, and also Kochhar, for up-to-date, objective discussions of thinking about the Indo-Aryans.

**p.278** "Fairservis's method" This is outlined in Fairservis, 1992: 23-24.

"Fairservis prefers to see a twist" Ibid: 50-51. The 'translations' are on p. 57.

**p.279** "Since there is little basic research" Possehl, 1996: 168.

"I believe that the script is now" Fairservis, 1992: preface.

"the matter of the direction of writing and reading" My account is based on Parpola, 1994: 64-67, and Possehl, 1996: 59-62.

**p.281** "Parpola's two volumes of photographs" See Joshi and Parpola (Vol. 1), and Shah and Parpola (Vol. 2). A third volume, with inscriptions from collections outside India and Pakistan and addenda to volumes 1 and 2, is in preparation.

"Mahadevan…says that Parpola's sign list" Mahadevan, 1998a: section 12.

"Mahadevan reckons" Mahadevan, 1989: 9.

"Parpola's…sign list" See Parpola, 1994: chapter 5.

**p.284** "Wells" See Wells, 1999a, and Kelley and Wells.

"admits Mahadevan" Mahadevan, 1989: 9.

"common sequence" Parpola, 1994: 69.

"writes Steven Bonta" Bonta: 25-29.

**p.285** "Application of the context criterion" Parpola, 1994: 69.

"examples of potential numerals" Bonta: 51, 54.

"Mahadevan did a frequency count" Fairservis, 1992:62.

"Bonta believes that the various 'fish' signs" Bonta: 79-88.

**p.286** "comment by Parpola" Parpola, 1994: 82.

"numerical system needs much further study" See Possehl, 1996: 104-05, and Bonta: chapter 5, for past and current studies.

"One of the most convincing techniques" The four seal impressions appear in Wells, 1999b.

p.288 "word dividers" The examples appear in Parpola, 1994: 83.

"more reliable method of segmenting words" The example appears in Mahadevan, 1989: 10-13 and pl. 6.

p.289 "writes Mahadevan" Ibid: 11.

"To quote Parpola" His discussion of his theory appears in Parpola, 1994:94-95.

p.290 "praise from John Chadwick" See Clauson and Chadwick.

"strong criticism" See Burrow.

"The latest theory...advanced by Mahadevan " See Mahadevan, 1998b.

"the complex issue of...the Indus language" See Parpola, 1994: chapters 8 and 9, and Mallory.

"system of Indus Valley weights" Kenoyer: 98-99.

"Indus language... related to the Munda languages" Michael Witzel of Harvard University has recently supported this theory, in the face of criticism from Parpola (personal communication from Asko Parpola).

"Chadwick's...phrase" Chadwick, 1994.

p.291 "If the Brahuis" Parpola, 1994: 165. The migration theory is supported chiefly by J. Elfenbein.

"Wheeler" See his *The Indus Civilization*.

"Knorozov and his collaborators" Their work is assessed, and criticized for its speculative nature, in Zide and Zvelebil.

"cultural evidence about Dravidian civilization" See Mahadevan, 1998a: esp. section 14.

"Heras" See Possehl, 1996: 110-15.

p.292 "Who that has seen the phosporescence" Parpola, 1994: 181.

"Parpola has extended Heras's small 'decipherment'" Ibid: 194-95.

p.293 "It is interesting to note" Mahadevan,1995: 11.

p.294 "Another of Parpola's several readings" See Parpola, 1994: chapter 13, and Parpola, 1997.

"It is very likely" Mahadevan, 1998a: section 12 (slightly edited). See also Mahadevan's own theory about Murukan in Mahadevan, 1999.

p.295 "uncertainty inherent in interpreting Indus signs" See, for example, the seal reproduced in Kenoyer (p. 117), which he interprets (p. 82) as two men fighting over a women, but which Parpola, 1999, interprets as a scene from a Vedic text involving the goddess of war.

"Many of the signs...are so simplified" Parpola, 1994: 278.

"archaeological project...at Harappa" See http://www.harappa.com

"inscription found at Dholavira" See Parpola: 110 and 113, and Wells, 1999b, for a controversial interpretation.

"Kenoyer is currently engaged" Personal communication.

## XI THE PHAISTOS DISC

p.297 "Bennett remarked" Bennett, 1998a: 139.

"*Economist*" 16 January 1999. The editor is Jerome M. Eisenberg of *Minerva*.

p.298 "*Le Disque de Phaestos*" Other editions are by Olivier and Godart.

"asks Bennett" Bennett, 1999: 27.

p.303 "hoax theory" See McEvedy, who is not a specialist in the Cretan scripts. It is discussed in Duhoux, 1977: 15.

"corrections [to the disc]" Ibid: 32-35.

p.304 "the world's first typewritten document" Hooker *et al*: 190.

"Chadwick and Duhoux...have disagreed" Chadwick in Hooker *et al*: 190-93, and Duhoux, 2000.

"Evans wrote" Evans, *Palace of Minos*, Vol. I: 649.

p.306 "plumed Viking cap" Ibid: 655.

"Chadwick preferred" Hooker *et al*: 192.

p.308 "Duhoux attaches much weight" Duhoux, 1977: 15 and 80-81.

"empirical formula" Mackay: 17. See also Jackson for a second statistical study of the disc.

p.310 "interesting speculative deduction" Hooker *et al*: 193.

p.311 "direction of reading [of disc]" Duhoux: 31; Chadwick in Hooker *et al*: 192.

p.312 "*The Bronze Age Computer Disc*" See Butler, and review of Butler in Bennett, 1999. See Faucounau for another recent 'decipherment', which derives the Phaistos disc language as a proto-Ionian dialect of Greek.

"Evans came perilously close" Evans, *Palace of Minos*, Vol. I: 662-63.

**p.313** "Hear ye, Cretans and Greeks" Fischer, 1997a: 115.

"Approaching each word" Ibid: 113.

"Fischer's work on the disc" See reviews in Coe, 1998 and Bennett, 1998a.

"another scholar" This was John Justeson (personal communication).

"utter fools of themselves" Chadwick to Bennett, 11 December 1984. The *National Geographic* editors went so far as to 'commend' Fischer, but the magazine did not publish his work.

**p.314** "Perhaps I subconsciously put together" Fischer, 1997a: 102.

"Chadwick sternly told the editors" Chadwick to Joseph Judge, 15 August and 8 November 1984.

"argument that finally carried the day" Personal communication from George Stuart, one of the *National Geographic* editors.

**p.315** "We must curb our impatience" Hooker *et al*: 194.


## XII    CONCLUSION

**p.317** "I have not made up my mind" Joseph Judge to Chadwick, 4 December 1984.

"Barry Fell" See Fell, 1976, and 1989-91. Fell offers complete translations of the Phaistos disc and *rongorongo* inscriptions.

"wrote Ventris" Chadwick, 1973: 13.

**p.318** "It is this quality" Chadwick, 1958: 4.

**p.319** "I love puzzles and codes" Feynman: 314-15. See also Sykes: 229-31.

**p.320** "Ventris remarked" Ventris, 1952: 57.

**p.321** "contemporary significance in decipherment" See Robinson, 2007: ch. 13.

"nature and significance of literacy" See Baines for a discussion of literacy in ancient Egypt.

**p.322** "calligraphy" See Gaur.

**p.323** "It is more like inventing" Personal communication.

"The worm thinks it ... foolish" See the Tagore anthology in the Bibliography: 382.

# FURTHER READING

Only books, articles and other items referred to in the main text and notes are listed in the Bibliography. Many of these are of course highly specialized. Good general introductions to the civilizations discussed in the text are to be found in many books. Recommended are:

a. Richard Parkinson, *Cracking Codes*, and Ian Shaw and Paul Nicholson, *British Museum Dictionary of Ancient Egypt* (for Egyptian hieroglyphs);

b. Oliver Dickinson, ed., *The Aegean Bronze Age*, John Chadwick, *The Mycenaean World*, and George Christopoulos and John Bastias, eds, *Prehistory and Protohistory* (for Linear A, Linear B and the Phaistos disc);

c. Michael D. Coe, *The Maya* and *Mexico*, Mary Miller, *The Art of Mesoamerica*, and Dennis Tedlock, *Popol Vuh* (for Mayan glyphs, the Zapotec and the Isthmian scripts);

d. P. L. Shinnie, *Meroe: A Civilization of the Sudan*, and Derek A. Welsby, *The Kingdom of Kush* (for the Meroitic script);

e. Massimo Pallottino, *The Etruscans*, Nigel Spivey, *Etruscan Art*, and Mario Torelli, ed., *The Etruscans* (for the Etruscan alphabet);

f. Georges Roux, *Ancient Iraq*, and Susan Pollock, *Ancient Mesopotamia* (for the proto-Elamite script);

g. Paul Bahn and John Flenley, *Easter Island, Earth Island* (for *rongorongo*);

h. J. Mark Kenoyer, *Ancient Cities of the Indus Valley Civilization*, and Jane R. McIntosh, *A Peaceful Realm: The Rise and Fall of the Indus Civilization* (for the Indus script).

The best book on successful decipherments is Maurice Pope's *The Story of Decipherment*.

There are many websites about writing and about ancient cultures and civilizations that include short sections on undeciphered scripts, somewhat fewer that deal only with undeciphered scripts, and these latter of course include sites offering 'decipherments' (beware). The normal search methods will quickly lead to the most important sites. The websites of journals and newspapers which cover archaeology, such as *Nature* and *The New York Times*, are also good places to begin searching.

Abdalla, Abdelgadir M., "A system for the dissection of Meroitic complexes", *Sudan Notes and Records*, 54, 1973, pp. 81-93

Adkins, Lesley and Roy, *The Keys of Egypt: The Race to Read the Hieroglyphs*, London, 2000

Agostiniani, Luciano and Francesco Nicosia, *Tabula Cortonensis*, Rome, 2000

Alsop, Joseph, *From the Silent Earth: A Report on the Greek Bronze Age*, New York, 1964

Anderson, Lloyd B., *The Writing System of La Mojarra and Associated Monuments*, 2nd edn, Washington DC, 1993

Andrews, Carol, *The Rosetta Stone*, London, 1981

Bahn, Paul
   1996a: "Making sense of *rongorongo*", *Nature*, 379, 18 January 1996, pp. 204-05
   1996b: "Cracking the Easter Island code", *New Scientist*, 150, 15 June 1996, pp. 36-39
   1998: "Who's a clever boy, then?", *New Scientist*, 157, 14 February 1998, pp. 44-45

Bahn, Paul and John Flenley, *Easter Island, Earth Island*, London, 1992

Baines, John, "Literacy and ancient Egyptian society", *Man*, 18, 1983, pp. 572-99

Barber, E. J. W., *Archaeological Decipherment: A Handbook*, Princeton, 1974

Barthel, Thomas S.
   1958a: *Grundlagen zur Entzifferung der Osterinselschrift*, Hamburg
   1958b: "Talking boards of Easter Island", *Scientific American*, 198, June 1958, pp. 61-68
   1993: "Perspectives and directions of the classical Rapanui script", in Steven Roger Fischer, ed., *Easter Island Studies*, Oxford, pp.174-76

Becattini, Massimo, "La tavola di Cortona", *Archeologia Viva*, 78, November/ December 1999, pp. 74-78

Bender, M. Lionel, "Upside-down Afrasian", *Afrikanistische Arbeitspapiers*, 50, 1997, pp. 19-34

Bennett, E. L., Jr.
   1947: *The Minoan Linear Script from Pylos*, PhD thesis for the University of Cincinnati (unpublished)
   1950:"Fractional quantities in Minoan bookkeeping", *American Journal of Archaeology*, 54, pp.204-22
   1951: *The Pylos Tablets: A Preliminary Transcription*, Princeton, 1951
   1971: [Entry on Alice Elizabeth Kober], in Edward T. James, ed., *Notable American Women 1607-1950: A Biographical Dictionary*, Vol. 2, Cambridge (Massachusetts), pp. 344-46
   1994-95: [Review of Parpola, *Deciphering the Indus Script*], *Minos*, 29-30, pp. 386-89
   1998a: [Review of Fischer, *Evidence for the Hellenic Dialect in the Phaistos Disk*], *Written Language and Literacy*, 1, 1998, pp. 261-64
   1998b: "The 3 R's of the Linear A and Linear B writing systems," *Semiotica*, 122, 1998, pp. 139-63
   1999: "The writing's on the disc—but no one can yet read it", *Times Higher Education Supplement*, 12 November 1999, pp. 26-27

Boas, George, trans., *The Hieroglyphics of Horapollo*, Princeton, 1993

Boltz, William G., *The Origin and Early Development of the Chinese Writing System*, New Haven, 1994

Bonfante, Giuliano and Larissa Bonfante, *The Etruscan Language: An Introduction*, Manchester, 1983

Bonfante, Larissa
   1990: *Etruscan*, London (in Hooker *et al.*, *Reading the Past: Ancient Writing from Cuneiform to the Alphabet*)
   1997: *Corpus Speculorum Etruscorum: U.S.A. 3: New York, The Metropolitan Museum of Art*, Rome
   2000: "Etruscan history gets a rewrite", *Times Higher Education Supplement*, 19 May 2000, pp. 22-23

Bonta, Steven Christopher, *Topics in the Study of the Indus Valley Script*, MA thesis for Brigham Young University, 1996 (unpublished)

Brown, Ann, *Arthur Evans and the Palace of Minos*, Oxford, 1989

Burrow, T., "Dravidian and the decipherment of the Indus script", *Antiquity*, 43, 1969, pp. 274-78

Butinov, N. A. and Y. V. Knorozov, "Preliminary report on the study of the written language of Easter Island", *Journal of the Polynesian Society*, 66, 1957, pp. 5-17

Butler, Alan, *The Bronze Age Computer Disc*, London, 1999

Campbell, Lyle, *Historical Linguistics: An Introduction*, Edinburgh, 1998

Cavalli-Sforza, Luigi Luca, *Genes, Peoples and Languages*, London, 2000

Chadwick, John
>1958: *The Decipherment of Linear B*, Cambridge
>1973: *Documents in Mycenaean Greek*, Cambridge (1st edn by Michael Ventris and John Chadwick, Cambridge, 1956)
>1975a: "Introduction to the problems of 'Minoan Linear A'", *Journal of the Royal Asiatic Society*, pp.143-47
>1975b: "Scripts and their solutions", *Times Literary Supplement*, 15 August 1975, p. 918
>1976: *The Mycenaean World*, Cambridge
>1987: *Linear B and Related Scripts*, London
>1994: "Two bee oar not two bee?", *Times Higher Education Supplement*, 9 December 1994, p. 22

Christopoulos, George A. and John C. Bastias, eds, *Prehistory and Protohistory*, London, 1974 (first volume of the History of the Hellenic World)

Claiborne, Robert, *The Birth of Writing*, 1974, Time-Life Books

Clauson, Gerard and John Chadwick, "The Indus script deciphered?", *Antiquity*, 43, 1969, pp. 200-07

Clendinnen, Inga, *Ambivalent Conquests: Maya and Spaniard in Yucatan 1517-1570*, Cambridge, 1987

Codex Dresden, *Die Maya-Handschrift der Königlichen Bibliothek zu Dresden; herausgegeben von Prof. Dr. E. Förstemann*, Leipzig, 1880

Coe, Michael D.
>1993: *The Maya*, 5th edn, London
>1994: *Mexico: From the Olmecs to the Aztecs*, 4th edn, London
>1995: "On *not* breaking the Indus code", *Antiquity*, 69, 1995, pp. 393-95
>1998: "Phallus and fallacy", *Times Higher Education Supplement*, 27 March 1998, pp. 24-25
>1999: *Breaking the Maya Code*, rev. edn, New York

Coe, Michael D. and Justin Kerr, *The Art of the Maya Scribe*, London, 1997

Coe, Sophie D. and Michael D. Coe, [Review of Knorozov's trans. of de Landa's *Relación de las Cosas de Yucatán*], *American Antiquity*, 23, 1957, pp. 207-08

Coulmas, Florian, *The Blackwell Encyclopedia of Writing Systems*, Oxford, 1996

Crawford, Harriet and Michael Rice, *Traces of Paradise: The Archaeology of Bahrain 2500 BC-300 AD*, London, 2000

Dalby, Andrew, *Dictionary of Languages*, London, 1998

Damerow, Peter and Robert K. Englund, *The Proto-Elamite Texts from Tepe Yahya*, Cambridge (Massachusetts), 1989

Daniels, Peter T. and William Bright, eds, *The World's Writing Systems*, New York, 1996

Davies, W. V., *Egyptian Hieroglyphs*, London, 1987

DeFrancis, John, *Visible Speech: The Diverse Oneness of Writing Systems*, Hawaii, 1989

Dickinson, Oliver, ed., *The Aegean Bronze Age*, Cambridge, 1994

D'Imperio, M.E., *The Voynich Manuscript: An Elegant Enigma*, Laguna Hills (California), 1981

Doblhofer, Ernst, *Voices in Stone: The Decipherment of Ancient Scripts and Writings*, London, 1961

Drew, David, *The Lost Chronicles of the Maya Kings*, London, 1999

Duhoux, Yves
>1977: *Le Disque de Phaestos*, Louvain
>1998: "Pre-Hellenic languages of Crete", *Journal of Indo-European Studies*, 26, pp. 1-39
>2000: "How not to decipher the Phaistos disc", *American Journal of Archaeology*, 104, pp. 597-600

Duhoux, Yves, Thomas G. Palaima and John Bennet, eds, *Problems in Decipherment*, Louvain, 1989

*Economist*, "Message understood?", London, 16 January 1999, p. 10 (two letters about the Phaistos disc)

Elfenbein, J., [Review of Parpola, *Deciphering the Indus Script*], *South Asian Studies*, 14, 1998, pp. 185-88

Englert, Sebastian, *Island at the Centre of the World: New Light on Easter Island*, London, 1970

Englund, Robert K., "Proto-Elamite", in Ehsan Yarshater, ed., *Encyclopedia Iranica*, Costa Mesa (California), 1998, pp. 325-30

Evans, A. J.
>1909: *Scripta Minoa, Vol. I: The Hieroglyphic and Primitive Linear Classes*, Oxford
>1921-35: *The Palace of Minos at Knossos*, Vols I-IV, London

Fairservis, Walter A., Jr.
>1983: "The script of the Indus Valley civilization", *Scientific American*, 248, March 1983, pp. 44-52
>1992: *The Harappan Civilization and its Writing: A Model for the Decipherment of the Indus Script*, Leiden

Farmer, Steve, Richard Sproat and Michael Witzel,
"The collapse of the Indus script thesis: the myth
of a literate Harappan civilization", *Electronic Journal
of Vedic Studies*, 11:2, December 2004, pp. 19-57

Faucounau, Jean, *Le Déchiffrement du Disque de Phaistos: Preuves
et Conséquences*, Paris, 1999

Fell, Barry
1976: "The Phaistos disk", *Epigraphic Society
Occasional Publications*, 4: 79, San Diego
1989-91: "Deciphering the Easter Island tablets",
Pts 1-4, *Epigraphic Society Occasional Publications*, Vols
18-20, San Diego

Feynman, Richard P., *Surely You're Joking Mr. Feynman!:
Adventures of a Curious Character*, London, 1992

Finkelberg, Margalit, "The language of Linear A:
Greek, Semitic, or Anatolian?", in R. Drews, ed.,
*Greater Anatolia and the Indo-Hittite Language Family*, in
monograph series number 38 of the *Journal of Indo-
European Studies*, Washington DC, 2001, pp. 81-105

Finkelberg, Margalit, Alexander Uchitel and David
Ussishkin, "A Linear A inscription from Tel
Lachish", *Tel Aviv*, 23: 2, 1996, pp. 195-207

Fischer, Steven Roger
1988: *Evidence for the Hellenic Dialect in the Phaistos Disk*,
Bern
1997a: *Glyph-Breaker*, New York
1997b: *Rongorongo: The Easter Island Script: History,
Traditions, Texts*, Oxford
1998: "Reply to Jacques Guy," *Journal de la Société des
Océanistes*, 107: 2, pp. 233-34

Friberg, Jöran, "Numbers and measures in the earliest
written records", *Scientific American*, 250, February
1984, pp. 78-85

Gardiner, Alan H., "The Egyptian origin of the
Semitic alphabet", *Journal of Egyptian Archaeology*, 3,
1916, pp. 1-16

Gaur, Albertine, *A History of Calligraphy*, London, 1994

Godart, Louis, *Il Disco di Festos,* Florence, 1993

Godart, Louis and Jean-Pierre Olivier, *Recueil des
Inscriptions en Linéaire A,*Vols 1-5 ['*GORILA*'], Paris,
1976-85

Gordon, Cyrus H., *Forgotten Scripts: The Story of Their
Decipherment*, rev. edn, New York, 1982

Griffith, Francis Llewellyn
1909: "Meroitic inscriptions", in D. Randall
Maciver and C. Leonard Woolley, *Areika*, Oxford,
1909, pp. 43-54
1911: *Karanog: The Meroitic Inscriptions of Shablul and
Karanog*, Philadelphia

Guy, Jacques B. M.
1985: "On a fragment of the 'Tahua' tablet,"
*Journal of the Polynesian Society*, 94, pp. 367-88

1990: "The lunar calendar of tablet Mamari",
*Journal de la Société des Océanistes*, 91, pp. 135-49
1998a: "Un pretendu déchiffrement des tablettes
de l'île de Pâques", *Journal de la Société des Océanistes*,
107, pp. 57-63
1998b: "Easter Island—does the Santiago staff
bear a cosmogonic text?", *Anthropos*, 93, pp.
552-55
1998c: "Probable nature and contents of the
Santiago staff", *Rapa Nui Journal*, 12, p.109
1999a: "Rongorongo: le signe 76 signifie-t-il
vraiment 'pénis' (*ure*)?", *Bulletin du Cercle
d'Etudes sur l'île de Pâques et la Polynésie*, 27, March
1999, pp. 5-6
1999b: "Nouveau regard sur *Atua-Mata-Riri*",
*Bulletin du Cercle d'Etudes sur l'île de Pâques et la Polynésie*,
28, April 1999, pp. 2-3
2000: [Review of Fischer, *Rongorongo: The Easter
Island Script*], *Anthropos*, 95, pp. 262-63
2006: "General properties of the rongorongo
writing", *Rapa Nui Journal*, 20:1, pp. 53-66

Harris, Roy, *The Origin of Writing*, London, 1986

Homer
*The Iliad*, (E. V. Rieu trans.), London, 1950
*The Odyssey*, (Walter Shewring trans.), Oxford,
1980

Hooker, J. T., "Problems and methods in the decipherment of Linear A", *Journal of the Royal Asiatic
Society*, 1975, pp. 164-72

Hooker, J. T. *et al.*, *Reading the Past: Ancient Writing from
Cuneiform to the Alphabet*, London, 1990 (contains
Walker, *Cuneiform*; Davies, *Egyptian Hieroglyphs*;
Chadwick, *Linear B and Related Scripts*; Bonfante,
*Etruscan*)

Houston, Stephen D.
1989: *Maya Glyphs*, London
2000: "Into the minds of ancients: advances in
Maya glyph studies", *Journal of World Prehistory*, 14, pp.
121-201

Houston, Stephen D. and Michael D. Coe, "Has
Isthmian writing been deciphered?", *Mexicon*, 25,
2003, pp. 151-61

Iversen, Erik, *The Myth of Egypt and its Hieroglyphs in European
Tradition*, Princeton, 1993

Jackson, MacDonald P., "A statistical study of the
Phaistos disc", *Kadmos*, 38, 1999, pp. 19-30

Jansen, Michael, Máire Mulloy and Gunter Urban, eds,
*Forgotten Cities of the Indus: Early Civilization in Pakistan from
the 8th to the 2nd Millennium BC*, Mainz, 1991

Jaussen, Florentin Etienne (Tepano*), L'île de Pâques,
Historique: Ecriture, et Répertoire des Signes des Tablettes ou
Bois d'Hibiscus Intelligents*, Paris, 1893

Jha, N., *Vedic Glossary on Indus Seals*, Varanasi, 1996

Joshi, Jagat Pati and Asko Parpola, eds, *Corpus of Indus Seals and Inscriptions 1: Collections in India*, Helsinki, 1987

Justeson, John S. and Terrence Kaufman
1992: "Un desciframiento de la escritura jeroglí-fica epi-Olmeca: métodos y resultados", *Arqueologia*, 8, pp. 15-25
1993: "A decipherment of epi-Olmec hieroglyphic writing", *Science*, 259, 19 March 1993, pp. 1703-11
1997: "A newly discovered column in the hiero-glyphic text of La Mojarra stela 1: a test of the epi-Olmec decipherment", *Science*, 277, 11 July 1997, pp. 207-10 (a fuller version appears at http://www.sciencemag.org)
2004: "Epi-Olmec", in Roger D. Woodard, ed., *The Cambridge Encyclopedia of the World's Ancient Languages*, Cambridge

Kelley, David H., "The decipherment of the epi-Olmec script as Zoquean by Justeson and Kaufman", *Review of Archaeology*, 14, 1993, pp. 29-32

Kelley, David H. and Bryan Wells, "Recent progress in understanding the Indus script", *Review of Archaeology*, 16, 1995, pp. 15-23

Kenoyer, Jonathan Mark, *Ancient Cities of the Indus Valley Civilization*, Karachi, 1998

Keyser, Paul, "The origin of the Latin numerals 1 to 1000", *American Journal of Archaeology*, 92, 1988, pp. 529-46

Kinnier Wilson, J. V.
1974: *Indo-Sumerian: A New Approach to the Problems of the Indus Script*, Oxford
1987: "Fish rations and the Indus script: some new arguments in the case for accountancy", *South Asian Studies*, 3, pp. 41-46

Knorozov, Yuri V.
1958: "The problem of the study of the Maya hieroglyphic writing", (Sophie D. Coe trans.), *American Antiquity*, 23, pp. 284-91
1998: "Relación de las cosas de San Petersburgo: an interview with Dr. Yuri Valentinovich Knorozov", Pts I and II, by Harri J. Kettunen, *Revista Xaman* (web magazine of the Center for Ibero-American Studies, University of Helsinki), March and May 1998

Kober, Alice E.
1946: "Inflection in Linear Class B: 1—declen-sion", *American Journal of Archaeology*, 50, pp. 268-76
1948: "The Minoan scripts: fact and theory", *American Journal of Archaeology*, 52, pp. 82-103
1949: "'Total' in Minoan (Linear Class B)", *Archiv Orientalni*, 17, pp. 386-98

Kochhar, Rajesh, *The Vedic People: Their History and Geography*, London, 1997

Lamberg-Karlovsky, C. C.
1978: "The proto-Elamites on the Iranian plateau", *Antiquity*, 52, pp. 114-20
1999: "Multi-storied pasts", *Times Higher Education Supplement*, 3 December 1999, p. 26

Larsen, Mogens Trolle, *The Conquest of Assyria: Excavations in an Antique Land*, London, 1996

Lee, Georgia, *The Rock Art of Easter Island: Symbols of Power, Prayers to the Gods*, Los Angeles, 1992

McEvedy, Colin, "Piltdown man and his printing set", *Independent*, 2 August 1989

MacGillivray, J. Alexander, *Minotaur: Sir Arthur Evans and the Archaeology of the Minoan Myth*, London, 2000

McIntosh, Jane R., *A Peaceful Realm: The Rise and Fall of the Indus Civilization*, Boulder (Colorado), 2001

Mackay, Alan, "On the type-fount of the Phaistos disc", *Statistical Methods in Linguistics*, 4, 1965, pp. 15-25

Macri, Martha J., [Review of Fischer, *Rongorongo: The Easter Island Script*], *Written Language and Literacy*, 2, 1999, pp. 152-56

Macri, Martha J. and Laura M. Stark, *A Sign Catalog of the La Mojarra Script*, San Francisco, 1993

Mahadevan, Iravatham
1989: "What do we know about the Indus script? *Neti neti* ('Not this nor that')", *Journal of the Institute of Asian Studies*, 7, Madras, pp. 1-29
1995: "'An encyclopaedia of the Indus script'", *Book Review*, 19, New Delhi, pp. 9-12
1998a: [Interview with Mahadevan by Omar Khan], available at http://www.harappa.com/script/mahadevantext.html
1998b: "Phonetic value of the 'arrow' sign in the Indus script", *Journal of the Institute of Asian Studies*, 15, Madras, pp. 69-73
1999: "Murukan in the Indus script", *Journal of the Institute of Asian Studies*, 16: 2, Madras, pp. 3-39

Mallory, J. P., *In Search of the Indo-Europeans: Language, Archaeology and Myth*, London, 1989

Man, John, *Alpha Beta: How Our Alphabet Shaped The Western World*, London, 2000

Martin, Simon and Nikolai Grube, *Chronicle of the Maya Kings and Queens: Deciphering the Dynasties of the Ancient Maya*, London, 2000

Métraux, Alfred, *Ethnology of Easter Island*, Honolulu, 1971

Miller, Mary Ellen, *The Art of Mesoamerica*, rev. edn, London, 1996

Millet, Nicholas B., *Meroitic Nubia*, PhD thesis for Yale University, 1968 (unpublished)

*Minerva*, "Earliest alphabetic writing discovered in Egypt", 11, 2000, p. 2

Moore, Oliver, *Chinese*, London, 2000

Morkot, Robert, *The Black Pharaohs*, London, 2000

Nagy, Gregory, "Greek-like elements in Linear A", *Greek Roman and Byzantine Studies*, 4, 1963, pp. 181-211

Niemeier, Wolf-Dietrich, "A Linear A inscription from Miletus", *Kadmos*, 35, 1996, pp. 87-99

Nissen, Hans J., Peter Damerow and Robert K. Englund, *Archaic Bookkeeping: Writing and Techniques of Economic Administration in the Ancient Near East*, Chicago, 1993

Nuttall, Nick, "Language of Easter Island deciphered", *Times*, 13 June 1996, p. 9

Olivier, Jean-Pierre, "Le disque de Phaistos: edition photographique", *Bulletin de Correspondance Hellenique*, 99, 1975, pp. 5-34

Packard, David W., *Minoan Linear A*, Berkeley, 1974

Page, R. I., *Runes*, London, 1987

Palaima, Thomas G.
1987: [Review of Godart and Olivier, '*GORILA*'], *American Journal of Archaeology*, 91, 1987, pp. 336-37
1999: "Ancient prescriptions in tablet form", *Times Higher Education Supplement*, 20 August 1999, p. 23

Palaima, Thomas G., Elizabeth I. Pope and F. Kent Reilly III, *Unlocking the Secrets of Ancient Writing: The Parallel Lives of Michael Ventris and Linda Schele and the Decipherment of Mycenaean and Mayan Writing*, Austin, 2000

Pallottino, Massimo, *The Etruscans*, rev. edn, London, 1975

Parkinson, Richard, *Cracking Codes: The Rosetta Stone and Decipherment*, London, 1999

Parpola, Asko
1994: *Deciphering the Indus Script*, Cambridge
1997: "Dravidian and the Indus script: on the interpretation of some pivotal signs", *Studia Orientalia*, 82, Helsinki, 1997, pp. 167-91
1999: "Industrious habits of cities past", *Times Higher Education Supplement*, 3 December 1999, p. 24

Pollock, Susan, *Ancient Mesopotamia*, Cambridge, 1999

Pope, Maurice, *The Story of Decipherment*, 2nd edn, London, 1999

Pope, Maurice and Jacques Raison, "Linear A: changing perspectives", in Yves Duhoux, ed., *Etudes Minoennes I: Le Linéaire A*, Louvain, 1978, pp. 5-64

Porter, Roy and Marilyn Ogilvie, consultant eds, *The Hutchinson Dictionary of Scientific Biography*, Vol. II, Oxford, 2000

Possehl, Gregory L.
1996: *Indus Age: The Writing System*, Philadelphia
1999: *Indus Age: The Beginnings*, Philadelphia

Postgate, Nicholas, Tao Wang and Toby Wilkinson, "The evidence for early writing: utilitarian or ceremonial?", *Antiquity*, 69, 1995, pp. 459-80

Potts, D. T., *The Archaeology of Elam: Formation and Transformation of an Ancient Iranian State*, Cambridge, 1999

Pozdniakov, Konstantin, "Les bases du déchiffrement de l'écriture de l'ile de Paques", *Journal de la Société des Océanistes*, 103, 1996, pp. 289-303

Proskouriakoff, Tatiana
1960: "Historical implications of a pattern of dates at Piedras Negras, Guatemala", *American Antiquity*, 25, pp. 454-75
1961: "The lords of the Maya realm", *Expedition*, Fall 1961, pp. 14-21

Rao, S. R., *The Decipherment of the Indus Script*, Bombay, 1982

Ratnagar, Shereen, *Encounters: The Westerly Trade of the Harappa Civilization*, New Delhi, 1981

Ray, John D.
1998: "Aegypto-Carica", *Kadmos*, 37, pp. 125-36
2007: *The Rosetta Stone*, London

Richter-Ushanas, Egbert, *The Symbolic Conception of the Indus Script*, 1988, Bremen

Rilly, Claude, "Assimilation et determination en meroitique: le determinant masque du mot *qore* 'roi'", *Meroitic Newsletter*, 26, 1999, pp. 79-86

Robinson, Andrew
2002: *The Man Who Deciphered Linear B*, London
2006: *The Last Man Who Knew Everything*, Oxford
2007: *The Story of Writing: Alphabets, Hieroglyphs and Pictograms*, 2nd edn, London
2008: "A century of puzzling", *Nature*, 453, 19 June 2008, pp. 990-91 (on the Phaistos disc)

Roux, Georges, *Ancient Iraq*, 3rd edn, London, 1992

Salvini, Mirjo, "Linear Elamite", in Ehsan Yarshater, ed., *Encyclopaedia Iranica*, Costa Mesa (California), 1998, pp. 330-32

Saussure, Ferdinand de, *Course in General Linguistics*, (Roy Harris trans.), London, 1983

Schele, Linda and Peter Mathews, *The Code of Kings: The Language of Seven Sacred Maya Temples and Tombs*, New York, 1998

Schmandt-Besserat, Denise, *How Writing Came About*, Austin, 1996

Schneider, David, "Pot luck: Linear A, an ancient script, is unearthed in Turkey", *Scientific American*, 275, July 1996, p. 14

Shah, Sayid Ghulam Mustafa and Asko Parpola, eds, *Corpus of Indus Seals and Inscriptions 2: Collections in Pakistan*, Helsinki, 1991

Sharer, Robert J., *The Ancient Maya*, 5th edition, Stanford, 1994

Shinnie, P. L.
  1967: *Meroe: A Civilization of the Sudan*, London
  1996: *Ancient Nubia*, London
  2000: "Dynastic upheavals in the shadow of the pharaohs", *Times Higher Education Supplement*, 9 June 2000, p.32
Singh, Simon, *The Code Book: The Science of Secrecy from Ancient Egypt to Quantum Cryptography*, London, 1999
Skinner, Henry Devenish
  1932a: "Undeciphered scripts", *Nature*, 130, 1 October 1932, p. 502
  1932b: "The Easter Island script", *Journal of the Polynesian Society*, 41, p. 323
Solé, Robert and Dominique Valbelle, *The Rosetta Stone: The Story of the Decoding of Egyptian Hieroglyphics*, London, 2001
Spivey, Nigel, *Etruscan Art*, London, 1997
Stephens, John L., *Incidents of Travel in Central America, Chiapas, and Yucatan*, Vols I and II, London, 1841
Stuart, David
  1987: "Ten phonetic syllables", *Research Reports on Ancient Maya Writing*, 14, Washington DC
  1988: "The Rio Azul cacao pot: epigraphic observations on the function of a Maya ceramic vessel", *Antiquity*, 62, pp. 153-57
Stuart, George E., "The carved stela from La Mojarra, Veracruz, Mexico", *Science*, 259, 19 March 1993, pp. 1700-01
Sykes, Christopher, ed., *No Ordinary Genius: The Illustrated Richard Feynman*, London, 1994
Tagore, Rabindranath, *An Anthology*, (Krishna Dutta and Andrew Robinson eds), New York, 1997
Tedlock, Dennis, *Popol Vuh: The Definitive Edition of the Mayan Book of the Dawn of Life and the Glories of Gods and Kings*, rev. edn, New York, 1996
Tetlow, Simon, Ben Harris, David Roques and A. G. Meredith, *Michael Ventris Remembered*, Stowe School, (Buckinghamshire, UK), 1984
*The Times*, "On the threshold?", London, 25 June 1953 (leader article about Linear B)
Thelwall, Robin, "Meroitic and African language prehistory: prelude to a synthesis", *Meroitica 10*, Berlin, 1988, pp. 587-615
Thompson, J. Eric S.
  1950: *Maya Hieroglyphic Writing: Introduction*, Washington DC
  1963: *Rise and Fall of Maya Civilization*, Norman
  1972: *A Commentary on the Dresden Codex*, Philadelphia
Thomson, William Judah, "Te Pito te Henua, or Easter Island", *Annual Reports of the Smithsonian Institution for 1889*, Washington DC, 1891, pp. 447-552
Torelli, Mario, ed., *The Etruscans*, London, 2000

Török, Laszlo, *The Kingdom of Kush: Handbook of the Napatan-Meroitic Civilization*, Leiden, 1997
Trautmann, Thomas R., *Aryans and British India*, Berkeley, 1997
UNESCO, [no ed.], *The Peopling of Ancient Egypt and the Deciphering of Meroitic Script*, Paris, 1978
Urcid (-Serrano), Javier
  1992: *Zapotec Hieroglyphic Writing*, Vols I and II, PhD thesis for Yale University
  1997: "La escritura zapoteca prehispánica", *Arqueología Mexicana*, 5: 26, July-August 1997, pp. 42-53
  1998: "Codices on stone: the genesis of writing in ancient Oaxaca", *Indiana Journal of Hispanic Literatures*, 13, pp. 7-16
  2001: *Zapotec Hieroglyphic Writing*, Dumbarton Oaks
Ventris, Michael
  1940: "Introducing the Minoan language", *American Journal of Archaeology*, 44, pp. 494-520
  1948: "Group working", *Plan*, 2, pp. 6-18 (conversation between architects edited by Ventris)
  1952: "Deciphering Europe's earliest scripts", *Listener*, 10 July 1952, pp. 57-58
  1953: "A note on decipherment methods", *Antiquity*, 27, pp. 200-06
  1954: "King Nestor's four-handled cups: Greek inventories in the Minoan script", *Archaeology*, 7, Spring 1954, pp. 15-21
  1988: *Work Notes on Minoan Language Research and Other Unedited Papers*, (Anna Sacconi ed.), Rome
Ventris, Michael and John Chadwick, "Evidence for Greek dialect in the Mycenaean archives", *Journal of Hellenic Studies*, 73, 1953, pp. 84-103
Walker, C. B. F., *Cuneiform*, London, 1987
Wells, Bryan
  1999a: *An Introduction to Indus Writing*, 2nd edn, Independence (Missouri): Early Sites Research Society
  1999b: "Unbroken seal secrets", *Times Higher Education Supplement*, 3 September 1999, pp. 20-21
Wells, H. G., *A Short History of the World*, London, 2000
Welsby, Derek A., *The Kingdom of Kush: The Napatan and Meroitic Empires*, London, 1996
Wheeler, Mortimer, *The Indus Civilization*, 3rd edn, Cambridge, 1968
Wilkins, John, "Etruscan numerals", *Transactions of the Philological Society*, London, 1962, pp. 51-79
Zauzich, Karl-Theodor, *Discovering Egyptian Hieroglyphs: A Practical Guide*, London, 1992
Zide, Arlene R. K. and Kamil V. Zvelebil, *The Soviet Decipherment of the Indus Valley Script: Translation and Critique*, The Hague, 1976

# ILLUSTRATION CREDITS

All maps (pages 13, 82, 85, 108, 110, 142, 152, 153, 160, 161, 184, 202, 222, 246, 250, 266-67, 277) were drawn by Simone Nevraumont and are copyright © Nevraumont Publishing Company. Sources for illustrations in published works fully referenced in the Bibliography are given here in an abbreviated form, e.g. Evans, *Palace of Minos*; Barthel, *Grundlagen*.

# INDEX